THE
ENCHANTMENTS
OF LOVE

AMOROUS AND EXEMPLARY NOVELS

Maria de Zayas

Translated from the Spanish by H. Patsy Boyer

UNIVERSITY OF CALIFORNIA PRESS

Berkeley / Los Angeles / Oxford

Fic

The publisher wishes to acknowledge the generous assistance of the Program for Cultural Cooperation between Spain's Ministry of Culture and United States Universities in the publication of this book.

University of California Press
Berkeley and Los Angeles, California

University of California Press
Oxford, England

Library of Congress Cataloging-in-Publication Data

Zayas y Sotomayor, María de, 1590–1650.
   [Novelas amorosas y ejemplares. English]
   The enchantments of love : amorous and exemplary novels /
Maria de Zayas ; translated from the Spanish by H. Patsy Boyer.
     p.   cm.
   Translation of: Novelas amorosas y ejemplares.
   ISBN 0–520–06671–5 (alk. paper)
   I. Title.
   PQ6498.Z5N6813   1990
863'.3—dc20   89–36559
                                        CIP

Printed in the United States of America

1 2 3 4 5 6 7 8 9

The paper used in this publication meets the minimum requirements of American National Standard for Information Sciences—Permanence of Paper for Printed Library Materials, ANSI Z39.48–1984 ∞

¿Por qué, vanos legisladores del mundo, atáis nuestras manos para las venganzas, imposibilitando nuestras fuerzas con vuestras falsas opiniones, pues nos negáis letras y armas? ¿El alma no es la misma que la de los hombres? Pues si ella es la que da valor al cuerpo, ¿quién obliga a los nuestros tanta cobardía? Yo aseguro que si entendierais que también había en nosotras valor y fortaleza, no os burlarais como os burláis; y así, por tenernos sujetas desde que nacemos vais enflaqueciendo nuestras fuerzas con los temores de la honra, y el entendimiento con el recato de la vergüenza, dándonos por espadas ruecas, y por libros almohadillas. ¡Mas triste de mí! ¿De qué me sirven estos pensamientos, pues ya no sirven para remediar cosas tan sin remedio?

Why, vain legislators of the world, do you tie our hands so that we cannot take vengeance? Because of your mistaken ideas about us, you render us powerless and deny us access to pen and sword. Isn't our soul the same as a man's soul? If the soul is what gives courage to the body, why are we so cowardly? If you men knew that we were brave and strong, I'm sure you wouldn't deceive us the way you do. By keeping us subject from the moment we're born, you weaken our strength with fears about honor and our minds with exaggerated emphasis on modesty and shame. For a sword, you give us the distaff; instead of books, a sewing cushion. Woe is me! What good do all these thoughts do? They don't solve my hopeless problem.

"The Power of Love"

Contents

ACKNOWLEDGMENTS ix
INTRODUCTION xi
HISTORICAL BACKGROUND xxxii
TRANSLATOR'S NOTE xxxvi
FRAME CHARACTERS xl
TO THE READER 1
PROLOGUE BY AN OBJECTIVE READER 3

BEGINNING 7

Everything Ventured (Lisarda) 12

Aminta Deceived and Honor's Revenge (Matilda) 47

SECOND NIGHT 77

The Miser's Reward (don Alvaro) 80

Forewarned but not Forearmed (don Alonso) 115

THIRD NIGHT 157

The Power of Love (Nise) 159

Disillusionment in Love and Virtue Rewarded (Phyllis) 182

FOURTH NIGHT 213

Just Desserts (don Miguel) 215

Triumph over the Impossible (don Lope) 242

FIFTH NIGHT 271

Judge Thyself (don Juan) 274

The Magic Garden (Laura) 296

Acknowledgments

I should like to acknowledge support from the College of Arts, Humanities, and Social Sciences at Colorado State University for support of various stages of my work on this translation in the form of a sabbatical leave in 1982 as well as a Joseph Stern research grant, which enabled me to have the dog-eared typescript transferred to disk. Joyce Criswell typed from my longhand and Kay Short typed to disk. Without Jay Bodine's patient and generous advice, the computer might have swallowed it all up.

Numberless students, colleagues, and friends have contributed to the improvement of my work, in particular Mary Crow, Barbara Lakin, Jon Thiem, Marion Freeman, and Maria Pilar Perez Stansfield. A word of special appreciation goes to Ruth El Saffar who, as director of a National Endowment for the Humanities summer seminar that I attended in 1979, encouraged me to undertake this task and who has provided invaluable support ever since. The participants in that seminar and in the first NEH Translation Institute at Santa Cruz (1987) helped in solving numerous ticklish problems. Finally, I wish to express particular thanks to Kathleen McNerney for her many insights, Russell Coberly for being a faithful reader, and Scott Mahler at the University of California Press for his guidance.

Introduction

The life of Maria de Zayas y Sotomayor remains largely a mystery. The only facts known about her are that she lived in Madrid during the first half of the seventeenth century and was a recognized literary figure. She wrote much occasional poetry, at least one play, *The Betrayal of Friendship*, and two best-selling collections of framed novellas, *The Enchantments of Love: Amorous and Exemplary Novels* (*Novelas amorosas y ejemplares*, 1637) and its sequel, *The Disenchantments of Love* (*Desengaños amorosos*, 1647). It is believed that she was noble, probably the daughter of don Fernando de Zayas y Sotomayor, a captain in the army and member of the elite Order of Santiago, and of doña Ana de Barasa. As a girl, she may have spent time in Naples when don Fernando served under the Spanish viceroy, the count of Lemos (1610–1616). The only contemporary references to Zayas pertain to her literary activity; her works were highly acclaimed by such notable contemporaries as Lope de Vega, who praised "her rare and unique genius." The first such mention occurs in 1621; there is no further reference to her after the publication of the *Disenchantments* in 1647. The dates and places of her birth and death have not come down to us.

With so little known about Zayas's life, it is no wonder that scholars have set forth an amazing amount of conjecture about this intriguing woman. Interpreting statements made by characters in the novellas, critics have debated whether Zayas was beautiful or ugly, whether she married, remained a spinster, or suffered a devastating love affair and took refuge in a convent like so many of her characters. What stands out is that Maria de Zayas was a remarkable woman for her time and is acknowledged by Hispanists as one of the foremost writers of Spain's Golden Age. She is among the first secular women writers in Spain and certainly the first to achieve such great fame.

Zayas's novellas became instant best sellers in Spain and remained so for two hundred years, rivaled only by Cervantes's novellas in popularity. During the 1650s, Scarron and Boisrobert translated and adapted them into French without attributing them to Zayas. Consequently, the widespread diffusion of Zayas's novellas in France and England has redounded to the fame of her French adapters. Often her works were attributed to Cervantes, but never, outside of Spain, have they achieved recognition as hers. The only direct translations of her work into English are Roscoe's "The Miser Chastised" (1832) and Sturrock's *A Shameful Revenge* (1963), in fact a lively adaptation of two enchantments and six disenchantments.

With the rise of subjective criticism in the nineteenth century, the popularity of Zayas's works waned precipitously. Renowned historian of Spanish literature George Ticknor wrote of the *Enchantments* in 1849: "Although written by a lady of the court, the work is the filthiest and most immodest that I have ever read." In 1929, the famous German Hispanist Ludwig Pfandl wrote: "Can there be anything more gross and obscene, more nonaesthetic and repulsive, than a woman who writes lascivious, dirty, sadistic, and morally corrupt stories?" This kind of masculinist criticism resulted in a total eclipse: her works at last disappeared. The twentieth century has produced a few editions, which soon went out of print. Agustin G. de Amezua published authoritative editions of the *Novelas amorosas y ejemplares* in 1948 (used for this translation) and the *Desengaños amorosos* in 1950; Maria Martinez del Portal reedited these two scholarly versions in a popular edition in 1973; at present the *Novelas amorosas y ejemplares* is not available in Spanish; the *Desengaños amorosos* has recently appeared in Alicia Yllera's superb scholarly version (1983). So, despite the long popularity of Zayas's work in Spain and its intrinsic merit as a Spanish and a world classic, this is the first complete translation of the *Enchantments* into English. The fate of her work reflects historical attitudes toward women through time and culture.

Remarkable, then, is the fact that, in an age when women received little if any formal education, Zayas managed to become highly literate and set pen to paper. She published her works in a society where, as a rule, women had no place in public life and had no voice. Zayas felt it necessary to defend herself as a woman writer in her foreword to the *Enchantments*, "To the Reader." The need for formal education of girls and the importance of women having a voice, of being able to communicate, inform both collections of novellas. Because of her commitment to these tenets, Zayas has been recognized as a women's advocate and a feminist in the modern sense of the term.

Zayas read widely and knew thoroughly the literature of her day, which she used as a base for her fictions. To appreciate her art, it is helpful to have some information on the genres she cultivated. Cervantes, in the prologue to his *Exemplary Novels* (1613), affirmed that he was the first in Spain to write the exemplary novella modeled on the Italian Renaissance novella. This elegant genre differs substantially from the ancient and naive folktale which has persisted down through the ages in that the stories are longer, more complex and sophisticated. Cervantes's novellas stem from the tradition of Boccaccio's *Decameron* (1350), a work that radically influenced the development of the narrative in Europe. In England, France, Italy, and Spain, many great writers made artful use of Italian tales, including Chaucer, Shakespeare, Marguerite de Navarre, Scarron, Moliere, Masuccio, Bandello, Cervantes, Lope de Vega, and Tirso de Molina. Maria de Zayas wrote in the same fashionable Italianate tradition.

Characteristic of Zayas's art, as of all Renaissance literature, is the ingenious reworking of accepted plots and literary conventions to create a new work. We recognize in her stories motifs reminiscent of Chaucer's *Canterbury Tales*, Shakespeare's Italianate plays, Moliere, and Cervantes, because they derive from the same Renaissance tradition. The modern reader, formed within this common literary heritage, is familiar with the reiterated plot elements, stylized language, and artificial conventions, while the scholar finds it difficult, if not impossible, to point with certainty to the original source of these elements.

Zayas drew from all the narrative and poetic literature in vogue in her day: chivalric, sentimental, pastoral, picaresque, Moorish, and Byzantine as well as the Italianate love story. She also made extensive use of motifs from Spain's most popular genre during the Golden Age, the *comedia*. We still delight in the tantalizing stage device of the woman disguised as a man, and anyone familiar with Calderon's bloodcurdling honor tragedies will recognize very similar scenes in Zayas's works, especially in the *Disenchantments*. Even the rich and popular ballad tradition finds echo in her poems. Many scholars, most notably Edwin Place, have studied her use of sources to conclude that her stories have a highly original and unique stamp.

Before discussing her stories, a brief explanation of terminology and the titles is in order. The term "novella," as in the original title *Novelas amorosas y ejemplares*, designates a fairly extensive, complex, prose narrative based on the fashionable Italian model. Undoubtedly the primary inspiration for Zayas's work was Cervantes's *Exemplary Novels* (1613). The genre became immediately popular in Spain as it already was elsewhere in Europe. In the author's "Beginning" to *The Enchantments of Love: Amorous and Exemplary Novels*, we learn that, by 1637, the term was so overused that it had lost its appeal. The organizer of the soirees, which make up the frame for the stories, instructed the storytellers to tell "enchantments" instead: "In using this term, she wanted to avoid the common term 'novella,' so trite that it was now entirely out of fashion." So, in spite of the work's title, the stories themselves are called "enchantments."

The Spanish word I have translated as "enchantment," *maravilla*, accords with the oft-stated aim of Golden Age literature to "fill with wonder, to amaze" (maravillar). In place of the literal "marvel," I have chosen to use the word "enchantments" for the stories and have also added it to the original title in order to underscore the relationship between the first and the second parts of Zayas's work (*The Enchantments of Love: Amorous and Exemplary Novels*, 1637, and *The Disenchantments of Love*, 1647) and to emphasize the word "disenchantment." This term constitutes a primary theme in all twenty novellas, designates the stories of the second part, and is the Spanish title of the second part, *Desengaños amorosos*.

The Spanish word *desengaño* has no good equivalent in English; it does not quite mean "disenchantment," just as *maravilla* is not the same as "enchantment." *Desengaño* is the negation of the word *engaño*, which means "deceit-deception" so, literally, *desengaño* means the state or process of being "un-deceived," "disabused of error," "seeing the light." This concept, then, adds meaning to the term "exemplary"; from reading the novellas, the reader should learn and take example, should "see the light." Hispanists use the term *desengaño* to describe the overall theme of seventeenth-century Spanish literature, particularly when studying its baroque aspects. The most moving illustration of *desengaño* occurs in Alonso Quijano's deathbed disavowal of books of chivalry, of knight-errantry, and of his identity as don Quixote. He recovers his sanity and "sees the light." *Engaño*, how men deceive or enchant women, and *desengaño* how women should see through the deception, are fundamental themes in both parts. To stress the importance of these two concepts and to reiterate the reciprocal relationship between the two parts, I refer to them as the *Enchantments* and the *Disenchantments* and use the term generically to differentiate the novellas from each of the two parts.

Inextricably intertwined with the pervasive theme of *desengaño* is the theme of love between a handsome gallant and a lovely lady. It appears in myriad forms from raw lust, rape, and eroticism to ritualized courtship, true love, and marital relationship. Love is not treated philosophically but rather is taken as an inevitable fact of life, a powerful and irrational force beyond the individual's control. Problems arise because men and women have vastly different notions of what love is. According to literary convention, the instant a man sees a beautiful woman, he desires simply to enjoy her favors without having to commit himself to marriage, and he calls this love. A woman, when she sees herself courted by a handsome gallant, wants to select for herself a man who promises to be a loving husband (thereby confusing suitor and husband), and she calls this love. Generally, Zayas's men are characterized as fickle and her women as constant. Men deceive in order to get their way and women, inexperienced and credulous, let themselves be deceived. The clash between their intentions produces disenchantment.

This agonistic approach to love is further complicated by the issue of honor. In Zayas's novellas, honor conforms to the rigid literary code of honor, which reflects social attitudes that still persist in our society—namely, that men (father, brother, husband, church, and state) have the right and the responsibility to control women's sexuality. The tension derives from the fact that a woman's purity, her chastity, must remain intact while men, whether single or married, devote their energy and their cunning to the conquest of that fortress. Traditionally, a promise of marriage made in the presence of a witness was considered binding. (It was not until 1545 that marriage became a sacrament.) In Zayas's work, a man's most vile deception was the abuse of this sacred promise that allowed him to have his pleasure while it left the trusting woman dishonored and, like Aminta, faced with death. Interestingly, however, in "Aminta Deceived and Honor's

Revenge," Aminta avenges her dishonor and finds a happy marriage, as does doña Hipolita in "Just Desserts," suggesting that the loss of virginity does not necessarily ruin a woman forever.

In 1609, Lope de Vega wrote that honor was the best dramatic subject, and every one of Zayas's novellas treats some aspect of this unhappy theme. (It is important to distinguish between conventional literary treatment of courtship, honor, and marriage and actual social practices.) Zayas's characters, unlike Calderon's, do not typically rail out against the bloody honor code, although several do accuse men of exaggerating its importance in order to oppress women, as we see in the epigraph to this book. In the novellas, honor represents women's vulnerability, that which gives men power over them. For this reason, there is insistence that women assume responsibility for their own honor, to such a degree that they should be trained in swordsmanship so they can properly defend themselves and women's good name. This message underlies the enchantments, as in "Aminta Deceived and Honor's Revenge," and becomes explicit in the disenchantments.

The honor code may strike the modern reader either as too artificial and literary, or as characteristic of a barbaric, "macho," society. Nevertheless, given that men's violence against women is still a reality in even the most advanced societies, honor, insofar as it represents men's power over women, continues to be a deeply emotional issue. For that reason, the theme of honor is rich in dramatic and tragic potential, particularly when presented from the woman's point of view. In the *Enchantments*, we find female characters deceived and sometimes dishonored, but the emphasis is on how these women cope with deception. They explore their options and attempt to control their destinies in a variety of ways, not the least of which is withdrawal into the convent. The *Disenchantments*, however, focus almost exclusively on unjustified wife abuse, torture, and killing, often in the name of honor. In this work, the central theme is women's powerlessness and inability to cope, expressed in extreme and bizarre cases of female victimization and male cruelty.

Zayas's artfully focused examination of sex roles as depicted in literature makes her work coherent and unique. Whereas earlier writers, like Boccaccio and Marguerite de Navarre, playfully exploited the battle of the sexes and a less rigid version of the honor code, Zayas refined the issues and their implications. She did, however, use her renowned predecessors as models in structuring her two collections around one central frame, which gradually develops into an exemplary tale in itself. While both collections clearly come from the same pen, their stories are as different from each other as day and night. The *Enchantments* contains ten courtly novellas narrated by five women and five men at a series of five lavish Christmas soirees held for the purpose of entertaining the lovely Lysis, ill with the quartan fever. This courtly frame develops the character of the ten narrators, provides opportunity for commentary on the stories, and, because it continues throughout the second part, serves to unify Zayas's two collections of novellas. The *Disenchantments* repeats the structure of the first part in that there are ten exemplary tales narrated by characters from the original frame story.

In the *Enchantments*, the frame seems mostly decorative as it describes costume and elaborate entertainments consisting of music, skits, masked balls, and sumptuous banquets. The plot presents the amorous intrigue of don Juan's change of affection—from the hostess, Lysis, to her cousin Lisarda—and is complicated by the fact that don Juan's friend, don Diego, begins to court Lysis. At the end of the *Enchantments*, the Narrator concludes: "I end my well-intentioned and entertaining soiree, promising a second part if this one is received with the pleasure I hope. In the second part, we shall see don Juan's ingratitude, Lisarda's change of heart, and Lysis's wedding. I hope my work is appreciated, valued, and praised, not my rough style, but the will with which it has been written."

The second set of soirees was planned for New Year's Day to celebrate Lysis's marriage to don Diego. The occasion gets postponed for over a year in the frame, although ten years separate the publication of the two parts. On this occasion, the hostess Lysis establishes rules: only women will narrate; the tales must be true "case histories" to enlighten, or disenchant, women about men's deceptions; and they must be in defense of women's good name. After hearing the ten disenchantments, told according to her stipulations, Lysis sees the light and decides not to marry her adoring suitor. She prefers to retire from the world to live a secular life in the convent. Four other ladies join her. After the soirees end, the Narrator concludes the book by stating: "this end is not tragic but rather the happiest that one could have asked for, because she, wanted and desired by many, did not subject herself to anyone." This stunning conclusion, so similar to the end of Mme de La Fayette's *Princesse de Cleves*, was published some thirty years prior to the French masterpiece.

A principal difference between the two parts, then, is the way the *Disenchantments* unfolds from the *Enchantments*; the frame story elaborates a coherent feminist message, which produces a greater unity and homogeneity in the ten stories. The *Enchantments*, on the other hand, is characterized by the variety of the ten stories and a highly subtle feminism. The distinctions between the five tales narrated by women and the five by men, and the variation in plots, tones, and textures demand reader interpretation. As in Cervantes's *Exemplary Novels*, the ten enchantments represent a mix of very different kinds of novellas: there are a pastoral and a Byzantine tale, two satires, two miracle stories, and honor pieces with cloak and dagger elements. When read from a feminist perspective, these stories and their ironies raise a host of questions which are left to the reader to answer. What, for example, do we know about the frame narrator? How are male and female characters depicted? Who is the central character? What does the end mean?

Besides raising provocative questions, each of the ten enchantments relies on some sort of catchy device intended to enchant and amaze (maravillar). There are, for example, several powerful and prophetic dreams ("Everything Ventured"), and two miracles, interestingly worked by Christ and not by the Virgin ("Triumph over the Impossible" and "The Power of Love"). God sends an awesome warning to Juana through the ghost of a former lover in "Disillusionment in Love and Virtue Rewarded." The devil plays a key part in "The Magic Garden" and in the first edition ending of "The Miser's Reward." Magic and the supernatural are pervasive in medieval and Renaissance literature and in Zayas's novellas. Treated sarcastically at times, magic seems to represent a fashionable and flashy literary device, but we should bear in mind that this was the age of witchhunts in northern Europe. (In Spain, there were few witch trials, as the zeal of the Spanish Inquisition was directed against heretics rather than witches and magicians. Magic and witchcraft are significant feminist issues in that the persecution of witches was, in fact, a persecution of women, and the phenomenon points out women's lack of power in posthumanist societies.) Don Marcos is fooled by a farcical magician ("The Miser's Reward"). Laura ("The Power of Love") and Juana ("Disillusionment in Love and Virtue Rewarded") seek the aid of a magician in their futile efforts to hold the affections of their lovers. Lucrecia, in the latter story, exercises powerful spells to keep her don Fernando enchanted. An appealing dramatic device is the woman disguised as a man who sets out to redress some wrong ("Everything Ventured," "Aminta Deceived and Honor's Revenge," and "Judge Thyself"). The two witty satires ("The Miser's Reward" and "Forewarned but not Forearmed") derive much of their humor from deliciously exaggerated situations, as we see in the description of don Marcos's rude awakening the morning after his wedding night, or when don Fadrique teaches his simple bride her marital duty.

The *Disenchantments*, on the other hand, relies on violence and irrationality for effect. Because of the ground rules that define the disenchantments, the differentiation between men's and women's stories is eliminated and there is less irony and less left to the imagination. The disenchantments seem to raise questions about human behavior rather than about how the tales are told. They are bizarre and shocking, even to the modern movie-goer, in their depiction of female victimization and male brutality. Through a meticulous process of undeception, or disenchantment, these novellas deconstruct the familiar and seemingly conventional literary universe established in the *Enchantments*. Six of the ten enchantments, for example, end in an ostensibly happy marriage, two women enter the convent, and the two satires end with the death of the foolish male protagonist. In contrast, six of the ten disenchantments end in vicious wife murder, and the other four depict traumatic torture and persecution of the female protagonist before she takes refuge in the convent. The enchantments generally treat courtship in a way reminiscent of Lope de Vega's cloak and dagger plays, while the disenchantments treat marriage in the style of Calderon's honor tragedies, but in both cases stressing gender perspective.

The grounding of the novellas in well-known literature is fundamental to Zayas's creative technique and her originality in that one of her aims is to demonstrate how literature written by men projects a negative and damaging image of women, an aim that brings to mind the modern concern about the influence of the media on thinking and values. This is summed up in the "Beginning" to the *Disenchantments* as Zelima begins the first tale: "My lady, you have commanded me tonight to tell a disenchantment to caution ladies about men's deceptions and their cunning, and also to defend women's good name in an age when it has fallen so low that no one ever hears or speaks a good word about them. *Without a single exception, there is no play staged or any book printed that is not a total offense against women* [italics mine]." There was, of course, at least one exception: Zayas's own *Enchantments*, published ten years before.

New in Zayas's work is the conscious feminization of a tremendous array of motifs taken from a highly refined, male-produced literature. In the *Enchantments*, this feminization is seen in the difference between the five stories narrated by women and the five narrated by men, in the perspective of the protagonists, in the way the character-narrators portray male and female characters, and in the pervasive irony. All five of the women's stories have strong female protagonists who are noble in character, constant in love, and perform some heroic deed. The men's protagonists reveal serious moral flaws. Only two of the five men's tales have female protagonists: doña Hipolita, in "Just Desserts," is of dubious moral fiber, and Estela, in "Judge Thyself," attributes her heroic valor to her love for don Carlos, as opposed to the women's self-motivated protagonists like Aminta. Ironically, after Estela becomes viceroy of Valencia and reveals that she is, in fact, a woman, the honors she has won through her heroism are transferred to her less valiant husband. In the other three men's tales, the women in some way deceive or betray the male protagonist.

In "Triumph Over the Impossible," don Rodrigo stands out as one of the more ambiguous of the men's protagonists. In order to merit the hand of his true love, doña Leonor, he goes off to war in Flanders, where he indulges in a highly unconventional dalliance. He neglects to write to doña Leonor and returns home more than a year later than he had promised. Then he blames doña Leonor for her betrayal in marrying another man, even though he knows that her parents, in order to force her into the undesired marriage, treacherously told her that he had married in Flanders. This tale, narrated by a man from the perspective of its flawed male protagonist, brings into contrast the adventuresome, novelistic, lives of men and the cloistered, restricted, and uninteresting, lives of women.

The men's tales differ significantly from the women's in many other ways. They have a more artificial, literary quality, with a polish and an intellectual control in their manipulation of traditional sources which tend to distance the reader from the action and the characters. They seem more ambiguous, perhaps because they are narrated by those "masters of deception," perhaps because of the ironic undermining of masculinist discourse. Of the twenty novellas, the only three that contain humor are men's tales. "The Miser's Reward" is a witty satire of a man's avarice. "Forewarned but not Forearmed" satirizes a man who, fearing that a clever woman will dishonor him, deliberately marries a mindless woman and, too late, learns his lesson. With delicious humor, both focus on the male protagonist who deceives and is himself deceived. Both were translated into French by Scarron and so, indirectly, came to serve as inspiration for Moliere's *L'avare* and *L'ecole des femmes*. It is interesting to note, from a cursory review of Zayas's stories adapted into French and English, that the five men's tales have far outstripped in popularity the fifteen women's tales.

Another frequently adapted men's tale with several highly comic moments is "Just Desserts." The protagonist, doña Hipolita, deceives her good husband, ultimately causing his death. She is raped by her brother-in-law, whom she murders. In the end, she marries the compassionate gentleman who rescued her from certain death, and, we are assured, they lived happily ever after. When we ponder what he knows about her character, however, we must wonder what kind of marriage they will have. The conventional happy ending with marriage as the solution to a woman's problems, as well as the title itself, appear to be highly ironic.

As the men's tales vary in type, so do the women's. Several stress what happens after marriage ("The Power of Love" and "Disillusionment in Love and Virtue Rewarded"). Husbands are all too often unfaithful, neglectful, and physically abusive. Wife battering is, in fact, the theme of "The Power of Love" and later becomes the central focus of the *Disenchantments*. This story is one of the most moving of the enchantments in its description of don Diego's transformation from loving suitor into abusive husband, and of Laura's solitude and helplessness. In the end, her husband realizes the "power of her love," but she has learned her lesson; unable to trust him, she chooses life in the convent.

In tone, the five women's stories seem more serious, intimate, and human, allowing the reader to identify more closely with the characters, which are better developed than in the men's stories. In women's tales as well as men's, female characters tend to be depicted as helpless and driven to resort to magic or needing a compassionate man to rescue them. Contrary to the Italianate tradition, the only women who deceive men occur either in the men's tales or as secondary, and evil, characters. Once enamored, the women's protagonists are invariably constant in their love. Some undertake heroic action and so, in effect, rescue themselves, albeit with the assistance of a man. Because the novellas tend to be bipartite rather than unitary, with two separate parts to the plot and at least two distinct messages (e.g., "Disillusionment in Love and Virtue Rewarded"), it is difficult to characterize them in simple terms, but, significantly, the women's tales present a wide range of female experience and feminine fantasy.

The contrast between the two kinds of enchantments is enhanced by the fact that men's and women's tales occur on alternate nights. On the last night, the concluding stories are don Juan's "Judge Thyself," a reworking of a novella by Lope de Vega, and Laura's "The Magic Garden," a reworking of a Boccaccio tale. To the modern reader, these two may seem the most contrived, but, as the final enchantments, they represent a culminating irony in the way they treat their sources and in the posture of their narrators. "Judge Thyself," told by the arrogant don Juan, is a prototypical feminist tale. It is based, not only on Lope's novella, but also on the historical-legendary precedents of Joan of Arc, Queen Christina of Sweden, and Spain's lady lieutenant, Catalina Erauso, three viragos made popular by the *comedia*. The Byzantine adventures of the protagonist, Estela, include abduction, enslavement, sexual assault, and timely rescue by the Prince of Fez. By dint of her extraordinary valor, she becomes a captain in the Emperor Charles V's cavalry and rises so high in his favor that he appoints her viceroy of Valencia. The first case brought before the new viceroy is her own disappearance. When she reveals her true identity, her titles and honors are transferred to her unheroic husband. Why is it that the arrogant don Juan narrates the tale of an improbably heroic female protagonist, a woman disguised as a man who achieves great military and political power? And why does this tale follow on the heels of don Lope's characterization of doña Leonor, in "Triumph Over the Impossible," as a woman who has no means whatsoever for controlling her life?

The final tale, "The Magic Garden," further exemplifies the subtle feminism of the enchantments which must be extrapolated from the action, characters, narrative points of view, ironies, and from what is *not* said. At the end of this final story, the frame characters debate who is noblest: the husband, the lover, or the devil. Each has behaved ignobly. None of the frame characters, however, defends the genuine nobility of the faithful wife, Constanza, who preferred death to dishonor. Indeed, they blame her for setting an impossible price on her honor when the true cause of the crisis is the lover who courted an honorable married woman and resorted to a pact with the devil to get his way with her. This tale, narrated by the hostess's mother, is in fact a prototypical masculine story recounted in similar form by Boccaccio (X, 5) and by Chaucer ("The Franklin's Tale"). Since it is told by the most important female narrator and is the concluding story in the first part, we cannot fail to perceive that the true protagonist is Constanza; the other characters, including Constanza's sister, Theodosia, reveal serious moral flaws. Nor can we overlook the irony of the frame characters' misinterpretation of the story which culminates in the arrogant don Juan's winning the prize for playing the devil's advocate so "divinely." (His name may be ironic as well, since Tirso de Molina's famous don Juan play was produced in 1630, only seven years before the publication of the *Enchantments*.) The subtlety of this subversion of a masculinist story and a masculinist interpretation of it keeps Zayas's readers on their toes. These nuances would have been easily understood by a seventeenth-century audience, accustomed to deciphering the riddle of meaning by looking beyond deceptive appearances.

As previously mentioned, the enchantments cause the reader to ask questions. Tales like "Judge Thyself," "The Magic Garden," and "Triumph Over the Impossible" could and, perhaps, should be narrated from a different point of view. That is, the fact that a female narrator tells a masculinist story, and a male narrator tells a feminist story, accentuates the importance of the identity and reliability of the narrator and, consequently, of the author. One of the more intriguing questions we can ask is: why this detail? Each story contains puzzling and seemingly gratuitous details that may be fraught with significance. In the men's stories, generally more tightly knit, the questions refer to flaws in character (e.g., doña Hipolita, don Rodrigo) whereas, in the women's stories, the questions usually relate to plot elements. Why, for example, doesn't Jacinta marry her rescuer Fabio at the end of "Everything Ventured"? Or, why did Laura spend three hours in the charnel house? This kind of question, so exploited by television series, brings alive the character of the narrators, involves the reader, and removes the stories from neat predictability.

In her feminism, Zayas wrote within the tradition of the medieval "woman question" debates that flourished in Spain and elsewhere in Europe and inspired a number of amusing *comedias* (see Matulka's article). What is new is that Zayas wedded the philosophical arguments in defense of women with exemplary fiction, a genre of rising popularity. Although the *Enchantments* and the *Disenchantments* differ in the way they present their feminist message, both collections were written primarily to entertain and to entertain both men and women; they did, in fact, become best sellers and remained so for over two hundred years. In "To the Reader," we see that Zayas was concerned from the very beginning to explore the gender implications of the message inherent in literature: what does literature communicate to men and women, about men and women, and how? On the basis of the amazing success of the *Enchantments*, it would seem that she felt encouraged to strengthen the defense of women in the *Disenchantments*.

In the disenchantments, it is easier to identify subtexts, or elements drawn from other works, such as Cervantes's "The Man Who Was Too Curious for His Own Good," or Calderon's "Surgeon of His Honor," as well as reworked elements from the *Enchantments*. All the novellas, however, stress the interplay between a masculinist perspective and a feminist perspective in text and subtext. This conscious pastiche technique of reworking recognizable motifs is fundamental to Zayas's feminization of Golden Age literature and to her resoundingly modern feminist message.

In both parts, the compelling criticism is directed against a society whose social institutions (courtship, the rigid honor code, marriage, the family) and cultural institutions (education and the arts, which we should equate with the media) conspire to oppress women and to deny them access to power. Zayas created her masterpiece primarily to entertain, but to entertain at the expense of a literature and a theater whose popularity was rooted in the negative depiction of women, so evident in Tirso's don Juan Tenorio, who has come to be one of Western literature's most widely interpreted heroes.

In seventeenth-century Spanish society, as opposed to literature, the well-to-do girl had only one decision to make in her lifetime: whether to marry or to enter the convent. Normally, even this decision was made for her by her parents, who typically determined a daughter's future, be it marriage or convent, before puberty. As we see in the epigraph, a woman's status, indeed her very identity, was controlled by her parents, by her husband, or by the church, and there was no place in Spanish society for the respectable single woman except the convent. This explains why the choice of a husband and marriage represented the crucial events in the life of a Spanish woman. It also explains why women's powerlessness is such an important theme in Zayas's novellas. Aminta's revenge, Estela's heroic exploits, even

Clara's constancy, represent fantasies rather than options available to the average Spanish woman.

In contrast, a man's life, his identity, was not circumscribed or even limited by marriage. Given the age-old double standard, men were always free to womanize, to engage in the chase in an effort to conquer a woman's chastity. To a masculine public, the "happily ever after" marriage in literature symbolized the male conquest of the female (otherwise called "social order restored"). Marriage, as a literary device, was a celebration of masculine triumph while, for a feminine public, marriage was only the beginning of what might turn into an excruciating honor tragedy, as is powerfully depicted in the disenchantments (see the entry on "marriage" in Barbara G. Walker's *The Woman's Encyclopedia of Myths and Secrets*). A woman's only sure exercise of self-determination and self-protection lay in the decision to enter the convent.

It was not uncommon for an upper-class Spanish woman to retire to a convent. This did not necessarily mean that she became a nun or took vows, but rather that she chose to live her life in an environment protected from a society that had no place for the single woman. The convent represented a safehouse for those who wished to abandon the arena of amorous struggle, which is how Zayas depicted life in society. In feminine literature, to enter the convent symbolizes a return to sisterhood, to the feminine. A few of her characters do take their vows, but many, like Lysis, simply withdraw from the world while continuing to live a secular life filled with all the comforts their rich estates afford: elaborate dress, servants, music, soirees, even suitors.

With regard to the religious dimension of the novellas, it is difficult for us in the twentieth century to understand the nature of Catholicism in Golden Age Spain. Dominant and omnipresent, based upon a complex theology, seventeenth-century Spanish Catholicism differs vastly from twentieth-century Protestant ethic. Following upon the Council of Trent and the Catholic Counter-Reformation, Spanish Catholicism permitted moral freedoms unthinkable to the Victorians at the same time that there was dogmatic control and harsh repression of heresy under the Inquisition. Zayas's novellas are in no way unorthodox and were lauded as exemplary by the censors, yet they treat moral issues and present material (e.g., rape, battering, murder) with a frankness that seems shocking to us. The spirit of the novellas is secular and the language conventional. Even in the miracle stories, like "Triumph Over the Impossible," there is little religious sentiment. Few of the characters who enter the convent express a vocation although all seem to find happiness in that way of life.

Many scholars have described Zayas's stories as "realistic" depictions of life in seventeenth century Spanish society which, to my mind, is like saying that television accurately reflects the life of the average American. There are, however, many elements in Zayas's stories which make them appear "realistic." The stories are set in specific places at precise moments in contemporary Spanish history and include references to well-known historical personages. Sometimes we feel as if we are glimpsing a moment in a real life, especially in the characters' monologues. Graphic descriptive detail contributes a painterly quality that brings to mind Zurbaran's paintings, as when don Fadrique watches doña Beatrice descend the staircase. The lavish descriptions of feminine attire, like the spectacular portraits of the time, depict the external constraint that characterized women's lives. But, when we consider the derivative plots, the courtly characterizations, and Zayas's aim to entertain and instruct by exposing the gender messages in literature and drama, we must acknowledge the primacy of the literary and the aesthetic over any desire to depict life as it really was. Certainly art reflects life, as was suggested in my comments on the meaning of love, courtship, and marriage for men and women, but art also filters and purifies the way such concepts are presented, in accord with the cultural climate of the time. In practically every story the character narrating it insists that it is a *true* tale and often provides elaborate proof, but this conventional insistence upon the literal truth of the tales has a Borges-like ring when it is followed by the ironic disclaimer: only the names and the places have been changed.

Even if we resist the temptation to believe that Zayas is speaking personally when, in fact, her characters are speaking, we can still draw parallels between the novellas and her experience. Clearly the oft-repeated pleas for the formal education of girls reflect a deep personal conviction. Reiterated is the statement that women should have access to culture through literacy and access to power through learning and swordsmanship. There is insistence that women must be responsible for their own honor and be able to defend it with the sword. Zayas wielded her pen as a sword. The remarkable existence of the *Enchantments* and the *Disenchantments* attests to the importance of women having a public voice with which to defend their good name and their honor. These two works added a new, feminist dimension to the recognition of the ways literature affects perception, thinking, and values, a theme central to the Spanish masterpiece, *Don Quixote*, as well. Zayas's genius lies in her masterful use of masculine discourse to subvert masculine literature.

The novellas are courtly and pertain to the life of the nobility, as opposed to the variety of social classes we find depicted in Boccaccio, Chaucer, Marguerite de Navarre, and Cervantes. This is undoubtedly the only world Zayas experienced directly. Her class and gender denied her freedom of movement; she could not get out and make contact with other ways of life as could any man. Given the traditional cloistering of women in Spain, the sheltered leisure and astonishing isolation of Zayas's female characters most likely reflect her own life. This might explain why there is not a shred of biographical information about this remarkable woman. Zayas's unflattering treatment of the lower classes indicates an elitist attitude. Servants and other "ordinary" people, be they courtesans, matchmakers, or nobles come down in the world, tend to act ignobly, but then so do a surprising number of the nobles. Shocking to us is the racism we find in "Forewarned but not Forearmed," a story that also presents women in a dubious, if comic, light, in the spirit of the *Decameron* and the *Heptameron*.

Zayas's narrators apologize for their inexperience in telling stories, for their use of everyday language, and their artlessness, as she herself does in "To the Reader" and in the concluding words of the *Enchantments*. Repeatedly, they urge their audience to appreciate the substance of what they say and their "will," which we would call message, meaning, or intention, and not criticize how they say it, because they are unschooled women. These statements are, I believe, both accurate and ironic appraisals of the style of both parts. While we would not consider her elegant prose "everyday" language, it is prose, and it does seem "everyday" in comparison with the refined and hermetic poetic language of her contemporaries like Quevedo and Gongora.

The novellas are liberally laced with a wide variety of poetry, some of which is so complex that it defies adequate translation. The poetry of the *Enchantments* varies greatly and is of high quality, particularly the long love ballads. It serves several purposes. First, in the Renaissance and in seventeenth-century Spain, prose was regarded as an inferior genre, demonstrating little art in comparison with poetry. In this connection, we will recall that the *comedia* was quintessentially poetic and the public went to the theater to "hear" a play rather than to "see" it. For this reason, writers dressed up prose with poetic adornment to prove their art and also to complement the content, to add variety and emotional nuance. Also, as the novellas often stress, competence in singing and composing music and verse were hallmarks of the well brought up nobleman and, sometimes, noblewoman. They were an important dimension of courtship and of everyday diversion. Zayas achieved renown as a poet beginning in 1621, and, by including so much poetry, she offsets criticism of her "rough style," she depicts the importance of poetry and music in the life of the nobility, and she revels in her own talent. Some technical aspects of Spanish poetry will be further described in the "Translator's Note."

The style of the two parts is powerful; the language is sparse, dynamic, and vigorous. The dialogue is lively, the description vivid, the narration fast-paced. The stories have a dramatic, oral quality that almost demands that they be read aloud, acted out, that the songs be sung. Given the widespread illiteracy in that day and especially among women, this is undoubtedly how the book was read. We can envision a group of women doing their needlework while one read aloud from Zayas's novellas. With this scene in mind, we can imagine the listeners' discussion of the stories, which would contrast sharply with the frame characters' commentary.

Another, more subtle, aspect of Zayas's writing is that each of the character-narrators has a distinctive manner of narrating consistent with his or her characterization. This contributes to the rich texture and variety of the two works. The characterization of the frame narrators develops more fully in the *Disenchantments*, but, even so, there are marked stylistic differences between the novellas. This can be seen, for example, in the way narrators do or do not use such elements as poetry, poetic language, classical allusion, visual imagery, exclamations, humor, irony, parenthesis, and subjective editorial commentary. Some of this variation derives from the nature of the stories but much reflects conscious differentiation.

As a result of the multiple layers of discourse in the novellas, it is sometimes difficult to identify the speaker. The omniscient Narrator controls the frame and seems to speak for Zayas at the conclusion of both books; this voice may also intrude on the stories themselves. The nature of the frame characters determines the kind of story they tell, and their personality is revealed in their attitudes toward characters and events, expressed when they introduce or conclude the story and editorialize or comment on it. From within the stories, the perspective of the protagonist contrasts with that of the other characters in the story. Any of these perspectives may be subverted by irony. Beyond the text are recognizable subtexts, or elements reworked from other sources, which serve as counterpoint. We may also include the imagined dimension of commentary by a seventeenth-century audience, such as a sewing circle or a men's club. In addition to these interpenetrating levels, there is a strong sense of authorial presence in many of the tales which has led scholars to affirm that "Zayas says this or that." The sporadic exclamations, "Poor girl, if only you knew what you were getting into!", comments such as "I don't know if it was caused by . . ." or "when I think of where she went, it fills me with horror," serve to remind us of the fiction within the fiction. The complex structuring and articulation of Zayas's two collections of novellas attest to her mastery of the form, despite her apology for her rough style.

Above and beyond the complex stylized literary world depicted in these novellas there are characters and moments of immediate and touching humanity, for example, Laura and her plight in "The Power of Love." Zayas's characters are not simple types; there is a wide range of sensible and good characters, both male and female, just as there are evil men and evil women. A significant number have unsettling flaws, particularly in the men's tales. There is harsh criticism of evil women, like Flora and Claudia who betray their sex ("Aminta Deceived and Honor's Revenge," "Judge Thyself"); of the deceits and abuses of unscrupulous men, like Celio and don Jacinto ("Everything Ventured," "Aminta Deceived"); of parents, especially fathers, who neglect and deceive their daughters (lack of parental support typifies almost all of the stories); of blabbing servants and greedy matchmakers.

Most striking in Zayas's stories is the development of character through monologue. This technique was unusual in Golden Age literature, which stressed external action over character development. Most of the novellas contain at least one moving monologue that humanizes the character and makes the situation poignant, as we see in don Diego's lovesick sleeplessness, and later in Laura's desperate hopelessness in "The Power of Love," part of which appears as the epigraph. Besides these touching moments, the use of seemingly minor or incongruent detail also serves to particularize the characters in such a powerful way that the reader gets caught up in the fiction. Just as the characters vary, so too the plots and styles maintain a vivid freshness, avoiding the predictability or monotony one might expect of an "unschooled woman." Evil often goes unpunished and good may or may not be properly rewarded. Indeed, contrary to all the rules of poetic justice, the most repeated motif in the twenty novellas is the victimization of an innocent woman sacrificed on the altar of love, or honor, a motif reminiscent of stories of the early Christian martyrs.

What strikes us as "truest" in the novellas is the presentation of love from the woman's point of view. The treatment of this complex emotion is much more than a cliche or a pretext for a message. Zayas magically succeeds in bringing this age-old theme to life and in capturing its powerful effects on men and women. The modern reader surely will respond with wonderment and sometimes shock at the passion and suffering depicted in these stories. The *Enchantments* are enchanting, and it is my hope as it was Zayas's, that the reader will be both edified and entertained.

Suggestions for Further Reading

Bourland, Caroline. *The Short Story in Spain in the Seventeenth Century.* (1st ed. 1927). New York: Burt Franklin, 1973.

Foa, Sandra. "Humor and Suicide in Zayas and Cervantes," in *Anales Cervantinos* XVI (1977): 71–83.

———. "Maria de Zayas: Sibyl of Madrid," in *Female Scholars: A Tradition of Female Scholars Before 1800*, ed. J. R. Brink. Montreal: Eden Press, 1980, 54–67.

Griswold, Susan C. "Topoi and Rhetorical Distance: The Feminism of Maria de Zayas," in *Revista de Estudios Hispanicos* XIV, no. 2 (1980): 97–116.

McKay, Carol. "Maria de Zayas: Feminist Awareness in Seventeenth Century Spain," in *Studies in Language and Literature*. Richmond, Ky: Eastern Kentucky University Press, 1976, 377–381.

McKendrick, Melveena. *Woman and Society in the Spanish Drama of the Golden Age.* London: Cambridge University Press, 1974.

Matulka, Barbara. "The Feminist Theme in the Drama of the Siglo de Oro," in *The Romanic Review* XXVI, no. 3 (1935): 191–231.

Miller, Beth, ed. *Women in Hispanic Literature.* Berkeley, Los Angeles, London: University of California Press: 1983.

Morby, Edwin S. "The *Difunta pleiteada* Theme in Maria de Zayas," in *Hispanic Review* XVI (1948): 238–242.

Ordoñez, Elizabeth J. "Woman and Her Text in the Works of Maria de Zayas and Ana Caro," in *Revista de Estudios Hispanicos* (1985): 3–15.

Place, Edwin B. "Maria de Zayas: An Outstanding Woman Short Story Writer of Seventeenth Century Spain," Boulder: *University of Colorado Series*, no. 13, 1923.

Scarron, Paul. *The Innocent Adultery and Other Short Novels* (Trans. Tom Brown et al. 1700) New York, London: Benjamin Blom, 1968.

Stackhouse, Kenneth A. "Verisimilitude, Magic and the Supernatural in the Novellas of Maria de Zayas," in *Hispanofila* 62 (Jan. 1982): 65–76.

Sturrock, John, trans. *A Shameful Revenge and Other Stories*. London: The Folio Society, 1963.

Sylvania, Lena Evelyn. *Dona Maria de Zayas: A Contribution to the Study of Her Works*. (1st ed. 1922). New York: AMS, 1966.

Welles, Marcia L. "Maria de Zayas y Sotomayor and Her *novela cortesana*: A Re-evaluation," in *Bulletin of Hispanic Studies* 55 (1978): 301–310.

Historical Background

With the discovery of the New World in 1492, Spain began a century of imperial expansion. The sixteenth century opened under the rule of Ferdinand and Isabella, the "Catholic Monarchs." They brought political unity to the disparate Spanish kingdoms. With the Conquest of Granada, they also sought to establish religious unity by expelling the Jews and Moors who did not convert to Catholicism, and they established the Inquisition in Castille to ensure orthodoxy. At the same time, the new thought and the new aesthetic of the Italian Renaissance began to flourish in Spain as a result of Spanish domination of Sicily, Naples, and Milan.

In 1516, their grandson Charles I of Spain, later Charles V, Holy Roman Emperor, succeeded to the throne. His reign was turbulent, characterized by almost constant wars in Europe and in northern Africa. Estela, protagonist of "Judge Thyself," participated in many of Charles's campaigns and rose high in his favor. Since the colonies in America are scarcely mentioned in Zayas's novellas, we shall only remind the modern reader that, in that age of discovery, exploration, and adventure, life surely seemed more fantastic than any fiction, even to the stay-at-homes who only heard or read about such marvelous exploits.

In 1556, Charles V abdicated the Spanish throne in favor of his son Philip II. This king continues to be a legendary and controversial figure probably because his was an age of extremes, a colorful and exciting period that served as inspiration to many nineteenth-century

Romantic writers. Philip II's rule also was characterized by constant warfare, especially in Flanders, the Netherlands, and Italy; many young gallants in Zayas's novellas go off to win fame and fortune in these wars, or, unhappy in love, to find glorious death. The multifarious effects of Spain's militarism on society in general hold a prominent place in Zayas's works. Jacinta is widowed because of military action; Aminta's betrothed is absent, doing military service in Italy; don Rodrigo engages in an unconventional dalliance while on duty in Flanders. The constant wars kept the government bankrupt in spite of treasure arriving from the Americas; wealth and poverty are greatly stressed in the novellas. Notable events in Spanish history were the naval victory over the Turks at Lepanto in 1571, the annexation of Portugal and its empire in 1581, and the disastrous defeat of the Invincible Armada in 1588. This moment traditionally marks the beginning of Spain's unrelenting decline.

Pirates ruled the seas—Drake in the Atlantic and the Barbary pirates in the Mediterranean. We should recall that Cervantes went as a soldier to fight in the Italian wars. He lost his hand in the naval battle of Lepanto, was captured by pirates, and spent five years as a slave in Algiers. The Moorish and Byzantine elements that seem like romantic exoticism to us were at that time a reality.

Philip II was not a warrior king like his father. He established the first permanent Spanish court in Madrid. The courtly novellas make frequent negative reference to the bureaucracy, corruption, and debauchery that became associated with the court. Legend paints Philip II as a repressive king closely associated with the Inquisition, which had gained new powers from the Tridentine Reforms (1545); less than a century after the introduction of printing, the Inquisition formalized the Index of Prohibited Books and this censorship may have led writers to produce a more "exemplary" literature. It is curious to note that the censors lauded Zayas's work, undaunted by a sexuality and a violence shocking to us. While witches were being burned in northern Europe, Spain persecuted heretics. The single mention of the Inquisition in the *Enchantments* criticizes the fact that in Italy there was only a light fine for sorcery ("The Power of Love"). It was an age of saints and mystics. People tended to believe in the supernatural, in miracles, in magic, and in diabolical powers, usually attributed to students, as in "Disillusionment in Love and Virtue Rewarded."

In 1598 Philip II was succeeded by Philip III, a weak king. It is supposed that Maria de Zayas grew up during his reign. The story that contains the greatest amount of historical detail, perhaps to offset the pastoral artificiality, "Everything Ventured," specifically refers to the tragic expulsion of the Moors in 1609, to the attack against Mamora in 1614, and names many important noble families. "Just Desserts" takes place in Valladolid at the time when Philip III moved the court there from Madrid (1600–1606).

Philip IV (1621–1665) was a pleasure-loving and capricious king who handed over the affairs of government to his "favorite," the count-duke of Olivares, so he could enjoy lavish court entertainments. Philip IV's reign is known for the great art that was produced, such as Velazquez' monumental royal portraits and Calderon's elaborate theater. This is the period of Zayas's maturity (1621–1647). In the year 1640, the Catalan Revolt takes place and Spain loses Portugal, marking the end of the great Spanish Empire. Zayas, sensible to current events, refers to these disasters in the *Disenchantments,* but there is no clear allusion to the reign of Philip IV in the *Enchantments.*

When the fortunes of the Spanish empire began to decline (1588), her artistic expression reached its zenith in the so-called Golden Age (1580–1680). This was a period when the arts bloomed in incredible profusion. For the sake of establishing a broader context for Maria de Zayas and for a reading of her works, I shall mention a few of Spain's great Golden Age artists whom she might have known personally, whose works she surely knew. I shall start with Cervantes, the author of *Don Quixote* (1605, 1615), who, in 1580, returned from his captivity in Algiers. Besides his masterpiece, Cervantes wrote plays and dramatic interludes, a pastoral novel, a Byzantine novel, and the *Exemplary Novels.* Cervantes's works represent a major source of inspiration for Zayas. Also around 1580, the mystics Saint Theresa of Avila and Saint John of the Cross were at their peak, as was the classicist Fray Luis de Leon. In Toledo, El Greco was beginning to paint. Lope de Vega was creating the *comedia* which, because of its enormous popularity, variety, and poetic depth is considered the quintessential expression of the Spanish spirit. Unbelievably fecund, he also wrote novellas, and Zayas used his "Fortunes of Diana" as a base for "Judge Thyself."

Other dramatists were Tirso de Molina, creator of the original don Juan, who also cultivated the Italianate novella, and Calderon de la Barca, famous for *Life Is a Dream,* for his honor tragedies, and many other finely crafted plays. These writers were all prolific, and the majority were active in the court city of Madrid during the first half of

the seventeenth century. The most famous poets, besides the dramatists like Lope and Calderon, were Gongora and Quevedo, whose refined and ornate expression made Zayas's prose appear "everyday."
Painters who flourished in the seventeenth century, besides Velazquez,
were Zurbaran (whose vivid but somber colors and dramatic com-
positions, particularly his portraits of women saints like Saint Casilda,
I associate with Zayas's style), Ribera, the painter of darkness and
shadow, and Murillo, famous for his Madonnas. Maria de Zayas grew
up and wrote in this teeming cultural environment, which was further
enriched by the influx of art and ideas from all of Europe and the
vast Spanish empire.

Suggestions for Further Reading*

Braudel, Fernand. *The Mediterranean and the Mediterranean World in
    the Age of Philip II*. Trans. Sian Reynolds, New York: Harper &
    Row, 1966.
Crow, John A. *Spain: The Root and the Flower*. (1st ed. 1963). Berkeley,
    Los Angeles, London: University of California Press, 1985.
Defourneaux, Marcelin. *Daily Life in Spain in the Golden Age*. Trans.
    Newton Branch. (Orig. ed. 1966). New York: Praeger Publishers,
    1970.
Dominguez Ortiz, Antonio. *The Golden Age of Spain: 1516–1659*.
    Trans. James Casey. New York: Basic Books, 1971.
Elliot, J. H. *Imperial Spain: 1469–1716*. New York: Mentor Books,
    1966.
Grierson, Edward. *The Fatal Inheritance*. London: The History Book
    Club, 1969.

*There is a vast amount of information in English about Spain's Golden Age. These
works are listed because they are readable, informative, readily available, and contain
useful bibliographies.

Translator's Note

Maria de Zayas wrote *The Enchantments of Love* in a "plain style" and primarily to entertain. I have made my translation in the same spirit. I have tried to use a language appealing to the general reader and useful to the scholar. Translating involves difficult decisions, as evidenced in the choice of the title. The English is faithful but, for the sake of readability, the long, complex, Spanish sentences have been broken down and reorganized. To show the effects of this restructuring on the English style, let us compare a literal translation of one average long sentence with the ten sentences of the finished version:

By this time the moon had completed her circuit, and hidden herself in her original home, so everything was in confused shadows and we [Hipolita and her husband don Pedro] surrendered to sleep; and so it happened that [my lover, don Gaspar], wandering through the garden [chanced] to come upon the bed in which my husband and I were; and because in his glance he saw that there were two people in it, and not believing it could be don Pedro, he lowered himself to his knees, saying to himself that his suspicion was not in vain, and carried away by rage he drew a dagger, and as he was about to strike my innocent master with it, a dreadful decision advised only by his rage, heaven who looks on things with more pity, permitted that at this moment, don Pedro, turning over in bed, sighed, with which don Gaspar recognized his error, and guessed what it could be, and giving thanks to heaven for its warning, moved to my side, and don Pedro's sleep and his audacity permitting it, he woke me. ("Just Desserts")

By this time, the moon had set and hidden herself in her original home so everything was in confused shadow. My husband and I were fast asleep.

It happened that, after sneaking all around the garden, he came upon the bed where my husband and I were sleeping. In the dim light, he could see that there were two persons, but it never occurred to him that I was with don Pedro. He knelt down beside us, saying to himself that his suspicions had not been false. Overcome by rage, he unsheathed his dagger. Just as he was about to plunge it into my innocent husband—a dreadful decision produced by his wrath—kind heaven which looks on things with compassion, caused don Pedro to turn over and sigh. Don Gaspar realized his mistake and guessed what must have happened.

He thanked heaven for the timely warning. Then, boldly taking advantage of don Pedro's deep sleep, he crept over to my side and woke me.

Because seventeenth-century writers paid little attention to punctuation, the text as it stands probably reflects the printer's or the modern editor's judgment rather than the author's original. Even so, I have exercised license for the sake of readability and in an effort to capture the oral rhythms that characterize the original text, so that the stories can be easily read aloud in English. The oral quality is reinforced by a variety of devices, such as the large amount of dialogue and indirect discourse, the informal subjective commentary, sometimes parenthetical, and such informal expressions as "Let's let him sleep and go back to . . ." or "more than you might imagine." Longer and more cumbersome sentences have, on occasion, been kept in English to slow down the pace, vary the rhythm, and remind the reader of the original complexity. On three or four occasions, I corrected blatant errors in the text, for example wrong names, or added clarification and it was often necessary to insert names in English to avoid confusion in pronoun reference.

One of the more delicate decisions that faces the translator is how to maintain a balance between the flavor of the original, in this case seventeenth-century baroque Spanish, and modern English. Within the text itself there are constant reminders of its time and place of origin, including the formulaic story openings that praise a place, the use of don and doña with the exotic names, the poetry, and the cliches like "pearly tears." I have normally retained the repetitive epithets "beautiful," "noble," "gallant," "wealthy." These words no longer have the same meaning for us as they had for the seventeenth-century public, and several, like "discreet" and "modest" seldom have good equivalents in modern English. A particularly difficult word is "will," whose meaning ranges from "will" to "passion," "love," "lust," "goodwill," "intention," "meaning," and so on. I preferred to let stand many of these words whose meaning was broader and more suggestive then than it is now, rather than limit or reduce them to a narrower sense.

The forty songs and poems which adorn the frame and the stories contribute an emotional and an aesthetic shading highly prized in Renaissance literature. Zayas displays a wide range of poetic artistry: there is a patriotic sonnet in honor of the king, a burlesque madrigal to "sister flea," several complex baroque poems that required explanatory notes, and several mordantly sophisticated personal attacks in the frame. My favorite poems are the long love ballads, which are highly lyrical and effective in communicating the feelings and pangs of love.

Zayas's poetry comes from the Renaissance Italian tradition and exploits its love themes, pastoral settings, Petrarchan imagery, and forms. All the poetry in the *Enchantments* is learned, or mannered, rather than popular, even though some popular forms are used. Spanish poetry differs from English poetry in several important ways. Rhythm is marked by syllables rather than feet, and the basic eight-syllable line that characterizes much of the poetry here is characteristic of the ancient and rich ballad tradition in Spain, a tradition that continues to inform Spanish poetry, as we can see in Lorca's brilliant "gypsy ballads." Another standard feature of the ballad form is assonant rhyme, that is, the repetition of only the ending stressed vowel and the final vowel in even lines, with odd lines being free. For example in the first poem of the *Enchantments*, there is the following rhyme (é–o) in all even lines of the ballad: vuelvo, contento, fresnos, Celio, celos, arroyuelos, cielo, presto, and so forth. Assonant rhyme, therefore, is subtler and more musical than consonant rhyme.

In translating the poetry, I have sought meaning first, because the poems usually relate to the characters and the action, and poetic effect second. For this reason, some of the translations may seem prosaic, particularly in the case of the more mannered and difficult poems like the sonnets. The Spanish sonnet is Petrarchan in form, with two quartets, ABBA, two tercets, CDE, consonant rhyme, and each line comprised of eleven syllables, sometimes followed by an extra stanza. The simpler love ballads tended to come across into English more lyrically. I tried to maintain an appropriate rhythm without counting syllables. When possible, I used irregular internal rhymes (for example sea–icy; again–feign–disdain) to suggest the subtle Spanish assonance. Because of an upsurge of interest in Zayas's work, her poetry is now receiving increased critical attention.

This translation is based upon Agustin G. de Amezúa's authoritative edition of the *Novelas amorosas y ejemplares* (Madrid: Aldus, 1948). Amezúa based his edition on the second edition, "revised and corrected by the author," published in the same year and by the same publisher as the first edition (Zaragoza, 1637). There seems to be minimal variation between the two editions except for the ending of "The Miser's Reward," which I chose to incorporate into the translation from the first edition.

Frame Characters

LYSIS, the hostess who is ill, provides the music and songs
LAURA, Lysis's widowed mother, tells tenth tale
DON JUAN, wearing brown, tells ninth tale and loves
LISARDA, Lysis's cousin, wearing brown, tells first tale
MATILDA, wearing walnut and silver, tells second tale
DON ALVARO, wearing Matilda's colors, tells third tale
DON ALONSO, wearing black, tells fourth tale; he loves
NISE, don Juan's cousin, wearing black; she tells fifth tale
DON MIGUEL, wearing black, tells seventh tale; he secretly loves
PHYLLIS, wearing green, tells sixth tale
DON LOPE, wearing Phyllis's green, tells eighth tale
DON DIEGO vies with don Juan over Lysis and doesn't tell a tale

Because Lysis is ill with quartan fever during Christmas, her best friends decide to entertain her on five successive nights. They ask don Juan to bring his friends and they plan lavish entertainments to cheer Lysis: singing, dancing, skits, feasting, and storytelling. The ten young people are each to tell an enchantment; Laura substitutes for her daughter and puts her in charge of the music. As the action unfolds, we see the conflict between Lysis and her suitor, don Juan, who spurns her to pay court to her cousin Lisarda. Don Diego begins to court Lysis, causing resentment in don Juan.

To the Reader

        Oh my reader, no doubt it will amaze you that a woman has the nerve, not only to write a book but actually to publish it, for publication is the crucible in which the purity of genius is tested; until writing is set in letters of lead, it has no real value. Our senses are so easily deceived that fragile sight often sees as pure gold what, by the light of the fire, is simply a piece of polished brass. Who can doubt, I repeat, that there will be many who will attribute to folly my audacity in publishing my scribbles because I'm a woman, and women, in the opinion of some fools, are unfit beings. If only out of common courtesy, however, people shouldn't take my book as an oddity or condemn it as foolish.

        Furthermore, whether this matter that we men and women are made of is a bonding of clay and fire, or a dough of earth and spirit, whatever, it has no more nobility in men than in women, for our blood is the same; our senses, our powers, and the organs that perform their functions are all the same; our souls the same, for souls are neither male nor female. How, then, can men presume to be wise and presume that women are not? In my opinion, the only answer to this question is men's cruelty and tyranny in keeping us cloistered and not giving us teachers. The real reason why women are not learned is not a defect in intelligence but a lack of opportunity. When our parents bring us up if, instead of putting cambric on our sewing cushions and patterns in our embroidery frames, they gave us books and teachers, we would be as fit as men for any job or university professorship. We

1

might even be sharper because we're of a colder humor, and intelligence partakes of the damp humor. This you can see in our spontaneous responses and in our clever thinking, for everything we do with skill, whether or not with erudition, shows talent.

If this explanation doesn't restore our credibility, let history demonstrate it. Let's examine what's been done by women who, by some chance, became writers. While their work doesn't excuse my ignorance, let it serve as a model for my daring. The poet Lucan relates of his wife, Argentaria, that she helped him in the revision of the three books of the *Pharsalia* and wrote many poems that passed as his own. Pythagorus' sister, Themistoclea, wrote a very learned book of aphorisms. Socrates venerated Diotima for her eminence. Aspano gave theoretical lessons in the academies. Eudoxa left a book of political theory; Zenobia, a compendium of oriental history; Cornelia, Africanus' wife, family epistles of exceptional elegance. There are infinite numbers of women from antiquity and from our own times whom I pass over in silence so as not to go on forever, and because you'll know about them even if you're an uneducated layman. After that, there were the *Polyantheas* in Latin and *Summas morales* in the vernacular so that women and lay people could become literate. Since these things are true, how can it be said that women aren't apt for book learning, particularly when women have my inclination? The moment I see a book, new or old, I drop my sewing and can't rest until I've read it. From this inclination came information, and from the information good taste, and from this the writing of poetry, and then the writing of these novellas, perhaps because they seemed easier or more interesting to write.

Books that aren't erudite can be good if they have a good subject, while many works filled with subtlety are offered for sale but never bought because the subject is unimportant or not pleasing. I don't need to caution you about the piety you should have because, if my book is good, you do nothing in praising it, and, if it's bad, you must respect it out of the courtesy you owe to any woman. Who can compete with women? The person who doesn't respect them is foolish because he needs them; the person who insults them is thankless, for he fails to appreciate his first home. Surely you don't wish to be rude, foolish, ignoble, or unappreciative. I offer this book to you, trusting your generosity and knowing that if it displeases you, you will excuse me because I was born a woman, with no obligation to write good novellas but a great desire to serve you well. Farewell.

Prologue by an Objective Reader

You, cruel or benevolent reader, in the tribunal of your sitting room, will judge modestly or boldly the least details of what you read. A brilliant talent in our country, a portent of our age, a wonder of all time, and a marvel among the living offers this book to you. I exaggerate little if you take into account the fact that heaven has placed such consummate abilities in the weak sex of a woman; abilities that surpass everything talent praises and applause celebrates. One normally expects only clear intelligence, noble respect, and prudent comportment in a lady (accompanied by the chaste modesty that accentuates these qualities to the enhancement of her noble upbringing), and we find in addition to these virtues that she has an exceedingly subtle wit, an admirable disposition, and singular charm in everything she thinks, says, and writes. Because of these qualities, we admire her as a phoenix of wisdom and accord her our highest regard for her many talents.

The lady doña Maria de Zayas, glory of the River Manzanares and honor of our Spain (whom the learned Madrid academies so applaud and celebrate), as proof of her pen, publishes these ten offspring of her rich mind called novellas. The moral they contain, the art they display, and the grace of their style are characteristic of her keen mind, as revealed in the ambitiousness of the undertaking. Because she is a lady, learned, and talented, you must, oh reader! examine with respect

3

her acute thought, stripped of the invidious affectation for which you censure those writers who don't bear the safe conduct of being a lady. Not only must you do this, you must also promote the author's fame. Your library should not be without her book, and not borrowed but purchased with your own money; no matter what it costs, it will be money well spent. While I'm on the subject, I want to describe those readers who read at no expense to themselves but at great cost to booksellers.

Parasitic readers are like gluttons at the table. They go to bookshops and, so as not to spend the pittance a book costs, they lean up against the counter and hastily gobble up a book with their eyes. The material goes through their minds as quickly as a cat walking on hot coals, which is what their commentary is like afterwards. They aren't bothered by the fact that people coming into the shop to buy books stumble over them while they're glued to the spot, or by the angry expression on the bookseller's face on seeing them so at ease, or by the snorting of his assistants. They'll put up with anything to read in this fraudulent way and study by sponging without ever having to spend a cent.

Others take advantage of the good nature and generosity of the bookseller by asking to borrow a brand new book and, after they've worn it out, instead of praising the work, they condemn it and speak ill of it.

Still others hope that those who do buy books will read them quickly so they can borrow them to read. The result of this is that, if they're ignorant or haven't understood the subject or haven't liked it, they disparage the book and make it hard for the bookseller to sell it. A book galloped through or hastily sampled before purchase is like secondhand love, which loses merit for the lover, or like cast-off clothing, which no longer serves its purpose.

Oh, dearest readers, let this book be exempt from this kind of treatment because of its great merit. Don't let the swindler get away with reading it for free. Make the parasite who wants to feast on it pay for it, and make the miser relax his mean and wretched avarice and spend his money. This book is not only good for the reform of customs, it's a tasty dish in and of itself. The provident wit of its discreet author is everywhere evident. Her praises deserve an eloquent pen, but the greatest praise my pen can offer is to refrain from applauding her, leaving her acclaim to silence which, from one who falls short, is the highest praise of the one we wish to celebrate. Farewell.

The Enchantments of Love

Beginning

It was one of those short December afternoons when bitter cold and terrible snowstorms make people stay indoors to enjoy a fire stoked up to produce enough heat to compete with the month of July and which even makes you thirsty. You want to please the ladies so they won't miss their walks in the Prado park or along the river or any of the other pastimes ladies enjoy in the court city of Madrid.

Lovely Lisarda, discreet Matilda, witty Nise, and wise Phyllis, all beautiful, noble, rich, and good friends, gathered together to entertain Lysis, a wonder of nature and a marvelous prodigy of this court city (her myriad charms had been attacked by a noxious ague). The ladies spent the afternoon in delightful innocent chatter to make Lysis forget her irksome illness in pleasant conversation with her good friends. (It was easy for them to get together at any time as they all lived in the same building, although in different apartments, as was the custom in Madrid.) Because it was so close to Christmas, a happy time perfect for the celebration of parties, games, and friendly joking, they decided among themselves to hold a soiree, a special entertainment for Christmas Eve and for the other days of the holiday season. In light of this agreement, they decided to invite don Juan. He was a handsome, rich, and clever young man, Nise's cousin, and the dearly beloved object of Lysis's affection. She was hoping to surrender to him in legal matrimony all the delightful charms with which heaven had endowed her.

7

Don Juan, however, was attracted to Lisarda, Lysis's cousin, and, since he wanted her to be the mistress of his affection, he did not return Lysis's love. The lovely lady resented having the very cause of her jealousy before her eyes and hated having to pretend to be cheerful and smile when in her heart she harbored mortal suspicions that had, in fact, occasioned her illness. Her depression was aggravated by the fact that Lisarda acted overjoyed to be the chosen one and proud that don Juan loved her. In amorous competition between the two cousins, Lisarda always won out because she was unprincipled in getting her way.

They did invite don Juan to the party and he, at the ladies' request and in appreciation of the invitation, brought don Alvaro, don Miguel, don Alonso, and don Lope, all his peers in nobility, elegance, wealth, and equally fond of passing their time in pleasant and witty conversation. They all gathered together and decided to make Lysis the president of the delightful entertainments. They asked her to organize everything and to tell each one what his or her part was to be. She tried to excuse herself from this duty because of her illness and, when they insisted, she nominated her mother to do it for her and thus she eluded the duties her friends had imposed on her.

Laura, which was the name of Lysis's mother, was a wise and noble lady whom death, life's bitter foe, had deprived of her beloved husband. The lovely widow organized the party like this: she exempted her daughter Lysis from actually participating because of her illness, but she put her in charge of organizing the music. Laura expressly commanded her daughter to give the musicians all the songs and ballads they were to perform on each of the five nights to make the entertainment more lively. She commanded her niece Lisarda and the lovely Matilda to invent a gay masque in which all the ladies and gentlemen could show off their elegance, gentility, grace, and talent. On the first night, after the masque, Lisarda and Matilda would each tell an "enchantment." In using this term she wanted to avoid the common term "novella," so trite that it was now entirely out of fashion. To keep the gentlemen from complaining about the ladies' preeminence, she would alternate their parts. On the second night, don Alvaro and don Alonso; on the third, Nise and Phyllis; on the fourth, don Miguel and don Lope; and on the fifth, don Juan and Laura herself would tell an enchantment. They would end their Christmas celebration with a sumptuous banquet, which Lysis, as hostess, wanted to offer all of her guests. They would invite the ladies' mothers and the gentlemen's fathers, for it just so happened that none of the ladies had a father and none of the gentlemen had a mother, as death does not accommodate the desires of mortals.

It was incumbent upon Lysis to inaugurate the festivities. She sent for the two ablest musicians she could find to accompany her angelic voice, for that is how she planned to contribute to the entertainment. She notified everyone that, as day took refuge and shrouded itself in night's dark mantle of mourning for the absence of the rubicund lord of Delphi, who had departed to take happy daylight to the Indies, thereby bringing dark shadows to our hemisphere, at that time they should assemble in lovely Lysis's sitting room to celebrate Christmas Eve with all the agreed upon entertainments. Her parlor was hung with heavy Flemish tapestries whose woods, groves, and flowers depicted exotic landscapes like Arcadia and the hanging gardens of Babylon. The room was crowned by a rich dais piled high with mountains of green velvet cushions ornamented with splendid silver embroidery and tassels. To one side of the dais was a luxurious couch that was to serve as seat, sanctuary, and throne for the lovely Lysis who, because of her illness, could enjoy this distinction. It was green brocade with gold trimming and fringe, the green symbolizing a hope she did not really feel. All around the hall were rows of green velvet chairs and numerous taborets for the gentlemen to sit on while enjoying the warmth of a silver brazier where incense was burned to perfume the dais.

At three that afternoon, the discreet Laura and the lovely Lysis welcomed the ladies with great pleasure. Not only did the special guests come, but many others as well who had heard about the entertainment and decided to attend and occupy the numerous extra chairs. Lysis, dressed in blue, the color of jealousy, was reclining on her couch. For the sake of modesty and appearance, she had insisted upon dressing up in spite of her quartan fever. The hall looked like a landscape illuminated by the fair sun god Apollo, so many were the candles that sparkled. It delighted all eyes that beheld the scene and echoed with laughter. The musicians took their seats next to Lysis's couch and began with a *gallardia,* inviting the ladies and gentlemen to move out onto the floor, each one bearing a flaming torch to give effect to the stately movements of the dance. The musicians had also prepared the ballad for Lysis to sing upon the conclusion of the dance.

Don Juan, as master of ceremonies and leader, started the lively dance alone. He was so handsome that the guests could not take their eyes from his elegant figure dressed in rich brown, with his golden chains and diamond buttons sparkling like stars. Lisarda and don Alvaro followed. She was wearing brown to match don Juan's colors. Don Alvaro wore Matilda's colors, as he was in her thrall. Matilda was dressed in walnut brown and silver and accompanied don Alonso, smartly dressed in black because that's the color Nise wore. Nise's dress was of soft velvet decorated with gold buttons. Don Miguel led her by the hand. He too wore black because, although he wanted to pay court to Phyllis, he did not dare don her colors for fear of don Lope, who was wearing Phyllis's green in hope of being accepted by her.

When Lysis saw in his colors how don Juan preferred Lisarda, she understood the message stated in his dress and felt disillusioned in her love for him. She concealed her sorrow by swallowing her sighs and stifling her tears and watched the grace and dexterity with which her friends danced the spritely masque with its pirouettes so intricate, its crosses, ribbons, and labyrinths so stately that everyone wished it would last a hundred years. Then, with tears still in her eyes, Lysis prepared to display her talent by accompanying the musicians with her lovely voice. Everyone took a seat to listen while she sang this ballad:

> Forests, hear my lament:
> listen while I sing my plaints,
> for happiness never lasts
> for the unfortunate.
> Long ago I testified
> to your elm and ash trees,
> to your crystal springs,
> about Celio's faithlessness.
> Tenderly you heard my plaints
> and distracted me from my jealousy
> with the loving music
> of your gently flowing brooks.
> Touched, he saw his folly,
> for heaven had wrought my constancy;
> briefly he sought to repay my affection
> but how soon he tired!
> Happy to see my love rewarded,
> I hoped to enjoy my good fortune,
> for even if he didn't really love me
> at least he seemed responsive.
> My soul judged its quarters

too small to contain my great joy,
for it mistook as favors
his discourtesy and disdain.
I adored his deception;
it served to increase my desire
to worship his charms,
what madness and folly!
Ungrateful lover, who would think
that these things I relate
would hasten and increase
your desire to forget me.
You are right to be cruel,
I complain unjustly,
because those who love least
are the most fortunate.
The village, seeing your thoughts turned
to a new mistress of your affection,
your eyes set on another love,
talks about your inconstancy,
while I, because I love you,
lament your neglect and rue your disdain.

Such an illustrious audience would not show proper gratitude if it did not praise the lovely Lysis for her beautiful voice. Don Juan's father, don Francisco, in refined and courtly language, spoke for everyone in saying how much they appreciated the great favor she had shown them. This caused the lovely lady to blush and, despite her illness, the suffusion of color that rushed to her cheeks heightened her beauty. Don Juan almost repented of his change of allegiance, but the moment he again looked at Lisarda, he became enmeshed in the bonds of her beauty as he watched her move to the special seat to tell her enchantment and thus begin this first night's entertainment.

She waited to begin until she saw everyone hushed and in suspense, hanging on each one of the well-chosen words her sweet mouth would utter. Searching her mind for just the right ones, very charmingly, she began:

Everything Ventured

Beautiful ladies and noble gentlemen, the name of my enchantment is "everything ventured" because in it you will see how, when a woman is unlucky, when her star leads her to misfortune, no example or warning can prevent it. Heeding the lesson in my enchantment should serve to keep a person from trusting in the frail bark of his weakness and from throwing himself into the ocean of unrestrained appetites lest he drown in it. This applies to the frailty of women as well as to the clear and heroic wisdom of men, whose deceptions are rightfully to be feared as you will see in my enchantment, which begins like this:

The craggy peaks of Montserrat are the manifestation of God's power on earth and of the wondrous miracles of His Holy Mother, manifested in Her divine mysteries, the effects of Her mercy. Here at Montserrat She holds up in the air the peak of a jagged mountain that has been abandoned by all other mountains so that it has no support whatsoever except that which heaven gives. No less amazing is the miraculous and holy church there, endowed with innumerable miracles and unbounded wealth. The greatest of these miracles is embodied in the true image of Our Lady Queen of Angels.

Our hero Fabio paid Her homage and offered Her his soul overflowing with devout love. He carefully examined the church walls covered with ex-votos, shrouds, crutches, and myriad other signs of Her power. Fabio is an illustrious son of the noble city of Madrid, a splendid example of her greatness and a credit to her fame. With his keen intelligence, his renowned nobility, his good nature, and refined manners, he adorns and enriches Madrid's fame as much as any of her brave founders of whom, as their mother, she is justly proud. Transported to this setting of Montserrat, Fabio set out to climb among the mountain's peaks.

What led this virtuous youth through such rugged terrain was the pious desire to visit the holy cells of the penitent monks who have died for the world in order to live for heaven. He visited several and received nourishment for body and soul. He meditated on the saintliness of these men who can even entice the fugitive birds to perch on their hands to eat the crumbs they feed them. He continued hiking into the most remote part of the wilderness to see the famous Cave of Saint Anthony, so-called because of its prodigious harshness and because of all the things that have occurred there, the remarkable penances of the saintly men who have dwelt there and resisted the devil's terrible temptations. One could say that to withstand these temptations requires as much spirituality as Saint Anthony himself showed.

Because the rugged terrain permitted passage only on foot, Fabio had left his mule and his servant back at the monastery. Weary from clambering up the narrow trail, he sat down beside a small crystalline brook that spilled forth its pearly drops across the tiny grasses as, with a gentle murmuring sound, it slipped down from a lovely spring that enjoys its splendid setting at the very top of the mountain. The crystal music and melodious laughter of that place seemed created by the hands of the angels for the recreation of the holy hermits who dwell there. Even unseen by the eye, it could not fail to delight the ear. The long walk on foot, the harshness of the trail, and the warmth of the sun had worn him out, so he decided to rest and recover his energy.

Scarcely had he caught his weary breath when there came to his ears a soft delicate voice whose low tones seemed not too distant, suggesting that their source was not far away. Thinking itself alone, that voice, as mournful as it was low, sang this ballad accompanied only by the humble stream:

> Who would think that my love,
> seared by so many sorrows,
> weary of such misfortune,
> would die a coward's death?
> Whoever saw it escape, fleeing
> from such harsh faithlessness,
> would believe it would come back

for new and greater sorrow?
Cursed be the naked truth
of all my misguided love,
and cursed be the one who called
all women fickle!
When I should, Celio,
complain of your mistreatment,
love will not let me forget you,
love wills for me to love you more.
From the time the dawn begins
until the sun departs
to bathe the Indian shores,
I cry, every constant, ever loving.
The sun reappears and finds me
renewing all my grief,
bewailing your folly,
lamenting your license.
I know well that I tire myself
in vain suffering such sorrow,
for tears shed in solitude cost a lot
and do very little good.
I came to this wilderness fleeing
from your ungrateful treatment
but, more constant than ever, I adore you,
for loving you is my nourishment.
I freed myself from the sight of you,
but I couldn't free myself
from my enemy imagination,
from my ever constant love.
One who's seen a castle besieged,
one who's seen a ship embattled,
one who's seen a captive in Algiers,
knows what I am like—unchanging.
Since I chose you for my master,
kill me, sorrows, kill me,
for then at least it can be said
she died without ever changing.
Alas, heartfelt woes,
you are powerful enough to kill me
but not powerful enough to end my love!

Fabio listened to the sorrowful voice and the heartrending complaints with great pleasure for, although the singer wasn't the most
gifted he had ever heard, still he was sorry when the song ended so
soon. The time, the place, the wilderness, and the sweetness of the
song made him want it to continue. His only consolation for the fact

that it did not last longer was the thought that he might soon delight his eyes and his soul with the sight of the sorrowful musician just as the voice had delighted his ears. No matter how humble the singer might be, hearing such a song in the wilderness when he had expected to hear only the roar of some wild beast was a great relief. So Fabio, feeling more energetic than before, went on his way hoping to catch sight of the singer. He thought that no one would express those emotions and sorrowful complaints in such a remote wilderness without some powerful reason. What remarkable compassion and generosity to sympathize with someone else's sorrow!

You can't imagine how eager Fabio was to speak with the unhappy musician! As he didn't want the unsuspecting singer to hide, he moved as quietly as possible. He followed along the edge of the brook seeking its beautiful source, for he suspected that that place would hold the jewel that in his mind he was envisioning, and that was exactly what he found.

He was not mistaken. He climbed up to the little meadow that was at the very top of the mountain, a place inhabited only by wild creatures or by the chaste goddess Diana. It was limited at one end by a large white boulder from which emerged a lovely glassy lake, savory sustenance for the perfumed flowers, the green rosemary, and the delicate thyme carpeting the meadow. Lying in their midst he saw a shepherd lad who appeared to be in the springtime of his years, dressed in brown breeches and a white wooly lambskin jacket, his pack and his staff at his side. The moment Fabio saw the lad he recognized him as the musician who had sung the verses, for he seemed sad and morose and still wept from the emotion he had just poured out in song. If the voice Fabio had heard did not indicate otherwise, he might have thought the lad to be a rare statue made to adorn the spring, so motionless was he in his grief. His white hands were clasped together in a knot and they were so white that they could have made the snow envious, if the snow, shamefaced, had not already abandoned the mountain. If the shepherd had exposed his face to the sun, it did not show from the little effect of its rays, nor had his face allowed the weather to work any harm against its great beauty. Scattered amongst the aromatic grasses was a flock of snowy sheep serving as a pretext for his dress. Given the amount of attention he was paying them, they seemed like a stage setting arranged for him in just this scene.

The suspension of the lovely lad was such that Fabio was able to get so close that he could see that the white flower of the lad's face belied his dress, for if he had been a man, golden down would have begun to shadow his lip. But, because the place was so dangerous for a woman, Fabio really doubted what he was seeing. He told himself that that doubt only accused him of not being very brave himself. He drew nearer and called out a courteous greeting to the shepherd lad. The lad started to his senses and uttered such a sorrowful sigh that it almost seemed to be the last of his mortal days. The wilderness had not yet roughened his manners, however, so when he saw Fabio, he stood up and courteously returned the greeting, asking how he had come to such a place. Fabio thanked him for his courtesy and responded in this way:

"I am a native of Madrid. I came to Barcelona on important business and, when I finished it and was returning home, I didn't want to pass by without visiting the miraculous monastery of Montserrat. To show my devotion, I visited the monastery and then I decided to see the hermitages here on the mountain. While I was resting in the fragrant thyme, I heard your sad song. It affected me deeply and made me want to see the musician who sang such a sorrowful lament. By your song I can tell that you suffer from true love and that you weep because of a faithless lover. I found you and I notice that in your face and in your bearing you are not what your dress indicates: your face does not match your clothes, nor do your words go with the disguise you wear. Your face gives everything away. You're too old to be a boy, and yet the lack of a beard reveals that you're not a man. So, with all due respect, I'd like to ask you to settle my doubts. Let me first assure you that if I can help to remedy your sorrows, don't dismiss that as impossible or send me away disconsolate. It troubles me to find a woman in this wilderness and wearing such a disguise but, without knowing the cause of your exile, I can do nothing to help."

The shepherd lad listened attentively to Fabio and, from time to time, a laggard tear would slip slowly down his cheek and drop to the ground. When he saw that Fabio had finished and was waiting for an answer, he said:

"Sir, heaven must not want my sorrows to remain hidden, either because there's someone who can help me to bear them, or because I'm drawing near to the end of my weary life and it wants my pain to serve as an example and a lesson for others. When I thought that only God and these boulders were listening to me, heaven brought your Christian compassion to this place to hear my laments and my sorrows which are so great and so varied, having come to me from every direction, that I think it would be a greater favor to you not to tell you than to tell you and give you cause to sorrow. Furthermore, my story is so long that if you stay to hear it, you'll lose a lot of time."

"On the contrary," Fabio replied, "you have aroused my interest and my sympathy. Even if I thought I'd turn into a savage from staying a long time high among these peaks, as long as you are here, I shall not leave until you tell me your story so that, if it's possible, I can extricate you from this way of life. I insist on it. From what I can tell, you are sensible enough not to make it hard for me to persuade you to choose a more appropriate and less perilous life. You're not safe here because of the wild animals and the bandits who inhabit these wilds. If they discover your beauty, as I have, you can be sure they won't show the same respect for your person as do I. Please don't deprive me of this favor. I intend to wait all the years of Ulysses' absence to hear your story, which I shall listen to with relish."

"Well, if that's how it is," the lad responded, "please, kind sir, sit down and listen to what, until this very moment, no one has ever heard me tell. Understand how much I trust in your good will and your discretion by telling you, when I have just met you, such pro-digious and unheard of things as happen only to those born to extreme misfortune. When you learn who I am, the honor and good name of my many noble relatives run great risk, as does my very life, for they will have to kill me to avenge themselves and cleanse their honor."

Fabio thanked him as best he could for confiding his secrets in him, and he did it very nicely. He told the shepherd his name and reassured him about any danger. They sat down together beside the spring, and the beautiful shepherd began his story like this:

"Discreet Fabio, my name is Jacinta. Your eyes were not deceived in recognizing me as a woman. I was born in Baeza, a noble city in Andalucia, and my parents were likewise noble, with sufficient prop-erty to maintain their nobility and their honor. A brother and I were born in my father's house, he is to its eternal sorrow and I to its dishonor. We women are brought up so deficiently that very little strength is expected of us simply because we have beautiful eyes. Were we born blind, the world would have less drama, for we would live safe from deception. My mother died at the worst time for me. Her loss was great because her company, upbringing, and vigilance would have been better for my modesty than my father's negligence in look-ing out for me and arranging my marriage. (It's a terrible mistake for parents to wait for their daughters to take such a step on their own.)

My father loved my brother dearly—he was my father's one and only passion. He never gave a thought to me and I have no idea what his intentions for me were. He had plenty of money to do anything he might have wanted or desired to do.

"I was sixteen when, one night while I was sleeping, I had a dream. (Woe is me! And even when I was awake I relived that dream.) I was going through a lovely forest and in the very depths of the forest, I met the most handsome man I had ever in my life seen. His face was shadowed by the edge of a fawn cape with silver hooks and catches. Attracted by his appearance, I stopped to gaze at him. Eager to see if his face looked as I imagined, I approached and boldly pulled aside his cape. The moment I did, he drew a dagger and plunged it into my heart so violently that the pain made me cry out, and all my maids came running in. As soon as I awoke from this dark dream, I lost sight of the fact that he had done me such injury, and I felt more deeply affected than you can imagine. His image remained etched in my memory. It did not fade away or disappear for ever so long. Noble Fabio, I yearned to find a man with exactly his appearance and bearing to be my husband. These thoughts so obsessed me that I kept imagining and reimagining that scene, and I would have conversations with him. Before you knew it, I was madly in love with a mystery man whom I didn't know, but you must believe that if the god Narcissus was dark, then surely he was Narcissus.

"Because of this obsession I could neither eat nor sleep. My face lost its color and I experienced the most profound melancholy of my life. Everyone noticed the changes in me. Who, Fabio, ever heard of anyone loving a mere shadow? They may tell tales about people who've loved monsters and other incredible things, but at least what they loved had form! I sympathized with Pygmalion who loved the statue that ultimately Jupiter brought to life for him, and with the youth from Athens, and with the lovers who loved a tree or a dolphin. But what I loved was a mere fantasy, a shadow. What would people think of that? Nobody would believe me and, if they did, they'd think I'd lost my mind. But I give you my word of honor as a noblewoman, that not in this or in anything else I'll tell you, do I add a single word that isn't the truth. You can imagine that I talked to myself. I reproved myself, and, to free myself from my obsessive passion, I looked very carefully at all the elegant young men who lived in my city and tried to grow fond of one of them. Everything I did simply made me love my phantom more, and nowhere could I find his equal. My love grew and grew so great that I even composed poetry to my beloved ghost.

"If it won't bore you, I'll recite a poem for you, for even though it's written by a woman, it's all the better—it isn't right to excuse the errors men make in their poetry because they are taught in all their studies how to refine and adorn their verses with art; but a woman, who has only her own instinct, deserves praise for everything that's good and pardon for any defects."

"Fair Jacinta, recite your poem for me," Fabio said, "it would give me great pleasure. I know how to compose fairly well but I've never taken it too seriously for, I swear to you, I always think other people's poetry is better than my own."

"Well," Jacinta replied, "if that's how you really feel, then for the rest of my story I won't interrupt to ask permission to recite the poems that are fitting. This is the one I composed for my phantom:

> I adore what I cannot see,
> I cannot see what I adore,
> I do not know the cause of my love,
> but I want to find that cause.
> My confusion—
> who can begin to understand it?
> I have come to love without seeing,
> by imagination alone,
> turning my affection
> to a shade who has no being.
>
> It would not be a wondrous miracle
> for a painting to inspire love
> and, although I don't approve of such a love,
> even so, in fact it is based on beauty.
> But to love a face
> that's an invention of the soul—
> no one can imagine such madness!
> To think that I will ever find
> the cause, still uncreated,
> how can I pray for such a miracle?
>
> The wound in my heart
> gushes blood but I do not die.
> Happily I await death
> to put an end to my passion.
> If I don't die, it would be good

at least to sleep;
but how can I ask
for life or death
from one who has no being
from one who only wounds?

    Heaven, if you created
the shade I love, grant me
the object of my love
who is loved before he is born.
But how can an unfortunate lover,
one who was born unlucky, make such prayer?
Who can comprehend
this strange miracle of love:
that I should overflow with desire
for a lover glimpsed only in a dream?

"Who would think, Fabio, that heaven could be so generous as to grant what I could not even pray for? Since I desired the impossible, I didn't dare express such an outlandish wish except in these verses which are more poetry than prayer. When one is fated to be unfortunate, heaven seems to countenance misfortune.

"In my city, there also lived a gentleman who came from Seville. He was of the worthy and renowned Ponce de Leon family. This gentleman had engaged in some boyhood mischief in his birthplace, so he left Seville and came to Baeza to marry a lady in every way his equal. They had three children. The oldest and the youngest were girls, the middle child a boy. The older daughter married in Granada, so only the younger daughter was left at home to make up for the absence of don Felix, their handsome son. To live up to the valor and bravery of his illustrious ancestors, don Felix had gone to serve in the wars, seeking by his brave exploits to make his many noble relatives of the house of the dukes of Arcos and the counts of Bailen proud of their relation with him. Before this noble youth had reached the age of twenty-four, he had earned the command of a company. After serving three years in Flanders, he returned to Spain to request promotion. While his relatives at court were handling his petition, he came home to Baeza to visit his parents, for it had been a long time since he'd seen them, and they all looked forward to the day of his return.

"Don Felix arrived in Baeza one afternoon while I was sitting on my balcony daydreaming. Since his house was on the same street, he had to pass right by my house. The grand entrance he made with his many servants distracted me from my daydreaming (otherwise I might never have noticed). The moment I set my eyes on his elegant figure, I stared more than was proper, for his appearance stunned me. To try to describe to you that moment would prolong my story and my heartbreak. What I saw, in fact, was the handsome lord of my dream, the lord of my soul. If it was not he, then I am not the Jacinta who loved him more than life itself. I did not know don Felix nor did he know me because, when he went off to the wars, I was such a little girl that I couldn't have remembered him despite the fact that his sister and I were good friends.

"Don Felix glanced up at the balcony and noticed how my eyes celebrated his arrival. Cupid found the right time and the right place to pierce his heart with love's golden dart. As far as I was concerned, it goes without saying that Cupid's work had already been done. As don Felix passed, he said to me: 'If this jewel be not mine, I shall surely die.' My soul yearned to reply 'I already am,' but my modesty was as great as my love, so I only hoped and prayed that Cupid would grant me good fortune now that he had at last granted me the object of my love.

"Don Felix did not miss a single chance that Fortune placed in his hands. The first thing that happened was that doña Isabel told me about her brother's arrival. Of course I had to go visit her to congratulate her. On that visit, don Felix let me know with his eyes and with his words that he loved me so clearly that I, loving him truly, wanted to celebrate my good fortune by not hiding my feelings from him. In so doing, I gave him permission to court me, to promenade by my house by day, and by night to serenade me with his guitar and with his sweet voice singing the love songs he composed so well. I recall, Fabio, that the very first time I spoke with him alone through the grating at my window was in response to this sonnet:

> To love the day, to hate the day,
> to call forth night and then dismiss her,
> to fear fire while drawing close to the flame,
> to feel sorrow and joy at the same time,

> for valor and cowardice to dwell side by side,
> cruel scorn and gentle pleading,
> for knowledge to tie
> reason in bonds and free audacity,

to seek a way to relieve sorrow
while refusing to abandon sorrow,
to desire without knowing what,

to feel pleasure and displeasure just alike,
and all the pain contained in hope,
if this isn't love, I don't know what it is.

"Love had already plotted my downfall; now it began to affix the bonds that would enchain me and dig the pit that would entrap me, and I sought a way to satisfy my desire. When I heard that sonnet, I went down to the room of one of my father's servants named Sarabia, who was greedier than he was loyal. Because his window opened onto the street, it was easy for me to talk with don Felix, and we could even hold hands. When I saw don Felix up close, I said:

" 'If truly you love as you say, then fortunate is the lady who merits your affection.'

" 'You know very well, my lady,' don Felix replied, 'from my eyes, from my great desire, that my love for you reveals my sweet perdition. I know better how to love than how to express my love. I don't sing to be a famous poet or musician but to tell you that you are to be my mistress for so long as I shall live. That is my only desire.'

" 'And do you think,' I asked, 'that I should believe what you say to me?'

" 'Most certainly,' my lover responded, 'because a woman has the privilege of allowing herself to love and be loved by the man who is to be her husband.'

" 'And what assures me that you will be my husband?' I asked.

" 'My love,' said don Felix, 'and this hand which, if you will accept it as the pledge of my word, will never fail you, even if it costs its owner his life.'

"How wonderful to find myself desired just as I'd imagined and wanted, friend Fabio! What woman ever refused the opportunity to marry the very man she loved, who didn't accept his offer right away? Well, there's no better bait for a woman than this, which will surely lead her to her downfall. I didn't want to jeopardize my good fortune, which is what I considered it then and shall always consider it when I recall that day. I put my hand through the grating and took the one my lord was offering to me, and said to him:

" 'This isn't the time, don Felix, for me disdainfully to play games or to hide my love with feigned resistance, sighs, and tears. I love you. I've loved you not just since that day when I first saw you, but even before. So that my words won't confuse you. . . .' and then I told him everything I've told you about my dream.

"All the while I was telling don Felix of my haunting dream, he kept kissing my hand, which he was holding in both of his, as consolation for all my sorrows. That day and this one would have caught us in that glory had our love not progressed to more. We took leave of each other with a thousand tender words, swearing our love and promising to see each other every night in that same place. It was easy to buy the servant with gold coins and, through my boldness, I managed to overcome the difficulty of getting there even though I had to walk right by the bed where my father and my brother were sleeping in order to leave my room.

"Doña Isabel visited me often because of her friendship for me and also to please her brother, and she served as the trusted intermediary to our love. For some time our courtship remained in this delightful state and during that time don Felix made no effort to return to duty in Italy.

"While virtually all the ladies in the city had been conquered by his magnificent presence, one in particular was his cousin, doña Adriana, one of the most beautiful women in the entire region. She was the daughter of don Felix's father's sister, who as I said before, was from Seville. Doña Adriana had four sisters and, when their father died, they had all come to Baeza. The two youngest entered the convent. The second daughter married here, and that left the eldest who had chosen neither to marry or to become a nun. She lived with her married sister who by now had become a widow and had inherited fifty thousand ducats. The widow loved her sister dearly as you can imagine since she was alone in the world and also because her sister, doña Adriana, was so very beautiful. Well, doña Adriana enjoyed frequent conversation with don Felix because they were cousins, and she fell madly and passionately in love with him and you'll soon find out what happened.

"Don Felix was aware of his cousin's love for him but, because he had his heart set on me, he passed it off and tried to avoid giving her encouragement or any pretext for loving him more. To every indication doña Adriana gave of her love he, with careless inattention, played disinterested. Finally, overcome by her frustrated love and deeply affected by his disdain, she fell ill and the doctors feared for her life. Besides not eating or sleeping, she refused to allow them to give her any remedies. This upset her mother terribly. Her mother, however, was a shrewd woman, and she began to suspect that her daughter's illness was caused by unrequited love. With this idea, she pressed doña Adriana's maid, in whom the girl confided everything, to tell her the truth. When she learned what the situation was, she planned how to remedy it.

"She called her nephew and, with tears in her eyes, told him of the great sorrow she felt because of her darling daughter's illness and explained the cause of her illness. Then she begged him most fervently to marry her daughter. She could answer for her brother's consent, and don Felix couldn't find a better match in all Baeza.

"Don Felix didn't want to be the cause of his cousin's death, nor did he wish to upset his aunt with a harsh reply. Therefore, trusting in the time it would take to make all the arrangements and to obtain a dispensation from Rome, he told her to take the matter up with his father and he agreed to accept their decision. Then he went in to visit his cousin and filled her heart with hope. As his aunt had requested, he went to doña Adriana's house regularly and showed satisfaction in her improvement. Doña Adriana recovered her health entirely.

"In order to visit his cousin, don Felix started missing his visits to me. I began to question his fidelity and despaired and wept my eyes dry. One night, in an effort to assuage my jealousy and also to avoid the neighbors' gossip, he arranged with Sarabia to come inside. When he saw my tears and heard in my complaints the rawness of my feelings, like a true lover above all suspicion, he told me what had happened with regard to his cousin. In telling me this he was loving but unwise because what, until then, had been merely fear became open jealousy, and the anger of a jealous woman is no small thing. I told him never to look at me again in all his life, let alone speak to me, unless he told his cousin that he couldn't be hers because he'd promised to marry me.

"I was so angry I tried to return to my room, but my lover wouldn't let me go. Very humbly and lovingly, he vowed he would not let a day pass without obeying me, that he would've done so already if he hadn't wanted to protect my decorum by speaking with me first. With the go-between servant as witness, he again gave me his word to marry me, and I gave him possession of my body and my soul, believing that in that way I could hold him more securely to his promise. That night passed more quickly than ever, for it was followed by the day of my great misfortune.

"The doctor had decided that that morning doña Adriana should drink a strong syrup and then take some exercise in the countryside. Unable to see the illness of her soul, he thought her loss of color was caused by anemia. On that very day, to satisfy my jealousy, my betrothed freed her from the illusions of her love. A man has only one body and one soul despite the fact that he may have many desires; no matter how many desires he has, he cannot be in two places at the same time and the night before my don Felix had been with me, which meant he wasn't with his cousin. The truth of the matter is that Fortune guided things in her own way, to the great detriment of my welfare, and arranged for doña Adriana to get up early that morning. She took her syrup and went for her walk with her aunt and her maids. Their first stop was her cousin don Felix's house. When doña Adriana entered, everyone was happy to see her so well. They all greeted her as if she were the sun and congratulated her on her improved health. She went off with doña Isabel to don Felix's room. He was still resting, making up for the sleep he'd lost in his amorous night with me. In the presence of his sister, doña Adriana began to take him to task for not having visited her the night before, just as if she were his wife. Don Felix made no response. Finally, in a few brief words, he managed to let her know that she was wasting her time; he was in love with me; we had exchanged vows; he was engaged to marry me, and, unless he lost his life, he would not fail to keep his word to me.

"These words caused doña Adriana to fall into a swoon. They had to carry her in to doña Isabel's bed. When she recovered her senses, stifling her tears as best she could, she took leave of doña Isabel, responding abruptly and drily to the comfort doña Isabel tried to give. She returned home, and, to avenge don Felix's rejection of her, she plotted the most cruel act against herself, against her cousin don Felix, and against me, that you can imagine. Oh jealousy! When you possess a woman's heart, what terrible things you do! In her fit of jealousy, the first thing doña Adriana did was write a letter to my father in which she informed him of what was going on and cautioned him to keep watch over his house, for his honor was in jeopardy. She waited until the next morning to give the letter to a servant for delivery to my father, with instructions to tell him that it came from Madrid. Then she put on her cloak and, ready to take her prescribed exercise, she went in to see her mother. More lovingly than you might expect, given her cruel plan, doña Adriana said to her:

" 'Mother dear, I'm going out for my walk now. God alone knows if I'll come back. Please embrace me, my lady, in case I should never see you again.'

" 'Hush, Adriana,' her mother said, alarmed, 'don't say such terrible things, unless you want to end my days. Why shouldn't you see me again? Why, you've recovered your health, I haven't seen you looking so well in a long time. Go, my child, don't wait till the sun gets so high that it might harm you.'

" 'Won't my lady please embrace me?' doña Adriana asked.

"She turned and left, her eyes filled with tears. She went to the front door, took two steps outside, uttered a heartrending cry, and collapsed to the ground. Her mother, her aunt, and all the servants rushed to help her. Thinking she'd fainted, they carried her to her bed and sent for the doctor to attend her, but her swoon was eternal; he declared her dead. When they went to undress her and place her in her shroud, the whole house suddenly exploded with screams. They unbuttoned her bodice of blue and gray tabby and between her beautiful breasts they found a letter she herself had written to her mother, explaining that she had taken her own life by putting corrosive sublimate in her syrup because she preferred to die rather than see her cousin don Felix in the arms of another woman.

"Doña Adriana's mother's grief would have broken anyone's heart! She was so grief-stricken that she was beyond tears. She was inconsolable, not only because of her daughter's suicide and the terrible desperation of her act, but especially because her body, when it got cold, bloated terribly and turned black. You can well imagine, Fabio, the reaction of the entire household and indeed of the whole city. Unaware of all that had been ordained against me and to keep doña Isabel company, I went to see this spectacle. I was feeling very confused about being the cause of that dreadful catastrophe as I'd learned what she'd done in a note from my betrothed.

"Don Felix didn't go to the funeral. He didn't want to arouse heaven to avenge his cruelty. I attributed his absence to his sorrow but either way his behavior was proper. The ill-fated woman was buried. Her family, because of its nobility and wealth, managed to overcome any obstacle that might have arisen from the fact that she died at her own hand.

"After the funeral I went home and waited for night to come, hoping to see don Felix. It was scarcely nine o'clock when Sarabia informed me that don Felix was downstairs in his room. Would to God his grief had prevailed and he had not come! That night seemed even more propitious than usual for a rendezvous because my crafty father, advised by doña Adriana's letter, had gone to bed earlier than normal. He had also made my brother and everyone else retire early. I pretended to go to bed. I waited a while, leaving time for my father to fall fast asleep and, despite his worry, restlessness, and rage, he did sleep soundly until four. As soon as I saw that he was sound asleep, I got up and, barefooted, wearing only my petticoat, I rushed to the arms of my beloved. We discussed with astonishment what doña Adriana had done and, through caresses and cajolery, I tried to assuage the grief he felt.

"Sarabia waited outside on the stairs, a vigilant spy in the cause of my misdeeds. Suddenly my father awoke with a start. He got up and went in to check my bed. When he didn't find me there, he woke my brother and told him briefly and succinctly what the situation was. He got his pistol and his sword. They were not so quiet, however, that the little dog we kept in the house didn't give warning to my servant with her barking. He listened closely, and, when he heard footsteps, he came down and told us that if we wanted to save our lives we should follow him quickly, as we had been found out.

"Terribly upset, we did as he said and before my father had gotten down the stairs the three of us had reached the street. We locked the door from the outside—our desperate plight inspired that clever trick.

"Just imagine, Fabio, me barefooted and wearing only my green damask petticoat trimmed with silver, just as I had come downstairs to meet my lover. Don Felix took me straight to the convent where his two aunts lived. By the time we arrived day had dawned. He knocked at the portal, and we entered through the turnstile. We told his aunts what had happened and in less than an hour I found myself behind bars, confused, and in tears. Don Felix encouraged me as much as he could; his aunts consoled me and assured me that everything would work out. They were positive that, as soon as my father's rage exhausted itself, he would agree to our marriage. Just in case he should try to charge don Felix with assault on his house, don Felix and Sarabia stayed in the same convent in a special room that his aunts prepared for them. From there he let his father and his sister know what had transpired.

"His father already knew from all the signs that don Felix was in love with me, and the idea did not make him unhappy, as he knew that in all Baeza his son couldn't find a better or a richer match. So he, too, believed that everything would work out and that I would become his son's wife. Accompanied by doña Isabel, he came to visit. He came especially to comfort and encourage me. She brought me dresses and jewels to make up for the lack of my own and to tide me over while I was having clothes made.

"While these events were happening to me, my father felt increasingly aggrieved by the scandal of my leaving his house. Of course it would have been worse if I'd stayed and born the brunt of his fury; it would have cost me my life at the very least. Instead of asking the law to investigate and thereby causing even greater scandal, he made up his mind to take upon himself revenge for the loss of his prize jewel and the star of his honor, now missing from his house. With this honorable intention, he set spies onto don Felix, so of course his plan was really no secret. Before too many days had passed, he found the chance he'd been waiting for, which brought as much misfortune as everything else except, in this instance, Fortune was on don Felix's side.

"It happened that one night, tired of being secluded and sure that I was safe in my cell with his aunts, who loved me as much as if I were their own daughter, don Felix easily overcame the objections of the servant who kept the keys to the convent and persuaded him to let him out. Don Felix only wanted to go visit his father; it wasn't far and he'd be right back. The disloyal guardian warned him about the danger, but then let him out. Well-armed and thrilled to be free, don Felix stepped outside. The moment he put his foot in the street, my father and my brother, with swords drawn, set upon him. As vigilant spies over their honor, they had been practically sleeping in the doorway to the convent. Don Felix was as cautious as my brother was reckless and consequently, with the first exchange of blows, don Felix pierced my brother's heart. He dropped dead without even being able to call on God. It all happened so fast that the doorkeeper hadn't even had time to close the door. He managed to get don Felix back inside before my father or the law could call him to account.

"Day came and the whole event became public. My ill-fated brother was buried and the gossip started. I, totally unaware of what had happened, went out to the visitors' room to see doña Isabel. She was terribly upset and in tears. She had hoped, because I was betrothed to her brother, that she in turn would become my brother's wife and she loved him dearly. She described to me what had taken place and told me that don Felix planned to leave Baeza and Spain. It was said that the mayor was negotiating to remove him from the sanctuary of the convent and that a chancery judge had been called in and was already on his way.

"Imagine, Fabio, my emotions and my tears at this sad news. It almost killed me. That very night my beloved lord was to depart for Flanders, haven for the unfortunate and refuge for criminals. He did just that, leaving orders for me to be well cared for. He charged his father with reconciling all grievances and arranging for his eventual return.

"They finally put an end to our tender farewells by transferring me, half-dead, from his arms into the arms of his aunt. By special permission of the vicar and the abbess, he departed through a back door to the nuns' living quarters which was seldom used. He took the road straight to Barcelona where the ships called home by Philip III for the expulsion of the Moriscos were harbored. These ships were now awaiting His Excellency Pedro Fernandez de Castro, the count of Lemos, to take him to the kingdom of Naples to become viceroy and captain general.

"My father soon learned of don Felix's absence. Since he could no longer take revenge directly on him, being wily, he plotted to take vengeance on me. The first thing he did was to take control of all the roads so that no letters could get through to don Felix's father or to me. It wasn't such a bad idea, because that way he knew don Felix's every move. He intercepted every letter, for money can do everything, and men of my father's standing have friends everywhere who will assist them in their vengeance.

"Don Felix had been gone some fifteen or twenty days, which seemed like twenty thousand years to me, and I had no news from my absent lover. One day, while my would-be father-in-law and sister-in-law were visiting me, a postman entered and delivered to my father-in-law a letter he said came from Barcelona. I later learned it had been mailed right there in the same city. It read:

I deeply regret being the first to inform your grace of the bad news. I wish I didn't have to, but my sense of obligation and my friendship leave me no other recourse. Last night, as Lieutenant Felix Ponce de Leon, your grace's son, was leaving a gaming house, he was stabbed twice. There is no information about who did it or why. It happened so suddenly that he never even saw his attacker. We buried him this morning and I am sending you this letter at once so that you will know the truth. May the Lord console you and grant you long life, as your humble servant desires for you. I shall take Sarabia with me to Naples unless your grace commands otherwise.

Barcelona, June 20.   Captain Diego de Mesa

"Alas, Fabio, what tragic news! I don't want to recall the grief I felt. Suffice it to say that I believed the letter because the captain was a very close friend of don Felix's. They had always kept in touch and they'd intended to make that trip together. So I believed it. You can imagine my tears, my sorrow. Don't ask why but, without asking questions or obtaining any other information, the next day I donned the nun's habit. So did doña Isabel, who loved me dearly and wanted to console me and keep me company.

"Don't forget, wise Fabio, that it was my own father who deceived me in this way. He appropriated all of don Felix's letters that came to the city and he wrote that fateful letter. When don Felix arrived in Barcelona, he found that the viceroy had already boarded ship, and so, with time for only a few short lines, he wrote to inform us that he and Sarabia were departing that same day. They traveled together because don Felix hadn't wanted to leave him in Baeza where his life would be in danger, He asked us to write him first in Naples where he was headed en route to Flanders. Because his father and I never received this letter, but instead the letter informing us of his death, which we believed to be true, we never wrote him or made any kind of investigation. After the year of our novitiate was over, doña Isabel and I took our vows. I was very pleased with the decision for, believing don Felix dead, I knew there could never be another man to win my love.

"My father died a month after I took my vows, leaving me heir to four thousand ducats in income. As he had no other children, he did not deprive me of my inheritance and, despite his rage, he was a Christian and fulfilled his obligations. This money I spent liberally on things for the convent and in that way I became mistress of it and nothing was done there that did not suit my pleasure.

"Don Felix arrived in Naples. Finding no letters there as he expected, he felt hurt and angry at my forgetfulness and neglect. So he stopped writing himself. Just at that time five companies were departing for Flanders. He was given a command and within a few days he set out again. When he got to Brussels, to get over his love for me, he devoted himself to gambling and womanizing. He spent six years like that, with never a thought for Spain or for the sorrowful Jacinta he had left back home. Would to God he had stayed there forever and left me to my peace and quiet and never subjected me to even greater misfortune!

"Six years passed and finally don Felix remembered his obligations and returned to Spain and to his birthplace to unleash the rest of my great misfortune. He arrived after nightfall and, instead of going to his father's house, he came straight to the convent. He arrived at the portal just as it was being closed for the night. He asked for Jacinta, saying that he bore letters from Flanders. The doorkeeper at this time was one of his aunts, and she was curious to know what the stranger wanted of me, finding it odd that anyone should ask for me except don Felix's father, who was my only visitor. She stepped back for a moment and then drew close and asked:

" 'Who is looking for Jacinta, for I am she.'

" 'You cannot deceive me,' don Felix said, 'for the soldier who gave me these letters described her voice to me.'

"Catching the deception, the doorkeeper immediately sent for me in order to discover the meaning of this mystery. The moment I arrived and asked who wanted to see me, don Felix recognized my voice. He came closer and said:

" 'Wasn't it time, my dear Jacinta, for me to come visit you?'

"Oh Fabio! What that voice did to me! Even now I think I can hear it and I feel exactly as I felt at that moment. The instant I recognized don Felix's voice, I immediately thought of the false news of his death, of my being a nun, and of the impossibility of ever marrying him. All the love that had been dormant in me reawakened. I uttered a heartrending cry and fell to the floor in such a cruel swoon that it lasted for three days. For three days I seemed dead; nonetheless, the doctors said I was alive even though none of the remedies they tried could bring me to my senses.

"Don Felix took lodging in a room in the convent, undoubtedly the same one he'd stayed in before. There he could visit with his sister, because this room had a grate through which we used to talk. From her he learned what had happened in his absence. When he found out that I'd taken my vows, it's a miracle he didn't die. He charged her to care for my health and to keep his arrival secret. He didn't want his father to find out; his mother had died in the meantime.

"I did finally recover from my swoon and my health improved. Heaven was saving my life for yet greater misfortune. At last I came to see my don Felix. We cried and cried. Finally we decided that Sarabia should go to Rome to seek permission for us to marry, given that my first vows were more binding than my second ones.

"Two weeks or a month passed while I collected money to send him on the long journey. During this time my love revived again and desire began to wax. Don Felix persuaded me to return to our former bliss and, in my weakness, I surrendered. Believing that the pope's dispensation was assured and trusting in the vows we had made to each other before I took my religious vows, I managed to get the key to the back door through which don Felix had escaped for Flanders. (Don't ask me how I did it, but you know how powerful money is.) When I gave the key to my lover, it made him happier than if I'd given him a kingdom. Oh, how terrible this is to describe! Every night, or almost every night, he came in to sleep with me. It was easy, for my cell was in that part of the convent. When I think about what we did, Fabio, I'm not surprised that misfortune has pursued me. I can only praise and laud God's great love and mercy that He didn't strike us both dead with a bolt of lightning.

"At about this time Sarabia left for Rome and don Felix remained in hiding, determined that no one should know he was there until the dispensation arrived. Sarabia got to Rome and presented to his Holiness the papers and the petition he was carrying which contained all the details of our situation and how I had entered the convent. This was a difficult case for the pope to decide, so he ordered don Felix, under threat of excommunication, to appear in person before his tribunal so the pope could hear the case in all its complex detail. Then he would consider granting the dispensation at the cost of four thousand ducats.

"When we were expecting happy news, Sarabia arrived with this. With great sorrow, I began to lament don Felix's absence, fearing he might forget me. He felt the same sorrow and asked me to leave the convent and go with him to Rome where, together, we might more easily obtain permission to marry. He asked that of a woman who was madly in love, so the decision wasn't difficult. The next night I took all the money and jewels I had and left a letter for doña Isabel. I entrusted to her the care and administration of my affairs. Then I placed myself in don Felix's hands. By the time day arrived, we were well away from Baeza on three mules that Sarabia had readied. Within twelve days we found ourselves in Valencia. We took a boat and, with a thousand difficulties and great risk to our lives, we got to Civita Vecchia. From there, we took a coach into Rome.

"Don Felix counted among his friends the ambassador from Spain and several cardinals who had been in the famed city of Baeza, a center of the holy faith. With their support, we dared to cast ourselves at the feet of his Holiness and he looked kindly upon our petition. He absolved us and ordered us to give two thousand ducats to the Royal Hospital of Spain, which is located in Rome. Then the pope himself wed us, with the condition that we not make love for a year under pain of mortal sin. If we did, he reserved the penalty and the punishment unto himself.

"In Rome we visited the holy sites and made general confession. After several days passed, don Felix learned that the countess of Gelves, Leonor of Portugal, was embarking for Zaragoza, where her husband Diego Pimentel had recently been appointed viceroy. This seemed like the perfect way to get back to Spain, back home, and rest from all the trials we had experienced, so he took me to Naples and, through the support of the marquis of Santa Cruz, I joined the ladies attending the countess and don Felix likewise joined their entourage.

"Fortune had it that because of a cruel gale, we were forced to travel by land, but we made it, Fabio. My husband and I finally got to Madrid. There he took me to the house of one of his relatives, a widow who had a beautiful daughter as ladylike as she was fair, as discreet as she was elegant. He planned to leave me in safekeeping with them, given the fact that we had to remain apart for the rest of the year. He went before the War Council to present his documents and to request reassignment to a company. He thought that with my income and his captain's pay, he could live like a king in Baeza.

"Don Felix received orders from his majesty that all soldiers seeking promotion should go serve in Mamora and, upon their return, the king promised to grant their promotion. But, since don Felix had done previous service, he was honored with the desired rank of captain. In this instance his patriotic sense of duty took precedence over his love for me. One afternoon, while he was visiting me in the company of his relatives, he said:

" 'My dearest Jacinta, you understand my duty to serve the king, which obliges all gentlemen and even the humblest man born with a sense of honor. This campaign cannot last long and if it should last longer than we anticipate, as long as a man carries true love in his heart and does not lack an honorable roof, be it in Algiers or in Constantinople, love will turn any countryside into a city, any hut into a palace. I tell you this because I must obey my orders. If I tried to evade my obligation, it would reflect badly on my name. The worthiness of this cause explains why I must now neglect you, if that's how you would describe my leaving you. The trust I have in you excuses me from taking you with me. If I didn't have such great confidence in you, I would take you in my company and you would suffer anew seeing me consumed by my work or maybe the journey itself would bring us both death.

" 'May God's will be done and as soon as these revolutions are put down I shall be free to enjoy you fully as my wife or, at the very least, to send for you so that I can occupy myself in serving you. I know well how much I owe your love and affection for me. You are my wife but we still have seven months until I can fully enjoy you as my own. All the honor and fame I shall earn will be yours. So, dear wife, please look kindly on this expedition and try to ease the sorrow we both feel. You shall stay here in my aunt's house and preserve our good name. I have taken care of everything necessary for your comfort. I'm leaving a letter for my father and sister in which I tell them our story. All my letters and money will come to you. Writing to you and receiving your letters will keep up my spirits and I shall live for the day when I see you again. I depart this afternoon. I haven't wanted to say anything to you until now to keep you from grieving too much. For your sake and for mine, please show the bravery you've shown in all our adversities and contain your feelings. With a sea of tears in my eyes, I beg of you, please don't deny me permission.'

"Discreet Fabio, I listened to my don Felix thinking that at that moment he was the most wonderful, handsome, and loving I had ever seen him, and my own love swelled greater. I was to lose him—how my misfortune ever worked things purposely to torment me! I tried to answer him, but my emotion wouldn't let me; I thought he was right in everything he'd said. With awkward words, I told him so, letting my eyes speak my feelings. It was clear that I consented to his decision and his desire, but my eyes expressed my sorrow. We exchanged very loving words, the more to increase our sorrow than to appease it. The moment came when I lost him forever. Don Felix departed.

"When he left, I was like a person deranged. I couldn't cry, I couldn't speak, I couldn't even hear the solace that doña Guiomar and her mother tried to give. They kept saying things to comfort me, trying in vain to break the trance that bound me. My beloved don Felix's departure cost me three months' illness, during which I came close to death. Would to heaven I had died! But when do the unfortunate receive such concessions, even from heaven which has in its power so many miracles?

"During those three months, I received no letters from don Felix, although letters from his father and sister did console me; they were happy to know the outcome of all our trials and they sent a thousand kind words, gifts, money, and fervent good wishes. They urged the two of us to come and stay in their company as soon as don Felix returned. None of this kindness, however, could fill the vacuum of my love, which made me fear a great misfortune. I believe that there is no better astrologer than a lover.

"For over four months I lived in torment. One night, sleep took greater power over me than usual (just as Fortune had given me don Felix in a dream, she took him away from me in the same way). I dreamt that I received a letter from don Felix and a box that appeared to contain jewels. When I opened it, I saw that it contained my husband's head! Imagine, Fabio, my cries and my wailing! I woke up weeping, so overwhelmed by fear, sorrow, and tears that I thought I would die. I fell into a faint. When doña Guiomar called out to me and threw water in my face, I returned to my senses. I was the most pitiful sight in the world. When I told them my dream, she, her mother, and the maids became so afraid that they didn't dare leave me alone. Everywhere I turned my eyes, I thought I saw don Felix's head.

"We spent the night battling my terror. In the morning, they decided to take me to my confessor so I could make confession. He was a very wise priest and well instructed in how to give comfort. As we were leaving the house, I heard a voice which the others didn't hear:

" 'It's true; he's dead. Don Felix is dead.'

"Because of these bad omens, you can believe that my confessor was unable to comfort me, nor was there solace anywhere on earth. I spent several days submerged in this terror. Finally came the news of what had happened in Mamora and, with the news, the story of the many who had drowned. Among the first of them was don Felix.

"A few days later Sarabia arrived, and he was the most reliable source of information. He described how the ships raced each other to enter port. Two of them collided and shattered. They split asunder and sank. It had been impossible to save even a single one of the men aboard. My don Felix had sailed on one of these ships. He was wearing armor so heavy that, when he fell into the sea, he never reappeared. Although they searched for him, no one ever saw him again. That's how his life ended in such a horrible way, the most gallant man of Andalucia! I say this without bias, for at thirty-four he was the handsomest man Nature could form.

"Given the close attention with which you listen to my story, it would be inconsiderate to tire you with my grief, my sorrows, my tears, and my mourning. I shall say only that for three years I didn't know what health or happiness were.

"When don Felix's father and sister learned the tragic news, they tried to bring me home and place me back in my convent. While I deeply lamented the death of my husband, I couldn't consent for, given the scandal I'd caused, I couldn't face my relatives, let alone the nuns, without his company. Besides, my poor health wouldn't have allowed me to travel or to suffer the rigors of being a novice and the weight of religious life. I sent Sarabia, whom I considered my companion in misfortune, back to manage my estates and I stayed with doña Guiomar and her mother, who treated me as her own daughter. This was not altogether surprising for, while I lived with them, I spent my income generously.

"Some friends advised me to remarry, but I knew I could never find another don Felix or any other man who could please my eyes or fill the emptiness in my heart. My memory was not empty, and it would not let me forget him. But, to my misfortune, I did find love, probably because I wasn't expecting it.

"A handsome, noble, rich, and very gallant youth named Celio, as clever as he was false, used to visit doña Guiomar. He knew how to love when he chose and how to forget when he pleased. In him virtue and deception grew together like the flowers in Madrid, all mingled together, perfumed carnations, lovely musk roses, mixed with wild flowers that have no beauty or perfume whatsoever. He spoke well and wrote better and was as skilled in loving as in scorning. During the long period of time he came to our house to visit, we never saw in this young man I describe any designs at all. He conversed openly and amiably and was perhaps one of the most assiduous in trying to relieve my sadness. Sometimes he and doña Guiomar would play music and sometimes he would recite poetry, at which he was very gifted. Time went by and he showed himself to be more accomplished in everything he did than I liked to admit. He praised doña Guiomar and me equally. He courted us both without offending either of us, first lauding the maiden, then praising the widow. Since I too composed poetry, he would challenge me and we would enjoy the competition. It didn't amaze him that I composed poetry. That's no miracle in a woman whose soul is just the same as a man's, and maybe it pleases Nature to perform this wonder, or maybe men shouldn't feel so vain, believing they're the only ones who enjoy great talent. What did amaze Celio was that I composed so well.

"It never occurred to me to love him or to scorn him. The fact was simply that he charmed me. I did, however, fear his indifference, which he himself had described to us on many occasions. One day, in particular, he described to us how a certain lady declared her love to him and now he despised her with the same intensity as he'd previously loved her. He boasted of the feckless ways in which he repaid her thousand kindnesses.

"Who would ever think, Fabio, that this would arouse my passion? I didn't exactly fall in love but I began to look at him more attentively than I should have! From noticing his fine figure, a tiny bit of desire was born in me. With that desire, my tears began to dry, and slowly I recovered my health. My memories faded, and so I came to love Celio and to wish he were my husband. In order not to seem forward, I waited to reveal my love until he himself brought up the subject. One day he asked me to compose a sonnet on the subject of a lady looking at herself in a mirror, struck by a ray of sunlight which dazzles her. Using this theme, I composed this sonnet:

> In the clear looking glass of disenchantment,
> Jacinta looks at herself, unconcerned,
> happy to be neither loved or in love,
> happy to see happiness where others see sorrow.
>
> She sees how all lovers are deceived
> when constant love is spurned,
> when the estranged lover, distant
> from his former passion, flees.
>
> Celio, the sun of this our age, envies
> the freedom in which Jacinta lives,
> exempt from offering spoils to love.
>
> Gallant, discreet, generous, loving,
> brilliantly daring,
> he appears in her mirror and dazzles her eyes.
>
> She feels a sweet annoyance
> and, setting aside the glass, she says:
>
> 'Before I saw Celio, I was free,
> But now, although he draws near to inflame me,
> I do not wish to retreat from his rays.'

"Celio received this sonnet with such pleasure that I felt confident that my good fortune was assured, when really it reflected only the fact that nobody feels averse to being loved. He raved about his good fortune and expressed appreciation of my love. He gave clear indication of his regard and told me that he had loved me from the first day he ever saw me, that he'd invented this trick to discover how I felt. He secured the snare into which I had just fallen by celebrating my beauty and his good fortune in a ballad of his own. Poor me! When I think about the tricks and strategies men use to conquer women and overcome their weakness, I consider them all traitors. Love represents a battlefield and a combat zone where, with fire and sword, it struggles to vanquish honor, guardian of the soul's fortress. I tell you, Fabio, that even though I seemed blind and captive to his will, I always knew what I lost in that battle. But I stopped being wise and fell in love with a man who despised women. This knowledge should have been enough to make me turn back, if only my sense of purpose had lasted.

"Celio was the most clever man in deception I've ever known. He began to give such color of truth to his love that even the shrewdest and wiliest woman, even one who prized her independence and knew the truth about him, would've believed him. He visited me constantly; morning, noon, and night he was at my house. His friends, when they noticed he was avoiding their company, realized that he was courting a woman of worth. He had one friend in particular who had your name, Fabio, with whom he maintained a closer friendship than with the rest. As Celio himself told me, he described all his tactics to that Fabio, who worried about my welfare and kept begging him not to lead me on if he intended to repay me the way he'd repaid all the other women he'd courted.

"Celio wrote me so many letters that they almost drove me crazy; he gave me so many timely gifts that it seemed as if he held heaven in his hands to give me the right thing at the right moment. He did everything possible to make me fall. Naively, I ignored his treacherous nature and heaped love on top of love. Of course I always behaved in accord with my belief that he would become my husband. Otherwise I would rather have died than let him know of my love. In all this I, being who I am, thought I was granting him great favor. Celio must not have thought about my position, or so it would seem, although he was not unaware of what he would gain by such a marriage. Totally taken in, I felt so happy to be his that I no longer thought about Felix. All of my senses were absorbed by Celio. I did fear his love because, from the moment I started loving him, I dreaded losing him. To calm these fears, one day when I saw him more attentive and more loving than usual, I told him all my thoughts. I said that, just as I had four thousand ducats a year in income, if I had all the money in the world and power over the whole world as well, I would make him master of all that.

"Celio acted true to form, and in that he was more fortunate than I was. He devastated all my hopes by telling me that he had spent his life studying the scriptures for the purpose of being ordained as a priest. That's what his parents wanted for him and it was also his own will. Consequently, I could command him to do anything I wanted and he would gladly obey, even at the cost of his own life. Anything, except marry. By way of consoling me for my loss, he gave me his word and swore by his faith that he would love me so long as he lived.

"How disappointed I was to see all my fears confirmed, all my hopes shattered! It was unthinkable for me, being who I am, to love anyone who could not become my legitimate husband; therefore our friendship had to end. Seeing Celio so cruel, I burst into tears. Although he couldn't ignore the fact that they were born of my love for him, instead of drying them, he got up and departed, leaving me bathed in more tears. I spent all that night and the next day weeping. He sent me none of the many messages he usually sent, not for lack of a messenger but for lack of will. The following afternoon, Celio came to make his excuses so coolly that, instead of dissipating my tears, he increased them.

"This was the beginning of his thanklessness toward me; after this start, much worse was to follow. He began to neglect my love. He came to see me only every now and then, and he ceased answering my letters, which formerly had merited his praise. As an excuse for this coldness, he blamed business and his friends. He caused me such sadness and distemper that soon my friends, who had previously enjoyed my company and my charm, fled from me, seeing me now so moody and peevish.

"Then Celio compounded his lack of affection by making me jealous. He began to visit other women and, what was even worse, to talk about them. This so aroused my rage and caused me such wrath that, to his mind, I turned into a carping shrew. Since his love had been feigned all along, before six months passed he found himself altogether free of any regard for me, as if he'd never felt anything at all. Heedless of his obligations to me, he began to visit a woman of easy virtue, one of the kind who sell pleasure for money. He really enjoyed this affair because it didn't make any claim on him or oblige him in any way. He didn't care that I knew about it nor did he heed the complaints I wrote to him or expressed to him on the rare occasions when he came to visit me.

"I learned about his affair and about all of his activities from one of my maids who followed him. I wrote that woman a letter begging her not to let him into her house. The result of this was that he never again came to my house and devoted himself more completely to her. Depressed and despairing, I spent my days and my nights weeping. But why tire you with these details? It's enough to say he closed his eyes to me.

"At this time, it became necessary for him to go to Salamanca. He planned to stay there a whole year, mostly to avoid seeing me. The result of this turn of events you can see in the clothes I'm wearing here in this wilderness where you have found me. And this is how it came about: shortly after he arrived in Salamanca, once again gallant and courtly, I heard that he'd become involved with another woman. This news so devastated me that I thought I'd lose my mind. I wrote him several letters and received no answer. Finally I decided to go to that famous city and try to regain his favor through being loving. If I couldn't break up his love affair, then I planned to take my life. Look, Fabio, how low I had fallen! But what won't a jealous woman stoop to?

"I told my plan to doña Guiomar in whom I confided all my misfortunes. When she saw that I was determined to go, she didn't want me to go alone. There was a gentleman who had visited our house whose frankness and friendship seemed like a brother's, so doña Guiomar and her mother asked him to accompany me. He instantly agreed. He rented two mules and we set out, departing from Madrid amply provided with money and jewels. I know very little about roads and traveling (the few times I had traveled with don Felix, I'd always been lavishly taken care of). This traitor who guided me took the road to Barcelona instead of the road to Salamanca. About half a league before we came to Barcelona, in the heart of the wilderness, he stole everything I had, including the two mules, and went back the way we had come.

"I was abandoned there in the open country all by myself, in despair and tempted to commit some foolish act. At last, however, alone and on foot, I walked until I came out of the wilderness to the Royal Highway. There I met some people and asked them how far it was to Salamanca. They laughed at this question and told me I was much closer to Barcelona. Then, of course, I understood the traitor's vile deceit in deliberately bringing me so far in order to rob me. I gathered heart and walked into Barcelona where I sold a ring for ten ducats. The wretch had overlooked it on my finger.

"I bought these clothes and cut my hair and, in this disguise, I came to Montserrat. I spent three days praying to the holy image of the Virgin to help me in my trials and begging food from the priests. They asked me if I'd like to work as a shepherd and keep the flock you see here on this mountain. That looked like a good opportunity to me, for not even Celio would know my whereabouts. Here I can bewail my misfortune and he can enjoy his affairs undisturbed. I accepted the job and have been here for four months, firmly resolved never to go back to where his faithless eyes might see me.

"This, discreet Fabio, is the cause of the sorrowful plaints that led you to discover me; love has brought me here and here I intend to end my life."

Fabio had been attentive to every word Jacinta said. When he saw she had ended her tale, he responded:

"I didn't wish to interrupt the thread of your sorry tale, discreet Jacinta, so well told and so heartfelt it was. I have waited until you finished to tell you that I'm Celio's friend Fabio, the very same one you said was anxious to meet you and upset about the way he treated you. You have painted Celio's portrait in such colors that, even if I hadn't known your misfortunes from him, and even before you named him, I would've known that you were the object of that mistreatment which I've lamented almost as much as you. I recognized your ungrateful lover immediately. I really can't blame Celio because it's his nature, it's so much a part of him that he never applies his intelligence to his love affairs, nor does he make any effort to change his ways. I have observed his behavior in many affairs, and in every case he's given the same treatment and gotten the same reaction from women. Besides telling you that I believe his star inclines him to love where he's scorned and to scorn where he's loved, I can assure you that I always heard great praise of you from him. He venerated your person and always spoke of you with the respect you are due, a sign of his regard for you. If only you'd loved him less, or if you hadn't revealed your love, or if you'd been less complaining, he might not have been so faithless.

"But it's too late now. If, being sensible and honorable as I know you to be, you love Celio with the intention of making him your husband, your desire is now impossible. He's closed the door to any such pretension by taking Holy Orders, which, as you know, prevents him from ever marrying. Given his nature, this was the only thing for him to do. I can imagine what would happen if Celio ever had a wife. He would kill her through sheer indifference and contempt, given the fact that he can't stand to stay in the same place or stick with the same thing for very long. Certainly your nobility, your honor, and your faith would never permit you to have any other kind of relationship with him! Nor would it be right for those who love you, don Felix's father, his sister, your relatives, the nuns in the convent where you spent so much time as a true religious, to learn of such weakness in you, because an affair like that would be impossible for you to hide.

"But it's not safe or decent for you to remain here. You're in danger of being discovered by the bandits who inhabit this wilderness or by the people who pass through to visit the holy hermits. If I heard you sing and managed to find you, others could too. Your estate is in a shambles, your relatives and your late husband's are worried and probably fear greater misfortune for you than you might think. Your amorous despair and the passion of your jealousy have so blinded you that you won't let reason counsel you to choose a more appropriate way of life.

"I, who look at the situation dispassionately, beg you to reconsider, to rethink your plans. I do not intend to leave here without taking you with me. If I didn't, I think heaven would call me to account for your life. Rather than doing anything so cruel as abandoning you here all alone, I will stay here with you myself, with no other motive than the obligation I feel toward you because you have confided in me and told me your story. Because I am who I am, I feel this obligation strongly. I also feel it's a debt I owe my friend Celio. I'm sure he'll thank me greatly if I succeed in changing your mind about staying alone in a place so dangerous to your good name and to your honor. I can't believe that he despises you so much that he doesn't care about your welfare, your life, and your honor as much as his own. May this oblige you, beautiful Jacinta, to revise your thinking.

"We shall go back to the Madrid where, in one of the best convents, you can live more in accord with your proper station. If you should ever find occasion to marry, you have ample estates to be able to do that and live in comfort, wisely cherishing the true caresses of your legitimate husband and forgetting the phony ones of a false lover. If you can learn about the faithlessness of men from the misfortunes you've experienced and forget Celio, you may decide to become a nun, knowing what that life is and realizing that it is the most perfect. This decision would give great pleasure to those of us who know you.

"And now, beautiful Jacinta, night is upon us. Let's go to the monastery. You can return the sheep to the monks, happy to have been pastured by such a beautiful shepherd. Tomorrow you will put on proper clothes, because these are not decent or befitting your person. We will take a maid to accompany you and rent a coach to return to Madrid. From this moment on, with your permission, I intend to be responsible for your good name, and I hope to feel pride in helping you solve your problems. If you can't live without Celio, I will make him visit you, replacing sinful love with brotherly love. While you deal with your amorous passion in this way, may heaven grant that you change your resolve and accept the solution I desire for you and toward which I shall guide you as if you were my sister. And as my sister you will travel in my company."

"Oh wise and noble Fabio!" Jacinta exclaimed, as her eyes filled with tears and she threw her arms around the neck of the kindhearted youth. "With this embrace I want to thank you and repay you for the favor you do me. Since heaven brought you to this uninhabitable wilderness at this time, I'd like to think that it hasn't abandoned me. I'll go with you more gladly than you expected. I'll obey you in your every command, which won't be repayment enough, since it's all to my advantage. And I agree to enter a convent. The one promise I can't make in obedience to you is to commit myself to becoming either a nun or a wife. Unless I suffer a change of heart, my love for Celio will prevent me from taking a husband, and my belonging to him prevents me from belonging to Christ. To give my love to the Divine Spouse I must be free and unattached. The rewards are different and I know that I risk losing heaven and gaining hell instead, but that's how strong my passion is. My love wouldn't be true love if it didn't cost so dear. I have money and I can easily remain in my present state; there's no need for me to change it.

"I am a Phoenix of love! I loved don Felix until death snatched him from me. I love and shall continue to love Celio until death

triumphs over my life. I made a commitment to love, and that's how
I shall die. If you could get Celio to visit me, I would be happy. All
I want is to see him, even knowing that he won't appreciate my passion
or my love. I'm willing to venture everything in spite of all I stand
to lose. I don't believe he'll ever change, because I know he's as thankless as I am constant. And I shall continue to be as unfortunate as I
have always been, but even so, my soul would enjoy the pleasure of
seeing him, in spite of his disloyalty and his displeasure."

With these words, they got up and returned to the holy monastery
where they rested that night. The next day, they set out for Barcelona
and Jacinta changed to appropriate dress. They hired a maid and took
a coach and returned to Madrid. Today Jacinta lives in a convent. She
is so happy that you'd think she desired to live no other way, that she
could ask for no greater pleasure. She has doña Guiomar to keep her
company because, when doña Guiomar's mother died, she begged
Jacinta to take care of her daughter until she married. Jacinta herself
told me this story so that I could put it in this book as an enchantment, which indeed it is. The story is so true that, if the names weren't
changed, they would be recognized by many, for the people are all
still alive except don Felix, who paid the price to death in the prime
of his life.

The lovely Lisarda told this enchantment with such charm and
grace that her listeners hung on each sweet word of the enchanting
tale. They wanted it to go on all night. Of one accord, they praised
her story and thanked her for such a notable favor. Don Juan, being
her suitor, outdid himself in his lavish praise, almost killing Lysis with
each word. To put a stop to his praise, she took up the guitar that
was beside her on the couch and made a signal to the musicians. They
silenced don Juan's praise and thereby ended her anguish by playing
the accompaniment to her sonnet. But Lysis's soul wept as her body
sang:

> My love doesn't grow faint from your neglect
> because it's a giant armed with constancy;
> don't tire yourself in rejecting me,
> for you will never see it overcome.

> The more thankless you are, the more I love you,
> for loving, because it is loving, gives great power.

I serve without reward, and I regard as wealth
what others consider valueless.

    When my eyes, bathed in tears
because they see others better loved,
deny themselves any respite,

    I say to them: "My friends, you are unfortunate
because you aren't picked or chosen;
but love, because it's love, is its own reward."

Few in the room missed the fact that these verses sung by the beautiful Lysis were aimed at the disdain with which don Juan repaid her love, given his obvious attraction to Lisarda. Naturally it grieved them to see the lady's love so poorly rewarded and to see don Juan so blind that he failed to prize such a worthy marriage. Although Lisarda was Lysis's cousin and they were equals in beauty and nobility, Lysis was the wealthier. But, if love is true, it takes no note of such details.

The one most struck by Lysis's plight was don Juan's friend don Diego, a noble and wealthy gentleman. He knew of Lysis's love and don Juan's disaffection because the lady herself had confessed her feelings to him. He knew her love to be so honorable that it didn't exceed the bounds of modesty. His soul filled with Lysis's beauty and he decided to ask don Juan's permission to court her and propose marriage. Meanwhile, and to begin with, he praised her verses and also her voice. Lysis, feeling gracious and magnanimous and perhaps also a bit spiteful, showed her appreciation of the favor he did her. This inspired don Diego to ask her permission for his servants to contribute some short plays and dances and for him to host the banquet for all the guests on the last night of the festivities. When she granted his request, he thanked her profusely and felt overjoyed but don Juan took umbrage at his temerity.

The guests had opened way for Matilda to tell her enchantment. After she changed places with Lisarda, she began with these words:

"In her enchantment, the lovely Lisarda has given tribute to women's constancy in love as evidenced in Jacinta's terrible misfortunes. It makes sense for me, in the same vein, to tell in my enchantment how we women are obliged not to let ourselves be deceived by men's trickery. Foolishly and without thinking, we fall into their snares, when we should be learning how to avenge ourselves, since honor stained can be cleansed only with the blood of the offender. The story I shall tell took place here in Madrid, and this is how it begins":

Aminta Deceived and
Honor's Revenge

Captain don Pedro (whose last name and lineage I do not mention out of respect to the family) was a native of the city of Victoria, one of the most important cities of Vizcaya because of its amenity, beauty, and nobility. From his earliest years, he had a leaning toward the military, an exercise proper to the nobility. He spent, if you can call it "spending," the flower of his youth serving his king in the wars with such valor and success that he attained high responsibilities from the prudent and most Catholic Philip II. His valiant service earned its proper reward when the Christian King Philip honored him by awarding him the habit of the Order of Santiago and a stipend of six thousand ducats which came with honor of the habit.

Segovia is a city as splendid in its architecture as in the greatness of its nobility, and rich in merchants who, through their business, spread its good name even to the most remote provinces of Italy. In this illustrious Castilian city, don Pedro married a lady his equal in birth and in wealth. From this marriage, he had only one son who inherited his father's brave and noble ideals. When the lad reached the age of discretion, in order to imitate his father and equal his deeds, he decided to employ his youth in proving his valor and accomplishing feats even in excess of his father's. And so, bearing the flag his father's courage had earned and with his father's blessing, he went to Italy to serve his king with the duke of Savoy in the famous Italian campaign.

Captain don Pedro had a brother who, because he was the elder, had inherited the family estate, which was not among the smallest in his land of Vizcaya. He had a beautiful daughter, the most beautiful in the whole province, who would inherit and become mistress of all his possessions. Aminta was between twelve and fourteen when death, cruel collector of lives, came knocking at her father's door. The Christian gentleman regretted leaving his beautiful daughter with no other help but that from heaven above even more than having to depart this world. Although his daughter had sufficient wealth to live comfortably and to marry nobly, it sorely troubled the gentleman's heart to leave her without a mother to guide and teach her in spite of his faith in his daughter's virtue.

Recognizing that the end of his life was near, he made his will and left his daughter mistress of all he possessed. He named his brother executor of his will. In a letter written just before his death, he begged his brother, don Pedro, to take charge of the beautiful Aminta and urged him insistently to marry her to someone worthy of her beauty and discretion—which he considered of greater value than her wealth, and rightly so, because Aminta was the epitome of all the gifts a lavish Nature could bestow. After the gentleman had made these arrangements, he went to his final sleep, surrendering his soul to his Creator and his body to the earth.

The captain received his elder brother's letter and responded to its tender news with tears. He decided it would be best for his niece to join his family so she could benefit from his wife's guidance and upbringing. The two agreed that she should marry their son, as it seemed to them, naturally, that they could find no better match. The captain set out to get her and soon arrived in Vizcaya. He spent several days putting the estate in order and arranging her affairs, naming a loyal administrator to take care of everything. Together they returned to Segovia.

Although too shrouded in mourning to be the sun, the beautiful Aminta entered Segovia to the marvel and wonderment of the whole city. She inspired such envy in the ladies and desire in the gallant youths that within a few days the city was resounding with her fame. The man who had not seen her considered himself unlucky. Each praised in her a virtue that he most prized: some her beauty, others her discretion, this one her wealth, that one her modesty. In sum, everybody called her the miracle of the age and the eighth wonder of modern times.

Of course there were considerable bold eyes and covetous desires, attracted by her charms and honest chastity, who hoped through marriage to become masters of such a jewel. Even after her uncle shut the door on all her potential suitors by announcing that Aminta was engaged to become his son's wife, a few, or maybe even a lot, hoped to win the lady's chaste heart through love. Aminta, happy with her uncle's plan to marry her so well, averted her eyes from all suitors and with pleasure awaited the arrival of her cousin and betrothed who was on his way home. Because she was a young girl, she knew nothing of love; indeed Aminta had no desire but to follow the will and pleasure of her aunt and uncle and thought there could be no pleasure except in the sight of her betrothed. While waiting for him to return home, Aminta led a delightful life, carefree and happy.

At her aunt's side, she so enjoyed the pleasures of the city and the fetes that, within a few months, she forgot her sorrow over her father's death. Her poor lovelorn admirers, denied any hope of ever possessing her, were overwhelmed by amorous desire and regret. They saw in her eyes the glance of the mythical basilisk that struck the beholder dead, leaving him no hope of surviving. Even knowing there was no hope at all, they didn't lessen or desist from their amorous courtship. In her street the music was continuous, the promenading constant, and the gallants without number. At nightfall her street resembled the mountains of Arcadia or the Jungle of Love. Over here you could hear sighing and over there music. Aminta, however, never listened and, if she heard, she laughed and made fun of it all.

But no one should trust in illusory power or freedom, for Love delights more in hunting a free will than in pleasing a captive one. The free man is always captive, the healthy man sick, the valiant vanquished, because Love usually begins in jest and ends in earnest. Let Aminta's eyes sleep relaxed and free. Before long she will learn, at the expense of many tears, how true my philosophy is.

It so happened, then, that one day a gentleman, whom I shall call don Jacinto, came to Segovia on important business. He was young, dashing, and more inclined to pleasure than to penitence. Indeed from Holy Thursday to Holy Thursday, he never thought of penance, like a man who dwells in the house of pleasure. In order to satisfy his own desires, he kept always by his side a woman freer and looser than any woman should be; if a woman does seek only her own pleasure, she should, at least, seem chaste. This woman always accompanied don Jacinto, and he brought her with him to Segovia as his sister. Because of this relationship, he had stopped living with his legitimate wife, who was as unfortunate as she was beautiful and as noble and intelligent as she was beautiful. Tired of having to put up with don Jacinto's license, she had gone back home to her parents who lived in Madrid.

Don Jacinto happened to go hear mass at the convent near Aminta's house where she customarily went with her aunt. Her beauty, her dress, and her attendants attracted so much attention that when don Jacinto set eyes on that beautiful sight, an intense emotion touched his very soul. Oh what power beauty has over vicious minds! Don Jacinto began to feel sick from the wound Aminta's beauty had struck in his heart. He informed himself all about her and, upon learning of her nobility, her wealth, and her purity, he considered his desires impossible. She was who she was and his being married complicated everything. His secret love was driving him mad; he felt like a mere ghost, like a man bereft of soul.

His passion so affected him that he ate little and slept less. He lost his health and fell sick from deep melancholy. He refused to be friendly or even talk with his mistress Flora. The mere sight of her became so loathsome to his eyes that he wished he were blind so he wouldn't have to look at her. Flora felt troubled by the sudden change in don Jacinto although, from what she did, you'd never guess it. She kept asking him over and over what was causing his depression but he refused to say. Finally, out of curiosity (I refuse to consider it love), she decided to keep close watch and eavesdrop until she found out. That wasn't hard for her to do. Since Love is blind and works only through the blind, both Love and the blind do things in such a way that they can scarcely be covered up. That's why lovers, themselves unseeing, think that others don't see either.

One day don Jacinto was absorbed in his thoughts of Aminta, and he thought Flora was out, for that was what she'd told him. He didn't love her any more so he didn't pay attention to her the way he used to. In fact, he had told her to go take a walk, to go see the city, because he wanted to be alone so he could give himself over completely to his thoughts of Aminta. Believing he was alone, he took up the lute, which he played well, and sang:

> Dido weeps for the fugitive Aeneas,
> for the cruel contempt in his departure,
> and, blind with rage, inflamed with wrath,
> she tears her face to avenge his scorn.

She calls out to her undeserving beloved;
her hand grasps the sword's hilt,
with it she cuts the flower of her sad life,
winning the laurels earned by her loyalty.

Beautiful Elisa Dido, although your sad fate
forced you to give yourself a harsh death,
I would exchange my life for your death;

because, if Aeneas had not loved you once,
he never could have spurned you;
since he loved you once, what a happy fate!

A famous deed it was,
a deed by which you made fame envious;
because you were loved once,
do not lament your being scorned.
With your sweet memory
comes no sorrow not leading on to glory.
But, alas, my great loyalty
is repaid only with disdain and contempt;
mine is true sorrow,
while yours is full of glory.
Thankless Aminta, take pity on one who's dying,
on one whose plight is desperate,
without hope of glory or end to all his pain.

Flora, who'd been hiding, emerged, and said:

"No longer, my dear don Jacinto, can you hide from me the cause
of your melancholy; you've just declared it in your song. To tell the
truth, I've suspected it for days because you've had such extravagant
praise for the captain's niece Aminta constantly on your lips. Don't
think I'm troubled that you've set your sights on her. I can't consider
it an affront for you to love a woman who excels me in every way.
Why, instead of anger, I feel pity that your desire is impossible unless,
of course, you use deception. If I loved you lightly, this love newly
born in you might make me jealous. But even if it were possible for
you to possess Aminta, I would not fear that you will forget me; when
you see how I seek and procure your pleasure for you, that will make
you love me all the more. I've always considered jealousy stupid. The
day I enlisted under Love's banner, I took a vow to rise above jealousy
so as never to know the horror that people say it is.

"The main obstacle I find to your desire is that Aminta will never
surrender except in marriage. Her haughtiness, however, is amusing.

If she were to read your letters and listen to your amorous speeches, who can doubt that she would love you? For women, there's no bond like marriage. Let her see your elegance. Impress yourself on her and you'll see how she falls. Despite the fact that everyone in the city says she's hoping to marry her cousin, a lover of your charms and attractions who's johnny-on-the-spot can accomplish more than a lover who's hoped for but absent. Dress splendidly and send her jewels.

"I, for my part, will lay out my snares and set my traps. Since I pass as your sister, I can become her friend and try to talk with her every time I see her in church. If she listens to me, I'll paint your amorous passion to her in such color that, even though it threatens her honor, she can't fail to fall. Once she loves you, it'll be easy for you, by promising marriage, to enjoy her. If your desire should persist, then take her from her uncle's house to a place where she's not known. If your desire should end as soon as you've enjoyed her, we can go home and she'll never know who the author of her downfall was. She'd never dare mention it to anyone for fear of being defamed and maybe even killed by her uncle. My only reward for doing all this for you is simply the pleasure that you will receive."

While don Jacinto listened to the song of that siren, he hung in suspense. Whether he thought she was doing it from love so as not to see him suffer, or to attain her own selfish desires, his response was to throw his arms around her. He called her his comfort, his solace, the savior of his life. He agreed to do everything just as Flora counseled. Don Jacinto was to begin his deception that very day. Eager, dashing, and very rich, he set out to press his courtship. During the day, he was by Aminta's door; at night he haunted her street. Sometimes he went alone, sometimes he went accompanied by Flora, who dressed as a man when they went to serenade Aminta.

In one of the downstairs apartments in Aminta's house, there lived a woman who wasn't exactly a lady nor was she really a servant. She'd been married to a merchant. She was an exceedingly curious woman, eager to know everything that was going on. She wasn't the kind to tell tales, however, not because she was a saint but because she hid her true nature beneath a veneer of virtue so successfully that the captain never questioned her visiting his house. She quickly noticed the new bird who came to nibble at the bait of Aminta's beauty. One evening when don Jacinto was by her door, she approached him and asked what he was seeking. Everybody in the whole city knew that

Aminta belonged to her cousin, who'd been in Milan and was expected to return home at any moment to marry her.

Don Jacinto had been waiting for just such an occasion. He seized the woman's arm and poured out his love to her, all in accord with the crafty plan he and Flora had devised. He led the woman to believe that he had an income of four thousand ducats. He told her he only wanted her to deliver a letter for him. He promised her impossible things. To back up his words, he placed a purse containing fifty escudos in her hands. Thanks to their miraculous power, doña Elena (that was the good woman's name) softened more than you might expect. She told him to go write the letter and bring it back. She would deliver it to Aminta and get a reply. Don Jacinto returned home and told Flora of his good fortune. He wrote the letter and took it back to where doña Elena was waiting for him. He gave it to her together with a magnificent diamond ring.

"This," he said, "you will give to beautiful Aminta as a gift and token of my love."

Doña Elena promised to do so and said she'd have the reply the next day. Don Jacinto left and immediately she went up to Aminta's room. Normally at night Aminta would be writing to her cousin and fiancé. Doña Elena went in and, placing the letter and the ring in Aminta's hand, she said:

"Beautiful Aminta, long may you enjoy your great beauty! Please read me this letter. It's from a lover who's courting me as if I were young and beautiful. He sent it to me with this jewel."

Aminta correctly assumed that the letter and the ring were probably from one of the many suitors who were courting her but, carried away by her curiosity and so as not to appear suspicious, or maybe fate was beginning to pursue her, she acknowledged doña Elena's words with a smile and read the following:

To Aminta from don Jacinto:
When will triumphs, fear is vanquished. Driven by my love and therefore not fearing your anger, sweet mistress mine, I dare to tell you of my love. I do not lie when I say that my love was born, not when I saw your beauty, but when I myself was born, for my heart tells me that heaven made you to be its mistress. Well do I know the impossibility of my suit because you await your fortunate cousin to make him your husband. Nevertheless, I don't want to die without your knowing, at least, that you are the cause of my death. If you are not as cruel as people say, while you wait for the fortunate man who

is to merit you, please give me life, if only by just allowing me to gaze upon you. Accept this ring, not as a token from me, but as a portrait of yourself.

"Who, my friend, is this mortally ill man seeking a cure in such haste?" Aminta asked.

"A man who deserves you," replied doña Elena, "more than the man who is to be your husband, because he's noble, gallant, rich, and intelligent. Your cousin may be of your blood, but don Jacinto is of the very best blood in Spain."

(Oh, greed and a purse full of coins, how quickly you inspire the mind of this woman to say things she doesn't even know!)

"I don't understand, most beautiful Aminta," the deceived and deceitful messenger continued, "how you can fail to appreciate a real offer that's so favorable to you in preference to the unknown. Consider the matter carefully and see that you make no mistake. Now then, what shall I reply to don Jacinto?"

"If it's not enough to tell him that you gave me the letter," Aminta responded somewhat tenderly, "tell him I read it, and that, my friend, seems no small favor to me."

As she said this, she slipped the ring on her finger.

Doña Elena would have liked to find don Jacinto immediately in order to give him the good news and receive her reward. But, since he hadn't anticipated such dispatch, not expecting a reply until the next day, he'd already retired to his lodging.

Can you imagine Aminta's confused thoughts? How many times she reread the letter? The speeches she made to herself? Her tossing and turning? How deeply love struck in her hitherto free and carefree heart? While she knew she was to become her cousin's wife, up until that moment, love had never touched her heart. She spent an exceedingly restless night waiting for day to dawn.

As soon as the sky began to lighten, she dressed, and perhaps she adorned herself with more than customary care and elegance in the hope of seeing the cause of her unrest. Now that she wanted to see him, she wasn't far from loving, not far at all! She was caught in the trap Love had set in doña Elena's words. Aminta listened and Love's cruelty brought her to the brink and into the snare she fell. (Poor girl, if only you knew what you were getting into!)

It was Sunday. When it came time for Aminta to leave the house with her aunt and the maids to go to mass, she found doña Elena talking with don Jacinto in the front entry. At the sight of the two of them and from their actions, she recognized him, as if her heart hadn't instantly told her who he was. If any part of her had remained free from the letter's message, she now gave herself entirely to his presence with clear signs of her surrender. Although don Jacinto was thirty, he was so handsome, elegant, and dashing that, if you didn't know he was married, his grace would charm anyone who looked at him. Being sharp, he recognized in the lady's face certain indications of love and began to promise himself success. As Aminta moved from the place where she first saw him until she got to the coach, her face turned a thousand colors and her eyes darted in a thousand directions to escape the boldness of his glance, especially when she heard doña Elena say:

"Go with God, don Jacinto, for my mission has progressed so well that it won't be long before it's accomplished."

At this moment, the beautiful Aminta tripped and fell almost at her suitor's feet as he was taking leave of the clever matchmaker. He planned to make his love known to its source any way he could. In this surprising situation, it behooved him to show proper courtesy, so he extended his hand to the beautiful Aminta and whispered:

"I want to be your husband, if Love and Fortune are on my side."

The lady responded more favorably than with words by extending her ungloved hand bearing the rich diamond. This sufficed for the gallant to feel more than optimistic.

Aminta's aunt thanked don Jacinto for helping her niece to her feet. To appear most courteous, he took down the step from the coach and helped his bright sun settle in among the other clouds of silk. He felt happier than he'd ever felt in his life.

Instantly he went to tell Flora his good fortune and to inform her that Aminta had gone to church. Flora took her shawl and accompanied her "brother" to the same church. She made a grand entrance and went to sit next to the beautiful but already deceived Aminta. Flora turned to don Jacinto, who was right beside her, and said:

"Wait, brother, let's sit here. You know my tastes are more those of a gallant than of a lady, and wherever I see a lady, particularly one as beautiful as this lady, I can't take my eyes from her beauty and my heart grows tender."

It wouldn't have been surprising for Aminta to thank Flora as a reward for learning that she was don Jacinto's sister. When she saw him enter the church with another woman, she had felt half dead; jealousy tore wide the wound and opened up love's door. Instead, Aminta said to Flora:

"With your great beauty, which certainly should cause envy rather than suffer it, I don't know why you seek any other. If you take a mirror in your hands and look at yourself, you will satisfy all your desire. Your beauty deserves more to be loved than to love. But I shall now have higher regard for myself; I'm flattered by the favor you've shown me because pure love gives pure fruit. I beg you, please tell me what it is in me that most pleases and delights you so that I may esteem it more and prize it in myself."

"All of you," Flora replied. "You are so splendid that I believe I'm not deceived in thinking that you must be the beautiful and discreet Aminta, whose elegance and beauty are the basilisk of the whole city."

"Aminta I am," the lady replied. "As for the rest, my lady, you can judge with what little reason they attribute this fame to me."

With great skill, the crafty Flora gradually placed bonds on the innocent Aminta to bring about her total downfall. Step by step, Flora led her to believe everything she wanted her to believe. She told Aminta how her brother don Jacinto had came from Valladolid, where he had a house and large estates, to verify the truth of her beauty, which fame had spread everywhere. If he found her as she'd been described, he hoped to make her his mistress. Don Jacinto had learned of her uncle's plans for her marriage, however, and hadn't dared approach her.

Flora extolled his love, his good blood, his wealth. Upon his marriage, he was sure to be awarded an order of nobility. Flora had asked him to bring her along so she could help him make Aminta's acquaintance and in case there were obstacles to the courtship. In sum, Flora painted Aminta's lover as so rich, so noble, and so in love that, to cap the climax, she thought if her brother didn't succeed in making Aminta his wife, he would surely die. Flora disguised her lies with such color of truth that it was no wonder Aminta believed every word, particularly when Love had already disposed her to surrender. Flora finished her speech begging Aminta to take pity on her brother. Now was the time for Aminta to act, before her cousin returned; otherwise, everything might have a disastrous end.

"Oh, my friend!" Aminta exclaimed. "How can it not end disastrously? For even if I wanted to satisfy your brother and make myself happy by marrying him, my uncle would never consent, as he intends me for his son. But I cannot deny that, ever since last night when I read your brother's letter and received this diamond, I've not been able to bring my thoughts back down to earth, that would be denying power to Love and betraying the loyalty I've sworn. If ever I had any desire to see my cousin, it has turned into a wish for his death or, at least, for his absence until my salvation comes or until the end of my days. Now I regret my disdain for all those who have loved me. Only for myself I feel no pity. I'm beyond caring about my reputation and my honor. That's the effect the sight of your brother has had on me. Now that I've declared my love, tell me what I should do. It's impossible for me to resist loving him. Any remedy is also impossible. My concern is to weigh how much I can afford to lose through my daring while rationally I'm afraid of what may happen."

That's all Flora wanted to hear, and she replied:

"Once you're my brother's wife, you'll no longer belong to your cousin. There's nothing for you to lose. Instead, you'll gain a husband who's his equal in station and wealth. If at first your uncle is angry, later, when he sees how much you gain, he will make peace with you. And, while I don't equal you in beauty, to pacify your cousin, the twenty thousand ducats I'll bring in dowry should make up for this deficiency, and you'll be his sister-in law. If things turn out so badly that none of this works, leave all your inheritance to them. My brother is content with only your person.

"You say that you can arrange nothing in your uncle's house, but there is one way: doña Elena, the woman who gave you the letter. She's a good friend and your family trusts her. You can talk with my brother in her house. That way you can make arrangements for your marriage. After you've gone before the vicar, you can come to our lodgings. By the time your uncle finds out what's been done, you'll already be in your husband's power. When your uncle understands the situation, he'll have no choice but to consider himself fortunate and you lucky."

Aminta was so blind that she acceded to everything, fearful of her cousin's imminent arrival. She told Flora that that afternoon she and her brother should come to doña Elena's room. While her aunt was receiving guests, they could talk at more leisure. Aminta took her leave with signs of eternal friendship and returned home with her accompaniment. Her aunt had noticed Aminta and Flora whispering together, but she assumed they were speaking of girlish things. Trusting in Aminta's modesty, she suspected nothing.

Flora described the arrangement to don Jacinto and, although her
elaborate deception caused him some doubt, she received for her efforts a thousand tender and loving favors. After dinner, Flora and don
Jacinto went to doña Elena's house together. She already knew of the
plan from Aminta. By this time, Aminta loved don Jacinto so truly
that she could think of nothing but becoming his wife, even though
there might be some worrisome obstacles between the "yes" and the
"no." She kept the secret to herself, not mentioning it to her servants.
She thought (and rightly) that no one reveals secrets like servants, and
the more you caution them to keep something quiet, the more apt
they are to make it public.

When the ill-advised lady was sure that her uncle had gone out and
her aunt was entertained with her friends, she excused herself and went
into the next room. There, she told the maids that, if she were called,
she'd be down at doña Elena's. Then she went to meet the authors
of her downfall.

Flora and Aminta greeted each other with an embrace, causing
proper envy in don Jacinto. He declared his love with all the right
words and offered himself to Aminta with extravagant promises made
believable by his tears. He increased Aminta's love by regaling her
with loving attentions and tenderness, and he gave her his hand in
marriage. By virtue of this pledge, he enjoyed some free and delightful
favors, gathering flowers and carnations in that garden untouched by
human hand which had been reserved for her absent cousin. Flora
and doña Elena witnessed these celebrations with a thousand jokes,
watching don Jacinto act as bold as Aminta reacted with embarrassment.

It was agreed that the next day, while her aunt and uncle were
sleeping their siesta, don Jacinto would bring a litter to take Aminta
to the vicar's house. She would disguise her name so that people
couldn't talk about her elopement. From the vicar's, she would go to
Flora and don Jacinto's lodgings, always in disguise until they got to
his city. From there, they would inform her uncle of what had been
done. Doña Elena was charged with keeping the secret. This she gladly
promised because she feared the captain's anger. It would be easier
for him to pardon Aminta once his rage had passed. When the plans
were finalized, they said good-bye with a thousand embraces. Don
Jacinto and Flora returned to their lodgings, well satisfied and pleased
with their success in the negotiations.

Oh, Aminta deceived! Plunged into such great evil, you no longer heed restraint, casting it aside and placing yourself in great danger! How deceitful you are, don Jacinto, unregenerate cause of the ruination of this poor girl! Your outrage will cost you dear! Oh, false Flora! In you, heaven created the epitome of deceit! May punishment fall upon you, you who act as your lover's matchmaker. Can anyone imagine how evil you are? Terribly evil because, as a woman who's evil, you have the advantage over men. Love excuses don Jacinto, deception excuses the unfortunate Aminta, but for Flora there is no excuse. Don't be amazed at men's deceptions any longer, for Flora surpasses them all in the expression of her love, if indeed it's really love. Whether she loves or not, she has done what you have seen.

The next day, which must have been Tuesday, if that has any significance, finally dawned. Aminta rose with the sun because the momentousness of her plans did not let her rest. She had dreamt about a thousand difficulties and misfortunes in accomplishing those plans. Stumbling here, falling there, hearing voices, all of which predicted disaster, she finally managed to get dressed. It seemed like forever until dinnertime. Totally absorbed in her thoughts and captive to her love, blind and deaf, she gathered up her jewels, wrapped them in a cloth, and placed them in the sleeve of her gown. She tucked her shawl into the other.

Nervously she dined with her aunt and uncle. The moment she knew they'd gone to bed, she went down to the entry. Again she charged doña Elena to keep her secret. Then she put on her shawl and entered the waiting litter. It carried her straight to the vicar's house because the bearers, don Jacinto's servants, had been well instructed in what they were to do. At the vicar's, Aminta met her lover. He could come and go wherever he wanted without being noticed because he wasn't known in the city; besides, it was flooded with merchants and travelers every weekday. The handsome couple appeared together before the vicar. Aminta kept her face covered to avoid being recognized. The moment the lovers clasped hands, a rich emerald ring she was wearing on her finger split in half and a piece flew out and struck don Jacinto right in the face. Although Don Jacinto noticed how much the ill omen upset Aminta, he ignored it.

After the marriage, don Jacinto took Aminta back to his lodgings. Flora received her "sister-in-law" (as we shall call her) with many embraces. She had a carefully planned and delicious supper served. Then, to ensure that Aminta was bound to her misfortune and that don Jacinto, once surfeited, would quickly tire of her, Flora took them to her own bed. She left them there and retired to another room at the same inn. As a reward for her resourcefulness, she expected to end up with her lover, abandoning Aminta to her misfortune and dishonor. Meanwhile, let Flora look on and suffer, for we can know or say no more about what transpired! Let's leave the three of them, the two traitors and the innocent girl, to pass this night. Each one will have to pay the consequences, for heaven keeps account of everything that happens.

Let's go back to Aminta's house where, by this time, everything was confusion, tears, threats, but in vain. Her uncle acted like a man deranged. When at last he realized that she was not going to appear and that no one had seen her leave, he began to make surreptitious inquiries to avoid making his dishonor public. Every effort was fruitless. Only doña Elena knew, and she said not a word, so he found out nothing. In the end, his wife's weeping and the maids' wailing caused the event to become public knowledge throughout the city. As a result, the police opened an equally fruitless investigation. The vicar reported that at two that afternoon he had married a lady and a gentleman. He didn't know who they were but he did suspect that the lady might have been Aminta. This news merely proved to everybody how much they didn't know.

The next day this information reached don Jacinto. Now that the flame of his passion had been assuaged, he began to consider the danger he was in and the punishment he faced. He feared that doña Elena, if she were pressed, would tell the whole story and reveal where he was lodging, which would greatly imperil his life and his reputation. That night he went to the window grating of doña Elena's apartment which opened onto the street. He knocked. While he talked with her and told her about the wedding, he pointed a pistol at her heart and fired. She gave up the ghost instantly, without time to confess her sins or call on God. She received a well-deserved reward for the evil she had done.

It's said that error follows upon error and one evil upon another. Don Jacinto's evil was so monstrous that his fear of the consequences increased. He realized that if the police searched the inns it would mean certain disaster for the sad Aminta to be found in his room. He felt sure that doña Elena's death would bring about such a search. Taking counsel from Aminta's fear, which was worrying her almost to death, from Flora's resourcefulness, and mostly from his own hindsight, the three decided that, while don Jacinto made arrangements for their departure, Aminta should stay at the house of an acquaintance of don Jacinto's, a noblewoman who lived on the outskirts of the city. He managed to convince the sorrowing Aminta that she would be better off there in case she were found and if so, they would announce their marriage publicly. If there were no search for her, he could easily arrange their journey to Valladolid and, once there, everything would work out the way they wanted. Aminta agreed to the whole idea.

To finish off his deception, don Jacinto went to the house of the woman who was a distant relative of his. She was a widow who had only one son to inherit her great wealth. His name was don Martin and he was one of the most gallant young men of his time. Don Jacinto told this lady that he had important business in Valladolid but would soon return. In the meantime, would she please allow a lady worthy of all consideration to stay in her company. Doña Luisa, for this was the lady's name, knew all about don Jacinto's peccadillos from the time she had lived in his province. She assumed that this was one of his many lady friends but, desiring to please him, she agreed to do what he asked.

He brought Aminta to doña Luisa's house that same night. Aminta was so upset and confused that don Jacinto was glad to be free of that burden. She brought along her own jewels as well as the ones her perfidious husband had given her. He immediately returned to his inn and, without wasting a minute, packed and left for his province in the company of his treacherous mistress Flora and their servants. Their overriding concern was to get home as soon as possible. Aminta stayed in doña Luisa's house using the name doña Victoria because her own name was so well known in Segovia. She was able to hide there very easily because doña Luisa hadn't lived in Segovia long, and she'd never heard a word about Aminta even though her story was now public knowledge in the city.

Doña Luisa's son had gone hunting four days before and hadn't been into the city, so he didn't know anything either. But the moment don Martin returned from hunting, he dressed for the street and went downtown. There he learned what his mother and the others in his house didn't know. After he got back from town, they sat down at the table for supper and his mother sent for her guest. The instant don Martin set eyes upon Aminta, he fell madly in love with her, thinking that he beheld an angel. All the while they dined, don Martin was transported, even as Aminta was oblivious both to this new passion and to her own misfortune. At the table he told his mother all the news he'd heard in the city: about how, the day before, the most beautiful woman in Castile, don Pedro's niece who was engaged to become the wife of his son who was in Milan, had disappeared from her home. No one had been able to ascertain any cause or motive for her disappearance. As far as her betrothal was concerned, she had accepted it with pleasure. Regarding her good sense and decorum, she was as discreet as she was beautiful. A public notice had been posted decreeing that no one should give her shelter under penalty of death.

"What's most shocking," he added, "is that this morning they found a neighbor, doña Elena, dead of a bullet through her heart. She lived in a downstairs apartment in the same house. Don Pedro and all his servants have been arrested. One of the servants reported that last evening, while looking out of a window, he had seen doña Elena talking with a stranger. Several others repeated that a maid said that her mistress, Aminta (that's the name of the missing lady), used to go often to doña Elena's house, being very careful that no one should know. This raised the suspicion that doña Elena was murdered because of Aminta. That's why the captain and his whole household have been arrested."

When Aminta heard this news, she began to tremble. Then don Martin (changing the subject), asked where their beautiful guest had come from. He wondered if she had descended from heaven. Doña Luisa replied:

"Don Jacinto brought her to stay with us while he does some business in Valladolid. When he finishes his business, he'll come back for her and take her home to his province."

"Is this lady his wife?" asked don Martin.

"God forbid!" doña Luisa exclaimed. "From what I know of her, it would grieve me to see her so ill-served."

"Speaking of wives," Aminta said with troubled voice, "is don Jacinto married, my lady, or betrothed?"

"Don Jacinto!" doña Luisa repeated. "That isn't really the name of the man who brought you here, my child. His real name is don Francisco, and he's married and lives in Madrid."

"Are you sure of that, my lady?" Aminta asked.

"I'm positive," doña Luisa replied. "Five or six years ago when I used to live in his province, where I'd lived ever since I married, I witnessed his marriage to a lady from Madrid. He'd fallen in love with her when he saw her at a cousin's wedding he'd attended with his parents. Within a year, of course, he no longer lived with his wife. I know his parents and his relatives, and I know that he's as depraved as he is rich."

"Doesn't he have a sister named Flora?" the confused lady asked.

"Ah, my friend!" doña Luisa exclaimed. "How mistaken you are! That woman has been his mistress for a long time now. She's the one who incites him to a thousand evil deeds. If he didn't enjoy the protection of his powerful relatives at court, he would've been executed long ago for the evil example he sets with his openly lascivious behavior, for vice in the nobility is more visible than in other people. Beautiful doña Victoria, please, for your own sake, explain this mystery to me. The tears you fight back are not without cause. Furthermore, if don Jacinto told you he's not married, he lied. His wife is named doña Maria. She went back home to her parents because she couldn't tolerate his evil ways."

"My troubles," replied Aminta, "are not such that they can be told without causing scandal. Please permit me to retire now. In time you will learn of greater treachery and deception than history recounts about Odysseus' cousin Sinon."

Doña Luisa could almost guess what must have happened but she had no idea who her guest was. Being prudent, however, she didn't wish to be importunate. She got up, took Aminta by the hand, and led her to her chamber. It was a beautiful room with windows whose balconies opened onto a lovely garden. It was next door to her son's bedroom with a door connecting the two, which she now locked to protect their privacy.

Like his mother, don Martin felt confused. He was so enamored of their guest that already he thought he couldn't live without her. Because she'd left the room in tears, and from her parting words, he suspected some amazing story. Knowing that doña Victoria's room adjoined his, he went to his own room. He noted that the connecting door was locked and understood his mother's precaution. He went out and, from among all the keys that lay on the desk, he selected the one to that door. Then he returned to his room and pretended to get ready for bed. But that's not what he did. Instead, he placed himself in front of the keyhole and tried to overhear what the mistress of his freedom might say. In her ignorance, doña Luisa was giving her guest misdirected comfort. Soon she left Aminta and went off to bed.

Alone in her room and unaware that anyone was listening, the desolate Aminta wept. In a voice neither loud nor soft, she began to pour forth her sorrows. Just as a fountain cannot spill its crystal drops when a hand covers its jet and restrains it, but spurts them forth violently once the hand is removed, this is what happened with all the words Aminta had been holding back. The moment she was alone, she poured forth her passion.

"Alas, Aminta!" she lamented, as she tore at the threads of her fine hair and gashed her white hands with the pearls of her teeth, drawing tiny red rivulets across her flesh. "How dire is your misfortune! I could become a legend all over the world, an example for all women and maybe even a lesson for them, if they are wise and not foolish as I have been! Alas! Woe is me! What disgrace and scandal I have caused through my folly! Just look at me—three days ago I enjoyed honor, wealth, a life of ease. I was adored by my aunt and uncle and respected by the whole city and today, hear all the gossip, see how the whole city is shocked! Alas, dear uncle! How can I make reparation for the grief and the dishonor you suffer, all because of me? How will you bear it when you learn the extent of my disgrace? Oh, doña Elena, cause of all my trials! I hope heaven punishes your soul as it has your body for ruining me! Oh, cruel Flora, more treacherous and iniquitous than your namesake! No wonder women with your whore's name are despised in Rome! Oh, don Jacinto, how could you have the heart to deceive a woman of my position, heedless of the fact that you would cause not only my death but your own as well. When my uncle finds out what you've done, he will surely track you down, if death doesn't strike him first. If he fails, my cousin and betrothed will, as my blood relative, avenge your offense against me. But how can I wait for that to come to pass and be patient when I have the courage and hands with which to end my life right now? It's preferable for the news of my crime to be broadcast together with the notice of my death. There's no other way: let the one who has lost her honor, lose her life."

As she uttered these words, she drew a knife from its sheath, meaning to slash the arteries in her wrists. She thought there was enough time left before morning for her to bleed to death and thus end all her woes. Don Martin, however, understood her determination and was amazed at her resolve, although, of course, he didn't really understand. Fearing a disastrous mishap, hastily he put the key in the lock, opened the door, and rushed in. The noise, combined with the intensity of her resolve, so upset the beautiful Aminta that she fell into a swoon. Don Martin picked her up in his arms, enjoying a liberty which, had she been conscious, would have been impossible, because her genuine modesty could never have been vanquished except by such deception as has been described.

With his sun eclipsed in his arms, don Martin felt exceedingly tender. He contemplated her youth, her beauty, and the violent emotions she was experiencing. This fed his love at a time when he had the opportunity to take some loving liberties. Carefully he arranged her tumbled hair and lovingly he dried her tears. In answer to her troubled sighs, he tasted delightful favors, gathering carnations in the garden of her beauty.

After a short while, Aminta came to her senses. Finding herself in don Martin's arms she withdrew from her new lover's possession with righteous anger. As she came to comprehend what her situation was, the strength and force of her grievance turned her love for don Jacinto into a desire for harsh vengeance. She had been deceived; now, suddenly, she was being courted. They say that there is no better bait to catch a woman spurned by an absent lover than tender love in the present, so now perhaps she was not quite as free as before. Recovering herself, she reacted angrily and said:

"Don Martin, what are you doing here? Do you think an unhappy woman requires any witness to her death besides her misfortune? Leave me alone. Go back to your room. With the death of this lone woman, the honor of many men will be restored."

"God forbid, beloved mistress mine," replied don Martin, "unless I accompany you in the act. From the moment I saw you, I have adored you. I have one life, which is yours, and this dagger which will do your will. If you don't want me to pay the ultimate price, then let me be your slave. That would make me happier than if I were master of all of Alexander's empire."

"Little do you know me," Aminta said, "since you state your desire so freely. Do not think, just because I'm in this compromising situation, I cease to be who I am. Although it may seem to you that I have lost my honor because of a traitor's deception, what happened to me could happen to the most reasonable and modest woman. You are not my husband and I will not give in to your desires. I beg you, please return to your room. Don't force me to call out to your mother and alarm the whole household. Don't make me publicize my unhappiness and deliver myself over to the sword of my family, who will find satisfaction for their disgrace only in my death."

Don Martin understood her determination and feared she would make an outcry. As she rushed toward the door, he stopped her and begged her to listen to him. It wasn't right for her to think he was trying to possess her without becoming her husband and, if she would accept him as such, he would consider himself very fortunate. The lady looked at him and noted the deep emotion with which he said these words. Besides offering to help, he asked her to explain exactly how she had been injured and by whom. For, if she had lost her honor as she said, some man was the cause. She should tell him everything and see how well he would serve her. He didn't expect her to marry him until her honor was fully satisfied, but he most fervently hoped she would marry him. Aminta, while grateful for her new lover's promises, still despaired of any remedy. She replied:

"I, don Martin, am Aminta, the very person who earlier this evening you said was the scandal of the city and disgrace to the captain don Pedro, my poor, injured uncle. I'll explain the reason why I am in your power; then, if you still want to do as you say, I'm willing to grant your wish."

Briefly she told him what is written here. Her story left him more enamored than before and deeply touched at seeing Aminta's innocence deceived. He wanted, even at the cost of his very life, to avenge her, providing that he not lose the beautiful prey he now had in his power. Again don Martin swore to avenge her honor and gave her his hand as husband. She willingly accepted, as she had no other choice.

"But that's not how my vengeance will be done," Aminta said. "I am the one offended, not you, and I alone must avenge my honor. I shall not be satisfied until my own hands restore to me what my folly has lost. While I give you my word to become your wife, you will not obtain your desire until I've killed that traitor. The only thing I ask is for you to take me where he lives, accompanying me to ensure the safety of my person. If you'll go with me, I'll change my dress— it's safer for me to go dressed as a man. Then I shall deceive him the very same way he deceived me. Once this is done, we can go to Madrid and there we can live in safety."

Don Martin agreed to her conditions. That wasn't surprising because he was in love and would have done anything to enjoy such a beautiful woman; he could almost understand don Jacinto's deception. They were agreed: Aminta expected to avenge herself and don Martin expected to be her husband. They planned their departure for the very next day and, with an embrace, he took his leave.

During the day don Martin arranged everything necessary for the journey. At last night came, although it seemed to the new lovers that it came more slowly than usual. After everyone retired and doña Luisa had gone to bed, don Martin entered Aminta's room bringing her clothing suited to her purpose. She donned the clothes and cut her hair to just the right length. She looked so beautiful that, if any part of don Martin's soul had remained untouched by love, he was totally overcome by the sight of her like this. He left his mother a letter in which he asked her to keep their departure a secret until their mission had been accomplished: it was important to his life and to the lady's honor.

They left the house and mounted two worthy mules; don Martin, in his dress, appeared to be a mule driver. They left Segovia and the next day at nightfall they found themselves in Madrid, the famous court city of the Catholic King Philip III. So great was Aminta's desire for revenge that she wouldn't take time to enter the great city and they pressed onward in their journey, which lasted several more days. I will simply say that one Saturday night they arrived in a city without a name, and it's important that it remain nameless. Taking safe lodging, they rested until morning.

Between themselves, they agreed that don Martin should remain in hiding at the inn since he was a native of that region and had friends there. He didn't want to risk being recognized by anybody. Aminta prepared to set out alone to begin her mission. Don Martin again begged her to let him satisfy her injury; she could count on great deeds from his love without having to take the slightest risk herself. But he couldn't convince Aminta. She said that if she was to be his, he must let her be his with honor.

"I am the one," Aminta said, "who, through my folly, lost my honor, and therefore I am the one who must recover it by shedding blood. You know that women, once they take a decision, seldom change their minds. Since this is the way it is, and it is, allow me to do this my own way. If you avenged my offense with your hands, you would think less of me."

She expressed herself so well and he listened so sympathetically that he had to give in, but not without feeling jealous. He said half-jokingly, half-seriously, that she was only using him to see don Jacinto again.

"The outcome will tell," Aminta said. She parted from him with greater emotion than don Martin would have liked. He felt afraid and the more fear he felt, the more he suffered. Aminta went off to find her enemy, followed and watched by her lover, who loved her more deeply than he willed.

Aminta went to the main church which was nearby. The very moment she entered, before she even had a chance to look around or to say her customary prayer, she saw her feigned don Jacinto and true don Francisco talking with several other gentlemen. She recognized him instantly. You must believe it took all the courage her masculine attire gave her to keep from showing her inner turmoil and weakness. Making an enormous effort, she screwed up her courage and approached them, hoping they would notice her. Don Jacinto asked her if he could do anything for her. When he looked at Aminta, he almost suspected who she was and abruptly his color altered. With as great an effort as her weakness could muster, she asked if there was anyone among their graces who needed a servant.

"Where are you from?" asked don Jacinto, scrutinizing her closely.

"From Valladolid," Aminta said. "I gambled away some of my father's money, and while he's getting over his anger, I've run away. When he misses me, he'll search me out and pardon me."

"You know a lot for such a young boy."

"I know very little, since I am where you see me."

"It seems to me that I've seen you before," don Jacinto replied, "or else you look like a woman I loved for twenty-four hours."

"A lot of love that person owes you," Aminta said. "It wouldn't surprise me if she'd want to get even with you."

"That's a foolish notion. There's no way she could even if she knew who I was. But, since you resemble her so closely, I want you to serve me. That way I can see myself served by the living image of one whom I served. It's a glorious feeling to see someone humbled who once was powerful, even if it's only play-acting."

So shameless was he that he felt pleased by what he had done! The enjoyment of sin is the first step to eternal damnation.

"What's your name?" he asked. "If you're to be my servant, I need to know your name."

"Jacinto," replied Aminta. "And if you take me into your service because I am a living portrait of that woman, I must thank nature who made me in her image because, for my part, I must say that, the moment I saw you, I liked you well."

"Did you come through Segovia?" don Jacinto asked.

"Yes, sir," the lady responded. "I didn't want to stop there, though,

because there was a terrible scandal. Some lady, whose name they said
was Aminta, had disappeared. They thought the earth swallowed her
because they couldn't find her dead or alive. To make matters worse,
a doña Elena, who they thought knew something about the missing
lady, was found murdered one morning. A lot of gentlemen are in
prison because of those mysteries."

"Don't they know," don Jacinto asked, "whether anyone carried her
off?"

"They didn't suspect that," Aminta said. "What they think is that
she herself ran away to keep from marrying her cousin with whom
the marriage contracts were already drawn up."

"Well, Jacinto, let's go home."

"That's a good idea," Aminta replied. "Let's go wherever you say,
and when I know where the house is, I'll go to my lodging for my
suitcase with my clean clothing."

Who can doubt that by this time Aminta was ready to collapse?
She wasn't stupid, however, so she kept up the pretense and accompanied her old enemy and new master to his house. There he presented
the false Flora as her mistress and lady. He told Flora to be kind to
their new servant and instructed the feigned Jacinto to serve Flora
with great care. Flora looked at "him." She looked at "him" again,
feeling increasingly disturbed and so faint she thought she might die.
She didn't dare say what she was thinking, although she really believed
she was looking at the deceived Aminta in person. She didn't mention
this to her lover because she didn't want to remind him of Aminta
now that he'd forgotten her so completely.

Aminta settled into her new house and then went back to tell her
lover don Martin of her quick good fortune. He felt terrible pangs of
jealousy over her position in the house of her first lover. She reassured
him with a thousand caresses, promised to hasten his relief, and went
back to her new masters.

She served them so delightfully that they were well pleased with
"him." "He" revealed "his" many talents, which were: reading, writing,
counting, a variety of other things and, best of all, playing music and
singing. Neither don Jacinto or Flora could be without "him" for a
minute. One day while they were dining, "he" took up the guitar at
Flora's command and sang this ballad:

> If you adore your beautiful Celia,
> and worship her image,
> sacrificing your pleasure

to her beloved beauty;
if her most beautiful eyes,
you regard as suns,
you look at as stars,
you celebrate as heavenly;
if you think her mouth
is a jewel box full of lovely pearls
and her hair pure gold,
beautifully spun in Arabia;
if you know that her hands
are snowy white mountains,
and that her grace, figure, and presence
belong to a second heavenly Venus;
if to her perfect beauty
and celebrated countenance
the beautiful apple were offered
which cost Troy so dear;
and, finally, if all your
sense, power, soul,
memory and will
are captive in her golden threads;
why, ungrateful Jacinto,
cause of my eternal sorrow,
with love false and feigned
did you deceive my innocence?

The deceived don Jacinto hung in suspense. He was not so amazed at the voice, which was very good, but at feeling the sense of the song as if he were actually seeing Aminta herself lamenting. At last he said to "him":

"This lady's plaints are very moving, friend Jacinto."

"That's how I treated her," Aminta replied, "but when she thought she'd caught a husband, I jilted her."

"Then you've been in love?" don Jacinto asked.

"Do I look that foolish?" the lady replied. "Be assured that I've known how to love and how to scorn. I'm also good at feigning passion and disenchanting because I'm more of a man than my beard might indicate. Even though mistress Flora says I look like a woman or a capon, some day I'll be a cock in spite of that knave who won my fortune and put me where I am today. But, since you like to hear the plaints of this woman, listen to these madrigals that treat the same subject:

It was when Phoebus wanted to offer
his rays to Diana

and she, beautiful and proud,
was returning from visiting India.
So that the beloved shepherd
should be consoled in their separation,
Matilda, eagerly went out
to seek her absent Jacinto.
With hastening step, she treads
the blossoms of the flowery meadow,
her face troubled because already
her heart warns her of her fate.
She comes to a beautiful valley,
watered by a gentle crystalline brook
where, taking his pleasure,
she sees Jacinto entertained with Isabella.
She slows her pace
and hears Jacinto saying:
"Maiden, I am burning up,
let your favor ease my sorrow."
Her hands he took in his
and, sighing tenderly, he kissed them.
Isabella said to him:
"What would Matilda say if she saw you now?"
"Hush, divine Isabella, don't say
such nonsense, and heed my passion;
you alone are worthy
of conquering proud hearts;
why, if Apollo should see you,
he would cease pursuing fugitive Daphne,
and for your beauty you would win
the apple from Venus, the divine goddess.
You would be for Jupiter
the Europa he conquered as a bull;
if you had been born in his time,
transformed into a swan he would enjoy you,
and as the golden rain he would descend
from his eternal chorus to visit you;
like Calixtus you would earn
a celestial seat among the spheres.
He would not enjoy Egina
as a shepherd in the lovely meadow
and much less Persephone,
because, enamored of your beauty,
he would devote himself entirely to you
and scorn all others in the world.
Even Juno would not take offense
to see her husband enjoy your sweet beauty."
This he said, and that's all it took,

for Isabella, now entirely vanquished,
has wrapped her arms
around his neck and measured
her mouth close to his.
Matilda went mad with jealousy
and, overcome by rage, she burst forth
like a doe wounded by the spear.
"Faithless, bold,
ungrateful, and most false of men,
here shall I end your life!"
she said as, with firm step,
she fell upon the lovers.
Then Morpheus fled her lovely eyes
weeping rivers of tears;
she believed that what she dreamt was true.
If this story had happened
while she was awake as it did while she slept,
she would have killed them with her tender hands.
Although he's only a child, Cupid,
when he's jealous, will do anything.

They praised the feigned Jacinto's song with boundless enthusiasm and showed their appreciation of "his" talents. Don Jacinto rewarded "him" with a suit and Flora with a ring, which Aminta gladly accepted.

With regard to her vengeance, Aminta was getting past the jesting stage. She did not fail to visit don Martin regularly and report to him on her progress. He kept begging her to hurry up or else let him do it. He could no longer stand staying shut indoors, nor could he bear the thought of her living in the house of the man who had been her first lover. It made Aminta angry that he was so suspicious. She told him that if he was losing faith in her he could go home. He owed her nothing and she owed him nothing. It had been only a gentlemanly act to accompany her.

She left without making up. He fell into a most impassioned state, more because of her anger than because of his jealousy, which was consuming. Aminta got home a little late and found her master and mistress already dining. They scolded her for her tardiness. Later on, don Martin came to the door and made the signal he'd used on other nights. Aminta went out and, after much arguing and pleading, they made up. He returned to his inn and she went back inside to retire.

Aminta stayed in her master's house one month. In the meantime, don Martin had written to a close and loyal friend of his in Segovia to find out what had transpired. The friend wrote him all the news from home and, after mentioning don Martin's mother's sorrow, the letter went on to tell how captain don Pedro had gotten out of jail on bond. As soon as he got home, he threw himself on his bed, saying "My honor is ruined," and died. His son don Luis had come home from Italy. He bailed the servants out of prison and was making an extensive search to learn the whereabouts of his cousin and fiancée, of whom there had been no news whatsoever.

The notice of her uncle's death and the vengeance her cousin don Luis's wrath promised redoubled Aminta's fury and wrath. It further enraged her to see don Jacinto enjoying Flora so freely, both of them the cause of all her misfortune. She didn't feel jealous but profoundly aggrieved. If you want to know whether you really loved, even though now you scorn, look at your lover in another's arms. Realizing that the time had come for deeds and not words, Aminta notified her lover don Martin that it would be that night. He awaited the outcome, knowing what he was supposed to do.

Aminta waited for just the right moment. When the city fell silent and everyone was sound asleep, she crept into her enemies' bedroom. This wasn't the first time; she had to go in every night to get her master's clothes for cleaning. Aminta drew her dagger. Two or three times she plunged it into the treacherous don Jacinto's heart, so sharply that his cry and his giving up the ghost were simultaneous. At the sound, Flora awoke and was about to scream but Aminta didn't give her time. She stabbed her in the throat, uttering these words:

"Traitor! Aminta punishes you and avenges her dishonor!"

She stabbed Flora in the breast three of four more times, sending her soul to keep her lover's company. Aminta closed the door to the room, took her cape and her suitcase and, using a new key she'd had made by pretending to lose the other one, she locked the front door and left. She went to don Martin's lodgings. When he heard how she had done them in, he said they should get on the road immediately.

Taking their clothing and the mules, they departed and traveled with haste to the first inn, where they stopped to rest. There Aminta dressed as a lady in an elegant gown she'd brought. Don Martin donned gentlemen's dress and hid the old clothes where they'd never be found. Two days they rested there. They confirmed the vows they'd made to each other and, with the vows, they confirmed their love. Aminta could no longer refuse don Martin, her true husband, any favor he might ask. Then don Martin hired a maid and two servants, rented a proper carriage, and they set out for Madrid.

By the morning after that terrible night, the sinful wretches were roasting in hell. Their evil lives had merited that death and their violent deaths were a fitting end to their lives. That morning, when the other servants noticed that the servant Jacinto didn't appear, and their master and Flora didn't get up, they went into the bedroom. As they beheld that awful scene, they screamed. The maids shrieked and soon everyone in the city joined in the clamor. The police took everyone's confession. Since the only clue was Jacinto's absence, and the fact that "he" had taken "his" suitcase, they took the other servants prisoner. The police searched every inn in the city and found the one where the authors of the crime had stayed, but they couldn't discover their names or where they were from. The only thing they found out was that the two had departed in the middle of the night. Because they'd said they were brothers, they often locked themselves in their room to talk.

With these slender clues, the mayor and several law officers set out after them. They didn't suspect a thing when they met up with don Martin and his lady, who were on their way to Madrid. They only saw two people traveling with composure and authority. Besides, they recognized don Martin as a noble from that city and knew that he now lived in Segovia. Don Martin informed them that he was traveling from a nearby town with the lady who was to become his wife, and they told him who they were looking for and why. The two acted astonished at the story. It's not surprising that the law officers didn't recognize the authors of the crime because, if you were looking for a muleteer and a young page, and you met an important gentleman and a beautiful lady, would you be suspicious?

The group had met on the road, and as they both carried provisions, don Martin and the mayor dined together. Not finding a trace of the fugitives he was seeking, the mayor decided to turn back to town while Aminta and don Martin went on their way. The mayor realized that the servants weren't guilty of the murders so they were set free. The estate of don Francisco (alias don Jacinto) was confiscated and part was given to the king, the rest went to his widow.

Don Martin and his bride arrived in Madrid. They arranged for a house and furnishings, took out a marriage license, and were wed. They had the banns published afterwards. As soon as they were settled, don Martin sent for his mother. She brought her entire household and all her wealth to Madrid. She felt happy to have such a daughter-in-law and, knowing who Aminta really was, she considered herself very fortunate.

The three still live in Madrid today. Aminta has kept the name doña Victoria. She is very happy with her adoring husband, don Martin. The only thing lacking for her to be completely happy is children. Her cousin don Luis is still alive, but out of respect for him, doña Victoria has not claimed the vast fortune left her by her father. Don Martin has not wanted to deal with this matter either. The secret of the story remains with these three, and if Aminta herself had not told it to me so it could be written with false names, no one would ever know. Now you all can see the deceived Aminta's great courage and how she avenged her own honor in this second enchantment.

The moment the lovely and discreet Matilda ended her enchantment, narrated with such wit and charm that she'd held her listeners totally absorbed and in suspense throughout, don Diego, Lysis's new suitor, signaled to the musicians. He instructed his two servants, who were both excellent dancers, to interrupt the applause for the lovely Matilda. Don Diego suggested that they get on with the entertainment because he felt that applause could not do her story justice, so it was better to omit it. The other ladies and gentlemen were of the same mind, so they all turned to watch the graceful turns and lively pirouettes being executed by don Diego's servants.

After the dance was over, the guests began a sumptuous meal that Lysis had arranged for her guests. As was customary at such evening affairs, a variety of sweet salads garnished with delightful fruits and conserves were served at the table. Each dish attested to their hostess's exquisite taste.

With prickly charm, Lysis darted a thousand scornful glances toward don Juan all the while she kept smiling favorably upon don Diego. This really burned don Juan up. Even though he was enamored of Lisarda, still he wanted to be loved by Lysis as well. To spite Lysis, he outdid himself in attention to Lisarda, just as Lysis was flirting with don Diego in order to wound don Juan.

When matins rang out at the Church of the Carmen, all the ladies and gentlemen decided to go hear midnight mass so they could sleep carefree and rise refreshed for the second night's entertainment. They said good-night to Lysis and her mother, who didn't want to go along.

They set out on their pious mission, the gentlemen accompanying the ladies. As he left, don Diego thanked Lysis for her great favor to him and offered to be her slave. This is how the first night's party came to an end.

Second Night

Phoebus Apollo was just taking shelter behind blue curtains and inviting night to cover the world with her black mantle as all the ladies and gentlemen who'd assembled for the first night's party again gathered at the noble Laura's house. This discreet lady and her beautiful daughter greeted them with great courtesy and delight. They took their seats in the order established on the previous night and don Diego announced that his servants would start the party with some lively dances and an improvised play they wanted to present.

When the ladies saw that they wouldn't be called upon to dance that night, they settled back in their places. Lysis was wearing a soft woolen gown of silvered purple and about her neck a diamond collar bearing don Diego's initial. He'd sent his new mistress the gift that very afternoon upon receiving the purple band she'd sent for him to wear with his green cross. These signals caused don Juan some uneasiness, although Lisarda sought to distract him with her numerous attentions.

The beautiful Lysis was readying her instrument and preparing to sing the ballad she'd composed and set to music that afternoon when the musicians begged her to save her song for the third night. They wanted to sing the song don Juan had composed especially for them to perform this evening. Everyone applauded this suggestion because they knew don Juan was as consummate in composition as in everything he did. The musicians took their places and sang this ballad:

One Sunday Anton goes
to Menga's house,
but Gila is sour-faced;
it must be jealousy.
The lad complains of her
and proper is his complaint,
for suspicion without fact
is an aberration of faith.
She blames him, innocent,
of course that's an offense;
she so freely accuses him
that it hurts him deep inside.
To speak with friendly Menga
is not wrong, well can you see,
for while there is no love without pleasure,
there can be pleasure without love.
Gila would like Anton to avoid
Menga, harsh demand,
for him to be discourteous
simply to show her favor.
The rules are not the same
for men as for women;
what is disdain in women
is rudeness in a man.
No one can reason
with jealousy, and, by heaven,
people who heed not reason
must be very foolish.
Empty fears, Gila,
mean nothing, except perhaps
that to fear without reason
may prepare one for a fall.
To forbid him to look at Menga,
I don't know if that's wise,
for, simply by being forbidden,
they say, it may create desire.
There is polite subjugation,
and, as I see it, it's enough for Anton
to be subject to his darling
without being bound to her error.
Thus is love for men;
their candor is duplicity,
their innocence a crime.
A curse on love, amen!

Anyone who watched the beautiful Lysis while the ballad was sung could easily detect in her restlessness the irritation she felt in listening. She caught the openness with which don Juan reproved her for her jealousy of Lisarda. She was on the verge of saying something, when she noticed how melancholy don Diego looked to see her so upset, and she recovered her composure. Her brow relaxed and her face brightened when, as president of the soiree, she commanded don Alvaro to tell his enchantment. He obeyed instantly, beginning:

"Avarice is the most pernicious vice a man can have. When a man is greedy then he's foolish, boring, irritating, and hateful to everyone. No one wants to cross his path, and rightfully so, as you will see in my enchantment, which goes like this":

The Miser's Reward

A gentleman from Navarre came to serve a grandee at
court, a man of lofty aspirations but humble earthly possessions, for
stepmother Fortune had endowed him with the single possession of
a meager bed to sleep on at night and to sit on during the day. This
young man, whom we shall call don Marcos, had lived with his ancient
father, so old that his many years had been their major source of
income, for he used his age to soften even the hardest of hearts. Don
Marcos was only twelve years old when he came to Madrid. That same
number of years had passed since he had lost his father, who died of
a terrible pain in his side.

Don Marcos found a position as page in a princely house and there
he had all the usual schooling in manginess, squalor, knavery, and
money-grubbing. Although don Marcos graduated in each of these
schools, it was in the last where he really shone. He willfully condemned himself to a penury more extreme than any hermit would
endure. He spent the eighteen coppers he earned so sparingly that he
was able to keep the total from diminishing hardly at all. This he
managed to do at the expense of his own stomach and his companions'
meals. If he did spend any money, it was so little you'd scarcely note
its absence.

Don Marcos was of medium height but, given the delicacy of his
eating habits, he turned from a youth into a stalk of asparagus. The
only time his stomach escaped from want was when it was his turn
to serve at his master's table. Then he would relieve the dishwashers

of their task, so thoroughly did he clean off the dishes that they were cleaner than when they went to the table. He would stuff his purse with absolutely every leftover he could safely use the next day.

In this wretched way he spent his youth. He also accompanied his master on his many travels when his master had important business in Spain or abroad. Don Marcos was finally promoted from page to servant. In making such a change, his master accomplished something that heaven could not. The eighteen coppers became five silver coins plus a few coppers; but don Marcos didn't change his way of life nor did he increase the rations he allowed his stomach. Indeed, now that he had more obligations he only knotted his purse more tightly. He virtually never saw a light in his house. If, on rare occasion he did splurge, it was only because his craftiness discovered a candle stub some careless butler had overlooked, which he would use parsimoniously. He would begin undressing the very moment he entered the front hall from the street so that, by the time he got to his room, he could drop his clothes and snuff out the candle in an instant.

When he got up in the morning, he'd take an old broken pot and go out to the street door and wait for the water-boys to pass. He'd ask the first one he saw to supply his need, and this would last him two or three days, so sparingly did he use it. Sometimes he would go out to where the little boys played and he'd give a copper to one to come make his bed and sweep the floor. When he did hire a servant, he'd make an agreement that the most he would give him was two coppers and a mat to sleep on. When he didn't have one, he'd find a jack-of-all-trades to do his chores and empty the unusual chamber pot he used for all his necessities. Having once served as a honey bucket, it was more battered than a worn-out well bucket. Even in the matter of doing his duty he was stingy.

He would eat a penny loaf of bread, meat scraps, or half a pound of stringy beef which he'd give to the cook with meticulous instructions on how to prepare it. This wasn't every day, only holidays. All he usually ate was a penny loaf and some cheese. He would enter the room where his fellow servants were eating and go up to the nearest one, saying:

"From the lovely aroma, that stew must be delicious. I think I'll have a little taste."

No sooner said than done. He'd grab a huge chunk. He'd go all around the table doing this, sampling each and every dish. It got so that when they saw him coming, everyone who could finished off his food in one gulp, and the ones who couldn't covered their plates with their hands.

He had one friend who was a servant in the same household. Don Marcos used to wait for this friend to go inside to eat and then, with his bread and cheese in his hand, he'd follow after, saying:

"I'll come bore you with my conversation while we eat."

Then he'd sit down at the table and scrounge as much as he could. He never bought wine in his life, though he did drink it every now and then, and this is how he obtained it: he'd stand in the doorway to the street and, when he saw a little boy or girl pass by carrying wine, he'd very politely ask them to let him taste it in such a way that they could hardly refuse. If the youngster was courteous, don Marcos would ask for another sip. Once when he was traveling on mule to Madrid a lad joined company with him and, to earn expenses, worked as his servant. To avoid paying him, one day don Marcos sent the boy off for wine. While the boy was gone, don Marcos mounted his mule and departed, leaving the boy to beg his way to the capital. At any inn he never lacked some relative from whom he could sponge and so avoid paying for his meal. Once he even fed his mule the straw stuffing from the mattress to keep from spending any money.

Many tales were told about don Marcos which entertained his master and his friends and so cheered their hearts that don Marcos became known throughout the city as the world's most temperate man. He was also chaste for, as he was wont to say, no woman is beautiful if she costs money and no woman is ugly if she's free, especially if she sews handkerchiefs and collars and other dainties typical of the fastidious woman.

Because don Marcos lived like this till he was thirty, everyone believed that he was rich and with good reason, for at the expense of his health and his good name, he'd managed to scrimp and save some six thousand ducats. He always carried them on his person as he greatly feared the wiles of bankers who, if they catch the slightest carelessness, clip a client quick as a fox. Because don Marcos was known not to be a gambler or a womanizer, almost every day he received an offer of marriage. He invariably shied away, fearful of some dreadful outcome. The women who sought him for a husband thought he could be a little more spendthrift, not quite so penny-wise—this is the word they used for his stinginess.

Among the many who aspired to become his wife was a lady who, although she'd never married, was considered a widow. A woman of good taste who, while a little older, disguised her age with artful makeup and dress. She was a merry widow who always wore a mourning dress of heavy silk and a chignon with a regal headdress. People said that doña Isidora, which was her name, was very rich and she certainly lived as if she were. But people always assume more than meets the eye. This match was proposed to don Marcos and the bride was described in glowing colors with the assurance that her wealth exceeded fourteen or fifteen thousand ducats. He was told that her late consort had been one of the finest gentlemen in the famous city of Seville in Andalucia, and that's how the lady always described him. When don Marcos heard all this, he considered himself as good as married.

The intermediary who negotiated the marriage was a cunning matchmaker who worked all kinds of deals and not just marriages; he trafficked in pretty faces and fat purses. He knew all the good and all the evil in the whole city, which is why doña Isidora promised him a fat reward if he could accomplish her desire. After the matchmaker made his proposition to don Marcos, he suggested that they visit doña Isidora that very afternoon to avoid any problem delay might cause.

When don Marcos entered doña Isidora's apartment, he was thunderstruck at all the rooms and all the beautiful and well-arranged furnishings. He examined everything very carefully because he'd been told that the woman who was about to become the mistress of his heart was mistress of all this. She'd surrounded herself with so much rich damask, so many furnishings like escritoires and pictures, that he thought it looked more like the house of a titled noble than an everyday house. The lavish parlor, the tidiness of the house, everything smelling so clean and fresh, seemed more like heaven than earth. Likewise, doña Isidora was so well dressed and neat that, as a poet friend of mine says, I think it was from her that well-attired ladies came to be known as "isidoras."

She had two maids who lived with her, one to do the sewing, the other charged with the general chores. If our gentleman hadn't been the kind of man he was, and if his meager diet hadn't diminished his energy, he might have married their mistress just to get the maids, so pretty were their faces. Especially the kitchen maid, she could've been a queen if kingdoms were granted on the basis of beauty.

Don Marcos was particularly impressed with doña Isidora's charm and her good sense. Because of her gentility and courteous manner, he thought she was grace personified. She spoke to him at great length and very pleasantly, and everything she said not only delighted don Marcos, it enamored him; so absolutely simple and without duplicity was he that his heart warmed in appreciation.

Doña Isidora thanked the matchmaker for the favor he'd done her in finding such a suitable match. She had arranged an elaborate and expensive luncheon to show off her many rich and aromatic dishes, set off by a white tablecloth and all the other tableware necessary to a sumptuous household such as Isidora's. This hooked don Marcos.

A handsome young man also came to lunch. He was debonair and so witty that he verged on being roguish. Doña Isidora introduced him as her nephew, whose name was Augustin. She obviously doted on him. Inez served the table while, at her mistress's command, the other maid, by name Marcela, took up the guitar, which she knew how to play very well. Indeed the best musician in the city played no better and, while she played, she sang in a voice more like an angel's than a woman's, as best don Marcos could judge. Without waiting to be cajoled, probably because she knew she sang well or else it was just her way, she sang this song with grace and charm:

Clear fountains,
since you whisper,
whisper to Narcissus
that he knows not how to love.

Whisper that he lives
free and unaffected
and that my affection
is written in water;
he should feel sorrow
if he knows my sorrow
which is the sweet prison
of all my freedom.
Whisper to Narcissus
that he knows not how to love.

Whisper that his heart
is made of ice,
and for his own solace
he makes me sorrow;
if I ask for his favor
he answers, "Let her suffer,"
and if I ask for mercy,
he feigns sleep.

Whisper to Narcissus
that he knows not how to love.

Whisper that he calls
other eyes his heaven
only to annoy me,
not because he loves them,
and he repays with disdain
my burning passion,
favoring her
to disfavor me.
Whisper to Narcissus
that he knows not how to love.

When, out of courtesy,
he responds to my love
his favor never lasts
more than a day.
He laughs gaily
at my sorrows
and shows me no mercy
even when he sees me dying.
Whisper to Narcissus
that he knows not how to love.

Whisper that for days
he has seemed loving
and has even made an effort
to respond to my attention:
my melancholy
makes him happy
and, when I change heart,
then he shows affection.
Whisper to Narcissus
that he knows not how to love.

Whisper that I've been
an unfortunate Echo
and, although scorned,
I've always followed him.
When I beg him
to hear my plaint,
disdainfully he lets
my eyes go on weeping.
Whisper to Narcissus
that he knows not how to love.

Whisper that, haughty,
disdainful, he lives free
while I live without peace
because of my love for him;
he does not accept
my eternal love,
instead, harshly,
he seeks my death.
Whisper to Narcissus
that he knows not how to love.

Whisper that his eyes,
serious and severe,
always quick
to cause me pain,
conquer many spoils
by their mere glance;
his haughty pride
knows no equal.
Whisper to Narcissus
that he knows not how to love.

Whisper that
with his happy smile
he has given to Belisa
glory that he took from me,
not as a lover
but as a traitor,
for although he feigns love
he deceives too much.
Whisper to Narcissus
that he knows not how to love.

Whisper my jealousy,
my wrenching sorrow,
oh, you lovely fountains,
heaven to my eyes!
whisper of my sadness,
my sorrow, and my pain,
my pleasure gone:
whisper, fountains,
and please tell Narcissus
that he knows not how to love.

I wouldn't venture to say which pleased don Marcos more, the spicy
empanadas, the tasty meat pies, the savory ham with flavorful fresh
fruit, or Marcela's sweet voice. The meal was accompanied by the poor

man's blessed remedy, wine, which, although well iced, was fiery. Maybe that's why one of its devotees called soda water a kind of fire extinguisher. All the while Marcela sang, don Marcos gorged himself, served by both doña Isidora and Augustin. He felt like a king because her voice was a treat to his ears just as the luncheon was a treat to his poor stomach, as bereft of treats as of nourishment. Doña Isidora also served Augustin, but don Marcos paid attention solely to the revivification of his stomach after its perennial fast. Without being able to swear to it, I think that luncheon saved him from six days of fasting and maybe even more, with all the tasty morsels doña Isidora and her nephew stuffed and crammed into the good gentleman's bottomless purse, enough provisions to last him a long, long time.

The meal ended just as day was ending, and four candles in lovely candelabras illuminated with their soft light the sweet music Augustin played on Marcela's guitar, while she and Inez danced several lively Spanish dances so nimbly and gracefully that the eyes and the hearts of their worthy audience danced along with their nimble feet. Now that don Marcos was full, he craved entertainment so, at his request, Marcela again took up the guitar and ended the party with this ballad:

> Blas has left his cottage,
> God knows if he'll ever return,
> since Menga is most devoted,
> and Blas is most ungrateful.
> He doesn't know how to be constant;
> whenever he sees himself loved, he turns faint;
> a person who doesn't know how to love
> doesn't even know how to appreciate.
> Menga hasn't made him jealous,
> she didn't know how,
> but if she had, perhaps
> she'd have been appreciated.
> Blas is a free spirit,
> he doesn't want to be tied down,
> so, seeing himself loved,
> he quickly turns neglectful.
> Not only does he seek out pleasures,
> he also makes them public,
> and, by making others suffer, he tries
> to improve upon his fame.
> It's certain that he won't come back,
> for love is a fine thing
> but when it turns sour
> it can never be the same again.

He's dying of love for another
but he won't really die,
for he knows how to feign love,
until he gets what he wants.
Pity the mountain lass
who sets her heart on him
for although she may sow love
all she'll reap is sorrow.
Menga is sure she's lost little,
for no matter how much she risks,
she cannot suffer more.
He is generous with disdain,
liberal with neglect,
extreme in excess,
scanty in affection.
Menga says she's glad;
I don't know if that is true,
it's a dubious illness
to be scorned and suffer so.
People usually boast of health
when they're close to death;
but I don't deny that it's smart
to know how to dissimulate.
Hiding to avoid being seen
or hearing him spoken of
without speaking in his praise,
these show signs of health.
But to live unhappy,
cry in secret and get upset
when he looks at another
are sure signs of love.
What I have gleaned
from all my theology
is that the person most insulting
is closest to granting pardon.
Menga boasts of being noble
and I doubt if she'll forget him,
for, once a choice is made,
it's ignoble to reverse it.
But she has told me
that now that she knows
jealousy, offense, insult,
to see him again would be an affront.

When the ballad ended, the trafficker in misfortune rose to his feet
and told don Marcos it was time for doña Isidora to retire. They said
good-bye to her, Augustin, and the two damsels and went to don

Marcos's house. As they walked down the street the enamored don Marcos described how much doña Isidora had impressed him. He expressed his desire to become her husband as soon as possible. In his conversation he revealed more interest in her money than in her person. He said he'd give a finger from his right hand to see the marriage a *fait accompli*. There could be no doubt that she suited him to a T, though he didn't think they would live so grandly, so ostentatiously, after they were married. That was fine for a prince but not for an ordinary man like himself. Just the necessary food and a few other things would be expense enough. His six thousand ducats and a like amount they could save by selling all the unnecessary items in doña Isidora's house would be plenty to support a gentleman's servant and his wife. All they really needed for their house would be four spoons, a jar, a platter, a good bed, and a few other essential items you can't live without. Everything else really was unnecessary and it would be better to sell it and invest the money, which would provide ample income for him to live like a prince and even have enough for his children to live honorably, if God so blessed him. If he had no children, doña Isidora had that nephew and it would all be for him, providing, of course, he was respectful and obedient and treated don Marcos like a father.

Don Marcos went along elaborating upon these thoughts and the matchmaker figured it was as good as settled. He told don Marcos he'd speak with doña Isidora the next morning and finalize the arrangements because, in these kinds of marriages, delay can cause more damage than death. They said good night.

Anxious to get his reward, the matchmaker hurried back to doña Isidora's to tell her every word don Marcos had uttered. Don Marcos went to his master's house and, since it was so late, everything was quiet. He took a candle stub from his purse, stuck it on the end of his sword, and lit it from the lamp illuminating a crucifix in the street. He said a short prayer that this new life he was about to begin would turn out well for him. He entered his room and went straight to bed, eager for the new day, yet fearful that his good fortune might evaporate.

Let's let him sleep and go back to the matchmaker, back to doña Isidora's house. As the matchmaker recounted the whole conversation, he commented on how well it was working out. Doña Isidora knew that better than he did, as you will soon find out. She gave the intermediary her official consent and four escudos as down payment.

She urged him to visit don Marcos first thing in the morning to tell him that she felt honored to become his wife. "Don't let him slip through our fingers!" she exclaimed, urging him to bring don Marcos to dine with her and her nephew so they could complete the arrangements and sign the papers that very afternoon. What double good news for don Marcos: to be accepted as bridegroom and to be invited to dinner!

Because he bore such good tidings, the matchmaker got up at the crack of dawn and went to greet our gentleman, whom he found already dressing. (Don Marcos's excitement about his lady love wouldn't let him rest an instant.) With arms open wide, he embraced his good friend, as he called that procurer of sorrows. His heart overflowed with joy when he heard of his good fortune. Quickly he finished dressing, donning the most elegant finery his penury permitted. Accompanying his guide to misfortune, he went to the house of his lady love and mistress, where that siren received him with the exquisite music of her loving words and Augustin, who was still dressing, greeted him with a thousand pleasantries. They passed the time until lunch in delightful conversation and the crafty youth, acting submissive, expressed effusive appreciation of his great good fortune, grateful that don Marcos treated him like a son. From the parlor they went into the dining room where the sideboard and the table were laid as you'd expect to find in the house of a great lord.

Doña Isidora didn't have to waste any words inviting don Marcos to take a seat at the table, for he beat her to it, himself urging everyone else to sit down, thus freeing them from any minor embarrassment. From the abundant and well-seasoned food elaborately laid out on the sideboard, the special guest satisfied his every desire. In his mind he kept going over and over the speeches he'd rehearsed the night before and some new ones as well, because he considered doña Isidora too lavish and extravagant. He thought her grandness and ostentation were entirely unnecessary and certainly a great waste of money if he had to pay for it himself.

The meal ended and, since they didn't have a guest bed for don Marcos, they asked him if, instead of taking a siesta, he would like to play a game of cards called *jugar al hombre* ("being a man"). He replied that he served in the household of a man so Christian and so virtuous that, if his master ever found out that one of his servants gambled or even played a single hand of blackjack, he wouldn't keep him in his service another instant. Knowing this, don Marcos had made it a rule always to please his master. Besides the fact that his inclinations were good and virtuous, he didn't know how to play that game *jugar al hombre*. Why, he wouldn't recognize a single card in the deck and, to tell the truth, he thought it just as well for it saved him many ducats each year.

"Well," doña Isidora said, "our friend don Marcos is so virtuous that he doesn't know how to play cards. I keep telling Augustin that's better for one's soul and for one's pocketbook. Now, son, run along and tell Marcela to hurry and finish eating so she can play the guitar and Inez her castanets and we'll entertain ourselves until Mr. Gamarra (that's the matchmaker's name) gets back with the notary to draw up all the papers."

Augustin went off on his aunt's errand and, while he was gone, don Marcos continued the conversation she had begun. Don Marcos said:

"Well, if Augustin truly wants to please me, he must give up gambling and going out at night. That way we'll be friends. If not, we'll have a thousand disagreements because I believe in going to bed early on those nights when there's nothing to do. When I get home, I not only lock the door, I nail it shut. Not that I'm jealous, for a man who has an honorable wife would be a fool to be jealous, but rich houses are never safe from robbers and I don't want some thief to clean me out by simply walking in and taking what has cost me such effort and hard work to earn. Anyhow, either he gives up his vices or there'll be the devil to pay."

Doña Isidora saw don Marcos becoming so angry she could hardly calm him down. She told him not to get upset, the boy would do anything to please him because he was the most docile lad she'd ever known, as time would tell.

"Good," don Marcos replied.

Augustin and the damsels entered, interrupting this conversation. Each one carried a musical instrument. The brassy Marcela started the entertainment with these verses:

> Lauro, when I loved you,
> your harshness offended me;
> sad by night and sad by day
> I lamented your ingratitude;
> nowhere did I find
> remedy for my grief,
> when only one single favor

would bring relief to my weary eyes,
but always in your thankless eyes
I found cruelty instead of love.

When I prayed to heaven
to die so as not to see you,
all of my efforts were spent
abasing myself and blaming you;
then I learned what jealously is
and, although worthy of being loved,
I sought to end my life.
Tell me, how can there be
greater misfortune than
being cruelly scorned?

I believe that that's worse
than living in oblivion
for, if I lived in oblivion,
my love would not annoy you.
I consider the sight of you a favor,
but your neglect offers me
a relief that one who scorns
usually denies to his adorer;
so oblivion will be
less harmful than it might seem.

Your attitude invites me
to ask the favor of your disfavor,
if, in the end, you will forget me
and be no longer offended by my love,
may your harshness some day
choose to love
and not ignore;
but if scorn me you must,
Lauro, then I prefer being scorned
to having have been scorned.

I cannot say whether Marcela's sweet voice or the words she sang
pleased her listeners more. When she finished, everyone praised the
song. Even though the verses were not the most polished or refined,
Marcela's verve lent them a spirit that made up for any deficiencies.
Doña Isidora then commanded Inez to dance with Augustin. She told
don Marcos that, as soon as they concluded their dance, she would
have Marcela sing again, she did it so marvelously. This is the ballad
Marcela zestfully sang, to don Marcos's great delight:

Now I see the culmination
of my misfortune,
and I see my jealousy
in favors you grant to others.

No longer can I expect love
from you, ungrateful Ardenio.
All my suffering
equals your disaffection,
so now may you be chilled by my fire,
may I not be inflamed by your ice,
may all my hopes die,
may I no longer live this torment;
since there is no relief or remedy
for my sorrowful confusion
no longer do I even seek it,
I suffer in despair.
Now I see the culmination
of my misfortune,
and I see my jealousy
in favors you grant to others.

What can I hope for now,
how can I try to oblige
one who boldly seeks
only to cause my death?
I imitate those brothers
who suffer in hell
and work in vain
to serve out all their time.
End my life, draw your sword,
and thrust it through my constant heart;
then I shall cease sorrowing,
unless this torture be eternal.
Now I see the culmination
of my misfortune,
and I see my jealousy
in favors you grant to others.

I love you well.
Fierce punishment for my crime!
But though I try
to obligate you
you free yourself;
who would believe that all my qualities,
considered divine by some,
seem hellish to your eyes

since you flee from them.
You men always say you seek
a woman who, in this age,
is a model of constancy,
but when by chance you find one,
you treat her in such a way
that to protect her honor
she has to risk it a hundred times.
Look at your love and at mine:
you can't ask for a clearer mirror:
in it you will see that there are women
who love and who suffer.
Now I see the culmination
of my misfortune,
and I see my jealousy
in favors you grant to others.

Until now I intended to remain silent
enduring all your madness
but since willfully you publish your love
how can I, so jealous, stay silent?
Let the world know I loved you,
let the world know you killed me,
and let that tyrant who is my lord
and my love know that as well.
As for Portia, flames are small,
as for Dido, steel is slight,
worse it is to die from jealousy,
the fire that burns deep within my soul.
Now I see the culmination
of my misfortune,
and I see my jealousy
in favors you grant to others.

Ungrateful Ardenio, my power is slight
and today I think it's even less
for my suffering does not obligate you;
never by suffering did I obligate you.
I want you to have your pleasures
but to enjoy them with respect,
for you once called me your own,
either truly or in pretense.
When I look for myself in your eyes
I see in them another mistress.
Can you tell me anything
that is truer than this?
Now I see the culmination

of my misfortune,
and I see my jealousy
in favors you grant to others.

Ingrate, if all your triumphs
no longer fit within your breast,
you can have them, for all I care,
they're really poisons, not triumphs.
But you must enjoy seeing me live
my days dying for your love,
since your scorn is so extreme.
If you enjoy killing me,
then kill me quickly and end it all.
Since I live in jealousy,
why do I seek any other death?
Now I see the culmination
of my misfortune,
and I see my jealousy
in favors you grant to others.

Since don Marcos was a typical Castilian rustic and as pure as silk from China, the ballad didn't seem long to him. Indeed, he wished it had lasted longer because his simple wit wasn't like the woolly wits at court who get bored after six stanzas. He thanked Marcela profusely and would have asked her to keep on singing if, just then, Gamarra hadn't arrived with a man he said was a notary, but who looked more like a lackey than anything else. They drew up all the agreements and papers. Doña Isidora put up her house and twelve thousand ducats as dowry. Because of his simplicity, don Marcos postponed the exercise of his authority and asked for no verification. He felt immensely pleased with the dowry, and his darling wife—that's what he called her now—made him feel so loving that he danced with her.

That evening they supped with the same lavish ostentation as at lunch, in spite of don Marcos's obsession with moderation in all expenditures. As master now of the house and the estate, he thought that if they kept on living like that the dowry wouldn't last four days, but he held his tongue for a more suitable occasion.

Finally it came time to retire and, to save himself the trouble of going back to his lodgings, he wanted to stay the night with his wife. She, very modestly, said that until she'd received the blessing of the church, no man would set foot in her chaste bed, which had belonged exclusively to her late lord and master.

So don Marcos had to go home to sleep. (It would be more accurate to say to stay awake, for the task of having the banns published had him up and dressed at five.) That was quickly done on three holidays, which Fortune luckily provided all in a row, so it must have been August, which brings holy days two by two. The banns were published and the wedding set for Monday, which is no worse a day for marriage than Tuesday. They held the civil wedding at the same time as they took their religious vows the way grandees do, all dressed up for the elaborate celebration and party.

Don Marcos humbled his nature and conquered his stinginess to buy a rich dress and an overskirt for his bride—on credit, so as not to diminish his six thousand ducats. He justified the expense by reasoning that it could also serve as her shroud, not because he wanted doña Isidora to die but because he thought that if she wore it only from Christmas to Christmas, it would last until Judgment Day. He invited a witness from his master's house, and everyone lauded his choice of a bride and his good fortune, thinking he'd really done well to find such an attractive woman who was also rich. Although doña Isidora was older than her bridegroom, she disguised it so well that it was a delight to see the art with which she fixed herself up, despite the dictums of Aristotle and other ancient philosophers.

Late in the afternoon following the wedding dinner, they celebrated. While Inez and Augustin kept things lively with their dances, doña Isidora asked Marcela to add her lovely voice. She didn't have to be asked twice. With grace and charm, she sang:

If the dawn laughs,
she laughs at me,
the one I adore is cold,
and I die constant.

When I see the dawn
with happy laughter
warn me of my sorrows,
I sigh over my troubles
but I am not surprised
to see her laugh
or to imagine
that she laughs at me.
The one I adore is cold,
and I die constant.

She laughs to see me
with a hundred thousand griefs

my eyes like oceans
on seeing myself scorned.
While my beloved master,
thankless, sleeps,
my sad grief
dismisses all my sleep.
The one I adore is cold,
and I die constant.

She laughs because I say
I'm not in love
and so I keep the secret
of his harshness
to see if I can turn
the terrible disdain
he employs to kill me
into kinder treatment.
The one I adore is cold,
and I die constant.

She laughs because I draw apart
from the man I pursue
and I complain,
calling him my enemy,
and I seek advice
loving him in absence,
cruelly I say farewell
to the others who pursue me.
The one I adore is cold,
and I die constant.

She laughs to see my eyes
announce my disaffection,
while my constancy causes
them a thousand woes,
promising rewards
while hiding my great passion,
glancing surreptitiously
at eyes that are free.
The one I adore is cold,
and I die constant.

She laughs that I try
to hide my jealousy
and I cannot sleep,
despite my vows and oaths,
and trying not to care,

this makes me sad
because love ordains
my sad death,
loving a cold man,
dying constant.

While they were enjoying these entertainments night came, the first night of don Marcos's possession, the first night of his many misfortunes. Even before he could take possession, Fortune began to work her way. The first thing that happened was that Augustin had an attack. I don't know if it was caused by seeing his aunt married, all I know is that it upset the whole household. Doña Isidora, disconsolate, went in to undress him and put him to bed, more lovingly than was proper. She was so solicitous and amorous that she almost made her bridegroom jealous.

After don Marcos saw the sick man become somewhat calm and, while his wife was preparing for bed, he scrupulously locked the doors and drew the bolts on the windows. This extreme caution upset his dear wife's maids. It inspired more concern and worry than you can imagine because they thought it was a question of excessive jealousy when it was really simple avarice. The good man had brought with him all his clothes and the six thousand ducats that had never seen the light of day, and he wanted to go to bed assured that his treasure was safe. When at last he went to bed with his wife, the two maids, instead of going to bed, began to whisper and cry, exaggerating the cautious nature of their new master. Marcela said:

"Inez, what has Fortune brought us? We always used to go to bed at three or four after a lot of dancing and flirting by the door or at the window, with money rolling into the house the way dust rolls into other houses, and now we see the doors locked at eleven and the windows practically nailed shut and we don't dare open them!"

"No, we can't open them," Inez said, "as the Lord is my God. Our new master promises to lock everything up as tight as the legendary cave of Toledo. So, sister dear, the party's over, as the saying goes. We might as well take the veil. But this is what our mistress wanted, despite the fact that she had little need to marry. We had everything we needed, she shouldn't have done this to us. And I really don't understand why it didn't upset her to see poor don Augustin's outburst tonight. Why, it's clear to me that his fit came from seeing her married. It doesn't surprise me because he's used to a life of indulgence, to being pampered, and now suddenly he's caged in like a little finch. Of course, I'm sure he regrets it as much as I do! If these aren't bad times, you could string me up with a silken cord."

"At least you, Inez," Marcella replied, "get to go out and do the shopping; you don't have any reason to cry. It's much worse for me. Playing the wretched chambermaid, along with all the rest of this hoax, means I have to put up with the fretting of a jealous man who thinks ants look like giants. Well, I'm going to do something about it; I'm sure I can figure out some way to keep from starving to death. A pox on you, sir don Marcos, if you think I'll play your game!"

"Well, Marcela, I'll have to bear with it," Inez said, "because, to tell you the truth, what I want more than anything is don Augustin. Until now the mistress hasn't given me a chance to say a word to him, though I do think he doesn't look on me with disfavor. From now on though, things will be different because she'll have to pay attention to her new husband."

Thus went the conversation of the two maids. The fact was that don Augustin was doña Isidora's gigolo, and he ate, dressed, and gambled at her expense under the guise of being her nephew. He enjoyed other things as well, such as the pleasant social intercourse between ladies and gentlemen that took place in her house, the dances, the games, and all the other little things of the sort. And suddenly he had to adjust to this new game of her having a husband, and his naughty habit of always sleeping in doña Isidora's company left him tossing alone and sleepless that night. The moment Inez had confessed her love for him to Marcela, she decided to go see if he needed anything, and she left Marcela preparing to go to bed. It was her good fortune that, since Augustin was so young, he felt afraid of the dark and he said to her:

"Please, Inez, come to bed with me, for I'm experiencing the greatest terror in the world and if I have to sleep alone I won't be able to shut my eyes from this dreadful fear."

Inez was exceedingly compassionate and felt such pity for him that instantly she obliged him and even rewarded him for arranging things to her liking.

The next morning, Tuesday, after all, Inez feared her mistress might get up first and catch her red-handed with her plunder, so she got up much earlier than usual and went to tell her friend Marcela all about it. Not finding Marcela in her room, she searched the house looking for her. When she got to the little back gate hidden way out behind the corral, she found it standing wide open. It appeared that Marcela had had a date and, in order to keep it, she'd taken the key and run off with her man, thus escaping from the mess they were in. On purpose, just to annoy don Marcos, she'd left the gate wide open. When Inez saw this, she ran screaming to her mistress, which woke up the poor bridegroom.

Half dead of fright, he leapt from the bed and called out to doña Isidora to hurry and get up to see if anything was missing. He flung open the window expecting to see his wife there in the bed, but what he saw was a phantom, a deathly ghost. The good woman's face showed each and every wrinkle she had so carefully covered with makeup, successfully disguising her years, which surely were closer to fifty-five than the thirty-six she'd declared on her dowry agreement. Her hair was thin and gray from the many snowy winters she had lived through. This deficiency wasn't serious, thanks to artful arrangement and the chignons, which she sorely missed on this occasion. Much to her annoyance, they had fallen onto the pillow in her sleep. Her teeth likewise were scattered all over the bed—as the prince of poets once said "her teeth were like pearls scattered before swine." Don Marcos even had several caught in his mustache, which looked like a rooftop sprinkled with hoarfrost. They had gotten caught there because of his mustache's friendship with his wife's mouth.

How all of this affected the poor gentleman we shall leave to the imagination of our kind reader so as not to extend our tale excessively with things that are better left to the imagination. All I shall say is that doña Isidora, not accustomed to being seen so early in the morning and upset that her charms had been so brusquely exposed, grabbed her wig and jammed it on her head. She looked worse with it on than without it because in her haste she got it on askew, setting it down over her eyebrows. Oh, cursed Marcela, cause of untold misfortunes! May God never ever pardon you, amen! Finally, recovering her aplomb if not her reason, doña Isidora reached for her pettiskirt to put on so she could go look for the fugitive maid, but it wasn't there. Neither was the rich dress she had worn for her wedding, or the embroidered slippers, or any of the jewels she'd left in a tray, or the chain worth two hundred escudos she'd taken from her hoard to wear the day before to solemnize her marriage. It was all gone. The clever Marcela had not wanted to depart empty-handed.

How do you suppose don Marcos reacted to this? What words can describe it, what pen can set it down? Only one who has earned his money at great cost to his health could understand how deeply he felt this, particularly when he couldn't even find consolation in his bride's beauty. It was enough to depress the devil himself. He looked at his wife and saw a terrible fright, he looked around and saw the loss of doña Isidora's rich clothes and the chain. In his nightshirt, he paced back and forth in the parlor in a state of shock, sighing and wringing his hands.

While he was pacing like this, doña Isidora repaired to all her magic makeup boxes in the miraculous Jordan of her dressing room. Meanwhile, Augustin got up. Inez had already gone to tell him the news and the two laughed at doña Isidora's appearance and don Marcos's stupidity and rage. Half-dressed, he came out to console his "uncle," uttering all the trite and malicious things he could invent and string together. He urged don Marcos to catch the culprit; he told him to forebear, they were only material things, and so on. Don Marcos finally came to his senses and got dressed. When doña Isidora reappeared, she looked so different that don Marcos wondered whether this was the same person and if he'd been mistaken. Don Marcos and Augustin went out together to search all of Marcela's hideouts as Inez described them.

They would have been smarter not to have gone, or at least don Marcos would have been, as I think Augustin was only playing him for a fool. As you may well imagine, Marcela was nowhere to be found. At last, they realized it was hopeless and returned home, resigned to God's will from on high and to Marcela's from here below, for there was no more they could do. Our wretched gentleman grudgingly performed his duties that day even though he felt terribly depressed; the loss of the chain really stuck in his craw.

Fortune was not yet satisfied and planned to continue her persecution of his stinginess. What happened was this: the moment they sat down to eat, two of the lord admiral's servants appeared, greeted them all, and said that their master kissed doña Isidora's hands and would she kindly return all the silver she'd had on loan for over a month. If she refused, they'd have to collect some other way. When that message was delivered to the lady, the only reply she could give was to surrender to them every piece she possessed—plates, platters, serving dishes, every thing in the house that shone, all the things that had so impressed don Marcos. He tried playing bold, saying that it all belonged to him, they had no right to carry it off, and so on. Finally one of the servants went to get the lord admiral's steward to help while the other one stayed to keep watch over the silver.

Ultimately they carried every bit of silver away. Don Marcos, blind with rage and fury, tore his hair in vain. He began saying and doing the craziest things. He complained about her deception and vowed to sue for divorce. Doña Isidora, very humbly, tried to calm him down, telling him he should thank her, not berate her. She explained that, to catch a husband like him, anything, even deception, was wise and proper and furthermore, it was unthinkable to dissolve the marriage, so he'd better learn patience.

Don Marcos had no other choice, but from that day on, they never knew a moment's peace nor did they eat another bite with pleasure. Don Augustin was present through all this. He kept very quiet and tried to make peace while continuing to eat at their expense and spending delightful nights with Inez. The two of them laughed at doña Isidora's wiles and don Marcos's misfortunes.

If Fortune had left them in peace with the misfortunes she had already wrought, don Marcos might have been content with what was left and gotten along honorably. But as soon as doña Isidora's marriage became known in Madrid, a man who rented furnishings came to collect three months' rent on the wall hangings and the living room furniture. He carried it all away, saying that a woman who'd married as well as doña Isidora no longer needed to rent and should buy furniture of her own.

This shock almost did don Marcos in. It brought him to blows with his wife. Her wig and her teeth flew every which way and she suffered no little pain. Worst of all, the insult of being abused so soon after her wedding made her cry and blame don Marcos for treating a lady like her so brutally only because of a few material possessions. Fortune gives and Fortune takes away, she said, and even if this had been a matter of honor, he punished her too severely.

Don Marcos retorted that to him money was honor. The arguing solved nothing; the owner of the furniture and the hangings carried everything off along with the money she owed for the rental, which don Marcos had to pay because his wife had given up all her customers and clients and no longer knew what color money was; indeed the only money she'd set her eyes on recently was don Marcos's hoard, which he spent sparingly, trying vainly to keep it intact.

With all the screaming and shouting going on, the owner of the house, which don Marcos believed belonged to him, came down. Doña Isidora had told him that the landlord had rented the upstairs apartment for a year. The landlord said that if they were going to make such a racket all day long every day, they'd have to look for another house and go with God, for he wanted the place quiet.

"What do you mean, go?" don Marcos asked. "You're the one who has to go, since this is my house."

"What do you mean, your house, you idiot?" the landlord exclaimed. "You lunatic, get out of here. I swear to God, if you weren't crazy, I'd throw you out the window this very instant!"

Don Marcos became furious and his rage emboldened him. Doña Isidora had to intervene and don Augustin enlightened him with the truth. They managed to calm the landlord down by promising to vacate the next day. What could don Marcos do? He either had to shut up or go hang himself; he didn't have the will to do anything else. He was dumbstruck, grief-stricken, beside himself. He took his cape and left the house. Augustin, at his aunt's insistence, followed after trying to pacify him. The two men finally found an apartment near the palace they could move into which wasn't far from the house of don Marcos's master. They made a deposit and arranged to move the next day. Don Marcos told Augustin to go home to eat, but he couldn't go back and face that treacherous, deceitful aunt of his. The youth went home and told her everything that had happened and together the two of them planned the move.

Our miserable hero finally came home to go to bed, down at the mouth and starving to death. Night passed. The next morning, doña Isidora sent him to the new house to receive their clothing while Inez went to get a cart in which to transport everything.

The moment the simple fool had gone, the treacherous doña Isidora, her nephew, and the maid gathered up every item in the house, loaded it onto the cart, and all three fled Madrid taking the road to Barcelona. The only things they left in the house were those things they couldn't carry, things of no value, like pots and pans and such.

Don Marcos waited till close to noon. Worried by their delay, he went back to the old house. Not finding them there, he asked a neighbor when they'd left. She replied quite a while ago. Believing they'd already arrived at their new quarters, he rushed back so as not to keep them waiting. Tired and sweaty, he found that they weren't there and almost died, fearing exactly what had happened. Like a flash, he went back again to their old house and kicked open the door that they'd left locked. The moment it flew open and he entered, he saw there was nothing there that wasn't worthless. He then realized the full extent of his misfortune. He cried, he shouted, he raced through all the rooms and banged his head against the walls, saying:

"Woe is me! All my fears have come true! What a cursed idea to arrange this blasted marriage that has cost me so dear! Where are you, you deceitful siren, you thief of all my possessions, of everything I saved up at such cost to myself so I could live a life of some ease?"

He shrieked these and similar laments so loudly that people came in from the street. Some servant who knew what had happened told him to accept the fact that they had gone far away, for the van that had carried off his clothes, his wife, her nephew, and the maid, was not a local moving cart but a highway van. He'd asked them where they were going, and they'd said they were leaving Madrid.

That was the last straw! But, as hope springs eternal even in the midst of disaster, don Marcos decided to try to find out which way the cart carrying his heart and his six thousand ducats had taken. He inquired but was able to learn nothing because the owner of the van wasn't very bright. He was just an ordinary working man from Madrid and the clever tricksters who had rented his van far outwitted him. Not knowing which road they'd taken made any attempt to follow them a dead end. Furthermore, don Marcos didn't have a red cent left. His only recourse was to take a loan, but given his indebtedness for the wedding dress and the chain for his bride, he didn't know how he was going to pay even that.

Shriveled by a thousand worries, he set out for his master's house. As he was walking down the Calle Mayor, he ran smack into the crafty Marcela. She tried to escape but couldn't. The instant don Marcos recognized her, he grabbed her. He lost all self-control.

"Now! You swindling thief!" our don Marcos shrieked, "you will give back to me every single thing you stole from me that night you ran away from my house!"

"Alas, sir," Marcela replied, in tears, "well did I know that misfortune would befall me when my mistress made me leave like that! Listen to me, for the love of God! Please don't destroy my honor! I have a good name and I'm engaged to be married and everything would be ruined if such tales were told about me when I'm really innocent. Here, let's go inside this doorway so you can hear my story, and you'll find out who has your clothes and your chain. I knew your grace would suspect me! I told my mistress so that night, but she's a mistress and I'm just a servant. Pity those who serve, how hard it is for them to earn their bread!"

Don Marcos wasn't very bright (as I said before), so he believed her tears and followed her into the doorway of a nearby house. She told him who doña Isidora really was, about her wheeling and dealing, about her business and customers, and explained why she'd married him. All along she'd planned to deceive don Marcos exactly the way she had and at such great cost to him. Marcela told him as well that don Augustin wasn't really her nephew but her gigolo, a conniving vagabond who'd taken up with a woman of her age and profession simply to get free meals and enjoy a life of leisure. In fact, doña Isidora was the one who'd hidden the clothes and the chain to give to don Augustin just as she gave everything to him. She had ordered Marcela to leave and hide where she couldn't be found in order to cover up her own complicity, so he would think Marcela had stolen everything.

Marcela thought don Marcos was harmless, that's why she dared to tell him all that without fearing what he might do to her. Or maybe she thought that by talking she might be able to slip out of his firm grasp and escape. Or maybe she didn't think about it at all because she was "just a servant," which is most likely. At any rate, the little traitor ended her speech warning him to be careful because, when he least expected it, they planned to steal him blind. Then she repeated several times:

"I've told your grace everything I know, everything my conscience dictates, so now, if it please your grace, I am at your command. I'll do whatever you say."

"Now, friend Marcela, is a fine time for you to warn me!" don Marcos exclaimed. "Now that it's too late! That treacherous woman and that son-of-a-bitch opportunist have already run off with everything I possess."

He then recounted all that had happened since the day when she'd disappeared.

"How can that be?" Marcela asked. "Can there be greater evil? Oh, your grace, not in vain did I pity you, but I never dared say anything. The night my mistress sent me from the house, I wanted to warn your grace, knowing what was going on, but I was afraid because, when I refused to hide the chain, she beat me up verbally and physically, as God can attest."

"Well, Marcela," don Marcos went on, "I understand what you're saying, but the awful thing is that there's nothing I can do about it now. I can't even find out where they are."

"Oh, sir, don't let that trouble you," the sly Marcela retorted, "I know a man and, I even dare to hope, God willing, that he'll soon be my husband, who can tell your grace where to find them just as if he could see them with his own two eyes, for he knows how to conjure up devils and all kinds of marvelous things."

"Oh, Marcela!" exclaimed don Marcos, "How grateful I would be! How indebted I'd be if he'd tell me where they are! Please have pity on my misfortune and see if you can arrange it."

It's in the nature of an evil person who sees a man down to help him sink even lower, just as it's in the nature of good people to be credulous. And so don Marcos believed Marcela. She'd decided to deceive and bilk him as much as she could, so with this in mind, she replied that they should go right then. The house wasn't far. While the two were walking down the street together, don Marcos ran into a fellow servant from his master's house; he borrowed four reales from the servant to give to the astrologer, intending that sum not just as a down payment but as full payment for his services. They reached Marcela's house where she lived with the man she called a magician who happened to be her current lover. Don Marcos spoke with him and they agreed on a price of one hundred and fifty reales. The magician told don Marcos to come back in a week and he would conjure up a devil to reveal where those villains were with such exactitude that don Marcos would easily find them. He warned don Marcos not to pursue the matter if he didn't have a stout heart. If he didn't have the courage to see the devil in his true form, don Marcos needed to decide in what form he did want to see the devil appear.

So powerful was don Marcos's desire to find out about his money that looking at the devil seemed as easy as pie. So he said the devil should appear in the very form he appeared in hell for, though the magician might see him cry like a woman over the loss of his money, in all other things he was very manly. With these words, don Marcos gave him the four reales he'd just borrowed and said good-bye to him and Marcela. Then he sought refuge at a friend's house, if the wretched ever have friends. Here he bewailed his sad fate.

Let's leave don Marcos at this point and go back to the enchanter (as we shall call him). In order to accomplish what he had promised and work an outlandish trick on the miser, about whom he knew everything from Marcela, the enchanter did what I'm about to describe to you. He got a cat and shut it up in a little room like a pantry. It had only one small window about the size of a sheet of paper and as high from the ground as the height of a man. The enchanter placed a strong cord net over the window. Then, with the "cat-hole" darkened, he went inside the pantry with the cat and beat it with a whip. When he got the cat frantically wild, he removed the shade from the cat-hole. The cat took off running and leapt up to the little window. Caught by the net, it was hurled back down. He did this over and over, until finally, without even being beaten, the cat learned to head straight for the window. When all this training was done, the enchanter advised the miser that everything was prepared for that night and, when the clock struck eleven, he would reveal to don Marcos everything he desired to know.

Much against his nature, our misguided friend had managed to borrow the one hundred fifty reales which he brought to the enchanter's house and placed in his hands, urging him to make the conjuration powerful. The latter, knowing the measure of don Marcos's courage and spirit, carefully seated him in a chair right beneath the pantry window from which he had now removed the netting. It was, as we mentioned, eleven, and the only light in the room came from a small lamp in a corner.

Inside the pantry, the magician had placed the cat all covered with firecrackers and a boy who, at a certain signal, was to light them and set the cat loose. Marcela left the room as she didn't have the courage to see the apparition. Then the crafty magician donned a heavy black cape and a matching hat. To make his trick more credible, he held in one hand a book in Gothic script on parchment which looked very old. Next he drew a circle on the floor and stepped inside it. Holding a wand in his other hand, he began to read, almost whispering, in a grave and ominous tone. Every now and then he would pronounce rare and outlandish words don Marcos had never heard before. Don Marcos's eyes were big as saucers (as the saying goes). At the slightest sound he would look all around to see if the devil had appeared to tell him everything he desired to know. Next the enchanter tossed sulphur, salt, and pepper into the fire in the brazier at his side, struck the floor with his wand, and said in a loud voice:

"Come, demon Calquimorro, come, you who watch over all travelers, you who know all destinations and hideouts! Here in the presence of don Marcos you will tell us where our quarries are going and how they can be found. Appear this instant or protect yourself from my punishment! Are you being rebellious that you refuse to obey me? I shall press you until you do my bidding."

After this conjuration, he read again from the book. Then he renewed the incense, struck the floor with his wand, and refurbished his conjuration. By this time, don Marcos was about to choke to death. When the enchanter was ready for the devil to appear, he intoned:

"Oh, you who hold the keys to the gates of hell, command Cerberus to send Calquimorro, demon of the highways, to tell us where our travelers are. If you fail to do so this instant, I shall punish you cruelly!"

At this cue, the boy who was holding the cat in the pantry lit the firecrackers and uncovered the hole. Because the cat had been trained to head for the little window, naturally it sought to escape the same way without any regard for don Marcos who, of course, was sitting in the chair directly underneath the pantry window. All aflame, roaring and howling, racing and tearing about, on its way to freedom, the cat bounded through the opening and landed right on don Marcos's head, scorching his whiskers, his hair, and even his face. Don Marcos thought he'd seen not one devil but all the devils in hell. He shrieked and fell to the floor in a dead faint, without ever hearing the voice that said:

"You will find them in Granada."

The cat's howling, don Marcos's shriek, and the sight of a flaming cat streaking down the street brought people running, including the police. This crowd came to the door, burst in, and found Marcela and her lover desperately throwing water on don Marcos, in an effort to revive him, but he didn't move till the next morning. The constable made inquiries into the case. Even though Marcela and her lover explained the whole trick, he was not satisfied. Because don Marcos had no place to stay, the constable made the enchanter put the unconscious man in his own bed and two guards were stationed in the house with Marcela and the half-dead don Marcos. The magician and his helper, who was found in the pantry, were handcuffed and carried off to jail. The magician was charged with murdering a man in his own house. The next morning a report on the case was given to the justice of the peace. He ordered the two prisoners brought before him and sent for Marcela to find out whether the man had recovered or died.

By this time, don Marcos had, in fact, returned to his senses. Marcela described the whole trick to him and he realized he was the world's biggest fool. The constable brought them both to court. When don Marcos was interrogated by the officials about the details of the case, he told the truth as best he knew it. He recounted the whole story of his marriage and how the girl Marcela had taken him to her house promising that the enchanter would tell him the whereabouts of the scoundrels who had run off with all his possessions. That's all he knew because, after the elaborate conjurations of the magician reading from the great book, such a terrible ugly demon had emerged from a black hole and come at him roaring horrifically, and his soul hadn't been strong enough to hear whatever it had said. It had rushed straight at him and scorched him, as they could see. He could remember nothing more after that because his heart had failed and he hadn't recovered his senses till that morning.

This account astounded the law officers. The enchanter disenchanted them by explaining how the whole trick worked, as we have already described. Marcela and the boy corroborated his explanation and the police brought in the dead cat from the street, where it had fallen, burned to a crisp. They also brought in two or three books from the enchanter's house and asked don Marcos if he recognized the book of conjurations. He picked one out and handed it to them. They opened it and saw that it was the popular novel *Amadis of Gaul*. Because the book was old and printed in Gothic script, it had passed for a book of spells. After they heard the whole case, they laughed so hard that the hall didn't become quiet for a long time. Don Marcos felt so ashamed that he wished a thousand times he could kill the enchanter and then himself. The judges warned him not to be so credulous, not to let himself be so easily fooled. Then the case was dismissed. Don Marcos felt so miserable that he didn't even look like the same man. He sighed, so deeply did he sigh that he seemed almost crazy. His grief was so profound that everyone who saw him felt sorry for him.

He returned to his master's house where he encountered a mailman looking for him to deliver a letter, for which he had to pay a real. He opened it and it read:

To Mister Miser Marcos:
  Hail! Any man who doesn't eat and robs his body of its nourishment to save money, who marries for money without even ascertaining that his bride really has money, well deserves the punishment your grace has received, a punishment that has been storing up for you a long, long, time. Your grace, never eat except at others' expense, never pay your servants, scrimp on half a pound of beef, bread, two coppers for the lad who helps you, cleans for you,

and empties the battered chamber pot in which you do your duty. Save up another six thousand ducats and contact me immediately. Then, lovingly, I'll come back to you and be your wife, as such a parsimonious husband certainly deserves.

Doña Isidora the Vengeful

This letter put Marcos into such a fit that it brought on a high fever.* [Everyone who saw him believed that his end had come. He was like that until eight that evening. Then he took his cape and left his friend's house, heading toward the famous Colegio de Santa Maria de Aragon. Because it was summer, the sun was still pursuing its course toward the Indian beaches. As the sun gradually withdrew its light from the earth, the moon, which was waxing, went filling the corners deprived of sunlight with her silvery rays. The despairing don Marcos was walking down the highway toward the new bridge when he ran into a man he recognized as Gamarra, the very one who had drawn up the contracts for that black marriage. Gamarra spoke first:

"What are you doing, don Marcos, in these parts at this hour?"

"What do you think a man as unfortunate as I am would do here," he answered, "except hang himself from one of these trees. That's how I'll end my misfortunes. Oh, Mr. Gamarra, what a disastrous marriage mine was! How I wish all the ill I've suffered would befall you and make you as miserable as I am! I give you my word, this place is perfect, and if I were wearing my sword, I'd take vengeance for the terrible deception your grace perpetrated on me in marrying me to that treacherous woman!"

"I heard about that," Gamarra replied, "about what happened to you and, I swear, your misfortune touched my soul! If this weren't such a bad time for me, I'd avenge your affront with my own hands and save you the trouble. But I'm suffering the greatest grief a man can suffer. I left home intending to hang myself. I decided to die at my own hand rather than on the public gallows."

"That same worthy intention, friend Gamarra," don Marcos said, "has brought me here. I feel so ashamed to face people that I no longer care about my life or my soul. I can't believe there's another more unfortunate than I, so you must tell me what's happened. Then together, as good friends, we can dispose our lives and our deaths."

"What more do you want to know?" Gamarra replied. "If I don't

*The bracketed material that follows comes from the first Spanish edition (Zaragoza, 1637); it was omitted in all subsequent editions.

kill myself here and now, tomorrow I'll be hanged in Madrid's main square. This is how it came about: I work as a servant to the duke of Osuna and he has great confidence in me. He had so much confidence that he entrusted me with some jewels he intended to present to a lady. While I happened to be carrying them, I went to a gambling house and began to gamble. Things always go from bad to worse when you play with another person's money so, in short, I lost everything. When I realized I'd lost more than a thousand ducats, I almost went crazy and began to despair.

"A friend of mine, who's wardrober for the duke, asked me what was wrong and I told him my misfortune. Moved by my plight, he handed me the keys to the wardrobe and told me to go in and take whatever I wanted. He'd keep watch. I thanked him for the great favor and did just that. I took some silk tapestries, some gold, and a few other things to make up the price of my loss. As I was leaving, the chief steward came upon me and, seeing me so laden, he grabbed me. Realizing it was vital for me to get away, I fled and left him holding the goods, the keys, and my life in his hands. When I left home, they'd taken the wardrober prisoner. If they press him, he'll tell the truth, and I'll face the death penalty. Fearing that, I got this rope and came out here where a tree, and now you, will witness my unhappy end instead of all the eyes in Madrid. If you've come with the same intention, there are plenty of trees and ample rope for the two of us."

As he said these words, he drew the rope from his purse. Don Marcos thanked him for his generosity and asked him to make their nooses. He did this swiftly and with ease, placing them in two trees right next to each other.

The entire conversation had been overheard by a man who was relaxing under a tree, resting from having gone down to the river and back. While he could see don Marcos talking and hear the answers, he couldn't see the other man. This so upset him that he scarcely dared breathe. Then he saw that poor desperate man place the noose around his neck and leap from the branch where he'd climbed. At that very moment he heard a great roaring sound, which made him take off up the hill running faster than the eagle flies. He never stopped till he got to the mayor's house. Once in the mayor's presence, he described everything he'd witnessed: how a man had hanged himself and maybe another one, too, from what he'd heard them say, although he'd seen only one of the men.

He went on to recount the conversation. The other man was named

Gamarra, who said he was the duke of Osuna's servant, and the witness described how the wardrober had been taken prisoner. The mayor and all the men he could muster accompanied the witness back to the place. Because the moon was setting, they brought along lights. They found the wretched don Marcos hanging from a tree and discovered a noose hanging from the next one, but it was empty. Feeling great pity for his soul, they took don Marcos down and carried him back to the jail. There they left him and held the man who'd reported the case until morning.

They investigated to learn the identity of the dead man, which was easy because they found papers in his purse including doña Isidora's letter, and someone recognized him as a servant from his master's house. They went to the duke of Osuna's house to find out about the man named Gamarra, but they'd never heard of him. They found not a trace of any such man. None of his tale proved true: his being the duke's servant, losing the jewels, the jailing of the wardrober.

Based on the testimony of the man who'd heard the conversation and saw no one, they decided that the other man must have been the devil who'd come with those lies to drive don Marcos to despair and, it appeared, he had succeeded.

They gave full account to don Marcos's master, and he arranged the funeral. He got permission for him to be buried in holy ground, giving as excuse that his despair had driven him crazy. Such is the vanity of the world that it honors the body of a man even though the poor wretch's soul was probably burning in hell. His master also commanded that this story be written down, together with what happened to doña Isidora, and so it has come into my hands.]* Within several days he died a totally miserable man.

In Barcelona, while doña Isidora was waiting for the boat to take the threesome to Naples, one night don Augustin and his darling Inez left her asleep and absconded with the six thousand ducats and everything else she possessed; they boarded the boat for Naples without her. Upon their arrival, he enlisted as a soldier and the beautiful Inez, now on her own, became a courtesan. That's how she supported her don Augustin with rich gifts and all kinds of finery.

Doña Isidora returned to Madrid. She gave up her wigs and her elegant costumes and now she begs alms. She herself told me this enchantment and I decided to write it down so that misers can see

---

*The first edition variation ends here.

what a bad end this one had. Maybe they can learn a lesson from another's experience and not make the same mistakes.

Everyone had listened to don Alvaro's enchantment and heard about don Marcos's bad end with relish. As don Alonso was changing places with don Alvaro and preparing to tell his enchantment, don Juan signaled to the musicians, who sang the following ballad:

> Anton visits Menga
> even in her house;
> by my faith, if this offends Gila
> there is good reason why.
> He anticipates her complaints,
> a very suspicious sign,
> for the one who makes complaints
> is trying to forestall them.
> In feeling offended,
> she has more than cause,
> for such an affront kills;
> and one will never see,
> lads, a woman spurned
> who is pleasant, but believe me
> conversation and pleasure
> are marks of true love.
> Disregarding all the signals
> means something, and now you see
> that talking together today
> is fruit of yesterday's effort.
> Insincere in their courtesy,
> men know all the ways
> of belying their falsity
> by using extreme courtesy.
> There is no fear, only blunders,
> but Menga seeks him out,
> just the two alone, and she beautiful;
> who knows if this is a blunder.
> If forbidding him to see her
> is to risk losing Anton, let me say
> that such a finicky love
> is close to collapse.
> People call jealousy foolish,
> surely they've never experienced it;
> the jealous man errs only
> in his scruples and suspicions.
> Anton will enjoy these delights

only with Gila;
a shaky reputation strays
the scales from balance.
Oh, how well men know how
to offend with their excuses,
but, since love reveals all,
long live love, amen!

I wonder if don Juan, at the risk of Lisarda's annoyance but fearful of Lysis's indignation, sought in this second ballad to make up for his affront to Lysis in the previous one? As Lisarda had gloried in the first ballad she felt offended by this one. She showed her displeasure in a charming frown at don Juan which delighted the inconstant lover. If he hadn't been a flirt, he would have treated Lisarda's affection more gently and discreetly and not so insensitively. Don Juan took pride in being Lisarda's suitor and in rejecting Lysis.

Lysis, however, had grown tired of struggling with his deceptions and disappointments. She decided that as soon as all the parties were over, for she didn't want to spoil her friends' enjoyment of the celebrations, she'd tell don Juan not to come to her house any more, as his visits only added insult to injury. Besides, he spent most of his time at Lisarda's apartment, morning and evening, day and night. Furthermore, if don Diego wanted to become her husband, she would close her eyes to all other adventures.

Don Diego felt exactly the same way. He could hardly wait for the parties to end so he could begin to court Lysis. Don Juan (for very different reasons) was thinking the same thoughts. He felt aggrieved that his friend don Diego had set his sights on Lysis knowing that she had been the object of his attention, albeit now of his inattention. With all these different thoughts, the four preoccupied lovers turned their full attention to don Alonso, who began his enchantment like this:

"Illustrious audience, it usually happens that the most anxious, the most compulsive person falls exactly into the trap he fears most, as you shall see in my enchantment. A man shouldn't rely solely on his own judgment, let alone dare to test a woman. He should watch out for himself and take each woman for herself and accept her as she is. In the final analysis, an intelligent woman is no dish for a foolish man, nor is a foolish woman right for an intelligent man, and as proof of this, I shall tell my tale":

Forewarned but
not Forearmed

Don Fadrique was a son of the illustrious city of Granada, a marvelous wonder among all the splendors of Andalucia. It would not be proper to mention his name and lineage because of his many noble relatives who still live there today. We shall content ourselves with saying that his handsome appearance was matched by his nobility and wealth. Because of these superlative qualities, he enjoyed renown as the "rich and gallant don Fadrique" not only in his birthplace but everywhere he went. He was very young when his parents died; despite this loss, he conducted himself with such great moderation that people marveled at this degree of discretion in so tender a youth.

As if to prove the old saying that lads without love are like dancers without music or gamblers without money, one day he turned his attention toward an elegant, beautiful woman from the same city. Her name was Serafina and, although she was not as wealthy as don Fadrique, her beauty was indeed angelic. He fell passionately in love with her, but she disdainfully rejected him because she was already infatuated with another gentleman from their city. (It's truly a shame that a man of don Fadrique's qualities should fall in love with a woman who has already given herself to another.) Don Fadrique was not unaware of Serafina's other love but he believed he could overcome all obstacles with his wealth, especially as her suitor was not from one

of Granada's richest or noblest families. Don Fadrique felt sure that
the moment he asked Serafina's parents for her hand in marriage, she
would be his.

But that's not how Serafina felt. She thought that getting married
required exchanging letters and flirting the way characters do in those
romantic tales that thrill the heart and enchant the soul. And don
Fadrique wanted to win Serafina's affection before asking her parents'
consent. Since desire is the basis of love, he believed he could win her
for himself because his own desire was so great in spite of the fact
that he saw his rival favored. She seemed so modest and virtuous, it
never occurred to him that her desire might have led her to exceed
the bounds of propriety.

With high hopes, he began to pay court to Serafina and to her
maids as well; she showed him more favor than previously because,
although she loved don Vicente—that was his rival's name—she didn't
want don Fadrique to spurn her. Because her maids encouraged his
hopes, our lover thought he'd been right in thinking he could win
out over her other suitor, and he was happy with this hope. One night
when the maids had promised him to bring their lady out to her
balcony, he sang this sonnet to the tones of his lute:

> Oh tyrant! Let me die for your eyes
> and may your eyes enjoy their slaughter;
> may you then console me with your eyes,
> may your eyes cause me a thousand woes.

> Let me surrender my eyes to yours
> as a prize, while they, instead of loving me
> or cheering me in my sorrows,
> turn all my flowers into thorns.

> May your eyes kill me with scorn,
> cold harshness, rejection,
> while my eyes die for yours.

> Alas, thankless one! In your eyes I see
> as much ingratitude as beauty
> aimed at the eyes that love your eyes.

Everyone who heard the song thanked don Fadrique and praised
his music and the grace and ability with which he sang. But we cannot
swear that Serafina was at her window. From that night on she denied
don Fadrique even a glimpse of herself. Despite his insistent efforts,

he didn't set eyes on her for days, nor could he elicit any answer to the letters he sent. To his inquiries and pleading, her servants said only that Serafina had become terribly melancholy, that she didn't enjoy even an hour of peace. Don Fadrique suspected that the cause of her illness was that she had been disappointed in her hope of marrying don Vicente. Don Fadrique no longer saw him frequent her street the way he'd done in the past, so he concluded that don Vicente had desisted because of his own courtship. Confident that with his good looks and his wealth he could make up for her sorrows and her lost happiness, don Fadrique felt personally obliged to restore the pleasure he had caused his lady to lose: he asked her parents for her hand in marriage.

Her parents saw the heavens open, as the saying goes, and not only did they say yes, they expressed their infinite appreciation and even offered to be his slaves. They then informed their daughter of this arrangement and she, being discreet, led them to think that she was very pleased and willing to accede to their wishes when her health would permit. She asked them to put don Fadrique off for a while until she felt better, and then she would do as they commanded.

The lady's parents considered this answer sufficient and it satisfied don Fadrique. He did beg his future parents-in-law (which is how he now considered them) to pamper his future wife and take special care of her so she'd recover her health as soon as possible. To show the great love he felt for her, he would do his part by sending her presents and by spending time in her street even more assiduously than before. Despite the fact that his rival's recent neglect had somewhat calmed his fears, he did still feel jealous of don Vicente.

Occasionally Serafina would come to her window to encourage her lover's hopes with a glimpse of her beauty. Her lack of color and her mournful expression clearly revealed the illness that made her keep to her bed. Even though she was confined to bed, he would occasionally visit her because he already considered himself her husband. Of course her mother and her maids were always present to restrain any liberties he might have taken. Several months passed like this and finally don Fadrique began to despair because of Serafina's illness. He decided to marry her whether she was ill or well.

One night he was standing on the corner keeping watch over the walls that housed his beautiful mistress and pondering his suspicions as he had on so many other nights. Some time after two o'clock he saw the front door of her house open and out came a woman who, in her figure and bearing, seemed to be Serafina. He was astounded. Half dead of jealousy, he moved closer until he recognized her clearly. Suspecting that she was going to a rendezvous with his rival, he followed her. He watched her enter a vacant lot where the house had fallen down and now wood was stacked. Because the outside walls had all fallen in and there weren't any gates or doors, it was used by those who wanted to hide some amorous mischief.

Serafina ducked into the dark space. Certain that don Vicente must be inside, don Fadrique became enraged to the point of violence: such behavior required a just and honorable vengeance. He circled around to the back and entered the lot. He saw that his lady had gone down into a little tumbledown room. There she struggled to stifle her moans and she cried out to God and all His saints to help her. These cries undeceived her lover with regard to any and all doubts he may have had: Serafina gave birth to a baby. As soon as she saw herself free of her burden, she gathered up her skirts and returned home, abandoning the little creature to its fate.

But heaven, much to the detriment of Serafina's good name and don Fadrique's love for her, had arranged it so that at least the child wouldn't die unbaptized. Don Fadrique went over to where the baby lay crying on the ground. He picked it up and wrapped it in his cape, all the while crossing himself. He now realized that this was the cause of Serafina's illness and that the father was don Vicente, who'd disappeared because of her pregnancy. He thanked God over and over for miraculously saving him from the misfortune of marrying Serafina. He carried the little creature to a midwife's house and asked her to take care of the baby and find a wet nurse for it as soon as possible, for it was very important that the baby live.

When don Fadrique and the midwife examined the baby carefully they saw that it was a beautiful little girl; she seemed more like an angel from heaven than a human baby. The midwife followed all his instructions. She found a nurse and the next day don Fadrique spoke with a relative of his and asked her to bring up Gracia—this was the name they gave the baby when she was baptized—in her own home.

For now we shall let her grow up and deal with her when the right time comes, as she's the most important person in this story. Let's return to Serafina who, within two weeks recovered entirely from her illness and, with all her former beauty restored, told her parents that whenever they liked they could celebrate her marriage to don Fadrique. In the meantime, he, having learned a frightening lesson from this experience, went to the house of the relative who was caring for Gracia. He told her that, since he was young, he felt a great desire to visit other parts of Spain, travel that would take several years. Therefore he wanted to leave her the authority to administer his estate as she thought best. His only request was that she take good care of Gracia, treating her as if she were his own child, because she held a great secret. If God preserved her life until she was three, then he entreated her to place the child in a convent where she would grow up innocent of the ways of the world, for he had certain plans that he would reveal in due time.

After making these arrangements, don Fadrique packed all his belongings and had them taken to his aunt's house. He gathered up a large amount of money and many jewels and, accompanied by his servant, he set out on horseback for the rich, noble city of Seville. Before departing, he wrote a sonnet and sent it to Serafina. Serafina received his letter, which read:

If, when you could have made me your equal,
oh thankless one, you treated me coldly,
and tried, through harshness,
to show what little love you had for me;

if, deceitfully you withheld from me
the sight of your glorious beauty
and on every occasion you showed me
the mountain of snow in your cold heart;

now, when you have lost your power,
why do you seek a flame among the embers?
Let things be and have pity on my youth.

You offer me the impossible: you are false.
You err in trying to revive the flame
because, to your misfortune, I have seen the light.

This mysterious message frightened Serafina terribly because she'd tried in vain to find out what had become of the baby she'd abandoned in the empty lot. Don Fadrique's sudden change of heart confirmed her myriad fears. His hasty departure also worried her parents, who feared it was based on something untoward. Given that Serafina felt an inclination to become a nun, they supported her in that desire and she entered a convent, still feeling very troubled and worried about what had taken place. She was haunted by the nightmare of the abandoned baby, for, if it had died or the dogs had eaten it, her conscience would have to bear that crime. These fears motivated her to try, through penitence and a devout life, not only to achieve forgiveness for her sin, but even to live the life of a saint, and that's how she came to be considered in Granada.

Don Fadrique went to Seville feeling so embittered by the lesson of Serafina that, because of her, he railed against all women without exception. His generalizations go entirely contrary to the real nature of women because there are a hundred good women for each bad one; not all women are bad, and it isn't right to confuse the good with the bad and blame them all. Nevertheless, he asserted that you can't trust women; above all you can't trust a clever woman because, if she's clever and intelligent, she'll become mischievous and wicked and use all her wiles to deceive men. A woman should tend to her sewing and her prayers, keep her house and care for her children; everything else is idle artifice that only brings about a woman's ruination more quickly.

Firm in these convictions, he came to Seville, as I said, and went to stay with a relative of his, a very prominent, wealthy, and important personage. He planned to stay several months to enjoy the many wonders for which this city is famous. One day when he was out walking down one of the main streets with his relative, he saw a lady in widow's weeds descend from a coach in front of a magnificent house. He thought she was the most beautiful woman he'd ever seen. Not only beautiful, she was also young and had an elegant figure. His relative informed him that she was wealthy and very noble; she was from one of the best and most illustrious families of Seville. Although don Fadrique had been badly burned by his experience with Serafina, it wasn't enough to keep him from being captivated by the beauty of doña Beatrice, as the beautiful widow was called.

When don Fadrique passed her on the street, there he left his heart. As he didn't want to lose it forever, he asked his companion to walk by the house one more time. At this, don Mateo (for this was his name) said:

"I think, don Fadrique, my friend, that you may not leave Seville so soon; you seem love-stricken. By my faith, the sight of that lady has affected you!"

"You're right," don Fadrique replied. "I'd spend my whole life here if I thought I could be hers."

"If that's your intention . . ," Mateo responded, "but let me warn

you, this lady's position, nobility, and virtue admit nothing but marriage, even if her suitor were the king himself. For four years she was
married to a gentleman in every way her equal, and she's been widowed for two years. She's twenty-four. When she was a maiden, not
a soul piqued her interest; after she married, nobody even caught a
glimpse of her; as a widow, no one has captured her attention. She's
had more suitors than hairs on her head, all wanting to win her love
and marry her. But, if your love is as you say and you want me to
recommend your many fine qualities to her, I will, and it may so
happen that you'll be chosen, for you're not lacking in the qualities
she might want in a husband. She's related to my wife, so I have
occasion to visit her. Now I'm sure I'll be successful for, look, she's
come out on her balcony. It's no small favor that she responds to your
interest instead of shutting her door in our faces."

"Oh my friend!" exclaimed don Fadrique. "How can I, a stranger,
dare to court a woman who has rejected so many gentlemen from
Seville? But if I'm to die of love, it's better that I die from her scorn
and rejection than without her even knowing of my love. Speak with
her, friend, and tell her of my nobility, my wealth; tell her I'm dying
of love for her."

The two continued down the street again and, as they passed her,
they made a respectful bow. (Upon descending from the coach, the
beautiful doña Beatrice had noticed the attention with which don Fadrique looked at her.) She knew the man accompanied by don Mateo
was a stranger and he seemed very enamored. Quickly she removed
her cloak and went to the window. She observed that while the two
men talked they kept looking at her so, when they greeted her with
such courtesy, she made a bow no less ceremonious.

They walked on by her house, delighted to have seen her so ame-
nable. They agreed that don Mateo should speak with her the very
next day to try to arrange their marriage. Don Fadrique was so in
love that he wished he'd do it that very instant. The night didn't pass
quickly enough for the enamored gentleman, and the next morning
he pressed his friend to hurry and find out the life-or-death news that
awaited him, which don Mateo did.

He spoke with doña Beatrice and praised her suitor's many fine
qualities. The lady replied that she greatly appreciated the attention
he accorded her as well as his friend's desire to honor her with the
offer of his person in marriage, but, she said, the day she buried her
husband she'd made a vow not to marry for at least three years to

show the respect that her love owed his memory. That's why she harshly dismissed everyone who approached her on this subject, she didn't want any commitments. But, if this gentleman wished to wait out the year that remained, she would give him her word that no one else would become her husband because, if she were to tell the truth, his unaffected appearance and all the qualities don Mateo described had pleased her greatly. She wanted someone just like him to become her master, a man without pretense, modest, and in no way pompous. Don Mateo went back to his friend very happy with this answer, thinking he hadn't negotiated badly.

With every passing hour, don Fadrique was falling more and more in love. Although the idea of having to wait such a long time disappointed his imagination, he decided to spend the whole year in Seville. He considered the lovely widow a worthy reward if he could indeed manage to win her. Since he had a lot of money, he fixed up an apartment in his relative's house and hired servants and began to live in gracious style in order to quicken his lady's interest. Occasionally, in don Mateo's company, he would visit her. She wouldn't grant him such favor otherwise. He tried to send gifts, but they weren't accepted; she wouldn't accept even a pin. The only favor she granted him was to appear on her balcony when informed he was in the street. She did this at her maids' request (the gentleman from Granada had won their loyalty because, what their mistress refused to accept, they accepted eagerly, and so aided him in his courtship). Her presence would light up the whole world with the splendor of her eyes. Sometimes in the evenings she would join her servants while they listened to don Fadrique sing, which, as I said, he did very well.

One night he serenaded her as usual but that evening doña Beatrice didn't come out onto her balcony. She was angry because she'd seen him speak to another lady in church. He sang the following ballad, which he himself had composed:

> Like the tall tower of Babel,
> Nimrod's construction
> which was meant to reach heaven
> but instead tumbled into the abyss,
> that's how my hopes appear:
> I'd hoped their
> yearnings would reach
> the heaven of my love.
> But, since their foundation
> was rascally Cupid,

who doesn't deserve to be
worshipped as a god,
like a little child, in the end,
he changed his fickle nature
and became blind to the quality
of my undying love.
Oh, ill-fated love,
plummeting down like Phaeton,
how did you hope to drive
the chariot of the sun?
Hopes shattered and dashed,
withered like a flower,
happy times now transformed
into sorrowful times.
Bold imagination,
where did you think you'd go
if your wings were made of wax
and under the sign of Leo the lion?
Affection, you thought
you'd be given a helping hand;
but trusting in that,
your trust was in vain.
Today my sun has not appeared
on her eastern balcony;
she has shrouded behind clouds
the light of her perfection.
Love sells his pleasures dear
and, when he grants pleasures,
they bear a high price,
for they're only leased and then withdrawn,
which is a great misfortune.
Child god, blind as a lynx,
may you burn up in my fire:
but no, let love pardon my offense
as humbly I kiss your feet.

The favor don Fadrique received that night was hearing doña Beatrice tell her servants it was time to retire, thereby letting him know
that she'd heard his song. This made him happier than if he ruled the
universe.

Our lover spent over six months like this, without ever receiving
permission from doña Beatrice to visit her alone. Her extreme modesty
so inflamed him that he could scarcely rest. One night, when, as on
every other night, he was in his lady's street, he noticed the door
standing open. Hoping to look upon her beauty from closer up, he
very cautiously ventured to enter her house. It worked out so well

that he got all the way to her apartment without being detected. From the doorway in the hall he could see her sitting on her bench surrounded by maids keeping her company. When she gave signs of wanting to prepare for bed, the servants asked her to sing a little, almost as if they were in a league with don Fadrique and knew he was watching. Doña Beatrice demurred saying she wasn't in the mood, she was feeling melancholy. One of the maids, who had more spirit than the others, got up and went into the next room to fetch a harp. She said:

"Heavens, my lady, if you're melancholy, this is the best relief. Sing just a little and you'll see how much better you feel; it will cheer you up."

As she said this she placed the harp before her mistress. To please her maids, doña Beatrice sang this song:

When the dawn shows
her happy smile,
when, cheerfully, she removes
the dark curtain
from her eastern balcony
so the day may enter,
when she looses her
beautiful rich tresses
and scatters pearls
across full bloomed carnations,
when the countryside
pours forth happiness,
jealous Marfisa laments
the absence of Albano.

When happily dawn readies
the lavish chariot
for Phoebus, who comes
from the Indian shore,
when among clear
crystalline springs
that murmur of deception
and distill pearly drops,
when to the gurgling of the spring,
the nymphs sing, then
jealous Marfisa laments
the absence of Albano.

When among carnations
dawn paints her eyes
with their clear dewdrops

of silvery decoration,
when with resonant lyres
the birds sing
their welcome to Phoebus
at the splendid sight of him,
when across the mountains
a thousand delights are seen,
jealous Marfisa laments
the absence of Albano.

That lass used to be
the marvel of the village,
death to all eyes,
and a living death,
fierce basilisk,
cause of misfortune
because her scorn
was like poison.
They said her charm
was like salt; now
jealous Marfisa laments
the absence of Albano.

Her pride surrendered
to the attractions
of an ungrateful peasant lad
who, far away, thinks not of her.
When he happily
turns to a new mistress,
and defends her beauty.
and praises her splendor,
and conquers her beauty,
and aspires to glory,
jealous Marfisa laments
the absence of Albano.

When she ended, doña Beatrice set aside the harp and asked her
maids to help her undress for bed. (Her voice, the sweetness and
charm of the music had bewitched don Fadrique.) The poem apparently meant nothing personal because often a poet writes what he
wants to please the musician. Still absorbed, he stayed there in the
darkness. When he realized that Beatrice had retired, he went downstairs to leave the house, but he couldn't. The coachman, who had a
little room next to the front door, had locked up and retired when
he saw that no one else would be entering or leaving that night.

Don Fadrique was quite upset but there was nothing he could do so he sat down on a bench to wait for morning. Of course he could have called to have them open for him, but he didn't want to give cause for the servants to gossip or risk any danger to doña Beatrice's honor. So he concealed himself there in the entrance to wait until the coachman opened in the morning.

He must have been there about two hours when he heard the door to his lady's room open. From where he was sitting, he could see the stairs and the hall, so he tried to focus on where the sound had come from. He saw doña Beatrice emerge from her room, very surprising since he assumed she was sound asleep. Over her nightgown she was wearing a petticoat of red silk embroidered with silver trimming that sparkled like stars. The only other garment she had on was a mantilla of the same silk lined in blue plush, thrown on with such negligence that you could see the whiteness of her nightgown and its silvery handwork—an art for which Seville was famous. Her golden hair was caught in a blue and silver silk net, although a few loose strands curled down to frame the beauty of her face. Around her throat, she wore two heavy strings of pearls, matched by the pearls she wore on both slender wrists. Their whiteness was visible because the sleeves of her gown were open like the sleeves of a monk's robe.

The gentlemen from Granada didn't miss a single detail because, in one of her white, white hands, doña Beatrice was carrying a wax candle set in a silver candlestick. By the light of the candle, he could contemplate her angelic face. He would have considered himself most fortunate if he were the person she was coming out to meet. In her other hand, she carried a silver salver with several dishes of conserves, some biscuits, and a small carafe of wine, covered by a white napkin whose rich embroidery and lace made a lovely sight.

"Heavens above!" don Fadrique exclaimed to himself, watching her emerge from her room and descend the stairs. "I wonder who the fortunate soul is who'll be served by such a beautiful butler. I'd give everything I possess to be that person!"

He thought this just as she reached the bottom of the stairs. He realized that she was heading straight for him, so he slipped back toward the stables and went inside, hoping to hide more safely. When he saw doña Beatrice heading for the same place, he hid behind one of the coach horses. The lady entered that filthy place so unsuitable to her beauty. Without even glancing toward don Fadrique, crouched behind the horse, she approached a little room at the back of the stable. Don Fadrique thought some sick servant must have inspired her piety and charity in performing this act, although it was really more appropriate for one of her maids than for their mistress. Attributing it to her devout humility and religiosity, he wanted to see where it would end, so he came out from behind the horse and found a place from which he could observe what went on in the little room that was scarcely large enough for a bed.

Great was don Fadrique's forbearance on this occasion. As soon as he drew close and beheld what was taking place in that room, he found his lady in such a terrible situation that I don't know how he endured it! Inside the little room I've described, lying in the bed, was a negro so black that his face seemed made of black silk. Although he looked to be about twenty-eight or thirty, his aspect was hideous, abominable. Don Fadrique thought the devil himself couldn't have looked more awful, though it's hard to tell whether this was true or simply the result of don Fadrique's sense of outrage. The negro's arched chest gave him a grotesque appearance, and his emaciated face indicated that he would die before long.

As doña Beatrice entered, she placed the candle and the other things on a little table beside the bed. She sat down on the edge of the bed and began to smooth the covers. Her great beauty made her look like an angel ministering to a fierce devil. She placed one of her exquisite hands on his forehead and began to speak in a tender, mournful tone:

"How are you feeling, Antonio? My love, won't you speak to me? Listen, open your eyes, look, your Beatrice is here. Come, dear, have a taste of these conserves. Take heart if you love me, and do as I say, or do you want me to join you in death as I have loved you in life? Don't you hear, my darling? Won't you answer or even look at me?"

While she said these words, she shed pearly tears. She leaned her lovely face close to the devilish black face. Don Fadrique, who was watching all this, felt closer to death than the negro. He didn't know what to say or do. Several times he almost revealed his presence, but then, when he thought about it, he realized the best thing was just to get out of it all. While he was vacillating, the negro opened his eyes and looked up at his mistress. With both hands he pushed away that face so close to his own and said in a weak voice:

"What do you want of me, madam? Leave me alone, for the love of God! How can you pursue me even as I lie dying? Isn't it enough that your lasciviousness has brought me to this end? Even now you want me to satisfy your vicious appetites when I am breathing my last? Get yourself a husband, madam, marry, and leave me in peace. I never want to see you again! I won't touch the food you bring me; I want only to die, that's all I'm good for now."

When he finished speaking, he turned his back to her, refusing to respond no matter how lovingly and tenderly she addressed him. Maybe he'd already died or maybe he just refused to heed her tears and her pleading. Doña Beatrice finally tired of trying and returned to her room, the saddest, most tearful woman in the world.

Don Fadrique waited until the front door was opened and, the moment he saw it clear, he fled from that house. He felt confusion and disgust to the same degree as previously he had felt delight and glory. The moment he got home, he went straight to bed without saying a word to his friend. Later that afternoon he went out to survey the virtuous widow's street to see if anything was happening. He got there just in time to see them bring the negro out for burial.

He went back home, always keeping this terrible secret to himself. For three or four days he walked her street, no longer inspired by his love, but simply trying to learn more about what he still couldn't believe despite the fact that he'd seen it with his own eyes. He never did catch sight of doña Beatrice; she remained withdrawn and grief-stricken over the death of her black lover.

Then one day after dinner while he was chatting with his friend, one of doña Beatrice's maids entered. Very happy to see him, she courteously placed a letter in his hands. It read:

Where there is love, there is little need for intermediaries. I am grateful for your attentions and satisfied with your love, so I've decided not to wait out the rest of the year to grant you the well-earned possession of my person and my property. We can celebrate our marriage whenever it pleases you, under any conditions you determine. Your worthiness and my love for you have brought me to this decision. May God keep you.   Doña Beatrice

Don Fadrique read the letter over three or four times and still he couldn't believe it. In his mind, he kept going over and over that dreadful scene. Deep down he felt amazed by what had happened to him. Twice he'd been on the verge of falling into grievous error, and twice heaven had revealed momentous secrets to him just in the nick of time. He understood clearly that doña Beatrice's new determination had been caused by the loss of her black lover. He made up his mind to do the honorable thing. Telling the maid to wait, he went into the next room, called in his friend, and said succinctly:

"My friend, it's important to my life and to my honor that I leave Seville within the hour. No one shall accompany me except the servant I brought with me from Granada. After my departure, you are to sell the clothing I leave here and with the money you get from the sale, you can pay the other servants. The why and wherefore I cannot tell you because others' reputations and honor are at stake. When I settle down, I'll write to you. This is very serious, so don't ask anything or even comment. While I write a letter, please have two mules prepared for me and, beyond that, don't try to learn more for the present."

He then wrote a letter to doña Beatrice and gave it to the maid to take to her mistress. The mules were brought around and he left Seville, headed for Madrid, repeating his former diatribes against clever women who, trusting in their ingenuity, seek to deceive men.

Let's leave him for a while and return to doña Beatrice. She received the letter, opened it, and read as follows:

The love that I felt for your grace was not simply desire to possess your beauty. I also valued your good name and your honor, as demonstrated by my attentions and courtesies to you. I, my lady, am somewhat scrupulous, and take it as a matter of conscience that only yesterday you were widowed and today you wish to remarry. Your grace should mourn at least one year for your ill-fated negro. In time your grace's proposal will be answered. May heaven protect and console you.

This letter almost made doña Beatrice go crazy but, seeing that don Fadrique had already left town, she soon said yes to another gentleman who had proposed to her, in that way making up for the loss of her late lover.

Journeying with forced marches (as the saying goes), don Fadrique soon arrived in Madrid and went to stay in the house of one of his uncles who owned property in the Carmen district. This uncle was a wealthy gentleman whose only son, don Juan, was his heir. Don Juan was a handsome, elegant youth, intelligent, high-spirited, and very charming. His father had betrothed him to a wealthy cousin but the marriage was to be delayed until she came of age, since at the time she was only ten.

Within a few days, don Fadrique and this youth came to treat each other like brothers. The two became such good friends that their closeness went way beyond mere family affection. Don Fadrique noticed that don Juan seemed exceedingly melancholy. In an effort to find out why, he stated that true friends don't keep secrets from each other and, to encourage don Juan further, don Fadrique told him about his own life and his strange experiences, but without mentioning any names. Then he begged don Juan to tell him what was causing his sadness, so unusual given his basically happy nature. This was exactly what don Juan had wanted don Fadrique to ask. He knew he'd feel his sorrow less if he could share it with his friend, and he replied:

"Friend don Fadrique, I dearly love a woman here in this city. When her parents died, they left her a lot of money and the obligation to marry her cousin who is away in the Indies. Our chaste love hasn't gone beyond simple conversation but we hope to enjoy love's reward when her betrothed returns. Right now neither her situation nor my own permits us to enjoy greater amorous indulgence. We are both betrothed and cannot risk our honor. Although I don't enjoy possession of my own betrothed, she serves as a chain that keeps me from being free.

"To describe this lady's beauty to you would be like reducing beauty itself to a cipher. Her intelligence is so keen that no one betters her in humanistic learning. Doña Ana, for this is her name, is the wonder of this age. She and her cousin, doña Violante, are the sibyls of Spain: both are beautiful, witty, both are musicians and poets. In conclusion, these two women possess the sum of all the beauty and intelligence scattered among all other women in the world.

"Well, someone told doña Ana that I was courting a woman named Nise, all because last Sunday I was seen talking with her in the Church of San Gines, which is Nise's church. Yesterday, very jealous, doña Ana told me to go away and never darken her door again. Besides that, because she knows I burn up with jealousy every time she mentions her betrothed—despite my hope that he will serve as intermediary to my success—she told me that she adores him alone and that she lovingly longs for his arrival. I can't bear the thought of anyone but myself enjoying possession of her beauty. I wrote her a letter on the subject of jealousy and she's sent me an answer that I'll show you. Given her talent for poetry, as for everything else, it's in ballad form." He took out doña Ana's letter and handed it to don Fadrique, who read:

Your mad behavior, Lisardo,
is such that my grief
forces me to blame you
while I suffer all the pain.
I don't want to count or make

a list of your thankless deeds,
because ingrates leave only
zeros, never pluses.
Lust alone prevails,
Lisardo, and my fears are just,
for you count on my loyalty
while denying your own.
I don't want to remind you
of all my many sorrows,
since you never gave me a receipt
for my priceless gift to you.
Sighs yearn to join the air,
for air is what they are,
and don't trouble to count
how many thousand sighs there are.
Tears yearn to join the sea,
sorrow yearns to join my complaints,
as my affection yearns for your icy disdain
hoping that your scorn will lose its force.
To say, Lisardo, that I
indulge my passion
to while away your absence,
is a chimera of your imagination.
If I wanted to be entertained,
the village has shepherds
and, while I do not show them favor,
they celebrate and sing my humble charms.
I could choose from them
one who would delight me
with his entertaining love
and make me extremely happy.
Yet you, Lisardo, although you enjoy
favors that others desire,
you do not value those favors,
indeed you even scorn them.
Lisardo, I believe
that a woman of my charms
grants you favors and rewards,
with merely a gentle glance.
But since you have always been
ungrateful for my affection,
you do not prize my love
or reward me with your own.
You don't even know what love is,
this I know for certain,
before you even start to love
already you seek to end it.

In harmony with my nature
I favor you; do not ask
more of me, it is enough that
your charm marks the limit of my pleasure.
Do you fear that the shepherd
who is to be my master will return?
If you spurn my favors,
Lisardo, why do you complain?
You ask for health and when I
give you medicine, you despair;
love is like being bled
without having your veins cut open.
The truth is, Lisardo,
another beauty has conquered you
so now you find my love a bother;
I understand, I am not stupid.
Lisardo, may heaven curse
one who makes his beloved jealous
by using the charms of another;
may the same fate befall him!
The musician sings in the street,
the poet makes his verses,
the lady falls in love
and ignores the one who courts her.
I know your tricks
I know your deceptions,
since I praised Nise to you
how much you love her now!
Ungrateful Lisardo, may you enjoy
her beauty a thousand years;
may as many favors delight you
as the sorrows that are killing me.
Drink in her sweet deception,
leave me my bitter beverage.
I intend to hang my chains
in the temple of my faith;
from there I will be watching you
the way a person watches a gambler
play the card on which he bets
truth against falsehood.
I do not complain about your offense,
Lisardo, because my complaints
would not make you love me again,
you would only make me pay for them.
I understand your attraction,
for her coal black hair
is ebony on which is etched

her beauty and your affection,
her black eyes, stars
in whose mischievous pupils
your war will find peace,
your storm, calm weather.
You wear her color, black,
and you appear more elegant
than when you're wearing mine,
which it pleases you to spurn.
To find solace for your sorrows
you could become a regular worshipper
in the glorious church of San Gines
where your Nise always goes.
With this song, I ask Love
to lament your faithlessness.
May God keep you. From my house.
From one who desires your happiness.

"You don't have a lot to fear from this enemy," don Fadrique said as he finished reading. "From what this poem says, she's more impassioned than angry. The woman writes well and if she's as beautiful as you say, you're foolish not to persevere until you reap the fruit of your love."

"The poem," don Juan replied, "is just a speck, a scratch, a nothing, compared to her great beauty and intelligence; she has often been called the Spanish sibyl."

"By God, cousin," don Fadrique said, "I fear women who know so much, more than I fear death itself. I'd like to find a woman who's as ignorant of the ways of the world as this one is wise in them. If I ever do find such a woman, as God lives, I shall devote myself to serving and loving her. But nowadays women are all so sharp you can hardly keep up with them. They all know how to love and how to deceive, but clever women have taught me such a lesson that I want to win only an ignorant one."

"You can't really mean that!" don Juan exclaimed. "I can't imagine any man wanting a foolish woman to talk with for fifteen minutes let alone to love! Why, the most famous philosophers in the world say that knowledge is food for the soul; then, so long as eyes feed on white skin, graceful hands, lovely eyes, a striking figure, in short, on beauty that's worthy of being loved in a woman, it's not right that the soul's desire should be denied or should have to feed itself only on nonsensical boring dullness! Since the soul is pure, we should not nourish it with unrefined food."

"Let's not discuss this anymore," don Fadrique replied. "There's a lot to be said on the subject, but I know what's best for me in this regard. Let's answer doña Ana's letter, though the best answer would be to visit her, for nothing is as effective and moving as the lover in person. Besides, I'm curious to see if her cousin interests me; maybe I can have some fun with her while I'm here in Madrid."

"Let's go," don Juan said. "To tell you the truth, that's exactly what I was wanting to do. But let me warn you: doña Violante is not dumb! If clever women displease you, you don't have to come with me."

"I'll manage," don Fadrique replied.

With this understanding, they went to visit the two beautiful cousins and were received with real pleasure. Although doña Ana still acted jealous and haughty, don Juan didn't have to do much to temper her resentment.

When don Fadrique saw doña Violante, he thought she was one of the most beautiful women he'd ever seen, even in comparison with Serafina and doña Beatrice. She was having her portrait painted (quite a fad here in Madrid), and for that reason, she was elegantly attired. It seemed, however, as if she'd dressed with such extravagance and elegance especially to conquer don Fadrique. She was wearing a full black skirt covered with sequins and gold buttons, a belt and a necklace glittering with diamonds and circling her brow a band of rubies. After much courtly praise, don Fadrique, inspired by the muses, took up a guitar and sang this ballad, which he improvised to suit the occasion:*

> Shepherdess whose beauty
> delights, enamors, slays,
> you are a wonder from heaven,
> the glory of our village.
> What paintbrush exists,
> even if it's guided and governed
> by the great Apelles himself,
> that can capture your beauty?
> What rays, even those the sun
> sends forth from his crown,
> can equal the splendor
> of your lovely chestnut tresses?
> What can match the radiance
> I see in your bright stars,

*In this ballad, Violante is compared with Campaspe, Alexander the Great's mistress, whose famous portrait was painted by the artist Apelles.

a light more brilliant
than the diamond's glitter?
What lilies compare with your white brow?
What Cupid's bows with your fine eyebrows?
What darts with your lashes?
What arrows with your eyes?
What alexandrine roses
match your cheeks?
All these are inferior to your beauty,
vanquished by your carmine.
Shepherdess, what rubies match
the color of your mouth?
Without any doubt,
the rubies in your hair seem false
when compared with your lovely lips.
Your words are carnations,
your white teeth pearls
with which the dawn, weeping,
bedecks her meadows.
Your lovely neck a column
of crystal which holds up
the heavenly home of Love,
where Cupid dwells.
What snow matches your hands
on whose snowy peaks
the bold who seek
adventure lose their way?
Of everything your dress reveals,
beautiful shepherdess,
I'd like to sing fullest praise,
but my tongue dares not.
Just like a second Campaspe,
you exhibit such heavenly graces,
poor Apelles simply gazes at you
without hope of capturing them!
Shepherdess, tell Apelles,
whose brushes seek
to bring your beauty
from heaven down to earth
that both he and I fall short;
both brush and pen remain
unable to capture an image
that can match the model.
Since the world no longer
possesses the mold
in which wise Nature formed you,
there will never be

another equal to you.
Diamonds, gold, crystal,
bright sun, roses, lilies,
heavens, stars, rubies,
carnations, jasmine, pearls,
everything, in your presence,
loses its beauty and its value.
What brush, what pen,
can do justice to such beauty?

Both doña Ana and her cousin praised don Fadrique's verses and his voice. Doña Violante in particular began to look favorably on this gentleman from Granada because of his lavish praise of her. From that afternoon on, Cupid's game was on the table. In this instance don Fadrique didn't hold true to his determination to spurn clever women and fear sharp ones. He fell head over heels in love. The next day, before he and don Juan set out to visit the beautiful cousins, don Fadrique sent this sonnet to doña Ana:*

You are a string on love's instrument,
beautiful, heavenly first string, and love so esteems
your sweet tone that now it raises you
from first to third and changes key.

Discreet was all thought of love,
and through your value love's tone gains courage,
for being first, love wants to impress
its sovereign tone on your being.

The third string often shifts to first
but, being first, for it to become third
is heavenly, wonderful, strange, miraculous.

And so I say that if Orpheus
had used you to make his divine music
he would have filled with love all he lulled to sleep.

But why, my pen,
do you sing of love for this
beautiful first string
when love already possesses her?

*This sonnet is based on a conceit impossible to translate into English. The central metaphor derives from musical imagery punning on the word *prima*, first string of an instrument and also cousin, and on *tercera*, the third string and also matchmaker or go-between. There is also punning on *cuerda*, meaning cord, string, wise.

What I beg of you,
being the third string,
please tell your lovely first string
to love me.

Doña Ana's answer to don Fadrique was that in this regard she
wouldn't have to do much for doña Violante was very impressed with
him. This news made him feel so proud and happy that he forgot all
about his experiences with Serafina and Beatrice and the lessons he'd
learned. Don Fadrique and doña Violante spent many days courting
in the same formal manner, their love never venturing to other kinds
of amorous experimentation. They enjoyed only that intercourse that
held no risk to their honor, and this restraint so impassioned don
Fadrique that he soon came to the point of wanting to marry doña
Violante. She, however, never mentioned such a thing, for she truly
abhorred the thought of marriage, afraid of losing the freedom she
enjoyed.

One day while the two cousins were dressing to go visit "their"
lovely cousins, they received a message from the ladies saying that
doña Ana's betrothed had arrived so secretly that they'd had no word
of his arrival. This suddenness frightened them both; doña Ana feared
her fiance had come secretly either because he felt suspicious or else
because he had some fearsome design. Anyhow, for them all to be
safe, they'd have to be very careful. She begged don Juan to arm
himself with patience, as the two women themselves were doing. Not
only should he and don Fadrique not visit them, they shouldn't even
walk down their street until they received further instruction.

This was a terrible blow to don Juan and don Fadrique but, despite
their great distress, they had to bear it. They felt even worse four days
later when they found out that doña Ana had gotten married. Furthermore, her new lord and master, being over forty and experienced in
the ways of the world, was a jealous man. He had imposed harsh rules
to protect the honor of the house. It would be impossible for the
gallant lovers to see the lovely cousins even at their window, nor could
don Juan and don Fadrique send any word, not even to inquire about
the ladies' health—in the case of doña Ana because of her new husband's protectiveness and in doña Violante's for reasons we shall soon
find out.

Don Juan and don Fadrique spent a whole month in despair, waiting for some news, impatient, anxious, unhappy. It appeared that the
two lovely cousins felt no concern about their sorrow. At last they

decided, regardless of the risk, to walk down the street where their
ladies lived, on the off chance that they might see one of the ladies
or at least one of the maids from the house. One day the two men
strolled down the street and again the next day and both times they
saw doña Ana's husband enter the house accompanied by his brother,
a handsome young student. It was impossible for them to glimpse the
ladies or anything else that resembled a woman: some male servants,
yes, but they didn't know them so they didn't dare speak to them.

Anxiety kept the two men up late each night and woke them early
in the morning. Luck had it that very early one Sunday morning they
saw one of doña Violante's maids leave on her way to mass. Don Juan
approached to speak to her. Fearfully she looked all around. Then she
told the two lovers how jealous her new master was and described
how circumspectly they lived. She took the letter don Juan had written
previously in case he should find just such a chance to deliver it and
she told them to return the next day. She'd try to bring a reply. Then
she rushed off to take the letter to her mistress. It read:

I don't feel jealous because jealousy solves nothing. I could even bear jealousy
if you felt any affection for me. What most saddens me is that you've forgotten
me. If you still feel the least spark of our former flame, please have pity on
my love, be kind to me in this cruel situation.

After the ladies read the letter, doña Ana gave a reply to the same
maid who, when she saw the gentlemen in the street below, threw it
to them from the window. Doña Ana's letter read:

The master is a jealous man and newly wed so he hasn't had time for second
thoughts or to grow inattentive. Within the next week, however, he has to
go to Valladolid to see some relatives, and then I shall make my excuses
properly and pay my debts to you.

Don Juan and don Fadrique kissed this letter over and over, considering it a kind of happy prophecy that inspired a thousand fantasies
and conjectures. This euphoria lasted for several days. But when they
didn't receive further instructions as the letter had promised, and there
was no change in the habits of the ladies' house—it remained impossible to glimpse them either in the street or at a window—the two
men fell into the same despair they had felt before they received the
letter. They haunted the street at all hours of the day and spent many
a night from sunset to sunup in front of the house.

One day when don Juan chanced to go hear mass at the Church

of the Carmen he saw his beloved doña Ana enter (a sight he considered nothing less than miraculous). He watched her enter a side chapel to hear mass. In spite of the fact that she was accompanied by a footman, he followed her and knelt down at her side. There were lengthy complaints and brief excuses. Doña Ana explained that her husband, although he'd said he was going to Valladolid, hadn't gone. Given the nature of their meeting place, she saw no way to talk more with him unless he could come to her house that very night. She herself would open the door for him. But he had to bring his cousin with him so don Fadrique could take doña Ana's place in bed with her husband. What made the whole thing possible was the fact that she was furious with her husband, so furious she hadn't spoken to him for days. Her anger was that great and, besides, he slept so soundly that she was certain he'd never notice the substitution. While her cousin doña Violante might have taken doña Ana's place, she couldn't because she was ill. If don Juan didn't obey these instructions, then there was no way to satisfy his desires.

This plan confounded don Juan. On one hand, he knew don Fadrique would never go along with his part, and on the other, he saw the chance he'd be losing. Mulling over these thoughts, he went home and, after much urging and pleading by don Fadrique, don Juan finally told him everything doña Ana had said. Don Fadrique asked don Juan if he was crazy. He couldn't believe don Juan would repeat such nonsense if he were in his right mind. Then don Fadrique cracked a thousand jokes and began to rave about the great favor doña Ana did him in fixing him up with such a lovely bed partner.

The two spent several hours arguing back and forth, one begging, the other refusing. Finally don Juan reached his limit and drew his sword, intending to kill himself. Very unwillingly, don Fadrique gave in and agreed to take doña Ana's place in bed with her husband.

Don Juan and don Fadrique went to doña Ana's house. The lady had been worried but, when they arrived together, she understood that, in coming along, don Fadrique had agreed to the plan. Doña Ana let them in and led them to a room right next to her bedroom. She commanded don Fadrique to undress. All in the dark, he obeyed. He was in a terrible temper. Then she led him, barefoot and wearing only his shirt, into the adjoining room. She stood him next to the bed and whispered to him to get in. There she left him and happily went off with her lover to another room.

Let's leave don Juan and doña Ana and return to don Fadrique.

As soon as he found himself in bed next to the man whose honor he was offending by substituting for his wife so she could dally with a lover, he began to think about what might happen to him, what such audacity might cost. He remained so wide awake and fearful that he would have given everything he owned not to be in such a dreadful situation. The offended husband sighed in his sleep. Then he turned toward his supposed wife and threw an arm around don Fadrique's neck, acting as if he wanted to make love. Even though the husband did all this in his sleep and didn't persist, don Fadrique felt very threatened. As gently as he could, he took the sleeping man's arm and removed it from around his neck and huddled over in a corner of the bed. He upbraided himself for having gotten into this mess simply to satisfy the whim of the two crazy lovers.

Don Fadrique had just survived the first test when the deceived husband stretched out his feet and rubbed them against those of his terrified bedmate. Don Fadrique thought each one of these contacts was almost like dying. To be brief, the two spent all night long like this, with one trying to snuggle up and the other trying to slither away. When light began to show under the crack in the door, don Fadrique became more fearful than before, realizing that all he'd suffered would be in vain if it grew light and the deceived husband awoke and saw his bed partner before doña Ana rescued him. Don Fadrique felt sure he wouldn't get out of this bind alive. He got up as quietly as he could and groped his way to the door. Just as he was about to open it, doña Ana appeared. When she saw him, she said in a loud voice:

"Where are you going in such a hurry, don Fadrique?"

"Oh, my lady!" he exclaimed in a whisper. "Knowing the danger I'm in, how can you be so reckless? For God's sake, let me get out of here! If your master wakes up, we'll lose everything!"

"What do you mean, get out of here?" The clever lady asked in a loud voice so she'd be heard. "By heaven! I want my husband to see who he slept with last night so he'll know what his jealousy and his passion have caused."

Then, without don Fadrique's being able to stop her, because the room was small and he was dumfounded, she reached over and jerked open the window. With the curtains pulled back and standing by the bed, she said:

"Look, my lord husband, look who you slept with last night!"

Don Fadrique looked down at the figure in the bed and instead of Ana's bearded husband, who had, in fact, departed six days before, he saw the exquisite doña Violante. The lovely woman looked like dawn when she draws back the curtains of the night and sallies forth to scatter her pearls across the flowering meadows. This trick of the two lovely cousins so mortified don Fadrique that he couldn't utter a word. He couldn't think of a thing to say, and doña Ana and doña Violante celebrated their success with gales of laughter. Doña Violante described in detail how she had tormented him all night long.

The gentleman from Granada soon recovered from his embarrassment and doña Ana arranged it so he could savor the fruit of all the flowers whose seeds he had sown. He enjoyed many delightful pleasures with his lady, not only while doña Ana's husband was absent, and he was delayed by lawsuits, but even after his return. Don Fadrique bribed one of her maids to let him in so he could spend most nights in doña Violante's company, to don Juan's great envy, since he couldn't be with his doña Ana and begrudged his cousin's good fortune.

Don Fadrique enjoyed his affair with his lady for several months, giving more and more indications of his growing love, more than you might expect. Compelled by this love, a thousand times he decided to make her his wife if ever she showed any desire to marry. But each time he brought up the subject of her changing her status, she cut him off with a thousand persuasive pretexts.

Then, just when don Fadrique was feeling most confident and least apprehensive about her love, doña Violante's interest began to wane. She began avoiding him as much as she could. Out of jealousy, he blamed some new infatuation and his complaints became increasingly boring and bothersome. Despairing because of his fall from favor just when he thought he'd reached the peak, he bribed the servant with gifts and promises of great rewards and found out what he didn't really want to know. The treacherous maid told don Fadrique to feign illness that night and to tell doña Violante he was sick in bed so she wouldn't prepare for his visit as she usually did. He should come to the house and she'd leave the door open so he could let himself in and see what he might see.

This was simple because, ever since her cousin's marriage, doña Violante had lived in an apartment separated from the rest of the house where she could stay out of doña Ana and her new husband's

affairs. Doña Violante couldn't stand doña Ana's husband and, besides, she was used to having her freedom and didn't want anyone
keeping watch over her. There was a door connecting their two
apartments and often doña Violante would eat with doña Ana
and her husband because he was charmed by doña Violante's conversation.

Doña Violante believed in don Fadrique's feigned illness and it
suited her well that she wouldn't have to bother to entertain him as
usual. She decided to retire early.

Now the thing is that doña Ana's husband's brother usually spent
most of his time with the three of them and he had taken a great
liking to doña Violante. She, already obligated by don Fadrique's attentions, hadn't acceded to his desires. Now, either tired of don Fadrique or pleased by her new lover's gifts and jewels, she put behind
her any sense of obligation to her former lover. Her new dalliance
inspired her to deprive don Fadrique of his possession altogether by
no longer submitting to his love and desires. So, on this night when
she thought she was safe because of don Fadrique's indisposition, she
sent a message to her new lover. He notified his brother that he
planned to stay home that evening and wouldn't be spending it with
him and doña Ana. Immediately he came to visit doña Violante to
take advantage of this great opportunity.

Don Fadrique arrived and found the front door unlocked. His heart
wouldn't let him wait. Hearing voices, he rushed to the door of doña
Violante's apartment. He burst into her room and found his lady
already in bed and the young student undressing, preparing to join
her.

At this moment, don Fadrique's wrath could not have been rational;
he rushed in determined to tear his rival to shreds with his bare hands
rather than dirty his sword on such a young boy. When the callow
lover saw a man burst in furiously and he was naked and without a
sword, he leaned over and picked up a shoe that was on the floor and
held it in his hand as if it were a pistol. He told don Fadrique that,
if he didn't stand back, he'd shoot. The youth then darted out the
door and down into the street, leaving don Fadrique shaken by the
suddenness of his charge.

Doña Violante was firmly resolved to divest herself of don Fadrique's attentions. She looked at him standing there, frozen, staring
at the door through which his rival had just disappeared. She began

to roar with laughter, finding the trick with the shoe particularly hilarious.

The gentleman from Granada felt more humiliated by her laughter than by anything else. His rage exploded; he rushed over to doña Violante and struck her in the face, bathing it in blood. Furious, she told him to get out, she'd call her brother-in-law, she'd make don Fadrique pay dearly. Heedless of her threats, his rage increased. He grabbed her by the hair and beat her until she was forced to scream. Her screams brought doña Ana and her husband to the connecting door.

Don Fadrique was afraid of being caught, especially if the police should come, because they could charge him with anything. He fled from the premises and went back to don Juan's house. He told don Juan what had taken place and immediately set about arranging his departure. He knew that the duke of Osuna was about to become the new viceroy of Sicily and hoped to join him for the passage over. Within four days, don Fadrique set out, leaving don Juan very dejected about what had happened and grieved to lose such a good friend.

Although don Fadrique left Spain intending to go to Sicily, he ended up in Naples, and the beauty of the city held him quite some time. He had a variety of adventures, all of which confirmed his belief that women exercise their intelligence with great cleverness to destroy men's good name and honor. (Keep on believing that, don Fadrique, some day you'll learn just the opposite.)

In Naples he had a mistress who, every time her husband came home, made him pretend he was a hutch backed up against the wall. From Naples, he went to Rome where he had an affair with a woman who one night, for his sake, murdered her own husband, stuffed him in a sack, carried him on her back down to the river, and dumped him in.

He spent many years involved in these and numerous other affairs. After sixteen years away from home, weary of traveling and short of money—indeed he hardly had enough left to get home—he decided to return. He landed in Barcelona and rested for several days. Carefully he checked his purse and then bought a mule to take him to Granada. The next morning he set out alone, for he didn't have enough money left to hire a servant.

Don Fadrique traveled slightly over four leagues, intending to eat and rest further down the road. It was around nine in the morning when he passed through a beautiful place that belonged to a duke of Catalonia and his beautiful wife from Valencia, who had retired to live on their lands to save money. The beautiful duchess happened to be out on her balcony just as don Fadrique was passing. She noticed the traveler hastening by and was struck by his jauntiness, so she sent a servant after him to tell him she desired to speak with him.

As soon as this message was given to don Fadrique, he turned back to see what the beautiful duchess wanted of him. He'd always prided himself on being considerate and particularly with ladies. Impressed by the duchess' beauty and elegance, he greeted her with great courtesy. She invited him to take a seat and, very charmingly, inquired where he was from and why he was traveling with such haste. She emphasized the pleasure it would give her to know his answer because, the moment she'd set eyes on him, she'd felt inclined to love him. That's why she decided to invite him to be her guest while the duke was away hunting.

Don Fadrique, who wasn't at all shy, thanked her for the favor she showed him and told her who he was and about the experiences he'd had in Granada, Seville, Naples, Rome, and everywhere else he'd been. He ended his tale saying he'd run out of money and was tired of traveling so he was returning home with the intention of getting married, if he could find a wife to suit his taste.

"What kind of woman would she be," the duchess asked, "the woman who would suit your taste?"

"My lady, as I've told you, I'm noble," don Fadrique replied. "I have more money than I need to last me the rest of my life, so it doesn't matter to me if the woman who is to be mine isn't wealthy so long as she's beautiful and well born. What most pleases me in a woman is virtue. That's all I require, for earthly goods God gives and God takes away."

"Then," the duchess said, "if you found a woman noble, beautiful, virtuous, and discreet, would you immediately place your neck in the delightful yoke of matrimony?"

"I promise you, my lady," don Fadrique responded, "I have been so chastened by the cleverness of discreet women that I would far prefer to be conquered by a mindless woman, even if she's ugly, as long as she has the other qualities you describe. If a woman must be knowledgeable, all she needs to know is how to love her husband, how to rear his children, and how to care for his honor, without any other pretensions."

"And how," the duchess asked, "will she know how to be honorable if she doesn't even know what honor means? Don't you know that a simpleton commits sins without even knowing it? An intelligent woman knows how to take care of herself. Your decision shows bad judgment, for a wise woman is something never to be forgotten. Some day you will remember my words.

"But, to change the subject, I am so attracted by your looks and your wit that I shall do something for you I never thought I'd do."

Then she invited don Fadrique to be her guest at dinner and she took him into her bedchamber to dine more intimately. This surprised him; indeed none of his other experiences astonished him as greatly. They dined and entertained each other and had a delightful time together enjoying the warm afternoon and the solitude. Don Fadrique was enchanted by the duchess' beauty and charm and wished he could stay forever, if he could've done so without scandal.

Night was beginning to spread her mantle across the countryside when a maid entered saying that the duke had arrived, and so quietly that no one had seen him until he was inside the house. By now he'd be climbing the stairs. The duchess had no choice but to open a gilded cupboard where water was stored right in her own room. Quickly she put don Fadrique inside and locked the cupboard with the key. Then she reclined on her bed.

The duke, a man somewhat past fifty, came in. When he saw her stretched out on the bed looking as beautiful as a rosebud on a rosebush, he greeted her lovingly and asked her why she was in bed. The beautiful lady replied that the only reason was that she'd wanted to spend the hot siesta time resting quietly, and then she'd felt too lazy to dress so she hadn't bothered to get up.

The duke told the duchess that he'd come back with a tremendous appetite, so they ordered their supper brought up to her room and they dined with leisurely pleasure. Afterwards, the astute duchess decided to play a joke on her lover locked up in the cabinet, so she asked the duke to play a game naming all the things he could think of that were made of iron. He accepted the wager. After much haggling, they each bet a hundred escudos on whether he could guess the word she had in mind. He took up a pen and began to write a list of everything that's made of iron. The duchess's luck in pulling off her trick was so good that the duke never thought of keys. The duchess noted his oversight and even though she urged him to keep trying to think of other things, he said he couldn't. In this she saw her wish fulfilled. She placed her hand over the paper and said:

"Now, my lord, while you try to think of other things made of iron, I'll tell you a story, the cleverest one you've ever heard. Today, when I was standing on my balcony, a stranger passed by and he was the handsomest man I'd ever laid my eyes on. He was in a great hurry, and that made me want to speak with him and find out why he was in such a hurry. I sent for him and when he came back, I asked him who he was. He told me he was from Granada and that he'd left his birthplace for the following reason . . ." She proceeded to recount to her husband word for word what don Fadrique had told her about his experiences. "The stranger ended his tale saying that he was on his way home to get married, if only he could find a mindless woman, since he'd been so chastened by clever women. I tried to persuade him he was wrong, but he argued in favor of his convictions. Heavens, my lord, he dined with me and spent the siesta with me and then, when the maid told me you'd arrived, I put him in that cupboard there where the distilled water is kept."

The duke got very upset and immediately began to demand the keys. The duchess burst into laughter and said:

"Calm down, my lord, calm down. Keys are what's made of iron that you overlooked! You can't really believe that a man exists to whom such things have happened, or that a woman would be so foolish as to tell her husband such a thing if it were true! Why, if it were true, she'd never mention it. The story was to help you remember keys. And now, my lord, since you've lost your wager, hand over the money you owe me. I plan to spend it on a fancy dress so that what has cost you such fright will be a suitable reward for my cleverness."

"By heaven!" the duke exclaimed. "You're the very devil! What a way to remind me of my oversight! I give in!"

Turning to his treasurer, who was present with the other servants, he ordered him to give the duchess the hundred escudos immediately. Then the duke went out to receive several of his vassals who'd come to visit and ask how he'd fared on the hunt.

The duchess let don Fadrique out of his hiding place, still trembling from her crazy audacity. She gave him the hundred escudos she'd won and another hundred of her own. She also presented him with a chain and her miniature, which were worth more than three hundred escudos. She embraced him and asked him to write her, and then had him taken out through the back door. As soon as don Fadrique found himself on the road, he crossed himself repeatedly because of his narrow escape.

He didn't want to stay the night in that area so he traveled the two leagues to the place where he would've eaten lunch if what we've narrated hadn't occurred. While he rode down the road, he kept marveling at the duchess's astuteness and temerity and at the duke's kindliness and good nature. He thought to himself:

"I certainly was right that cleverness in women leads to their ruination. If the duchess didn't trust in her wit, she never would've dared offend against her husband, let alone tell him about it. I intend to avoid that kind of thing if I can, either by not marrying or by finding a woman so simple and innocent that she'll know nothing of love and scorn, a woman who doesn't know the meaning of cleverness or deception."

These thoughts entertained him all the way to Madrid, where he visited his cousin don Juan. His father had died and don Juan had come into his inheritance and married his cousin. Don Fadrique learned from him that doña Violante had gotten married and that doña Ana had gone to the Indies with her husband.

From Madrid don Fadrique set out for Granada, where he was received like a favorite son of the city. He went to his aunt's house and she welcomed him with a thousand kind words. He learned everything that had happened during his absence: Serafina had become a nun, was leading a penitent life, and everyone considered her a saint; don Vicente, feeling guilty for having abandoned her after she'd entrusted her honor to him, had died of remorse at seeing her a nun. Don Vicente had tried to take her out of the convent to marry her, but Serafina was determined never to marry. Five days after his fruitless attempt to marry Serafina had failed and helped along by a sudden fever, he paid for his ingratitude with his life. Don Fadrique learned that doña Gracia, the little baby he'd had left in his aunt's custody and who was now sixteen, had lived in the convent since she was four.

The very next day he accompanied his aunt to visit doña Gracia. In her beauty, in her innocence and simplicity, he saw the image of an angel. She looked like a lovely statue, but a statue without a soul, which was surprising, given that she'd been brought up by nuns and they're not stupid. As don Fadrique talked with her, he found in her conversation and ignorance precisely the woman he was looking for. He felt very attracted to the beautiful Gracia and his love was increased by the fact that she looked just like her mother, Serafina.

Don Fadrique told his aunt the whole story. When she learned that Gracia wasn't his daughter as she'd thought all along, she approved of his choice for a wife. Gracia accepted this good fortune placidly, like one who knows neither pleasure or displeasure, good or evil. She was naturally stupid, the only flaw in her beauty, although it was precisely the flaw her husband required.

Don Fadrique arranged the wedding, bought finery and jewels for his bride, and set up the house he'd inherited from his parents to be their home. He wanted his wife to live in her own house and not with his aunt, for he didn't want her primitive intelligence to develop. Given his obsessive belief that intelligence leads women to fall into a thousand errors, he hired all her maids with great care, selecting the least cunning and the most ignorant. I may have stated otherwise at the beginning of this story, but now I realize that he wasn't a wise man. I can't understand how a discreet man can desire his opposite. But perhaps his fears about his honor explain his error; perhaps, in order to protect his honor, he felt compelled to deny his pleasure.

The day of the wedding arrived and Gracia left the convent. Her beauty amazed all eyes, her innocence all sense. The wedding was celebrated with a banquet and party attended by all the principal citizens of Granada, as befitted the groom's nobility. The day passed by more quickly than the bride would've liked because she didn't ever want to take off all her finery and jewels. At last don Fadrique bade farewell to the guests, and the members of his family left him alone with Gracia. Determined to test his wife's ignorance, he took her into the bedroom and sat down on the bed. She had on her small clothes, as the saying goes, wearing only her bodice and pettiskirt and divested of her jewels. Fadrique asked Gracia to listen carefully to what he had to say, which was this or something equally foolish:

"My lady, you are now my wife, for which I give thanks to heaven! So long as we live, you must do what I'm about to tell you, and you must always perform this duty faithfully to keep from displeasing me and offending against God."

Gracia humbly replied that she would gladly do as he said.

"Do you know," don Fadrique asked, "what married life is?"

"No, my lord, I have no idea," Gracia said. "But you explain it to me and I'll learn it like the Hail Mary."

Don Fadrique was delighted with her simplicity. He showed her some golden armor and then put it on over her bodice: the breastplate and the backpiece, the gorget and the armplates, without omitting the gauntlets. He gave her a lance and told her that married life meant that, while he slept, she was to keep watch over him, pacing back and forth around the room.

Dressed in her golden armor, Gracia was a sight to see, so fetching and lovely was she! Whatever she didn't possess in the way of intelligence she made up for in her striking appearance; with the helmet pressed down over her curly locks and the sword in its sheath, she was the very image of Pallas Athena.

After the lovely lady was fully armed as I've described, don Fadrique commanded her to keep watch while he slept. Happily he went to bed and slept peacefully until five o'clock. He got up and, after he dressed, he took Gracia gently in his arms and very tenderly undressed her and put her to bed, telling her to rest and sleep. He ordered the servants not to wake her until eleven. He went off to hear mass and tend his business affairs, which were many, since he'd bought himself a position on the city council. More than a week went by with this routine, and don Fadrique never led Gracia to think married life might be any different. She was so innocent that she believed this was what all married women did.

Then it happened that some problems arose with city affairs and the council ordered don Fadrique to depart by the next stage to go speak with the king. Because of the urgency of the case and because they knew he had many friends at court, having spent so much time in Madrid, they didn't observe the usual courtesy toward newlyweds in this instance. The suddenness of this development left him time only to rush home, pack for the journey, and tell his new wife to be sure to keep up her married duties while he was gone just as she'd done before, for it was a great sin to breach them in any way. Gracia promised to do her duty regularly and devoutly, so don Fadrique departed quite happily. But, of course, one intends to go to court for a short time and ends up staying for a long time. That's what happened with don Fadrique. His stay lasted not days but months; his case dragged on for over six months. Gracia faithfully performed her marital duty.

One day a gentleman from Cordoba came to Granada to file a lawsuit before the chancellery. He was in no way stupid or unattractive. When he was idle, he would stroll through the streets of the city. One day, he saw doña Gracia out on her balcony where she spent her afternoons embroidering. The sight of her captivated him. He was stricken by the vision of her beauty and, suffice it to say, he began to frequent her street. The lady, being ignorant of all these things and knowing nothing about the laws of love and courtship, neither accepted nor rejected his attentions. Her lack of response saddened the gentleman from Cordoba.

One of doña Gracia's neighbors was observing this course of events, and she realized that the gentleman had fallen in love with the young bride. One day she called out to him and, discovering the truth of her supposition, promised to intercede with doña Gracia for him. There's always some abyss for virtue to fall into. The neighbor went to see doña Gracia. Extravagantly she praised the young bride's beauty, which marked the first step leading to doña Gracia's downfall. Then the neighbor told her how the gentleman who spent so much time in her street loved her greatly and desired to serve her.

"I truly appreciate that," the lady replied. "But I already have a lot of servants and, until one of them leaves, I shan't be able to satisfy his wish although, if he likes, I can write my husband to see if he might hire him just to please me."

"Oh, no, my lady," the crafty matchmaker exclaimed, beginning to realize how ignorant the young bride was. "This gentleman is very rich and noble; he has great estates. He doesn't want you to hire him as a servant, he wants to serve you with all his wealth, to send you some gift or jewel, if you'd like."

"Oh, my friend," doña Gracia replied. "I already have so much jewelry I don't even know where to put it all."

"Well, if that's the way it is," the matchmaker said, "and you don't want him to send you anything, then at least give him permission to visit you, which he greatly desires."

"Of course! Let him come!" the foolish lady said. "What prevents him from coming to visit me?"

"My lady," the neighbor answered, "don't you understand that the servants, if they see him come openly during the daytime, might think ill of it?"

"Well, then, here," doña Gracia said, "this key opens the back door entering from the garden and, indeed, I think it opens every door in the house because it's a master key. Give it to him and tell him to come tonight and climb the circular staircase that comes right up to the room where I sleep."

The woman could hardly believe such ignorance, but she didn't want to probe further. She took the key and went to get the reward for her work, which was a heavy gold chain. That night don Alvaro—this was his name—came through the garden as he'd been instructed, climbed the stairs, and was about to enter the room, when he saw doña Gracia in her elaborate armor holding aloft her lance. She looked like an Amazon. The light was dim and, since don Alvaro couldn't begin to imagine, let alone believe, the truth of what he was seeing, he thought he'd been betrayed. As quickly as he could, he turned tail and fled and the next minute he was in the street.

The following morning he described this scene to the matchmaker and immediately she went to see doña Gracia. The moment she entered, doña Gracia inquired about the gentleman. He must have been terribly ill since he hadn't come as he'd been instructed.

"Oh, my lady," she said, "of course he came. But he said he found a man in armor, carrying a lance and marching around the room."

"Good heavens!" doña Gracia answered, laughing merrily, "doesn't he know I was just doing my married duty? That gentleman must not be married if he thought I was a man! Tell him it's me and not to be afraid."

The matchmaker took this explanation to don Alvaro. That night he went again to visit his lady and, when he found her in her armor, he asked her to explain. Laughing, she said:

"Well, how else should I lead a married life if not like this?"

"What do you mean, married life, my lady?" don Alvaro asked. "You've been deceived; this isn't what married life is."

"Well, my lord," said doña Gracia, "this is how my husband taught me, and he says it's a terrible sin to violate it. But if you know an easier way, in truth I'd love to know what it is and learn how to do it, for this life I lead is very tiresome."

When the cavalier youth heard this naive request, he himself undressed her and took her to bed and enjoyed everything that her foolish husband had postponed in his desire to test his wife's ignorance. All the time don Fadrique was at court, don Alvaro and doña Gracia lived a true married life. At last don Fadrique finished his business and wrote that he was coming home. Don Alvaro finished up his business and returned to Cordoba.

Don Fadrique arrived home and was greeted by his wife with much pleasure for, just as she had no intelligence, she had no sense either. They dined together and, because don Fadrique was tired from his journey, he went right to bed. He assumed that doña Gracia would put on her armor as he'd commanded. When he saw her come out naked and get into bed with him, he was astounded at this novelty, and asked:

"Well, my lady, how is it that you don't perform your married duty as I taught you?"

"My, my, sir," she said, "what do you mean married duty and all that nonsense! I learned a much better way with my other husband who took me to bed with him and caressed me more than you do."

"You mean," don Fadrique asked, "you've had another husband?"

"Yes, my lord," doña Gracia answered. "After you left, another handsome, charming husband came along and told me he'd show me a different married life, better than yours."

She told him everything that had happened with the gentleman from Cordoba. But she couldn't understand what had become of him. After she'd received don Fadrique's letter with news of his return, she hadn't seen him again. In despair, the foolish don Fadrique asked her what the man's name was and where he was from. But doña Gracia answered that she didn't know, she never called him anything but husband.

Don Fadrique understood that in trying to prevent his dishonor, he had purposely married a fool who had not only offended against his honor but who even told him all about it. He realized the error in his thinking and recalled the duchess' words: discreet women know how to keep the laws of honor and, if ever they break them, they know how to keep their error secret.

For the rest of his life, don Fadrique praised discreet women who are virtuous, saying that they are priceless beyond all thought and, if they're not virtuous, at least they know how to behave prudently and modestly.

Realizing that nothing could be done about what had happened because it was his fault, don Fadrique covered up his misfortune. If discreet women sometimes fail in the test, what could he expect of a foolish woman? Trying not to let his wife out of his sight so she wouldn't offend against him again, he lived for several more years. When he died, since they had no children, he left all his wealth to doña Gracia, with the provision that she become a nun in the same convent as Serafina. He wrote a letter to Serafina explaining that this was her long-lost daughter. He also wrote his cousin don Juan in Madrid telling this story just as it is set down here.

In the end, no matter how don Fadrique tried to prevent the catastrophe he'd been forewarned about, in spite of all the lands he'd visited and all the adventures he'd had, he fell into the very situation he feared, and it was a foolish woman who ruined his honor.

Doña Gracia became a nun in the same convent with her mother, and the two were happy to know each other. Because doña Gracia was foolish, she readily found happiness and spent the huge fortune at her disposal in building a grand convent where she spent her days pleasantly.

I now take pleasure in ending this enchantment by warning all the ignorant people who condemn discretion in women: there can be no virtue where intelligence is lacking. Furthermore, if a woman is going to be bad, it doesn't matter whether she's foolish or not, but a good woman, if she's discreet, will know how to take care of herself. Be warned, you who would put a woman to the test, of the risk you take.

As don Alonso was reaching the final words of his delightful and entertaining enchantment his audience was caught up and absorbed by his words. They were roused from their rapture by the sound of many well-tuned instruments that began to play dance music in the adjoining room. Everyone turned to see who was making such sweet music. Twelve handsome lads dressed as shepherds and wearing purple satin caps trimmed with silver, each one bearing a lighted torch, tripped into the hall. After they did the stately dance all around the room, they separated into two columns. The most elegant and spritely lad began to dance alone with his torch held high. He danced all around the room and then approached the beautiful Lisarda. Making a deep bow, he invited her to dance. The lady stepped out and together they danced. He returned her to her place and next, as is the custom in the torch dance, the charming lad invited the discreet Matilda, and after her, Nise. He selected don Juan to be her partner. Leaving the torch in Lisarda's hands, the two couples together performed a slow and stately dance. When the two ladies returned to their seats, Lisarda danced, inviting first don Miguel, then don Lope, and finally don Diego. While don Diego danced with Lisarda, he urged her to include her cousin in the dance. Lisarda, thinking this was a good idea, approached the couch where Lysis was reclining. With a lovely curtsey and very formal words, Lisarda begged Lysis to honor the party by dancing for them, now that her quartan fever had tempered itself. In fact it hadn't troubled her greatly since the first day of the celebration.

Lysis accepted, thinking more to please don Diego than her cousin. She danced so divinely that she delighted everyone and above all don Diego. While the two danced, he expressed his love and, as he returned her to her place, she thanked him and granted him permission to make arrangements for their marriage with her mother and the rest of her family.

While don Diego's servants were preparing for their comic skit, all the ladies and gentlemen danced. Before the skit began they had to move some of the chairs to make room, and it happened that don Juan and don Diego sat next to each other. Don Juan, acting aggrieved, said to don Diego:

"I see that Lysis looks on you with favor. It troubles me because I've been her suitor, yet at the same time it suits me just as well because it will stop her from pestering me with her complaints. You, however, should have informed me of your intention, for it's better to have me for a friend than an enemy."

"That's true," don Diego replied, somewhat irritated. "It's terrible to have a poet as an enemy, for no sword can wound as deeply as the pen. I wish to serve Lysis, that's obvious. It's no crime for me not to ask your permission because Lysis is her own mistress and not yours, and I'm content with my mistress's permission for me to court her. Lisarda is your mistress; you content yourself with her and don't try to entertain two mistresses at the same time, one to praise and the other to put down. Lysis has given me permission to discuss our marriage with her mother and, if you consider that an affront, I stand ready to give you satisfaction at the time and place you determine."

"Fine," don Juan retorted. "I am satisfied, not about Lysis's decision to marry you, even though I don't want her for myself, but that you're willing to settle our difference. I want you to know, I'm a poet accomplished with the pen and a gentleman practiced with the sword."

"So be it," don Diego replied, "but we shouldn't spoil the ladies' pleasure in these celebrations, which are to last three more days. Let's wait until the parties end; then we can take care of this any way you please."

"I'm satisfied," don Juan responded, and the two men turned to watch the end of the skit.

Lysis had heard their conversation and, while she felt like interrupting, she let it pass, since don Diego and don Juan had set their duel for after the parties, leaving her time to change their minds.

When the skit concluded, it was time for supper. The guests went to the tables where they satisfied their hunger with the tasty dishes, their eyes with the ladies' beauty, and their minds with the witty conversation, commenting on don Alvaro's enchantment, "forewarned but not forearmed." Finally all the guests went home and so ended the second night.

Third Night

The ladies and gentlemen had had their appetites whetted by the savory entertainments of the first two nights so, scarcely had the afternoon of the third soiree begun when guests started gathering in beautiful Lysis's house. She greeted them with her accustomed courtesy. On this occasion, she'd dressed in black, sprinkled with countless diamond buttons; among so many twinkling stars, she looked like the sun, so radiant was her beauty. While the guests exchanged greetings and chatted pleasantly, the afternoon passed quickly. As night began to fall, it came time to start the entertainment, so Lysis signaled the musicians who, accompanying her divine voice, sang this sonnet in honor of our King Philip IV:

> Sun who draws from the heavenly sun
> courage, greatness, light, and radiance;
> pearl who drew his being from the love
> between the sun Philip and mother-of-pearl Margaret;
>
> phoenix who revives in our Spain
> greater glories to make Spain greater,
> garden filled with regal purple blooms
> to set off your royal fleur-de-lis;
>
> Jupiter who reigns over the holy choir,
> who bathes in sweet harmony as if in light,
> being the sweet musician to his nymphs;

and, if sight does not deceive truth,
a youthful Cupid with his golden darts
is Philip, our sun, and King of Spain.

Disappointed in love by don Juan and grateful to don Diego, the lovely Lysis had deliberately changed the style of her song to avoid the theme of love and jealousy and so discourage the rivalry between the two men. Lysis had made don Juan promise that they'd be friends because she loved don Diego, and they both were feigning courtesy toward each other.

It was Nise's turn to tell the fifth enchantment on this third night, so she occupied the special seat and began like this:

"No one can ignore the power of love, especially when it overwhelms noble hearts. Love is like the sun; it has a powerful effect wherever it goes. You will see this clearly in my enchantment, which starts like this":

The Power of Love

Naples, a famous city in Italy, is renowned for its wealth, noble citizens, splendid buildings, pleasant location, and great beauty. It is crowned with many gardens and adorned with crystalline fountains, lovely ladies and elegant gentlemen. Laura was born there, a rare miracle of nature, and so exquisite that, among the most beautiful and elegant ladies of the city, she was considered a heavenly wonder. Experts in the city had made a list of the eleven most beautiful women and selected from the eleven three, and Laura was one of the eleven and also one of the three. She was her parents' third child, following two brothers who were as virtuous and noble as she was beautiful. Her mother died giving birth to her, leaving her father as tutor and comfort to the three lovely children who, although motherless, had their father's wise concern to make up for this lack.

Their father, don Antonio was his name, was of the Garrafa family, closely related to the duke and duchess of Nochera. He was lord of Piedrablanca, an estate located four miles from Naples, although he maintained his house and center of activity in town.

Don Alejandro, don Carlos, and Laura were brought up with all the care and attention that their noble position required. Their father made every effort to see that they were worthy of their nobility and wealth, training the children in the manners and exercises appropriate to a lovely lady and fine gentlemen. The beautiful Laura lived with the modesty and decorum befitting such a rich and important young lady. She was the apple of her father's eye, her brothers' delight, and the splendor of the city.

The one who most doted on Laura was don Carlos, the younger of the two brothers. He loved her so dearly that he outdid himself to please her. This was not surprising given Laura's grace, beauty, charm, discretion, and above all her modesty, which charmed not only her relatives but even those people who had only casual contact with her.

Her modesty needed no mother, for not only did her father and brothers keep vigilant watch over her beauty, her own chaste and pure thinking carefully governed her behavior. When she reached the age of discretion, she could no longer deny her company to the prominent ladies who were her relatives. For this, her great beauty would have to pay its price to misfortune.

It was the custom in Naples for maidens to attend parties and soirees given in the viceroy's palace and in other private homes of the nobility. This practice isn't considered proper in other parts of Italy; indeed, in many places maidens aren't even permitted to go to mass, a custom imposed by long tradition despite the efforts of ecclesiastical and lay authorities to change it.

At last, endowed with her beauty and her modesty, Laura went forth to see and to be seen, although, if she'd remembered the goddess Diana, she wouldn't have trusted in her modesty. Her splendid eyes were mortal basilisks to men's souls, her grace, a monster to endanger their lives, her wealth and noble condition, bait to the desires of a thousand gallant youths of the city, all of whom hoped to enjoy her great beauty in marriage.

Among the many suitors who served Laura, the most notable was don Diego Pinatelo. He was a discreet gentleman of the noble house of the dukes of Monteleon, rich and so enviable in all his qualities that it wasn't surprising that, self-confidently, he felt sure he could win the beautiful Laura. He was certain that her family would want to have such a noble husband for their daughter because, among all the suitors for her lovely hand, don Diego was clearly superior. The moment he saw Laura, her beauty caused him to surrender his heart to her so passionately that he might have died, if it had been time for him to give up his life. (So powerful, sometimes, is the effect of beholding beauty.) He first saw her at a party given by one of the city's princes. Don Diego set eyes upon her and fell head over heels in love. His love was so intense at that moment that he felt as if he'd loved her forever, and he wanted to let her know this.

Another custom in Naples was that at parties there was a master of ceremonies who would lead the ladies out to dance and give them to a gentleman chosen by him. Don Diego took advantage of this custom; undoubtedly money was exchanged, and scarcely had he warmed the master's hands when he found in his own hands those of the beautiful Laura, just in time to dance a galliard. This arrangement did him little good, however, because his passion, inflamed by her icy aloofness, led him to blurt: "My lady, I adore you." Instantly, the beautiful lady excused herself, feigning some indisposition. She left him and returned to her seat. This made don Diego very sad, and everyone who was watching the dance wondered what had happened. Throughout the rest of the party, don Diego suffered deep remorse and despaired. He did not merit a single glance from Laura, not because the beautiful lady wasn't attracted by don Diego's appearance, but because she felt constrained to uphold her modesty as she always had.

Night came and the party ended, which was sad for don Diego because Laura went home and he likewise had to go home. He went to bed (a common recourse for the sorrowful, who consult their pillows as if pillows could offer comfort). He tossed and turned and complained bitterly about his misfortune—if indeed it was a misfortune to have seen the beauty who was driving him crazy. If Laura had heard his complaints on this occasion, she might have felt more kindly disposed toward him than she had shown herself that afternoon.

"Alas!" the wounded youth lamented. "My heavenly Laura, how cruelly you reacted to those ill-fated words I uttered! If only you could know that my soul is more yours than the one you bear within you. There can be no offense against your honor or your family for, clearly, if I intend to employ my soul in your service, I'll make you my wife and in no way will your good name suffer. Is it possible, beloved mistress mine, that one so beautiful can have a heart so cruel it won't let you understand that now I've seen you, I'm not the same person I was before? I've lost my heart and I feel empty. Everything I am I've surrendered to your beauty. If I offend you in doing this, blame your beauty, for once human eyes behold it, they must desire it. There can be no other choice but to love you. Nothing seems more rational than for me to call myself your slave.

"Poor me! But I complain without cause. Since Laura's careful about her modesty and decorum, she was obliged to treat me harshly. It would have been improper for her to accept my love the very moment it commenced. Scarcely had my desire been born when I declared it to her. I'm rich; in nobility, my parents are in no way inferior to hers, so why should I despair? If I formally ask for her hand in marriage, why should her father refuse to give her to me? Take courage, cowardly heart, just because you love, you shouldn't fear. My misfortune can't be so great that I won't obtain what I desire so much."

Don Diego spent the night thinking these thoughts, sometimes heartened by his hopes, sometimes discouraged by his fears, as is natural in lovers. Meanwhile, the beautiful Laura had been profoundly affected by the sight of the handsome don Diego. In her memory, she kept hearing him say, "I adore you." Thoughtfully, as if loving were a crime, she pondered her freedom and the risks to her reputation; she decided to love him. Then guiltily, she chastised herself, thinking that if she accepted his love she was endangering her reputation. But if she rejected him, she was threatened by the same danger. Laura was the most confused woman on the face of the earth, sometimes encouraging her desires and sometimes struggling to repress them. These thoughts and worries caused her to avoid pleasurable activities. She wouldn't even talk with the people in her household. Then she began to seek occasion to see the cause of her passion.

The days slipped by and don Diego could do nothing but complain about his beloved mistress's disdain, for, even though she was in love, she granted him no favors. She only permitted him an occasional glimpse of her, and this she did so casually and nonchalantly that he never had a chance to tell her of his suffering. Although her own feelings might have led her to allow his courtship, the care with which she disguised her emotions was such that she hid the secret of her love even from her closest and most affectionate maids. Of course her sadness made her father and brothers suspicious and quite apprehensive. Don Carlos, in particular, noted her melancholy. Since he loved her most tenderly and trusted in their close relationship, he kept asking her what was causing her unhappiness. Noting that don Diego kept passing by their house, he came close to suspecting the source of her sorrow. But Laura blamed her poor health and managed to satisfy any doubts he might have had through her modesty and discretion. Even so, her family did not neglect keeping careful watch over her honor.

On one of the many nights don Diego spent outside Laura's house waiting for dawn to arrive, he brought a servant with him to play music and serve as his spokesman, since he had no other way to express his love to her. This servant had one of the sweetest voices in that

city so famous for its fine voices. He was to sing a ballad that don
Diego had composed for this occasion about the love and fears he
felt. He was jealous of a rich, noble gentleman, a good friend of
Laura's brothers, who came to their house with frequency. Don Diego
feared that her inattention to him might be caused by her love for
this rival—a good example of how jealousy colors even innocent situations. On that night, the musician sang this ballad:

Oh, aspiring love,
if the mistress you have chosen,
already obliged, recognizes another
more fortunate master,
why do you wander lost,
following in her footsteps,
noting all her actions,
seeking to gaze upon her?
What good does it do
for you to ask favor from heaven,
the impossible from love,
change from time?
Why do you call on jealousy
when you know that
in the impossible love
jealousy favors the beloved?
If you desire to see your beloved
far away, you are foolish,
for it makes no sense to punish yourself
simply because you wish to punish her.
If you ask discord
to wound her breast,
clearly you will see pleasure
turn into grief.
If you tell your eyes
to state their feeling,
you see that they accomplish little
no matter how tenderly they look.
If the one who could bring you
remedy for your ills,
one who is a faithful friend,
always gracious,
is also a prisoner
to that proud angel,
how can he help you
in your amorous enterprise?
If only in your love
you were to receive a reward,

if your mistress were to say
I feel sorry for you.
You look at your mistress
and see her unloving,
but even this disappointment
cannot change your desire.
You are like Tantalus
who sees the fleeting crystal
that he can never taste
reaching almost to his lips.
If only you could merit
for your great feeling
some feigned deception,
for I fear you'll die;
your sorrows must be like
the suffering of purgatory;
but I see your pain so hopeless
that it equals the torments of hell.
But you've made your choice
and death is the only remedy
for it would be a cowardly act for you
to turn your back and flee.

Sitting behind the window blind, Laura had been listening to the song from the very beginning. She decided she had to defend her reputation, because the false suspicions expressed in don Diego's verses impugned her honor. And so, what love couldn't accomplish, her fear of losing her good name did. Her shame battled with her love and finally she made up her mind to defend herself. Seeing don Diego nearby, she opened the window and softly, so no one could hear, she whispered to him:

"My lord, don Diego, it would be a miracle if, being in love, you didn't feel jealousy. There has never been a love without jealousy, or jealousy without love, but the jealousy you feel is so unfounded that I feel obliged to speak with you, something I never intended to do. I'm deeply troubled to hear my reputation sullied by the words of your song and the music of the lute, and, worst of all, in the mouth of a musician who, because he's a servant, must be an enemy. I haven't scorned you for any other suitor; indeed, if anyone in the world merits my affection, it's you and you'll be the one to win me, if you're willing to take the risk. May your love pardon my daring and boldness in acting like this and in telling you that, from this day forward, you may consider yourself mine, just as I'll consider myself fortunate to think that I'm yours. Please believe that I'd never have spoken thus if the night, with her dark mantle, didn't cloak my shame and the color that rushes to my face while I voice this truth. It was born the first day I saw you and has remained locked up inside me ever since. You're the only one who knows this. It would grieve me sorely if anyone were witness to my confession, except you who obliges me to confess."

Overcome by his emotion, the enamored don Diego, the happiest man on earth, was struggling to respond and thank the beautiful Laura, when she heard the doors of her house open and saw two swordsmen assault him so suddenly that, had he not been prepared and his servant not been standing by with drawn sword, he might never have gotten to pursue his amorous desires any further.

Laura saw the attack and recognized her two brothers. Fearing they might catch her, she closed the window as quietly as she could, ran to her room, and quickly went to bed, not to seek repose but rather to dissemble for, with her beloved in such danger, she would certainly find no rest.

When don Alejandro and don Carlos heard the music, they had leapt from their beds and, as I've described, run out with their swords drawn. Although their swordsmanship was not necessarily better than that of don Diego and his servant, it was luckier. During the struggle, don Diego was wounded and had to withdraw. He complained of his misfortune, but it might be more appropriate to call it good fortune because, when his parents learned the cause of the fight, they saw how their son would profit from such a noble marriage. Knowing that this was his desire, they sought intermediaries to present their petition to Laura's father. When Laura feared that the whole episode of the duel might cause eternal discord, she suddenly found herself wed to don Diego, much to everyone's delight. Their marriage brought such joy to the two lovers that it would be foolish to try to describe it in this brief account.

Who, recalling don Diego's love, his tears, his complaints, the burning desire in his heart, can hear about this marvelously happy outcome and not consider Laura terribly fortunate? Who can doubt that everyone who has amorous hopes will say: how I wish I were so fortunate and my troubles could have such a happy conclusion as those of this noble lady? Particularly those ladies who think only of their own desires. Similarly, who can look at don Diego enjoying in Laura the epitome of beauty, lavish wealth, the culmination of discretion, and a prodigy of love and not exclaim that heaven has never created a more fortunate man? Given their correspondence in all these fine qualities, one would think at the very least that this love would be eternal. And it might have been, if Laura hadn't been unfortunate because of her beauty; if don Diego had not been mutable like all men—if his love hadn't been a prelude to neglect, if his nobility hadn't previously restrained his appetites. Laura's wealth didn't protect her from unhappiness, nor did her beauty from scorn, her discretion from neglect, her love from thanklessness. In this day and age, all these virtues are greatly prized but little valued.

What was lacking for Laura to be happy? Nothing. She trusted in love and believed that its power could overcome the greatest impossibility; but even though she was more beautiful than Venus, don Diego began to scorn her. Is it too much to ask that a man be faithful, particularly when he enjoys possession?

It happened that before don Diego fell in love with Laura, he had fixed his attentions on Nise, an attractive woman from Naples who, while not the "crème de la crème," was certainly not from the dregs of society. Her appearance, her qualities, and her estate were not so deficient that she didn't entertain high aspirations. She wanted to be don Diego's wife, as her noble condition might warrant, and so she had already granted him all the favors he'd sought and all she had to offer. During the early days and months of his marriage he had neglected Nise. She set out to discover the cause of his neglect and it didn't take her long, for there's always someone who'll tell. Since don Diego had never intended to be her husband, and the wedding had been public, he hadn't given a thought to Nise. She was terribly distressed by don Diego's marriage but, after all, she was a woman in love and always forgiving of offenses, even at the expense of her own reputation. Nise remained committed to don Diego; she thought she couldn't live without him. If she couldn't be his wife, at least she could continue to enjoy him as his mistress. To accomplish her goal, she barraged him with letters, she pressed him with tears and, finally, through her insistent pleading, she managed to get don Diego to come back to her house.

This was Laura's undoing. With all her art, Nise knew how to enamor don Diego all over again and now, because Laura was his, she seemed boring. Laura began to feel rejected because of don Diego's neglect, and she grew irksome with her jealous outbursts. Don Diego the solicitous, don Diego the persistent, don Diego the lover, don Diego who, at the beginning of their marriage, had said he was the happiest man in the world, not only denied that he'd ever been like that, he even denied to himself any acknowledgment of his obligations. Men who spurn their wives so flagrantly give wings to offense; when a man's immorality becomes flamboyant, he comes perilously close to losing his honor. Don Diego started by being inattentive, by missing bed and board. He refused to acknowledge the sorrow he was causing his wife, for it's far easier to deny one's actions than to face up to them. He disdained her favors and, in his speech, he showed contempt for her. When a man behaves so badly, what can he expect? I don't know if I ought to say that he should anticipate some offense to his honor.

Laura noted the changes in her husband's behavior, and she began to express grief, first with tears and then with words, in an effort to deal with his scorn. When a woman shows how much she's affected by her husband's errors, she's lost. When Laura felt it necessary to express her unhappiness, she gave further cause to don Diego, not just to abuse her verbally but even to lay hands upon her, heedless of the infamy of such an act. Indeed, so greatly had he come to hate and loath her that he came home only occasionally to keep up appearances. Having to face Laura was worse than death to don Diego.

Laura tried to find out the cause of these changes in behavior, and she soon learned the whole story. Servants don't have to be tortured to tell all about the failings of their masters, and they don't restrict themselves to telling only true things, they also know how to make up the most elaborate lies. Servants have been called "prose poets" because of their talent for invention, a weakness common in those who cannot help themselves. The only good it did Laura to learn the cause of her misfortunes was to make her feel her sorrows more deeply. Her situation looked hopeless to her. When the will falters there can be no hope, that's why the proverb says, "Will once twisted can never be straightened." If the remedy doesn't come from the source of the injury, no matter what the illness, there can be no cure. That's why, generally, those who are lovesick seldom want to get well.

What Laura gained from finding out the truth about don Diego's licentious behavior was to cause him to become even more shameless, pursuing his desire with greater abandon. When his vice becomes public, the vicious man knows no restraint.

One day Laura saw Nise in church. With tears in her eyes, she begged Nise to give up her claims on don Diego. Laura told her that the only thing she was accomplishing was destroying her own honor and making Laura's life a living hell. Nise had reached the point of no longer caring about her reputation, so she didn't fear falling any lower than she already had. She replied to Laura so sharply and rudely that what Laura had thought would be the solution to her sorrow left her feeling even more hopeless, and it left Nise even more determined to pursue her love at all costs. She lost all respect for God and for the rules of society. If previously she'd pursued don Diego quietly and modestly by sending him letters, gifts, and other little things, now, shamelessly, she and her servants openly came looking for him. This license increased Laura's torment and passion, for she saw even less possibility of solution than at first. She lived the most desolate life you can imagine, absolutely without hope. No wonder! She suffered from a jealousy worse than any ravaging illness.

Laura's father and brothers noticed her unhappiness, her strained appearance, and the loss of her beauty. (Naturally she hid her sorrow from them as best she could, fearing some tragic outcome.) Finally, however, they became aware of what was going on and of the evil life don Diego was leading, and they had many arguments and ugly disagreements with him about it, which ultimately turned into open enmity.

The sad and beautiful Laura spent some time in this torment. With each day that passed, her husband's liberties increased and her patience diminished. But you can't cry over your misfortunes all the time. One night she was up late, unable to sleep because of don Diego's tardiness and her constant worries; she was sure he was in Nise's arms. She decided to ease her sorrows by singing. (Some say this eases them, but I think it makes them worse.) She took up her harp, which Italian women play very well and, sometimes singing, sometimes bursting into tears, she sang this ballad, disguising don Diego's name as Albano:

Why, tyrant Albano,
if you worship Nise
and offer all the attentions
of your love to her beauty;
why, if your heart
is prisoner to her eyes,
and to your eyes her face
is such a beautiful image;
why if you entangle your love
in the prison of her hair
and she, so responsive to you,
rewards you with her love;

why, if from her mouth,
jewelbox full of lovely pearls,
you hear love's sweet sayings,
which greatly increase your joy,
why do you repay my constancy
with disloyalty and deception
when, because I love you,
I suffer such great torment?
And if truly you give
your heart to your Nise,
why don't you give me cruel death,
since you scorn me so?
Once you feigned for me
a loving tenderness;
why didn't you at least
let me live in ignorance?
But you have used your desire,
your will, and your power,
thankless lover, all to adore her,
and never even told me.
Can't you see it isn't right,
or just, or proper
to awaken one who sleeps,
especially one who loves,
just to make her sorrow?
Woe is me, so unfortunate!
What means do I have
to make this soul of mine
come home to its body?
Tyrant, give me back my soul;
but no, don't return it to me,
it's better for the body
to die for the sake of the soul.
Alas! if in your heart
Nise's soul dwells,
even though the soul is immortal,
the body still must surely die.
Heaven, pity me, for I am dying;
jealousy torments me
like ice that burns my soul,
like fire that chills my heart.
A thousand curses,
tyrannical Albano, on the one
who lets her soul get caught
in the prison of love.
Oh my eyes, let us weep
as many tender tears

as all the waters that the ocean deep
casts upon the sands.
And to the tune of jealousy,
instrument of my complaint,
while we weep, let us sing
sad mournful songs of love.
Listen carefully,
lofty, snowy, peaks,
and let your clear echoes
serve as my response.
Listen lovely little birds,
and with melodious tongue
you shall sing my jealousy
with your sweet voices.
My Albano adores Nise
and leaves me to my sorrows;
I suffer true passion,
I suffer real pain.
He lovingly celebrates
her heavenly beauty
and praises to the skies
letters written by her hand.
Ariadne, what say you
who weep and lament
the inconstancy of your lover,
his abuse, and his absence?
And you, afflicted Prometheus,
although you feel your flesh
ravaged by the eagle
and chained to the Caucasus,
you suffer, yes, but you do not feel
as much pain as I experience,
or any fears as great.
Unhappy Ixion,
you don't feel the wracking pain
of the wheel; what you feel
are all my torments.
Tantalus reaching for the water,
always unable to touch it,
never managing to taste it,
watching it retreat as you approach,
your grief is slight,
no matter how it's described,
for there is no greater pain
than that produced by jealousy.
Ungrateful wretch, may it please heaven
for you likewise to suffer jealousy,

and rage as I am raging,
and suffer as I am suffering.
And may that enemy of mine
cause you such jealousy
that, like Midas and all his gold,
you will be rich in sorrows!

Who wouldn't be deeply touched by Laura's complaints, sung sweetly and with such great feeling? Anyone but don Diego, who was proud of his infidelity. The moment Laura reached this part of her song, her faithless husband entered and heard her words. He well understood their meaning and reacted angrily to what should have affected him differently. What he should have prized and valued filled him with rage. He began to insult Laura and said such terrible, awful things that she burst into tears. Crystal torrents poured down her heavenly cheeks (scattering pearls the dawn might have used to decorate her May flowers and lovely spring meadows). At last, Laura said to him:

"What are you doing, you thankless wretch? How can you so abuse the freedom you enjoy with all your evil ways, with no respect for heaven and no fear of hell. What you ought to praise angers you. You should be ashamed that the whole world knows and the entire city is talking about your vicious excesses. It seems as if you were deliberately stirring my passion and driving me to offend against your honor. If it troubles you that I complain about your behavior, then remove the cause of my complaints or else end my weary life. I'm fed up with your sinful wrongdoing. Is this the way you treat my love? Is this the way you appreciate my affection? Is this the way you reward my suffering? Well, it's a wonder I haven't taken the cause of all my misfortune and torn her to shreds with my bare hands!

"Poor me, to be so unfortunate! No, I'm wrong to say 'poor me.' It would be more fitting to say 'poor you' because, with your vices, you're arousing heaven's wrath, which will surely descend upon you and open wide your way to hell. God will tire of putting up with you, the world is tired of having you around; and the one you idolize will surely give you your due reward. May all women who let themselves be deceived by men's promises learn a lesson from me. May women know that if all men are like you, then women are bound to suffer instead of live. What can any husband who behaves like you expect? Only that his wife, beyond caring about honor, may destroy his honor for him. Not that I'll do that, no matter what cause you give me in your behavior, because I am who I am, and also because, to my misfortune, the great love I have for you would never let me dishonor you. But I fear that your evil ways will inspire other men, vicious like yourself, to try to take up where you leave off. I fear that the gossips and scandalmongers will imagine my dishonor and spread rumors. What man can look at a woman like me married to a husband like you, who wouldn't be as determined to win me as you are neglectful of me?"

These were such strong words that don Diego opened up the eyes of his heart as well as the eyes of his face, and he saw that Laura was right. But his heart was so filled with Nise that it remained empty of any sense of obligation. Overcome by an infernal rage, he rushed over to her and struck her so violently that the white pearls of her teeth, bathed in the blood shed by his angry hand, looked instead like red coral. Not satisfied with this, he drew his dagger, ready to free her from the yoke as burdensome to him as it was to her. The maids, who'd been trying to separate him from his wife, screamed even more loudly at the sight of the dagger and cried out to Laura's father and brothers.

Furiously they dashed into the room. When don Carlos saw don Diego's frenzy and Laura bathed in the blood that was still gushing from her mouth, he thought her husband had stabbed her. With a sense of dreadful grief, don Carlos attacked don Diego. He wrenched the dagger away from him and was about to thrust it through his heart, when the brazen don Diego, seeing himself in such imminent danger, embraced don Carlos. Laura threw her arms around don Carlos and begged him to come to his senses, saying:

"Oh, dear brother, with his life goes the life of your unfortunate sister!"

Don Carlos checked himself, and his father intervened between the two men and calmed things down. They all returned to their separate rooms. Don Antonio was afraid that it would be his downfall if there were scenes like that every day. He decided he couldn't bear to see with his own eyes the mistreatment of his beloved daughter Laura. The next day, he gathered up his entire household and both his sons and they went to Piedrablanca, abandoning the poor Laura to her unhappy fate. She was so sad and disconsolate to see them go that she wished she could die.

Laura had heard that there were women in the region who, through sorcery, could make the unloving love. Finding her love more despised with each passing day, she decided to remedy her problem by this means, a mistake often made by passionate people. She arranged to have a sorceress brought to her. In Naples sorceresses enjoy such freedom to exercise their superstitions and schemes that they work their spells publicly. They do strange and amazing things that appear so true you almost have to believe in their powers. The viceroy and the clergy are concerned about this problem, as there's no restriction by the Inquisition or other punishment sufficient to frighten them, for in Italy the usual penalty is a small fine.

The intermediary whom Laura had charged with bringing the sorceress to her didn't tarry. The two were probably friends, for they all know one another. The woman came, and Laura sought to curry her favor with gifts (which is what these women really want). Encouraged by the sorceress's promises, Laura told her about her misfortunes and aroused her sympathy by her many tears. She used these words to make her request:

"My friend, if you can make my husband despise his mistress Nise and love me again as he did at the beginning of our marriage when he was more faithful and I happier, you will find in my satisfaction and gratitude how much I value your services. I'll give you half of all I possess. If this isn't enough, set your fee in terms of my need, state your own price and, if what I possess isn't enough, I'll sell my body to meet it."

The woman assured Laura of her qualifications and told her of the miracles she'd performed in similar cases. She made Laura feel that her request was so feasible that Laura believed success was a sure thing. The woman said she needed certain objects that Laura should obtain and bring to her in a little pouch: hairs from the head and beard and the teeth of a hanged man. With these tokens and a few other things, she would make don Diego change character so dramatically it would astound Laura. As for pay, she wanted only what the results were worth.

"Furthermore, my lady," the false sorceress went on, "all the beauty and all the wealth in the world aren't enough to make one happy without the help of spells such as mine. Why, if you only knew how many women enjoy peace with their husbands because of me, your fears would be allayed and you'd feel assured of your good fortune."

Laura felt very confused when she realized that the woman was asking her to obtain such difficult things. She had no idea how she could get hold of the hair and teeth of a hanged man. She gave the

woman a hundred gold escudos and, since money accomplishes miracles, she told her to find someone to obtain them for her.

The crafty sorceress (who wanted to prolong the cure in order to
bleed the lady's purse and cover up her machinations) replied that she
didn't know anyone she could trust and, besides, the power lay in the
fact that Laura herself obtained those objects and gave them into her
hands. Having said this, the sorceress departed, leaving Laura as sad
and troubled as you can imagine.

Laura kept wondering how she could get the things the woman
asked for, but every thought that occurred to her presented a thousand
difficulties. Her only remedy was to shed torrents of tears from her
beautiful eyes, because she couldn't think of a soul she could trust.
Laura thought it was beneath the dignity of a woman like herself to
stoop to such base activities. She was afraid of her servants' lack of
discretion, and above all she feared that don Diego might find out.
These thoughts only made her weep more and, wringing her hands,
she said to herself:

"Unlucky Laura! How could you ever have expected to be lucky?
Even when you were born, you cost your mother her life. Why not
sacrifice your life to death! Oh Love, mortal enemy of mankind, how
much evil you've brought to the world, especially to women who are
weak in every way and so susceptible to deception. It seems as if you
direct your full power and all your hostility against us women. I don't
know why heaven made me beautiful, noble, and rich, if these qualities
can't prevent misfortune. The many gifts nature and wealth have bestowed upon me have been powerless against the unlucky star under
which I was born. If I am truly unlucky, what can life have in store
for me?

"This wretched life is more sorrow than joy. To whom can I tell
my sorrows? Who will help me? Who will listen to my complaints
and be moved? Who will see my tears and dry them for me? No one.
My father and my brothers abandoned me and left me helpless to
avoid knowing about my plight. Even heaven, which comforts the
afflicted, is deaf to my pleas. Alas, don Diego, who would ever have
thought . . . ? But I should've thought, I should've known, for after
all, you're a man, and men's deceptions exceed even the exploits of
the devil himself. Men do greater evil than all the minions of hell.
Where can a true man be found? In what man, especially when he
knows he's loved, does love last more than a day? It's as if the more

a man knows he's loved, the more he scorns and abuses. Cursed be the woman who believes in men! In the end, she'll find her love rewarded just as I have. Seeing so many painful examples of the way men behave, what woman can be so foolish as to want to get married. And the very woman who thinks she's most likely to find happiness will be the one to fail most dismally.

"How can I have so little valor, such effeminate courage? How can I be such a coward that I don't strike dead the enemy of all my peace and the ingrate who treats me so harshly? But alas! I love him. I'm afraid to make him angry; I'm afraid I might lose him! Why, vain legislators of the world, do you tie our hands so that we cannot take vengeance. Because of your mistaken ideas about us, you render us powerless and deny us access to pen and sword. Isn't our soul the same as a man's soul? If the soul is what gives courage to the body, why are we so cowardly? If you men knew that we were brave and strong, I'm sure you wouldn't deceive us the way you do. By keeping us subject from the moment we're born, you weaken our strength with fears about honor and our minds with exaggerated emphasis on modesty and shame. For a sword, you give us the distaff, instead of books, a sewing cushion. Woe is me! What good do all these thoughts do? They don't solve my hopeless problem. What I must think about is how to get that sorceress the things she's asked for."

As Laura said this, she set her mind to thinking about what she might do. Again she began to lament. Anyone who heard Laura's laments would say that the power of love had reached its limit, but there were greater trials ahead. Night came, and it was the darkest and the most shadowy night of the winter (to show how night felt about her plan). She didn't take into account any risk or possible consequences of her acts should don Diego come home and find her absent from their house. She instructed her servants, if her husband did by chance return, to tell him she'd gone to visit one of her many women friends in Naples.

Laura put on one of her maid's cloaks, took a little lantern and, accompanied only by her vast fears, she set out down the street with greater courage than her few years warranted. She went to get what she hoped would solve all her problems. Just thinking about where she went fills me with horror. Oh, don Diego, cause of so much evil, why doesn't God take you to account for all your wickedness? You have driven your wife beyond fear of the dreadful place where she will go, disregarding the suspicions she might arouse in her maids and risking the loss of her honor and her life if she's discovered! If only you thought about it, you'd see how much you owe her!

About a mile from the city of Naples, there's a holy image of Our Lady of Arca much venerated in the whole kingdom. The image is in a chapel just a stone's throw from the main highway that goes to Piedrablanca. The chapel is about fifty feet long and the same across; its door faces the road. In the front of the chapel, there's an altar with the holy image painted on the wall behind it. The ceiling is about nine feet high, and the floor is a pit sunk about twenty feet deep. Surrounding this great pit there's just a ledge about eighteen inches wide along which you can walk around the chapel. At about the height of a man, and sometimes even lower, there are iron hooks in the wall. After criminals sentenced to death have been publicly hanged, their corpses are brought here and hung from these hooks. As the bodies decompose, their bones fall into the pit, which, being holy ground, serves as their tomb. A few days before, six highway bandits had been hanged.

This is the dreadful place where Laura went. With the incredible courage her love inspired in her, she entered. Ignoring the great danger, she was mindful only of her terrible need. She felt less afraid of the people she was going to do business with than of falling into the abyss. If that happened, no one would ever know what had become of her. What incredible heart in such a frail, weak woman! She got to the chapel about ten and stayed until one. Who knows if it was God's will or her own limitation, but she wasn't able to accomplish her mission in spite of the fact that she could easily reach the faces of the dead men. I shall now tell you how that came about.

I've already described how Laura's father and her brothers, to keep from seeing her mistreated and to avoid the risk of open warfare with their brother-in-law, had retreated to Piedrablanca. There they lived, if not forgetful of her, at least removed from the sight of her sorry plight. The night when Laura went to the chapel, don Carlos was fast asleep in his bed. Suddenly he awoke with a start and cried out so loudly that it almost seemed as if he might die. His cry upset the whole household. Confused and worried, his father and all the servants rushed to his room. Showing their grief in tears, they asked him what had caused his outcry, but it was a mystery even to the one who'd suffered it. After don Carlos recovered his composure, he said in a loud voice, "My sister is in danger!" He jumped up, threw on his clothes, and ordered his horse to be saddled. He leapt on the horse and, without waiting for a servant to accompany him, he took the road to Naples at full gallop. He rode so fast that by one o'clock he'd gotten to the chapel. At that point the horse stopped sharply and stood stock still, as if it were a statue made of bronze or stone.

Don Carlos tried to proceed but, no matter how he tried, he couldn't make the horse budge. He couldn't get him to move either forward or backward. Each time he spurred him on, the horse would utter a frightful snort. When don Carlos couldn't solve this mystery, he remembered that the chapel was nearby. He turned to look at it and saw the light from the lantern his sister was carrying. He thought some sorceress must have detained him there. To make sure, he decided to see if the horse would move toward the chapel; the moment he turned the rein, without any other urging, the horse did his master's will. With sword in hand, he rode up to the door. (The moment whoever was inside heard him, the mysterious person snuffed out the light and huddled close to the wall.) Don Carlos called out:

"Whoever you are there, come out immediately! If you don't, I swear by the king's life, that I won't leave this spot until I see who you are by the light of the sun and find out what you're doing in this place."

Laura recognized her brother's voice. Hoping he'd go away, she disguised her voice as best she could and replied:

"I'm a poor unfortunate woman come to this place for a certain purpose. It's none of your business who I am. Please, for the love of God, go away! And rest assured, kind sir, that if you insist on waiting until daylight, I shall throw myself down into the pit, even though that would cost me my life and my soul."

Laura couldn't disguise her voice well enough, and her brother hadn't forgotten her as completely as she thought. He gasped and cried out loudly, saying:

"Oh, sister, how dreadful for you to be here! Not in vain did my heart warn me of your peril. Come out of there!"

Realizing that her brother had recognized her, Laura used the utmost care she could muster to keep from falling into the pit. Hugging the wall and probably also clinging to the bodies of the dead men, slowly she managed to make her way out. When she reached her grief-stricken brother she threw herself in his arms. (Who can doubt that don Carlos, loving her as much as he did, felt heartsick as he embraced her?) Together they moved away from that dread spot, and then he

listened to Laura briefly relate what had brought her there. She learned
how her brother had chanced to come there at that very moment. He
considered the rescue miraculous, as did Laura, despite the fact that
she was feeling very ashamed of what she'd done. Don Carlos decided
to take her back to Piedrablanca on his horse.

Near dawn they reached Piedrablanca. After Laura's father heard
the whole story, he, the two brothers, and Laura got into a coach and
drove to Naples. They went straight to the palace of the viceroy, who
at that time happened to be don Pedro Fernandez de Castro, count
of Lemos. He was a very noble, wise, and devout prince whose rare
virtues and outstanding qualities should be written on bronze plaques
and on the tongue of fame rather than just on paper. Don Antonio
(as I was saying) placed himself at the feet of this eminent person. He
knelt down and told the viceroy that, in order to relate a most por-
tentous event that had occurred, it was necessary for his son-in-law,
don Diego Pinatelo, to be present, because the matter concerned his
authority and his domestic relations.

His excellency, well aware of don Antonio's valor and nobility, immediately sent the captain of the guard to fetch don Diego. He was
found in a state of despair and the entire household in turmoil. The
menservants had fled, terrified of his rage, and the maids had been
locked up. What caused the uproar was that he had come home late
the night before and found Laura gone. Thinking that his noble wife
had deserted him or run away intending to destroy his honor, he'd
tried to set the house on fire. He raged like a lion.

When don Diego was informed that the viceroy required his presence, he accompanied the escort, furious and glowering. He entered
the hall and was stunned to see his father-in-law, his brothers-in-law,
and his wife. He was even more astonished to hear his wife, in his
presence, tell the viceroy exactly what we have written here. Laura
ended her story and added that she was disillusioned with the world
and with men and didn't want to have to struggle any longer. When
she thought about what she'd done and the awful place where she'd
gone, she was horrified. For this reason, she wanted to enter a convent,
the only real sanctuary for the relief of the misery to which women
are subjected.

When don Diego heard Laura say this, it touched his heart to realize he'd caused so much pain. Being a well-intentioned man, he
prized Laura at this moment more than ever and feared she might
really do as she wished. He understood how aggrieved she was and
realized he could win no concessions from her, so he tried to use the

viceroy as intermediary. He begged the noble gentleman to intercede and ask Laura to come back to him. He promised to mend his way now that he knew the power of her love. To assure Laura of his own love, he would place Nise, the cause of so much misfortune, in his excellency's hands so he could put her in a convent. Separated from Nise forever and eternally grateful to Laura for the power of her love, he would adore his true wife and serve her always.

The viceroy approved of don Diego's plan, as did don Antonio and his sons. But it was impossible for Laura to accept his offer. She was too afraid because of the past. Ever more resolute in her determination, she told don Diego he was wasting his time. She wanted to give to God, who was infinitely more appreciative, all the love she'd previously devoted to her thankless husband.

That very day Laura entered the rich, noble, and holy convent of the Immaculate Conception. Not even the viceroy himself could make Laura reveal the identity of the woman who'd asked for those outrageous objects in order to have her punished.

In despair, don Diego went home. He gathered up all the jewels and money he could find and, without saying good-bye to anyone, departed the city. A few months later it was learned that while serving in the army of his majesty Philip III, king of Spain, in the war with the duke of Savoy, he was blown up by a mine. Laura, now entirely free, took the habit and soon thereafter made her vows. She lives a devout life in the convent. She still regrets her daring deed and, every time she recalls that awful place where she went, she trembles. I heard this tale from her own lips, and I tell it as a true story so that everyone will know the great power of love and the marvelous enchantment of its power.

Everyone had listened with amazement to the discreet enchantment narrated by the beautiful Nise. Some praised the power of Laura's love, others her intelligence, and everyone praised her courage. They all agreed that not one among them would dare to visit such a dread place as she had. This gave Nise the opportunity to reaffirm that every word she'd spoken was true.

Lysis noted that the lovely Phyllis was preparing to tell her tale so, accompanied by the musicians, she sang this burlesque madrigal:

> Let us understand one another,
> sister flea: who has given you
> such a tyrannical nature,

such courage and valor,
that you attack everyone?
Why are you the one who forgives no one?

And such a tiny little thing
to bite more than one poet, what a coup!
You bite people of all classes,
as a beautiful woman might confess,
that what she denied to others
the flea has thoroughly enjoyed.

When I consider your progeny
and ponder your humble lineage,
I'm amazed at your power
and so I'd call you a scandal-monger,
born, perhaps, in a stable, still
you bite and martyrize the whole world.

Tailor of human flesh
who makes everyone nervous,
worrying morning, noon, and night
about where you may be wandering;
you and Love are the appellate judges
of all mortal beings.

Oh, haughty commissioner!
Oh, harsh justice!
Oh, vengeful mayor!
Oh, heartless and designing bailiff!
Oh, tricky notary,
life and death are in your hands!

Please be grateful for my friendship,
for sometimes I let you bite me;
so let's be friends, and you go bite
the judges with all your might,
and may they give the prize to me
for I've already tasted it.

The prettily sung lyrics gave much pleasure to the audience, who
recognized that they'd been composed for some contest. They all
thanked the heavenly Lysis, most of all don Diego. With each word
the lovely lady sang, he became more passionately enamored, which
made don Juan terribly jealous, although he gave a different reason
for his dispute with don Diego, suggesting that it was because don
Diego feared his pen more than his sword. The truth was that he

loved Lisarda, still, he didn't dislike Lysis, and he didn't want to lose the affection of either woman. Such fickle men belong in solitary confinement.

While the illustrious audience was congratulating Lysis and singing her praise, Nise and Phyllis changed places. They all turned their attention to Phyllis, and she began:

"Since the lovely Nise has told all about the power of love in her enchantment, to continue in her style, I'd like to tell about the power of virtue in mine, about how a woman is disenchanted by the experiences of another woman and ultimately is rewarded. I tell this story so men will realize that there are virtuous women and that it's wrong for the name of good women to be tarnished by the deeds of bad women: all women should not be tarred with the same brush. Without departing one whit from the truth, my story goes like this":

Disillusionment in Love
and Virtue Rewarded

The imperial city of Toledo, ancient seat of monarchs and crown city of their kingdom, glories in its delightful setting, its beautiful construction, its noble gentlemen and splendid ladies. Their heavenly faces compete with their elegant wit as they join in amorous battle, the effects of which can be seen in the hearts of all who celebrate and delight in love. If each lovely lady is herself a sibyl, all of them together form a veritable squadron of angels. In these splendors and in many other wonders, this illustrious city is one of Spain's glories and nature's greatest miracles. More than any other place, it deserves the name of being the eighth wonder of the world.

Here, not many years ago, lived a gentleman we shall call don Fernando. He was born of noble, fairly well-to-do parents, and he seemed so gallant, high-spirited, and brave that, if he hadn't tarnished his natural graces by being more inclined toward mischief and vice than toward virtue, he might have been the pride and glory of his birthplace. (Oh, woe betide those men who don't do good as they were brought up to do!) From don Fernando's tenderest youth, his parents tried to rear him and teach him the manners required by his noble birth so that he would carry on the family tradition inherited from his ancestors. But such virtuous customs were too weighty for don Fernando. He invariably obeyed his mischievous inclinations; indeed he never even tried to resist them. As a result, he took little advantage of his good upbringing. Suddenly, at the very worst time, his father died and his mother was unable to give don Fernando the kind of attention he needed, either because she couldn't control him or because she had no other son and was afraid to lose his affection.

Thereafter don Fernando devoted himself even more wholeheartedly to his vices and mischief: he dueled, he gambled, and he womanized so wantonly that he never missed any incident that took place in the city. He was involved in every scrape and caused so much mischief that he prided himself on being the cock of the walk. Don Fernando had scarcely reached manhood when he became the abomination of men. He seemed to have been brought up purposefully to ruin and destroy the good name as well as the inheritance of his ancestors. There was no trouble from which he was absent, no disturbance of which he was not a part, and getting out of all these scrapes cost him a lot. His excesses were so notorious that he was watched, especially by the police, with whom he was constantly having brushes. These skirmishes consumed a fair part of his inheritance, which concerned him more than a little because it hadn't been very abundant to begin with.

In the midst of all these diversions and excesses, love struck our gentleman in the form of the beauty, grace, and discretion of a lady who lived in Toledo, fairly wealthy herself and incomparably beautiful, whom we shall call doña Juana. Her parents had both passed away, leaving her all alone. They had been strangers in the city and so she had no relatives there. Doña Juana was twenty, a dangerous age for a woman's virtue because at this time beauty, vanity, and folly are governed by the will, and a woman tends not to heed reason or judgment and, instead, lets herself be carried away by lascivious desires.

Doña Juana let herself be courted and served by several young gentlemen, thinking that in this way she could arrange her own marriage. Don Fernando took a fancy to our lady (quite unprecedented, given his nature). He courted her favor with letters, music, gifts, all the weapons men use to conquer the frail resistance of women. Doña Juana looked favorably on don Fernando and felt pleased to see herself courted by such a gallant and noble gentleman. She believed that, if she could oblige him to become her husband, she would be exceedingly fortunate. Although not unaware of his reckless excesses, she said, as do others (but they're wrong), that they were just boyish pranks, sowing wild oats. In the long run, however, you can expect little of the man who lacks principles in the beginning.

Don Fernando, being astute, knew that doña Juana would never surrender herself to him except in marriage, so he pretended to want just that. That is what he told everyone who might repeat it to her, especially her maids, whenever he spoke with them. The lady was equally clever and, knowing that there's no better bait for a man's affections than aloofness, in order to sharpen his desire, she played hard to get, enamoring him more and more with her coy disdain. Her distance really did affect don Fernando, perhaps because in the beginning he was only fooling around and now he really loved her, or maybe because he was determined to conquer her. Given his conviction that his good looks could conquer any beauty, he was afraid he might lose status unless he succeeded in vanquishing her disdain. So he set out to overcome her distance with his many charms. The crueler she was, the more loving he seemed, the more disdainful she was, the humbler he acted, the colder she was, the more lovesick he appeared to be.

One summer night, as on many other nights, love brought him to her street with some friends. As the saying goes, where the soul dwells, there you'll find the body. He came prepared with musical instruments for entertainment. He asked his friends to accompany him, and they all joined in and sang:

Of the two pains that love
can bring to an unhappy man,
worse than being forgotten
is being scorned;
for one can forget his oblivion
and love again another day,
but the one who's been scorned,
whenever he remembers
it will be to feel scorn again,
rather than to love well.

Oblivion is the lack of
insistent memory,
it's bad fortune
but not bad intention;
against all natural law,
one blinded by passion
who scorns in this situation
not only doesn't love
but actually desires evil;
worse than oblivion is disdain.

And so, to make my point, if scorn
is an offense, one understands
that the thankless lover
who scorns aggrieves;
and if someone wants to love
who has been scorned,
let him enter the game,
but if I'm to be mistreated,
rather than being scorned,
I prefer to sink into oblivion.

I confess that the one who scorns
holds a certain kind of memory,
but if that seems like glory,
it's more like hell to me,
because when you consider it well,
such a person only desires
to see himself happy and avenged;
and if this is the way it is,
then just because of the danger
it's better to be forgotten.

Don Fernando made no mistake in singing these verses, albeit un-
intentionally, because until this time he'd been unable to ascertain the
lady's will, to tell whether she was inclined to love him or to scorn
him. He didn't know whether his charms had found room in her heart
for, although he was reckless, he could boast of many charms. But
doña Juana had already decided to favor him. She had, until that
moment, remained hidden to listen to his music. Now she allowed
herself to be seen and even requested that he play more music because
it pleased her greatly. Happier for this favor than he'd ever felt before,
don Fernando took heart and sang this ballad unaccompanied:

Melancholy suspicion,
torment of my memory,
delight of my soul,
and eternal flame of my pleasure,
death of my hopes,
fear of my desiring,
tomb of my glory,
prison of my thoughts,
tears in my sad eyes,
and sighs in my breast,
if you are not love, you must be jealousy.

Fears of my misfortune
born before their time,
know, to my sorrow,
my mistress's disdain.
From her, with tender tears,
signs of my true affection,
sure indications of my love,
I humbly beg her remedy.
To see if my request
finds mercy in her heart,
the heaven of all my glory,
I seek glory in her heaven.
Who are you? But I suspect
if you are not love, you must be jealousy.

Hear my tender sighs,
oh, image I idolize,
as, weeping, I bewail
your neglect and my sorrow.
Mistress mine, I am
Tantalus to your favors;
when I try to taste
your delicious crystal chalice,
it slips away from my thirsting lips;
Sisyphus am I, carrying on my shoulders
the weight of my glory
and, when I reach the summit,
together we fall into the depths.
Who are you? But I suspect
if you are not love, you must be jealousy.

Alas! How many times I've tried
to suppress the illness I suffer;
how many times my boldness
overcomes my fears.
And how many times I have seen
my hopes flee from disappointment
but then, unheeded, they
go back where they came from.
And how many times, when I saw Cupid
fanning the flame
did I with reason
interrupt his chaotic plan.
Who are you? But I suspect
if you are not love, you must be jealousy.

So, indeed, I lost myself
to those bewitching eyes

that have snuffed out more lives
than the heavens have stars.
I feel like Etna erupting,
Mongibelo afire,
and the flames that burn me
are themselves inflamed by ice.
Sweet liberty lost,
it is right that we should cry;
you for my hopeless love
and I for your eternal captivity.
Who are you? But I suspect
if you are not love, you must be jealousy.

Because of the favors doña Juana granted him that night, don Fernando departed happier than you can imagine. Considering the scorn she had previously shown toward him and, since these were the first favors he'd received, he thought he'd done quite well. Continuing his courtship and his love, increasing his gifts, and exaggerating his courtesies, he gradually won the affections of the lady. Now she was hopelessly in love, and don Fernando became the one who let himself be loved and served (this is the nature of men who are loved and the fate of women who surrender). Even though don Fernando did love doña Juana, he was no longer beside himself with passion. His love certainly wasn't enough to make him give up any of his other pastimes for doña Juana (as is typical of the false lover). It's well known that those who enjoy possession are the very ones who know best how to deceive and least how to love truly, for the unhappy lover is never fickle while the successful lover seldom stays true.

Ultimately don Fernando won his desire and doña Juana surrendered herself to him. No wonder, when he placed her under obligation by promising to marry her, which is the prize men offer in order to sugarcoat the bitter pill of their deception. Don Fernando's mother was still alive, and this was the excuse he offered for not marrying doña Juana immediately. He said he was afraid his marriage would upset her so much that it might cause her death, so they'd have to keep their love secret until the right time. Doña Juana believed him and swallowed happily all the excuses he made. She believed that the most important thing, winning his affection, had been accomplished. She put aside all her fears because fortune seemed to favor her and, besides, she could no longer live without her lover, which was probably the real reason.

Their secret affair went on for six months, and don Fernando gave her everything she needed. He supported her household as if she were his wife because that was the agreement they had. During this time, doña Juana came to love him more and more passionately while don Fernando loved her as her possessor. But then the possession began to bore him.

Doña Juana had a friend who, although she'd passed her forty-eighth birthday, was still attractive and elegant. She hadn't lost a bit of the vibrant beauty she enjoyed in her youth. Her appeal was enhanced by the great wealth she possessed and had increased in Rome and in the other countries where she'd traveled. Everywhere she went, she had become known as a powerful witch, but not everybody knew it because she never exercised her powers on behalf of others, only for herself. Certainly doña Juana didn't know this, although she did have her doubts about Lucrecia—this was the good woman's name. Lucrecia was a native of Rome but as clever and Spanish as if she'd been born and brought up in Old Castile.

Because of her friendship with doña Juana, she came often to her house. You may well imagine that she fell in love with don Fernando, knowing how affection develops from frequent contact. Love is an enemy as unavoidable as it is powerful, for I agree with those who say that affection and disaffection are not within our power to control. Now this was not Lucrecia's first experience of this kind, and she wanted her beloved to know of her love, so she began to visit doña Juana more frequently and to look very lovingly at don Fernando.

At first don Fernando didn't catch on because he thought Lucrecia was beyond the age of flirtation and love affairs. She, now passionately in love, took note of doña Juana's great love and don Fernando's little love. Although doña Juana didn't suspect her friend's treachery, she did represent an impediment to the achievement of Lucrecia's desire because she was so in love she couldn't bear to be separated from her lover. Lucrecia decided to write him a letter, which she carried with her to have ready. She waited for the right time, place, and situation and, at the first opportunity, she gave it to him. It read as follows:

Don Fernando, knowing that doña Juana is to become your wife, it would be foolish on my part to try to separate you from her love. But I see in your behavior and in the other entertainments which engage you that your affection for her does not go beyond simple enjoyment of her beauty. For this reason, I've decided to reveal my feelings to you. I've loved you from the moment I first saw you. A love as determined as mine cannot be expressed less candidly; I possess great wealth with which to regale you; my wealth and my person are yours to command. You are all I want, all I care about. May God keep you.

Lucrecia

Don Fernando was by nature fickle—men like him require constant change for stimulation; when they tire of enjoying one beauty, they desire another, and sometimes even an ugly woman will appeal to them. At any rate, either because of his nature, his desire to have money to spend and to gamble with, or most probably because Lucrecia's magical spells and arts were beginning to control his will, he read her letter and accepted her offer. That very day he went to her house. Of course he didn't fail to show up at doña Juana's as well. He hid his visits to Lucrecia, who was now trying to break up his relationship with doña Juana and put an end to his visits to her.

Doña Juana noticed her lover's absences. She also detected changes in Lucrecia's behavior, noting in particular the fact that her friend didn't visit as regularly. Doña Juana began to suspect what was actually going on. To find out the cause for these changes for sure, she began to follow don Fernando. She soon discovered the whole situation and learned that Lucrecia had given him power over her estate. He could spend her money as he liked and even exhaust her fortune. Doña Juana began to argue with her ungrateful lover over his new affair, but that only made her less attractive and less loveable. Don Fernando had no intention of giving up his pleasure, and our poor lady had no recourse but to suffer her anguish. Realizing that her anger only drove him farther away, she decided to dissemble, hoping to win him back through her love, since she couldn't live without don Fernando and his neglect was driving her crazy.

Lucrecia began to use her powers to their fullest. When our poor gentleman was at doña Juana's house, Lucrecia would draw him instantly to her own house in whatever state her magic happened to catch him, whether he was dressed or not.

Doña Juana watched all this happening and noticed that don Fernando came irregularly and infrequently to her house. Usually he would visit her upon leaving his mother's (she, naturally, was troubled to see her son so preoccupied). All of a sudden some stronger attraction would draw him away from doña Juana. There were still a few burning embers among the ashes of his love for her, but they could not withstand Lucrecia's spells and charms. He would stand hesitating in the street unable to decide where to go, torn between love and bewitchment. In the end Lucrecia—or more precisely, the devil, who was very much on her side—would win out.

Finally, realizing that her beauty alone was not enough and that she was losing ground, doña Juana decided to fight fire with fire. She made inquiries about who could help her in this kind of situation. A friend told her about a student who lived in the famous and noble city of Alcala. The friend said that the student was so gifted in these matters that, just by listening to her tale, he could guarantee results. Because using an intermediary would delay the resolution of her problem, doña Juana decided to be her own messenger. Pretending to have made a vow, she asked don Fernando's permission, which wasn't very hard to obtain, to make a pilgrimage to the tomb of the glorious Saint James. She hired a coach and set out in search of what she hoped would be her salvation, carrying a letter of introduction from the friend who'd told her about the student.

When she got to the student's house in Alcala, he welcomed her courteously. She placed in his hands the sum of twenty escudos and the letter of introduction. The troubled lady described her misfortune and begged him to help her. The student replied that, before he could accept the money, it was necessary to find out whether don Fernando would, in fact, marry her. When she learned his intention, then she could reward the student for what he'd actually done. To accomplish this, he gave her two rings with green stones. He instructed her to return to Toledo and to keep the rings in safekeeping and not even to try them on until don Fernando came to see her.

When she saw him actually enter, she was to place the rings on the fingers of her right hand with the stones turned in toward her palms. Holding don Fernando's two hands in hers, she was to bring up the subject of their marriage and pay close attention to the answers he gave. Within the week, the student would come to her house and advise her as to how to proceed, just as if he'd taken the matter up with God Himself, who's the only one who really knows the future. The student warned her to take the rings off immediately and to guard them with her life because they were priceless to him. After receiving this advice, doña Juana gave him directions to her house and repeated her name so that he'd have no trouble finding her in Toledo. She returned home the happiest person in the world.

The moment she got back, she let don Fernando know of her arrival. He received this news with more regret than enthusiasm, although his obligation to her made him act pleased. To avoid giving her cause for complaint, he went immediately to see her. Doña Juana saw her chance. The instant don Fernando entered, she put on the rings the way the student had instructed and took don Fernando's hands in hers. With myriad caresses, she began to ask when the day would come when they would be united before the eyes of God. Given the open way they were living in sin together, they really should take God's displeasure into account. Why, when she thought about their not being married, she feared losing God's grace, and this fear ruined her happiness and made her mortally sad.

Don Fernando responded to her pleas more tenderly than usual. The explanation for this was that Lucrecia thought doña Juana was away. Unaware that she'd come home, she was not pressing don Fernando with her magical spells. Don Fernando replied that if he didn't think it would upset his mother, he would make her his wife that very night; but time would accomplish what now seemed impossible to her. His answer and the fact that he spent the whole night with her, made doña Juana think that fortune was on her side and that don Fernando was as good as wed to her.

Doña Juana removed the rings and gave them to the maid to put away. The maid thought they were so shiny and pretty that she put them on her own hands. Then she wore them when she went to draw water from the well and when she washed the dishes. The next day she wore the pretty rings down to the river where the maids were washing clothes to show them off. She wore them not only on this one day but every day until the student came to Toledo. She took them off only to go into the presence of her mistress because, of course, she didn't want doña Juana to see her wearing them.

As they had agreed, the student came to Toledo and doña Juana greeted him as if he were an oracle. She gave him gifts and rewarded him. Then doña Juana returned his rings to him and described how don Fernando had responded. The student, grateful for her many kindnesses, told her that he would study the whole matter with careful attention and let her know what the situation promised and what measures she should take to bring about a happy conclusion. He then departed.

But the wretch had gotten scarcely a league outside of Toledo when the devils who dwelt in the rings appeared before him. They knocked him from his mule and beat him up. They battered him until they almost killed him. As they fled, they shrieked:

"Fool! Traitor! You gave us to a woman who entrusted us to a maid who wore us down to the river, to the plaza, everywhere she went. She wore us on her hands while she scrubbed floors and lugged water. You're to blame and you're the one who must pay! And what answer do you intend to give that woman? Do you think her lover will marry her? No indeed, because living in sin together the way they are, they're already burning in hell's fire, and that's just where they'll go when they die! Neither you nor she can make her wish come true."

Having shrieked these words, the devils left the poor student for dead. He was in such bad shape that he was a pitiful sight to see. He had bruises all over his whole body.

The next morning, some bread-sellers on their way to Toledo found him on the verge of death. Moved by compassion, they placed him on a mule and brought him into the city. They placed him in the plaza to see if anyone recognized him, because the poor fellow was unable to say who he was or where to take him.

It so happened that doña Juana's maid went out to buy food just then, and she was among the many who flocked to see the battered student. She recognized him immediately. With this news, she ran to her mistress. The moment doña Juana heard it, she grabbed her cloak and rushed to the plaza where she found the poor student. She had him brought to her house to be taken care of. She put him in her own bed and called in her doctors to cure him. So, thanks to doña Juana, God's will was done; the student regained consciousness and, under her good care, he gradually recovered his health.

During his recovery, he told doña Juana the cause of his misfortune, repeating the statements the demons had made about her affair. His report that she was "already burning in hell's fire" right here in this world caused such terror in the lady that it was enough to disillusion her with her love. Disenchanted, she realized the danger she was in and decided to remedy it by taking an altogether different tack.

Eventually the student recovered completely from his illness. Before he departed for home, doña Juana asked him, since his knowledge was great, to help her in her new plan. The grateful young man promised to do everything that was within his power.

Now the truth is that when don Fernando had fallen in love with doña Juana and she, overwhelmed by this good fortune, had given him possession of her person, she was also loved and courted by a gentleman from Genoa, the son of a very wealthy man attending the

Spanish court. Through his business dealings in Italy, the father had earned a great fortune and a title of nobility for his sons. This son was the second son; he had one older brother and two sisters, one married and the other a nun, both of whom lived in Toledo. This young man, whose name was Octavio, spent all the time he could in Toledo with his sisters just to glimpse doña Juana. His father approved of his spending so much time there because of the pleasure his visits afforded his sisters. Early on, before don Fernando had begun to pay doña Juana court, she had favored Octavio. Then she captured don Fernando's attention. Octavio found out that don Fernando was the reason why his lady no longer looked on him with favor, so he decided to get rid of don Fernando. One night when don Fernando and his friends were in doña Juana's street, Octavio and his friends attacked them and the fight resulted in cruel wounds; several young men were injured on both sides, and neither side won. Octavio then challenged don Fernando to a duel, but by this time don Fernando was already enjoying doña Juana's favors, having promised to marry her, as I've said before.

When the lady heard about the duel she became afraid of losing don Fernando, so she wrote Octavio a letter telling him, among other discreet and moving things, that the greatest thing he could do to show his love for her was to protect the life of her betrothed even more than her own, that he should realize her life was sustained by her love for her betrothed. The love-stricken Octavio went into such a passion that he was ill for many days. To comply with doña Juana's pleasure and her command, he wrote her a letter filled with tenderness and laments. He even swore to protect don Fernando's life, as she would see in his deeds. That very afternoon, dressed for the road, the most gallant gentleman in the world (and, had not doña Juana's fancy been so taken by don Fernando, she would have felt attracted to Octavio), seeing her on her balcony, said to her with tears in his eyes:

"My ungrateful beauty, basilisk of my life, farewell forever."

With these words, Octavio forever left his sister's house in Toledo, his parents' home, and Spain. He went to Genoa where he rested several days before entering the army to serve the king in Naples.

Doña Juana believed the words the student had repeated to her. She thought that if only Octavio would return to Spain, he would make her a better husband than don Fernando. She explained this background to the student. She tried to put him in her debt with gifts and to encourage him by promises of other gifts, such as a hundred escudos for a new suit. Then she asked him to use all of his powers and arts to make Octavio come back.

The student, who'd learned his lesson from recent experience, replied that in this matter he could only tell her what she needed to do in order to obtain her heart's desire. Within the month he planned to come back to Toledo and, depending on her success, she could pay him then. He gave her a note and told her to lock herself in her room every night and do precisely as the note instructed. Because the note's words were scandalous and it's not necessary for us to know them, they won't be repeated here. Certainly doña Juana never uttered them to a soul except her confessor. The student, well rewarded and quite pleased with his ingenuity, returned to Alcala, leaving the lady fully advised as to what she should do.

Not wanting to waste a minute, doña Juana began that very night to exercise the spell. After three nights, the words the audacious student had written on the paper took effect or, more likely, God took advantage of this situation to regain doña Juana for Himself, using the devil and his wiles as a means to her conversion.

On the third night, doña Juana was performing her conjuration with all the concentration her desire could muster, when she heard a sound at the door. Suddenly she felt an icy draft on her face and was afraid to be alone. She looked over to where the sound had come from and saw Octavio passing through the locked door, dragging heavy chains and surrounded by fiery flames. Uttering terrifying moans, he moved toward her. In a frightful voice he said:

"What do you want of me, doña Juana, what do you want? Wasn't it enough for you to torment me during my lifetime? Must you also torment me in my death? Give up this evil life you lead. Fear God and fear the account you must give of all your sinful pleasures. Rest assured that even though the devil is the father of all lies and deceits, God may allow him to utter truths for the benefit and usefulness of men, to warn them of their perdition, as He has done with you. Through the voice of the student, He has warned you of your danger. Be fearful, for He has told you that you are burning in hell's fire, and give Him thanks because, sorrowful for your perdition, He has given you warning. You know that your sins cause Him to bleed and die on the cross, suffering great pain and injury.

"Take care of your soul, that's what you must do. Once it's lost, there is no greater loss, nor is there any way to make up for its loss.

Now leave me alone, for I suffer the greatest pain a miserable soul can imagine while I wait for God to have mercy on my torment. I want you to know that a year after I left this city, I met my death as I was leaving a gaming house, and God willed that my torment should not be eternal. Don't think I've come to tell you this because of the power of your conjurations, but because of God's great providence and mercy. He commanded me to give you this warning and to tell you that, if you don't take care of your soul, woe be unto you!"

As soon as Octavio uttered these words, he began to sigh and moan again. Dragging his chains behind him, he left the room. In his presence, doña Juana had listened to him bravely but, after he left, she was filled with fear and sorrow, not so much from having seen Octavio (a woman in love will brave anything) but from having heard his terrifying words. She understood them to be warnings from heaven, and she wondered if she might be close to death since such strange things were happening to her. So deeply did she feel this fear that she called out to her servants and fell to the floor, overcome by a cruel swoon. Her cry brought not only the servants but also the neighbors rushing into the room. Immediately they began to apply various remedies. Doña Juana would return to her senses only to faint again, over and over. This is how she spent the night, sometimes conscious, sometimes unconscious. The people who were attending her didn't dare leave her for fear she might die. They were also anxious to know what had brought on such a sudden illness. Sorrowing to see her so close to death, they kept asking her to tell them the cause, but all she would say was for them not to leave her alone because death was near. She kept begging them to call a confessor to give her the last sacraments.

In this confusion day came, and doña Juana showed no signs of improvement. By sheer force, they managed to undress her and put her to bed. When the lady saw it was day, she sent for don Fernando. He came and was amazed and saddened by her illness. He sat on her bed and asked her how she was feeling and what had happened. The beautiful doña Juana (shedding oceans of tears from her eyes) told him the story of the student and all about Octavio's apparition. She didn't omit a single detail and ended her story with these words:

"I, don Fernando, have only one soul. If it is lost, I have nothing else to lose. I have now received more than one warning from heaven, and it would be stupid for me to ignore these warnings until it's too late. I am aware of how faint your love for me is, and I know that you'll never marry me; you promised to marry me only to have your way with me. For two years now you've been deceiving me with your promises, and tomorrow will be no different from today. I've decided to end my days as a nun and, given the miracles that have happened to me, I don't expect to live much longer. Do not think I have chosen this path because I've been cheated of being your wife; I promise you that, even if you now were to try to marry me with all your heart and your mother's blessing, I wouldn't accept. The moment Octavio told me to watch out for my soul, I made up my mind to become Christ's bride and not yours, and this I have vowed.

"I need you to help me, to honor your obligation to me because of my love for you, which has not been small, considering the things I've done. You know that my estate is so limited that I don't have enough money for the dowry or for the other things I need to enter the convent of the Immaculate Conception, which is the convent where I choose to withdraw from all the trials and tribulations of this world. I need you to make up the difference and to negotiate my admission. As a woman disenchanted with the world, I beg you to watch out for yourself. Remember that one who suffers no trial or punishment in the pursuance of his vices has no sure salvation. What is sure is that God leaves us all free to go to hell."

Doña Juana fell silent, leaving her listeners astounded. Don Fernando felt as happy as if she'd given him a new lease on life, such was the power that Lucrecia had over him. He embraced doña Juana and praised her decision. Promising to help her in every way, he went to arrange her admission into the convent. They settled on a dowry of a thousand ducats, which don Fernando generously gave. He paid all the other expenses to outfit her properly and give the appropriate tips. The thousand ducats that doña Juana had inherited were to provide income for her expenses and to pay off the maids, to whom she gave her dresses, other clothes, and household goods. Within the week, she found herself wearing a nun's habit and happier than she'd ever been in all her life. She felt she'd found a refuge where she could seek salvation. By so narrowly escaping from the jaws of hell, she felt like she was in heaven.

Don Fernando thought it was incredible luck that he was free of the burden of his obligation to her because, if doña Juana hadn't miraculously withdrawn from the world, he would've had to marry her, a notion that had depressed him greatly, given his little love for her. He had, after all, been the one who had aroused her passion and won her through his deception. This is what often happens when love rules: men promise things they later deny when their desire has been satisfied and their passion has waned.

Now that don Fernando was free of doña Juana, he went more assiduously to Lucrecia's house. Seeing no obstacle to his devotion for her, she ceased using the full power of her spells, in the belief that she'd done enough already to keep him totally bound to her. This freedom gave don Fernando time to go to gaming houses where he gambled and squandered his own inheritance and Lucrecia's fortune as well. Neither source was sufficient to quench his insatiable thirst. He began to take loans, arranging the repayment for when he should inherit his full estate. In a very short time, he found that he had many ducats of debt. But he felt sure that, with his mother's death, he could fix everything and, given her age, he didn't think she'd last much longer.

His mother had known about his affair with doña Juana and, when she learned he was free of her, she thought he'd settle down. Now that don Fernando was not so bound by Lucrecia's spells, since she thought she had no rival to fear, don Fernando and his mother developed a plan. His mother wanted don Fernando to marry one of the most beautiful women then living in Toledo, whose virtue equaled her beauty. This lady, whose name was doña Clara, was the daughter of a merchant who'd made a great fortune through business not just in Spain but in Italy and in the Indies. Doña Clara was the merchant's only child, so all of his money was to go to her. There was, however, more falsehood than truth in the rumors of his wealth because the merchant had, in fact, gone bankrupt and was cleverly hiding his losses until he could marry off his daughter as her position merited.

Don Fernando's mother, as I said, set her sights on this lady. The eldest son and heir of a titled noble had also set his sights on her. He had no intention of marrying her even though he had fallen head over heels for her beauty. She granted him such small favors that even in Toledo she never gained a reputation for being either flirtatious or cruel. She permitted him to frequent her street, to serenade her, praising and celebrating her beauty, but never did she allow him any other liberty. The marquis (we shall call him by this title) tried in vain to overcome her distance, but doña Clara prized her virtue more than all his money could buy. Don Fernando's mother selected noble and clever intermediaries to arrange the marriage and, such was her good fortune, she had no trouble obtaining the lady's father's permission. Doña Clara understood the true intentions of the marquis and didn't trust him, so she promptly agreed to the proposed marriage. All the necessary arrangements were made, and she was wed to don Fernando. Her father gave her six thousand ducats as a present, explaining that the rest was tied up but, since she was his only child, she would ultimately inherit everything.

This is how the lamb fell into the wolf's power, we might say. Don Fernando was pleased to pay off his most pressing debts with this sum. Two months after doña Clara's marriage, her father realized that it was impossible for him to keep his promise and give as much money for the dowry as he'd promised. He gathered up all the money he had left after the six thousand ducats he'd given her and quietly left Toledo. He went to Seville where he took a boat to the Indies. This left his daughter with a thousand troubles because don Fernando had only married her for her money, and the six thousand ducats had already been spent on lavish clothes, things for the house, and paying off his debts. Within two days of learning she was penniless, he demonstrated his lack of love for her by turning the small attentions he had previously observed into open distaste and even hatred. The poor lady paid dearly for her father's deception, even though don Fernando's mother tried to shield and defend her because of her innocence and virtue.

Lucrecia learned of don Fernando's marriage when it was too late; it had already taken place. To avenge herself, she invoked her diabolical arts and drove him to his sickbed. She tormented him so he could scarcely move; all he could do was moan. For the six months the illness lasted, no one could discover what was causing it. The constant medications the doctors gave him only served to deplete his already meager estate. At last the sorceress realized that keeping Fernando ill contributed more to losing him than to avenging herself, so she ceased tormenting him and he began to get better. Lucrecia changed her treacherous intent, however, causing him to hate his wife. As a result, once he recovered he went back to his old ways and spent most of his time in Lucrecia's company.

The marquis, devastated by doña Clara's marriage, also paid for his sorrow with his health. He recovered from his illness but not from his love. He began to serve and court doña Clara anew, but she refused him any favor. She wouldn't even let him set eyes on her. Her distance only increased his passion.

Then don Fernando's mother died, and doña Clara lost her shield and her defense. Don Fernando likewise lost the restraint that had kept him from treating his wife as harshly as he would from now on. He spent whole days and nights without ever going home or seeing her. This treatment upset doña Clara so deeply that she knew no comfort, particularly when she learned the cause of her husband's crazy behavior.

The marquis was not unaware of doña Clara's suffering. Her face, her whole mien, revealed her deep sorrow, but her virtue and discretion were such that he could make no contact with her. He couldn't get her to accept a letter or even a jewel, despite the greatness of her need. Because of don Fernando's constant gambling and his incredible debts, their money had run out. There was nothing left and doña Clara was forced now to sell her dresses and her jewels in order to support the two little girls that the four years of her marriage to don Fernando had brought. She had to pay a maid to do the heavy work because don Fernando never came home any more. Despite these hardships, she would not give in to the marquis's pleading, nor could her friends or the maid get her to accept the gifts he tried to send through them. Whenever they broached this subject, she would say that the woman who takes soon must give.

At this point, the relationship between don Fernando and Lucrecia became public knowledge. The police began to follow don Fernando and set out to get Lucrecia. Someone warned Lucrecia in time, which gave her no choice but to flee from Toledo. Hastily she gathered up her household, which now included don Fernando, and they moved to Seville where they lived together as man and wife. He had long since forgotten all about his true wife and their daughters.

This new trial grieved doña Clara greatly. It was a miracle it didn't kill her. It seemed as if God were keeping her for even greater tests of her virtue. For over a year and a half she received not a word from or about don Fernando. She suffered such hardship that she could no longer afford the maid. She took to wearing humble clothing and worked day and night to support herself and her little girls. She kept her own house, and she herself collected and delivered embroidery for a shop, a job that is more available in the city of Toledo than anywhere else. One night when she was up late trying to finish some embroidery that she had to deliver the next morning, she sang to herself. She sang this ballad to express her love, sorrow, grief, and loneliness, and to keep herself awake:

Fugitive little bird
flying through the air,
inconstant to my attentions,
ungrateful for my love,
if you were infatuated
with a woman of your nature
such a sweet prison
would never tire you.
I never pretended not to know:
from knowing how to love
I came to know your love
to be half-hearted at the most.
One who loves is never deceived
even though he lets himself be deceived;
for Love, in his own court,
makes public disclosures.
What can the loving person do
when he knows he's been given
surreptitious poison
but drink it down in silence?
I let my fears be lulled
although I knew my weakness,
all the while you dissembled
until you tired of the deception.
I see you so distant,
cold, and faithless;
even when I call you back
you refuse to pay me heed.
Listen, my free little bird,
listen to my loving words
calling to you in sad tones,
hear my words.
Fickle little bird,
come back! Where are you going?
Come back to the cage in my heart,
have pity on my sorrows.
When you see me captive
you seek your freedom;
repay prison with prison,
then will you be complete.
As a wise man once said,
let love repay love;
and if your heart fails in that,
it is as hard as stone.
Because of you, my eyes
are an ocean of tears;
here you will find sweet drink

never failing.
My heart for your nourishment,
my freedom for your prison,
these arms your bonds,
while all this awaits you,
you flee without heeding my plaints.
God will that wherever you go
you are treated as you treat me,
never finding love!
I, lamenting my deception,
would end my life,
sensing in your madness
my death and your freedom."
This was said to a little bird
as he flew from his prison
by a heart sore wounded
but loyally devoted.
At the end of these sad plaints,
my heart, an instrument untuned,
sang to the free little bird
fleeing fugitive:
"Free little bird, you are the loser,
for the prize you leave behind
you will never find again."

The room where doña Clara was working was on the ground floor,
and it had a grated window opening onto the street. Outside, don
Sancho had been listening. This is the name of the marquis, her suitor,
or lover if you can call a man a lover who has so little hope of ever
being accepted. In a lovesick heart, love increases when it hears the
laments of the beloved, so, when don Sancho heard doña Clara's sad
plaints, her woes touched him to the depths of his soul. He knocked
at the window. The noise frightened doña Clara, and she asked who
it was.

"It is I, beautiful Clara, who else could it be?" don Sancho replied.
"Please listen a moment. Who could it be except the man who wor-
ships your beauty and considers even your disdain a personal favor
that gives hope to his life?"

"I don't know how you can hope, don Sancho," doña Clara said,
opening the window, "or what might make you feel any hope. Ever
since my marriage, I have never encouraged your friendship or acknowledged it in any way that might let you feel encouraged, in spite
of the intermediaries you send with gifts and letters. If you're counting
on the courtesy with which I allowed you to serve me before I mar-

ried, be aware that that was merely a maiden's way; I didn't love but let myself be loved, careful never to compromise my honor. Now I have a husband. Rightly or wrongly, heaven gave him to me, and so long as heaven doesn't take him away, I shall keep my faith with him as I have vowed.

"Because this is how things are, if you truly love me, the greatest proof you can give of your love would be to cease giving motive to what the neighbors might think of a powerful and gallant man like you besieging the doors of a young woman whose husband is absent. This is especially important because the whole city of Toledo knows my great need, and they might easily think that through it you have bought my honor."

"Your need is what I want to remedy, beautiful Clara," don Sancho said. "My only interest is to relieve your troubles. Please be so kind as to accept a thousand escudos. You need do me no other favor, for I give you my word, being the gentleman I am, that I shall never approach you again."

"There are no debts, don Sancho," doña Clara replied, "more easily repaid than those of affection, an example of which is your generosity. But I cannot trust myself, nor can I obligate myself for what I cannot repay. I have a husband. He will look out for me and for his daughters. If he doesn't, still I must believe that he will, and he cannot expect otherwise of me until the day he dies."

With these words, she shut the window. Her response left don Sancho so deeply in love that he could no more desist from his love than she could demean her virtue.

Don Fernando had left Toledo a year and a half before. No one knew his whereabouts until one day some gentlemen who'd been in Seville on business returned to Toledo. They told doña Clara they'd seen don Fernando in that city. This was such momentous news for doña Clara that there's no way to describe her reaction. From that moment on, she was determined to find him and try to make him come back home. First she needed to find somewhere to leave her daughters while she was away on this trip.

Doña Juana, now a nun leading a saintly life in her convent, with a comfortable income and the happiest person in the world, was not unaware of this turn of events. She thanked God that she hadn't been don Fernando's unfortunate victim. Somehow she learned of doña Clara's decision and her need to find a place to leave the girls who, by this time, were four and five years old. Doña Juana sent for doña

Clara and explained to her who she was, in case she didn't already know. Doña Juana described all the favors heaven had bestowed upon her by bringing her to her present situation. She went on to say how sorry she felt for all of doña Clara's tribulations, how much she admired her virtue and patience in bearing them. Doña Juana also informed doña Clara that she'd learned that doña Clara wanted to go to Seville and was looking for someone to care for her daughters. She asked doña Clara to bring the girls to her and she would keep them, not just while doña Clara was away, but always, as if they were her own and, when they grew up, she'd give them a dowry so they could join her in the religious life. Doña Clara should believe that she did this out of compassion and not because of the love she'd once felt for their father.

Doña Clara thanked doña Juana for her generous offer, which she accepted immediately. Not wishing to delay her departure a minute longer, she gathered up the few possessions she had left, including her bed, and took them and her daughters to doña Juana, who had obtained the archbishop's permission to take them under her care. The gatekeeper let them in. Doña Juana embraced doña Clara tightly and, her eyes brimming with tears, she placed in doña Clara's hands a purse containing four hundred silver reales. That very afternoon, upon saying good-bye, doña Clara set out for Seville in a cart, leaving doña Juana delighted with her new daughters.

Doña Clara got to Seville but, as she was on what you might call a wild goose chase, she had no idea where to find don Fernando. The city was huge and had so many inhabitants that she spent three months there without finding a shred of information about him. She had paid some bills in Toledo, which left her only a hundred reales, and now her money ran out. On the verge of starving to death, she despaired of finding any solution to her problems. Going back to Toledo wouldn't change anything, so she decided to stay in Seville until she succeeded in finding don Fernando. To keep body and soul together, she looked for a house where she could get a job as a maid. She approached various people, especially in church, and one lady said she knew a place where she might do very well serving as a companion to a lady now quite elderly. This lady might not want to hire her, however, because of the fact that doña Clara was very beautiful and the lady had a young husband.

Doña Clara (modestly and feeling ashamed) asked her for the address so she could try her luck. The lady gave it to her with a message for the mistress of the house who was her friend. Doña Clara went to the house, which was right by the main church. She entered and noted that it was beautifully furnished (a clear sign that the owners were rich). The door was standing open so she walked into the main parlor without knocking. Seated on a very rich couch she saw Lucre-cia, her husband's mistress. Doña Clara recognized her instantly from having seen her once in Toledo. Next to her sat don Fernando, in-formally dressed because of the summer heat. He was strumming a guitar and singing a ballad. In order not to interrupt, doña Clara waited to give her message, astonished at the sight she was seeing and particularly amazed that they didn't notice her.

Now over the eastern balcony
dawn begins to unfurl
and spill her copious light
across the flowering fields.
Now she captures
the lovely flowers
edged with dew;
enviously the springs
spill forth their crystal drops.
Now she calls her beloved brother
from lighting the Indies
in his golden coach, everywhere
sowing lilies and carnations.
Now the peaks of mountain ranges
stand silhouetted
by the heavenly music
of all the little birds.
Now the skies see themselves
reflected in the running rivers
as their clear crystal turns
to deep turquoise blue.
Now winter has become summer
and autumn spring;
the valleys lovely havens
and the meadows paradise,
because the heavenly feet
of Anarda tread their freshness;
Anarda, sweet prison of many hearts,
basilisk of the village.
A gallant shepherd
follows in her footsteps;
since he resembles Narcissus in beauty,
let him be called Narcissus.

He is the one who made Venus,
forgetful of her beloved Adonis,
descend from her heavenly couch
so she could gaze on him.
The one for whom beautiful Salmacis
in the loving company of nymphs
decided to become
an eternal hermaphrodite.
Foiling the fears
of her suspicious husband,
Anarda left her village
to meet with her Narcissus.
She comes to a clear spring
surrounded by myrtles and willows;
pleasantly they meet,
happily in love.
Tenderly they sit
by that divine tree,
triumph of the lord of Delos,
cruel punishment to his Daphne.
In this delightful place,
thirsting for each other's favors,
they drink in the nectar of their breaths
through the fine coral shells of their lips.
The child, son of Venus,
closed the gates to the meadow,
for only Cupid can enclose
a meadow within his gates.
Everything else that happened
only the tall trees saw,
turning their leaves into eyes
and their buds into ears.

The moment don Fernando ended his song, Lucrecia asked doña Clara what she was seeking. Doña Clara replied that her friend, the lady doña Lorenza, had sent her to see if she was suitable to be the maid Lucrecia was needing. Lucrecia commanded her to sit facing don Fernando. He looked straight at her but did not recognize her. It was as if he'd never before in his life laid eyes on her. This astounded doña Clara. To herself she gave thanks to God for having found for her what she had been unable to find on her own. She felt truly sorry to see him so estranged, so different but, being sensitive, she recognized that what produced this effect was the bewitchment of that Circe who sat before her.

Lucrecia, pleased with doña Clara's appearance and modesty, asked her where she was from.

"I'm from Toledo," doña Clara responded.

"Whatever brought you to this city?" Lucrecia asked.

"Madam," doña Clara said, "although I'm from Toledo, I didn't live there, but in Madrid. I came with a couple who were on their way to the Indies. Just at the time of departure, I fell ill and had to stay here, much to their disappointment. They left and my illness lasted for three months. I spent every cent I had. Seeing no other alternative, today I asked the lady doña Lorenza, whom I chanced to see at church, if she needed a companion, as is the custom in this city, and she sent me here. So if your grace has not yet found someone to serve her, rest assured that I know how to please because I'm an honorable and noble woman who once had her own house and lived in ease."

Impressed with such intelligence and virtue, Lucrecia was so pleased and delighted with Clara (she used her very own name) that neither one had any difficulty in coming to an agreement; they didn't even haggle. Clara stayed at the house, on one hand happy that she'd found what she was looking for and on the other troubled to see don Fernando so changed that he didn't recognize her. Furthermore, right before her eyes, he caressed and fondled a woman who in her age and in her appearance was not worthy of him. Arming herself with patience until the right moment should come, Clara made up her mind to bear everything she might have to witness.

Lucrecia gave her new maid the keys to everything and charged her with attending to the master and supervising the two slaves. She was only barred from entering one room up in an attic, because Lucrecia reserved this room for her own use. She kept the key and no other person ever went with her when she so cautiously entered that room. Although Clara tried to see what was inside, she couldn't. She suspected that this was Lucrecia's office for the sorcery by which she kept don Fernando so blind that he knew nothing, that he cared for nothing but loving and caressing his Lucrecia. He made such a good husband to Lucrecia that Clara would have been happy with half of those attentions.

More than a year passed with the three living together in this fashion, and Clara's masters became quite fond of her. In each regular mail Clara sent a letter to doña Juana describing the events in her life, and doña Juana would answer with encouraging advice so she wouldn't weaken in her resolution or give up until she had solved her problem.

Then one day Lucrecia took to her bed with a serious illness. Don Fernando became so upset that he almost went crazy. Lucrecia couldn't get out of bed, her fever was so high. After being bedridden for three or four days, she called Clara and spoke these words with genuine tenderness:

"Friend Clara, you've been with me for a year, and I've treated you more as a daughter than as a maid. If I survive this illness, I shall treat you even better in the future and, if I die, I'll leave you enough to get along on comfortably. I know you're grateful, but I remind you of these obligations so that you'll keep the secret that I'm about to tell you. Here, my child, take this key and go up to the attic to the room you already know about. Go inside and you'll find a large old chest. Inside it is a rooster. Feed him. Right there in the same room you'll find the grain. And, daughter, under no circumstances should you remove the blinders he's wearing. This matter is as dear to me as my life. If I should die of this illness, I beg of you, before your master or anyone else should find the rooster, dig a hole out in the corral and bury him just the way he is, wearing his blinders and the chain that ties him to the chest, and bury the sack of grain with him. This is the favor you must do for me."

Clara listened attentively to her mistress's words and instantly in her imagination a thousand thoughts began to whirl around, all leading to the same conclusion. To keep Lucrecia from suspecting any malice in her silence, she replied quickly, thanking her for the favor she showed by entrusting such an important and weighty secret to her. Clara promised to do to the letter exactly what she'd been instructed. She took the key and went to see the rooster with the blinders.

She climbed up to the attic. She entered the room and approached the chest, thinking seriously about what she was doing and about the reputation Lucrecia had had in Toledo. Covered with a cold sweat, she felt such great fear that she was about to turn back. But taking as much heart as she could muster and recovering the courage she had momentarily lost, at last she opened the chest. The moment she lifted the lid, she saw a rooster with a neck-ring chaining him to the chest. He was wearing little manacles on his feet and blinders over his eyes just like the ones that are put on horses to keep them from seeing.

So astonished and absorbed by this sight was Clara that she was unaware of what she was doing. She was both laughing hilariously and crossing herself at the same time. She suspected that most probably the rooster was the charm that bewitched her husband, rendering him so blind that he didn't even recognize her, his true wife. Since women desire what's forbidden, she felt a great temptation to remove the blinders. No sooner thought than done! After she took off the blinders, she fed the rooster and then shut everything up as it had been before and returned to her mistress, who was waiting for her. The instant Lucrecia saw her she said:

"My friend, did you feed the rooster? You didn't take off his blinders, did you?"

"No madam," Clara replied. "Why should I do anything contrary to your orders?" She added that Lucrecia should realize that Clara served her with great pleasure and cheerfully did as ordered.

When dinnertime came, don Fernando returned home. He asked Lucrecia how she was feeling and sat down at the table next to the bed where the slaves served him dinner. Clara was in the kitchen supervising everything and sending the plates to the table. When dinner was over, she went up to her masters' room. The instant don Fernando set his eyes on her, he recognized her. With great astonishment, like a man seeing a fantastic vision, he exclaimed:

"Doña Clara, what are you doing here? How did you get here? Who told you where I was? What kind of dress is that you're wearing? Where are my daughters? I must be dreaming! You're the wife I left in Toledo, helpless and penniless! What an unchristian and dastardly deed! Answer me! Don't keep me in suspense! I'm overwhelmed to see a sight I never expected to see again!"

Doña Clara replied:

"Well, husband, this is a fine time for you to show concern. I've been in this house for a year, serving you like a wretched slave, all because of the tricks of this Circe here, and now you ask me what I'm doing here!"

"You traitor!" Lucrecia shrieked at this moment. "You took the blinders off the rooster! But don't think you'll ever get don Fernando back! Your clever trick won't do you any good!"

She leapt suddenly from the bed with more energy than seemed possible, seeing her lying there so ill and weak. She ran to her desk and took out the wax figure of a man. Then she took a huge pin from the desk and jabbed it through the head so violently that it penetrated down into the body. She rushed to the fireplace and hurled it into the flames. She dashed back to the desk, grabbed a knife and, with the greatest cruelty you can imagine, she plunged it into her heart and fell dead beside the desk.

Lucrecia did all this so quickly that neither don Fernando, doña Clara, or the slaves could do anything to stop her. They were all in a state of shock.

They screamed and cried out, which attracted many people. Several police officers entered with the other people, and they held don Fernando and the other members of the household for questioning. First they took the confessions of the slaves, who recounted what they had witnessed. Next they heard the truth from don Fernando. He explained how Lucrecia had been his mistress and told the police everything that had happened between the two lovers from the first day they met until the present.

When doña Clara's turn came to make a statement, she said she wouldn't make a declaration except in the presence of the mayor. She also said that, rather than her going to his presence, in this case it was important to her honor for him to come to that house.

The police went to report the case to the mayor and informed him of her request. As soon as he heard the police report, he came immediately, accompanied by all the noblest gentlemen of Seville, who had heard about the strange case. In the presence of all those people, doña Clara told them who she was and what had happened, without omitting a single detail. Then she had the chest containing the rooster brought down from the attic. She herself opened it with the key hidden under the pillow on Lucrecia's bed. Everyone stared at the rooster with his manacles, his chain, and the blinders that doña Clara had removed and dropped beside him.

Astonished, the mayor picked up the blinders and put them on the rooster. Instantly don Fernando reverted to the way he'd been before. He didn't recognize doña Clara at all, it was as if he'd never seen her before in his life. When he beheld Lucrecia lying on the floor with the knife through her heart and bathed in her own blood, he rushed over and took her in his arms. He caressed her and uttered a thousand laments and demanded punishment for the one who had committed such a foul crime.

Then the mayor removed the blinders from the rooster. Don Fernando instantly recovered his right mind. Three or four times he performed this test, and every time was just the same. The mayor was finally convinced and acknowledged that everything they'd said must be true. He ordered everyone to leave the house and locked the doors. He had every desk and closet and even the most remote nooks and corners searched. In Lucrecia's desk, the police found a thousand charms and articles she used to make herself appear beautiful and attractive to don Fernando. These strange objects filled them with fear and wonderment. Satisfied at last with the truth, the police set don Fernando and doña Clara free. They kept the slaves in jail until they were sure that they'd had no part in the sorcery. The court confiscated the house for the Crown. Every item they found, including the rooster and the body of the wretched Lucrecia, was burned in the public plaza. Her soul was already burning in hell in payment for her sins, her wicked life, and her foul death.

The moment the charms were burned, don Fernando took sick. Gradually his health deteriorated and his life was consumed. Doña Clara sold the dress and other little items she'd acquired in Lucrecia's house. With this money and the salary the court had ordered her paid for her service in that house, she and don Fernando, now extremely ill, were able to board a coach for Toledo. They thought, and the doctors concurred, that don Fernando might recover his health there, because it was his birthplace and the air was more salubrious. But it was hopeless. As soon as they arrived in Toledo, he took to his bed and slowly began to die, suffering greatly.

If it hadn't been for doña Juana, who sent them food from her convent, they wouldn't have had a bite to eat. Don Fernando lasted for two months. During this time, he came to realize how much he owed to doña Clara. He loved her so deeply that he couldn't bear to be parted from her for a minute. Finally the hour of his death arrived. He received the sacraments with great sorrow and contrition for his many sins and gave up his soul to his Creator. The doctors found that he'd suffered from no physical illness but had been consumed and killed by Lucrecia's spells.

Doña Clara felt his loss so greatly that there was no solace for her, and she almost followed him in death. Even though she'd only enjoyed his love while he was ill and they were so needy, she had hoped don Fernando would live many years, especially when she saw how deeply he loved her during the last few days of his life.

At this point doña Clara found herself without a cent to bury don Fernando. Her only succor was God. She didn't dare make this request to doña Juana. Doña Juana had already done more than enough by keeping and supporting her daughters for so long. She decided to sell her poor bed, which left her no place to sleep. But God had not forgotten doña Clara's virtue or overlooked her great suffering. It so happened that just at this time don Sancho came back to the city. Ever since doña Clara had left Toledo, he'd lived in retirement (on the estate that he inherited upon his father's death. He'd chosen not to marry although he had ample opportunity to do so, being who he was). In letters from a servant who'd married in Toledo, don Sancho had kept up with what was going on in the city.

Yearning to see the beloved mistress of his heart, his true love and not just a passing fancy, he entered the city on the same day that doña Clara found herself in such a bind. When don Sancho learned what her situation was, the enamored youth couldn't bear it. He went to the lady's house to give his condolences. He himself arranged don Fernando's funeral to be as grand as possible. Don Sancho accompanied the body to the cemetery, just as if it were his father's funeral, accompanied by all the gentlemen in Toledo, who had paid no attention to don Fernando during his last days because of his poverty.

After the burial, he and the whole illustrious company returned to doña Clara's humble house. There, in the presence of so many noblemen, he said these words:

"Beautiful Clara, in burying the body of your late husband, I have done only what charity requires. You and the entire city well understand the will with which I have done this. My love comes from my heart alone, as you've never shown me more favor than your chaste respect. I have felt like this since before you had a husband. After you married, I was not even favored with a glimpse of you, in spite of my many efforts. All were fruitless thanks to your great virtue, and I love you all the more for it. I now have no father to obstruct my desire, nor do you have any reason not to be mine. It's proper for you to repay my love and the debt you owe my constancy by saying the simple yes that I beg of you and which I myself say first to you.

"I'm not alone in my high regard for you. All men in the world are indebted to women like you, who, by their great virtue, earn the love of those who had simply desired them. Please do not postpone my glory or deprive yourself of the reward you deserve. Your daughters will find a good father in me, and you will have a slave who forever adores your beauty."

The only answer doña Clara could give don Sancho was to throw herself at his feet, telling him that she was his slave and he should accept her as such.

Everyone who'd come to give their condolences, instead, gave their congratulations. The normal church procedures were followed, with the banns and everything else. In the meantime, doña Clara stayed with the mayor, who was a relative of don Sancho's. Don Sancho obtained the king's blessing for their marriage and, after the proper time, they were wed. It seemed as if at last heaven were on their side and trying to reward doña Clara's virtue.

After the wedding, don Sancho dowered doña Clara's daughters, who had decided to stay in the convent with doña Juana and become nuns. Doña Juana's wise decision inspired this enchantment and gave it the first part of its title, "disillusionment in love," for it isn't easy for one who loves to accept the truth.

Doña Clara lived many years with her don Sancho. They had beautiful children who inherited their father's estates. Because of her virtue, doña Clara was loved and appreciated beyond all imagining, for this is how heaven "rewards virtue."

Phyllis ended her enchantment late. The ladies and gentlemen praised it at length. They commented on doña Juana's wise awakening, on the astonishing part about the diabolical rings and Octavio's apparition, on doña Clara's virtue and constancy, on don Fernando's blindness and Lucrecia's willfulness, and especially on the funny part about the rooster with his little blinders. When supper was served, however, they didn't linger in leaving their places and getting to the table. They dined with great delight. Everyone felt good because Lisarda and Lysis prudently had asked don Juan and don Diego to promise to be friends. And this is how the third night ended.

Fourth Night

All the illustrious ladies and gentlemen assembled in beautiful Lysis's house much earlier than on the previous days because, to celebrate their reconciliation, don Juan and don Diego each wanted to host a dinner for all the guests on the two remaining days of the festivities. Tonight it was don Juan's turn. He wanted to be free on the last night, as he was to tell his enchantment then. With this understanding, he arranged a sumptuous meal, and every detail showed his exquisite taste and liberal generosity. The remainder of the afternoon was spent in dancing. With much grace and skill, the participants competed with one another in dress, bearing, elegance, and courtliness for, at this soiree, everyone knew who was courting whom. Don Diego and Lysis in particular were more open in expressing their feelings, now that don Diego had been formally accepted as Lysis's betrothed by Lysis and her mother.

As night fell and the time came to begin their delightful entertainment, Lysis, accompanied by the musicians, sang this song:

Now, Love, I am so afraid
from hoping and loving,
that I only know how to recognize
my disenchantment, albeit too late.
Reason may command me to protect
my life from your deceit;
already I am regretful,
for a woman of worth,

should she risk her love,
may find it's not returned.

I know, Love, what you're up to,
even at the expense of my love,
for to follow after your caprices
has certainly not been easy.
To love a faithless man,
can there be greater misfortune?
Curses upon the woman who tries
to attract the constant man
so as not to waste
her beauty and her worth!

When you hear a man tell
a woman she is fickle,
when he is like a weathervane,
can you fail to laugh?
They pretend loyalty
without seeing that they'll lose;
one should look carefully
when he pretends to be loyal,
that would be like a magic spell
that promises what it cannot give.

Lysis cut don Juan deeply with these three stanzas, and even don
Diego was saddened by them. Lysis reassured him with a thousand
discreet words, saying that they weren't her own verses but someone
else's she'd borrowed so she wouldn't have to compose her own. This
explanation satisfied her lover. Don Miguel saw that everyone was
waiting for him, so he took his seat and began like this:

"People get just what they deserve, that's common knowledge. Evil
always has its punishment just as good has its reward, if not in this
world, then certainly in the next. My enchantment shows this clearly,
and it goes like this":

Just Desserts

When the court of the Catholic King Philip III was in the rich and beautiful city of Valladolid, a certain gentleman left a club where he had gone to while away the tedious hours of the long December night in conversation. It was sometime after midnight. He was a noble son of the city of Madrid. The former capital, now bereft of her beloved king because of his disdain and neglect of her, decided to send her dearest and noblest remaining sons to serve the king and oblige him to love her as she loved him. The gentleman crossed one of the main streets in Valladolid on his way to his lodging and turned a corner at an intersection. Suddenly he saw the door of a rather modest house fly open. A white form was hurled violently outside. Because he was on the other side of the street, which was spacious and wide, he couldn't make out what that shape was, but he thought it was a person. It fell from the doorstep onto the ground and made a loud, heavy thud, as the ground was very hard from the heavy winter frost. The door slammed shut. The form remained motionless. Then he heard a low sobbing and a voice saying:

"Oh, heaven, have you abandoned me? Are you deaf to my sorrows? Untouched by my tears? Uncaring about my suffering?"

The form attempted to get up, but apparently the pain from the fall made it impossible. Don Garcia (this was the gentleman's name) felt deeply moved by these laments, so he approached and asked what was wrong, offering to help.

"Oh, sir," the shape cried out, "by the suffering of Christ, if you

215

feel greater compassion than the people who have put me in this situation, please help me get up and take me somewhere where my life
will be safe. Here it's not safe because, I assure you, I have more
enemies than friends."

When don Garcia heard these words, he was astounded because the
speaker appeared to be a woman. He drew closer and, by the dim
light of the cloud-covered moon, he saw that his suspicion was correct.
He was even more surprised to note that the woman was dressed only
in her petticoat. Curious to learn more about this intriguing situation,
he took her by the hand and helped her up. She was in such bad shape
that she could hardly stand. Don Garcia removed his cloak and
wrapped it around her. Encouraging her as much as he could, he
supported the poor woman in his compassionate arms, almost carrying
her battered body away from that street. When the lady realized he'd
stopped to decide what to do with her, sighing and weeping, she said
to him:

"Sir, now is not the time for you to desist from the great favor you
have done me. If I am found, my life is in peril, and by now there
must be many people looking for me. If you know of any safe hiding
place to put me up for the night, I beg you out of kindness please
take me there. Tomorrow I shall go to a convent. Do not stop helping
me now; when you learn who I am and hear my terrible story from
the beginning, you will see how fortunate you are to have found me."

"My lady," don Garcia replied, "I have only recently come to this
court; I've been here just two weeks, so I don't know anyone but
myself to whom I can entrust your care. If you're willing to come to
my lodging and aren't afraid to place yourself in the keeping of a
young stranger, then I will gladly serve you. If this is not to your
pleasure, tell me where you'd like me to take you, for in no way will
I disobey your command."

"Sir, let us go to your lodging," the lady replied. "Any place I know
to go would be discovered. Let's go quickly, before I'm found and
have to pay for a crime of which I am innocent. Mine was a crime I
only thought about committing, although people will blame me for
having restored my honor. I shall try to repay you for helping me."

As soon as she said this, they started off for don Garcia's inn. They
advanced with great difficulty because, in spite of all his encouragement, the lady could hardly stand on her feet. With much assistance
from don Garcia, they finally arrived at his room. The rest of the
house, occupied by the landlady and other guests, was dark, but the

landlady had left a light in his room. When they entered, don Garcia was able to see what he had found.

The moment he beheld his new companion, he thought she was an angel, not a woman, so great was the beauty, the purity, and composure of her face. She looked about twenty-four, and her beauty was so stunning that, without his being able to help it, the splendor of her eyes stole his heart. If don Garcia hadn't reminded himself of the faith she'd placed in him, he might have dared to play Tarquin to such a divine Lucrecia. Showing his nobility instead of his burning love, his sensibility more than his desire, his reason rather than his lust, with many gentle caresses he tried to make the lovely lady comfortable. It was and time to go to bed. The lady was improperly dressed and at the moment he had no clothes to give her. She was in such bad shape that he urged her to sleep in his bed.

The lady couldn't do otherwise. Not wanting to ask her anything about herself or about how he'd come to find her in such a situation at that time of night, don Garcia sat with her until she fell asleep. He left the room and locked the door from outside. He slipped into the room of another guest with whom he'd made friends, telling him that he'd lost the key to his own room and couldn't get in until morning.

The rest of the night seemed ages long to don Garcia, so attracted was he to the lovely lady and so eager to learn the cause of her great misfortune.

The moment day arrived he got dressed, told his friend he'd found the key, and went to his room to greet his beautiful guest. Apparently she'd slept little. Indeed her eyes looked as if she'd spent the whole night crying. The weeping hadn't diminished her divine beauty but it was clear that under happier circumstances she would have no equal.

Don Garcia sat down on the bed and asked her how she was. She thanked him for the help he'd given and asked if he'd gone out, if he'd heard what the news was in Valladolid.

"No, my lady," don Garcia responded, "because, if I'm to tell you the truth, my only desire was to see you and hear about your sorrows. I beg you not to keep me in suspense any longer, I'm very anxious to know."

"That doesn't surprise me, don Garcia," replied the lady, who by now had learned his name. "My story would amaze anyone who heard it. When you hear it from the beginning, it will really astound you. It's so strange you'll think it's one of those fabulous tales people tell in the winter by the fireside instead of a real story. It's about a woman who yesterday was the most highly regarded woman in Valladolid and today is the scandal and shock of the city. To keep you from being confused, I'll start at the beginning with my childhood, and someday you can tell my tale in your native city when it pleases God to take you back there. In return, I ask only that you keep the door locked; no one must know I'm here. I won't feel safe once my misfortune is known.

"My name, sir, is Hipolita. By this evening, you will hear about my nobility and my position. Even if you don't believe what I say about myself, one's status is never falsified when people gossip and recount shocking events. Everyone will tell you what you may not wish to believe from me, and you'll find out exactly who I am and who I have been. I was born here in this city to parents both noble and wealthy, and the misfortune that always attends beauty was born with me; I dare to give myself this praise because the whole city considers it true. As soon as I reached the age when beauty, elegance, discretion, and wit begin to flower in a woman, my parents had an infinite number of suitors who wanted to become members of the family. They sought to marry me more for my beauty than for my parents' rich estates, which were vast.

"Among my many suitors, the most outstanding were two gentlemen who were neighbors; there was only a wall separating their apartment from ours. They were brothers, and both wore the habit of the noble Order of Alcantara, to show how noble they were. When they began to court me, I knew nothing of love or of its power and sway; my only desire was to give my parents pleasure. My parents, well satisfied with both of the brothers, selected don Pedro, the elder, and rejected don Luis, the younger, who must have loved me more, since he was the more unfortunate. Don Pedro prized his marriage to me as a man who had won everything he'd ever wanted. I could tell how highly he regarded me from his many attentions and gifts. Would to God I had been sensible and grateful for his love, and so averted the misfortunes that have befallen me and the ones I have yet to suffer!

"For eight years I enjoyed my husband's caresses and he enjoyed my true love. I learned to love don Pedro despite my brother-in-law's courtship, which didn't stop even after he saw me married to his brother. Don Luis told me he loved me every time he had the chance. I don't think he expected me to return his love, he only wanted me to appreciate his attentions. At least that's how I understood it. He seemed sensible and Christian, though love often overwhelms the precepts of both. That's what I now think must have happened to him. I offered to marry him to my cousin, who's wealthier and more beautiful than I, so he had the opportunity to marry another woman and separate himself from my love, but he wouldn't. I bore this difficult situation as sensibly as I could. Sometimes I pretended not to understand his intentions; sometimes I reproached and cautioned him, and often I gave him the best and wisest advice my intelligence could provide. I would scold him and reprove him for his impropriety, swearing to tell his brother if he didn't quit his mad and unholy ways. Despite all this, don Luis, sometimes happy, sometimes sad, always loving and praising my beauty, nourished his love by looking at me, visiting me, and conversing with me. As our houses were next door to each other, his visits were quite frequent. With each visit, his love increased.

"Then, as you know, the court moved to this city. Would that God had heeded all the cries, tears, and complaints of those who rued this change but clamored out in vain. If the court hadn't come here, I would have been spared these misfortunes, for that was the cause of all my woes. Among the many parasites who follow the court, there was one whose name was don Gaspar. Portuguese in nationality, a soldier by profession, he hoped to receive his reward for the many services he'd done the Spanish king in Flanders and elsewhere. For that reason, he followed all the people who followed all the chancellors or, more accurately, all the chaotic confusion that the court and all its sycophants really are. Since their business is never accomplished as quickly as they would like, they have to wait month in, month out, year in, year out and don Gaspar's business was very long and drawn out. Idly, he began to frequent gambling establishments where he stood to lose his good name and his estate. Then, idly, he looked for someone to entertain him, who, to my misfortune, turned out to be me.

"One day he saw me in Our Lady of San Llorente church. He said I captured his heart. Soon what he'd sought for entertainment, he began to pursue from passionate love. Truly he robbed me of my love, my peace of mind, and my good name, all in the wink of an eye. Such was his gallantry, wit, and charm that even without the other graces that society calls gifts of nature, like music and poetry, his were enough to conquer and win the heart of any woman who saw him, let alone the heart of one courted and praised by him. Poor me! How his charms still affect my heart! I no longer cherish them but blame them for bringing me to my present situation. I can never again be the person I really am, nor can I ever go back to the happy life I enjoyed before I met don Gaspar.

"I learned of his love from one of my maids (fierce spy and crafty persecutor of my honor). From her, he likewise learned of my gratitude and affection. Through her, we wrote letters when we couldn't see each other in consideration of my honor and my husband's honorable nature. Although don Pedro wasn't a jealous man, he was scrupulous. That's how our love progressed.

"Don Gaspar really regretted that I was married, and I regretted it even more. There can be no greater misfortune for one in love than to be married already, especially if she no longer loves her husband. I came to feel resentful of my husband because I was in love with don Gaspar. Even if I hadn't resented don Pedro, his company couldn't give me pleasure because it kept me from my love. Don Gaspar first broached the subject of love with me in church, expressing a thousand endearments and sorrows. The more my love grew, the more my honor weakened and began to fall by the wayside. He expressed himself even more eloquently in his letters because in them he could state his love without restraint and say the most passionate things and write the saddest laments.

"I recall one night when I was fortunate to hear his divine voice singing sad verses. If you'd like to hear them, I can recite them, and you'll understand my weakness, for it's no miracle for a woman to surrender to a well-presented complaint."

"Please do," don Garcia responded, his heart completely won by the beauty and grace with which the beautiful Hipolita was telling her tragic tale. He didn't want her to omit a single thing; indeed he listened with such pleasure that he wished her story would last a hundred years.

"Well, since it pleases you," the lady said, "the verses went like this:

"My love is impossible;
for her, I am in torment,
for her, I utter a thousand sighs,
for her, my tears pour forth,
for her, I lose all pleasure,
for her, I seek sorrow,
desiring illness
and despising all good.
Oh, wretched plaints!
Oh, true love!

Oh, unfounded sighs,
love without effect!
Because Fortune ruled
that my mistress
is not free,
her will is held captive;
with what hope
can my wild desire live?
Oh God! Why don't
these sad thoughts vanish?
Happy shepherd,
sum of all good fortune,
because of you I cry, jealous,
because of you I fear, scorned.
The day when my ungrateful love
set her eyes on you
either she should have been blinded
or I should have been born blind.
If heaven created your grace
to bring me pain
it would have been kinder
had I never been born.
Or, since in the village
there are other pretty faces,
you could have exempted
my thankless love from triumph.
Since I was born unlucky,
unfortunate, what can I expect?
I suffer unreasonably,
I complain without cause.
Enjoy her—but what am I saying?
Don't enjoy her, for it kills me
just to think that everybody
calls her yours.
Be Tantalus to her desires,
let her neck be
the water you never taste
despite your pleas and plaints.
Let the angry hand
slice the Gordian knot
with which you hold her captive,
that jewel I prize the most.
Let my sighs go directly
to my ungrateful mistress
and set her breast
of marble aflame.
But if I love her truly,

how can I wish her ill?
It's better that I should die
since I'm the one who suffers."
Thus he sang, bewailing
his impossible desire,
his extreme sorrow,
his wild jealousy,
the loving peasant lad
following after his sheep
and lost in his thoughts
of how to attain his desire.
Then he heard a sound,
and ceased his tears,
silenced his plaints,
and stayed his step.
It was his ungrateful beloved
who feigned appreciation
and amorous delight
in his discreet company;
when she saw him depart
with his gentle lambs,
she had followed him
to calm his sorrows.
Her heart touched,
she had listened to him;
for love brings solace
to the constant lover.
She caught him unawares
with his arms spread wide,
his heart filled with tenderness,
and loving words upon his lips.
She said to him: "My dear,
now is not the time for crying,
for although I am not free,
I hate my prison.
I love your eyes
and seeing myself in them
I feel obliged
and confess that I am won.
Will love ever grant that someday
we can overcome these sorrows,
for, although you suffer them,
I feel them in my heart."
The shepherd who adores her
sets aside his fears
and like the ivy twines
around her lovely form.

In shells of coral
he drinks in her sweet breath
calming her fierce fears;
seated on the cool banks
of a laughing brook
they tell each other
all about their past.
Then Venus's little son
closed his gates on the scene:
Cupid alone is able
to close off the countryside.
To everything else that happened
only the weeping willows
were envious witnesses
and loving matchmakers.
But, oh God! all these glories
I enjoyed only in my dream;
filled with love and jealousy,
in sadness I awoke.

"The tender feeling within my breast and the force of my affection
could not bear to see don Gaspar suffer so terribly. I wanted to reward
his love if only with one day of favor and joy so that he might more
pleasurably bear all the sorrows that weighed upon him. My husband,
although he trusted me, allowed me little liberty, either because of the
nature of his love or because of his sensible and cautious jealousy,
which sometimes seemed quite foolish. Be that as it may, Love, who
sometimes takes pity on the suffering of his subjects and brings them
some brief pleasure, arranged for a friend to invite my husband on a
hunting trip that was to last two or three days. Don Pedro accepted
and, although I was immensely happy, I feigned surprise and displeasure at the unusual occurrence.

"When he departed on his hunting trip my maid, secretary to my
weakness, immediately went to inform don Gaspar of this wonderful
opportunity. In a letter I sent, he was invited to come that very night
to the back gate of the garden behind my house where he would find
the gate open and me. I didn't dare let him in the front door because
my parents, with whom my husband and I lived, might have heard
him.

"It was summertime. While I waited for my lover, I had two satin
mattresses brought into the garden and placed beneath the arbor, using the heat as an excuse, when I really just wanted to get away from
the maids. They wouldn't retire as long as they saw me dressed. I

didn't want them around while I was expecting my lover. I preferred solitude to company. I prepared to go to bed. After I'd undressed and they thought I was asleep, the maids finally left me and retired. Only the one who knew all my secrets stayed until I commanded her to withdraw and leave me alone in that place where my love and my honor were to do battle. Honor had already been vanquished, for love had conquered and triumphed. The gate was open. The garden was not very large, and no one could enter without being seen.

"Suddenly my maids came to tell me that my husband and master had returned home. His friend had suffered a great fall and injured himself so they couldn't continue the hunt and had had to come back.

"When I saw don Pedro home, I thought how great my fortune was that don Gaspar had not yet arrived. Aware of the danger to his life and mine if he should come now, I ordered my maid to lock the gate he was supposed to enter. I thought that, when he came and found it locked, he'd go away. Then, the next morning, I could tell him what had happened, and he would necessarily be satisfied, as no excuses are necessary where one's legitimate husband is concerned.

"Don Pedro came to me with open arms, and I had to receive him the same way, but with a very different spirit. He, delighted with the bed and the escape from the heat, told me that I really knew how to make the best of an occasion and enjoy life much more than he did. He explained his early return. Then he undressed and came to bed, occupying the place intended for my lover. Shortly after all this happened, my lover came to the gate and, finding it locked—which was clearly not our agreement—he became wildly jealous. He didn't imagine that what had really happened could be the reason for the gate being locked. Instead, he assumed I was with another lover. (Once a woman is easy, even the very man who caused her to err becomes suspicious of her.) With the help of his servant he leapt over the wall, which wasn't very high, and, treading quietly so as not to be heard, he boldly sought the cause of his betrayal.

"By this time, the moon had set and hidden herself in her original home so everything was in confused shadow. My husband and I were fast asleep. It happened that, after sneaking all around the garden, he came upon the bed where my husband and I were sleeping. In the dim light, he could see that there were two persons, but it never occurred to him that I was with don Pedro. He knelt down beside us, saying to himself that his suspicions had not been false. Overcome by rage, he unsheathed his dagger. Just as he was about to plunge it into my innocent husband—a dreadful decision produced by his wrath—kind heaven, which looks on things with compassion, caused don Pedro to turn over and sigh. Don Gaspar realized his mistake and guessed what must have happened.

"He thanked heaven for the timely warning. Then, boldly taking advantage of don Pedro's deep sleep, he crept over to my side and woke me. Shocked by his temerity, I signaled him to go away. Seeing my great fear he left, but he carried with him as a souvenir the gift of an embrace and the flowers of my lips, a different fruit from the one he'd intended to pluck that night. He jumped over the fence, which is lower from the inside, and returned to his inn. He fervently prayed to attain his frustrated desire while I rued and cursed my bad luck.

"The next day I received a letter from don Gaspar in which he revealed all his charms by describing how he'd felt in that situation. The letter affected me so deeply that, had I not already succumbed, it would have won me completely, so splendid did his words seem to me:

Who can feel wrath,
and rage against heaven,
if, whenever he expresses his feelings,
he has them all fly back in his face?
Who, unarmed,
can enter the fray
against one who is armed
and sure of victory?
Who, being of humbler caste,
even if aggrieved,
can take vengeance
against the powerful?
What poor man against a wealthy man
can, in like manner,
live a long life
in banqueting and elegance?
Who, when love persecutes him,
courting one who doesn't love,
even though she speaks of love,
can have any hope?
Who, against the fortunate one
who enjoys possession,
simply because he is unfortunate
can obtain the object of his desires?
Oh, heaven! When I sought

to enjoy her beautiful face
that belongs to another master
my misfortune discovers him!
My fortunes faded,
my hopes doubtful,
are more proper to the master
who possesses your grace.
Who before has ever experienced
such great misfortune
as the man who comes to possess you
and finds you already possessed?
Come Death, why do you delay;
living with misfortune is true tragedy.

"My attempt to enjoy my love was so disastrous the first time that I feared to try again, but my lover's pleas were so insistent and so moving that I had to make up my mind. I consulted with my maid, the secretary to my affair, and she was amazed at a woman who said she was in love but had so little spirit, was willing to risk so little. She suggested that don Gaspar should come in the evening and enter before the doors were locked. She'd keep him hidden in her room (until after don Pedro had gone to bed), and I could pretend some malady and leave my bed.

"I agreed to his entering early and meeting him in her room, for there's no true lover who won't attempt anything to obtain his heart's desire. I informed don Gaspar of the plan and what he was to do.

"Night came, and then my problems began. First, don Gaspar and my husband arrived almost at the same moment. My maid hid don Gaspar in her room. I pretended to be feeling unwell and sleepy and made everyone retire early, including my husband who was disconsolate to see me indisposed. If my passion had taken his genuine love into account, I would never have offended against him. While I waited for don Pedro to fall asleep so I could get up, I heard shouting in the street and then knocking at the door and voices crying: "Fire! Fire! Your house is on fire! Don Pedro, look, it's burning down! Save yourselves! The flames are shooting up through the roof!" Frantically I leapt from my bed, went out into the hall, and saw my house burning down. So huge was the fire that I couldn't see the sky for the smoke and the flames. Recognizing how great the danger was, I began to scream and called out to don Pedro and he to the servants to come help. My alarm was timely for at that moment the fire was at its height. What had happened was that the servant in charge of the kitchen had stuck a candle on a board in her room right next to the bed. She had fallen asleep and the candle fell on her, igniting the bedclothes and the board. She paid for her carelessness with her life. The flames didn't go out but caught the whole room on fire and the room next door where coal and firewood were stored. When this went up in flames so did the whole house. It passed through the door to my mother's maids' quarters, and it wasn't possible to save the four of them.

"This new disaster and the great peril I'd experienced caused me to faint. When I regained consciousness, it was close to morning and I was in my brother-in-law don Luis's house, where I'd been taken to save my life. The fire had been put out although I lost most of my things. I inquired whether my maid had escaped with her life, hoping to learn if the fire had harmed don Gaspar. While I was going through my ruined clothing, my maid came to me, and I learned that because of all the people who'd come to the fire, don Gaspar had been able to escape without being noticed.

"After the excitement of the fire, the excitement in my heart burned greater, and I sent for news of don Gaspar. Lamenting his unluckiness and grieved by my indisposition, he wrote me a letter filled with a thousand tender complaints. I answered with a thousand crazy things, promising him that, the next time, he'd have the chance to make up for all our catastrophes.

"It took some time to repair the damage caused by the fire and to restore the house. During this time, I stayed in my brother-in-law's house, as I said, and my lover and I had to be content to write letters. When I finally returned to my own home, very moved by don Gaspar's pleas, I gave in a third time to his urging, unmindful of the past failures that heaven had set in my way (not to mention the situation heaven has placed me in now). I decided to repeat the last plan, so I wrote don Gaspar to come early the way he had the previous time.

"Well, it so happened that on that night don Pedro returned home much earlier than usual because, as it turned out, the police were trying to arrest a friend of his for a murder. Because our house was so noble that it was respected as if it were an embassy, my husband had brought his friend home. To keep him safe, don Pedro had the doors locked early and ordered that they not be opened for any reason. When don Gaspar arrived, the door was locked and everyone had retired. Discovering his bad luck, he made a signal, at which my maid went out on the balcony and told him what had happened and blamed him for arriving so late. She told him it was impossible for her to open the door, but maybe he could get in through a little window on the ground level.

"Don Gaspar thanked her a thousand times and, promising to reward her, he asked her to unlock the window for him. It didn't have a grate because it opened on a blind alley and was very, very small. My intermediary went to the little window, and she warned him that he wouldn't fit. His love, however, made him think everything was possible, and he felt sure he could get in. He poked his head and his shoulders through the opening and then got stuck in the frame, halfway in and halfway out, so he could move neither forward nor backward.

"My maid saw the bind he was in and realizd that the only way out was to remove the frame. She went to call a friend and told her that the man was her lover. Between the two maids and don Gaspar's servant, using daggers and other tools, they removed the frame from the wall. They couldn't help making noise, however, which the other servants heard. Thinking it was thieves breaking in, they called out. This upset the whole house, and don Gaspar had to run quickly away, still stuck firmly inside the windowframe. Don Pedro gave orders to close off the window the next morning and the servants retired. Don Gaspar went to a carpenter who had to saw off the frame, thus freeing him from that impediment.

"I was totally unaware that my lover had been the thief who had upset a whole household. When I heard that a man had been trying to break in through the window, I didn't think to ask any questions. The next morning after my nusband left the house, my maid came to dress me and she described the whole scene to me (I swear, don Garcia, I laughed so hard I could hardly let her finish). My maid was roaring with laughter too.

"Misfortune doesn't come without reason. I believed that don Pedro wouldn't return home any time soon and by then, determined to reward don Gaspar for so many trials and labors, I sent my maid for him. He came right away, as he didn't live faraway. The moment he entered my room I embraced him. This was the second favor I'd granted him during the year our affair lasted; the first one was the kiss he stole the night he almost killed my husband.

"The two of us laughed heartily about his getting stuck in the window. All of a sudden my maid, who'd been acting as lookout and spy, rushed in crying":

" 'Alas, my lady, we're lost! Your husband has come home and in such a hurry that by now he's inside the house!'

"This news might have thrown me into confusion, but I couldn't let it because it would cost us our lives if my husband were to catch my flagrant infidelity and the great offense against his honor. I ran into my dressing room next door, yanked open a huge trunk, pulled everything out, and threw it all on a pile of pillows. I urged Gaspar to get inside. He managed to fit by curling up.

"Just at that moment, don Pedro rushed in asking urgently for a chamberpot, for it was this discomfort that had brought him home at such an unusual hour. It took him over an hour and a half to do this and eat his breakfast, which he hadn't done that morning. He dawdled so that I didn't think he'd ever have left if he hadn't heard the bells ringing for mass. As he left the house, I felt the keenest pleasure knowing that at last, fortune could not deny me the pleasure of enjoying my love. I opened the trunk but, to my horror, don Gaspar was dead!

"I couldn't make him move his hands or his feet. I placed my hand over his mouth and he wasn't breathing. He felt so cold I was sure he'd suffocated. How can I describe to you, don Garcia, what my feelings were at that moment? How can I express in words my tears, my sighs, my sorrow? I can only say that I decided to take my own life using my lover's dagger, like Thisbe. I was about to plunge the weapon into my heart when my maid came in. As upset as I was, she burst into tears. Finally she shut the trunk and led me out of the room. Weeping and wailing, we kept asking each other what we could do, how were we going to get his body out of the house. Every idea we came up with presented great obstacles and a mountain of difficulties.

"The two of us were still lamenting the death of the unfortunate don Gaspar, when my brother-in-law, don Luis, came in. Finding me so upset and tearful, he began to inquire as to the cause. I decided to trust in the great love he had always felt for me, going back to before I'd become his brother's wife; I told him the truth. Feeling desperate and at the end of my strength, I began:

" 'Don Luis, the greatest misfortune on the face of the earth that can happen to a woman has happened to me. Because I'm powerless to do anything about it, I dare to tell you.'

"So I described to him what I've just told you and ended with these words:

" 'You're a gentleman and, if you truly wish to help me, let my misfortune oblige you. As God is my witness, I swear to you that I haven't offended against my husband and your brother's honor in deed, even though I may have in intention. If you're so cruel and harsh that you choose not to believe me and you decide to tell don Pedro, do as you please. I'm willing to pay with my life.'

"Don Luis was astounded by my words. He told me to calm down, that he'd take care of the matter. He called a servant and had the trunk removed. Quickly they carried it to the house of a friend to whom he told the whole story. The two men opened the trunk, took don Gaspar out and laid him on the bed. They undressed him and felt his pulse and heart and discovered that he wasn't really dead. They put him into bed and placed wine compresses on his wrists, on his heart, and over his nose; they put hot water bottles all around him and noticed signs of life. Then they locked him in, leaving him alone and unaccompanied, as I learned afterward.

"Don Gaspar came to his senses as night was falling. He found himself naked in a strange bed in a house that he realized was not mine. He could recollect only that I'd put him inside the trunk. He pondered his situation and tried to find some explanation for this mystery but, no matter how he tried, he couldn't figure it out.

"While he was deep in these thoughts, he heard the door open and looked to see who it was. He recognized don Luis. The sight of my brother-in-law frightened him so terribly that he almost died on the spot. Don Gaspar was even more astounded when don Luis came over and sat down on the edge of his bed and said:

" 'You do recognize me, don Gaspar? You do know that I am don Pedro's brother and doña Hipolita's brother-in-law?'

" 'Yes, I do,' don Gaspar replied.

" 'You are also aware,' don Luis continued, 'of the nobility of our house? Do you remember what happened today? Well, I swear to you by this Cross' (and he placed his hand on the Cross he wore on his breast), 'that the day I find out you've even thought about renewing your courtship of doña Hipolita, or even walked down this street, I'll take the vengeance that I don't take today. I'll release you now simply because a crazy, distraught woman has trusted me and because I know that the offense against my brother has not been executed in fact, although the intentions are worthy of punishment. Remember, I'll know your every move, even in the deepest bowels of hell.'

"Don Gaspar reassured don Luis with a thousand oaths; he vowed he would obey and thanked him with a thousand civilities for having granted him his life, which had been and was still in don Luis's hands to take away. Don Gaspar dressed quickly and left that house. He was determined never again to set his eyes upon me and to his ears my name became the most hateful thing on earth, as you will see later in my story.

"I was terribly worried about what had happened but didn't dare ask don Luis what disposition he'd made of that unfortunate corpse. He never said a word to me about it. I charged my maid and trusted secretary to inquire at don Gaspar's lodgings as discreetly as possible to find out what had happened to him. She got to his inn just at the moment when he was sending his effects to another inn far away from that district, in order to keep his promise to don Luis. When don Gaspar saw Leonor (that was the maid's name, secretary to my madness), he told her to go with God, that he'd had enough of my tricks and deceptions. Briefly he recounted to her the events of that fateful day and told her about his promise to don Luis. Don Gaspar ended with a message for me: he had never imagined in all his life that a woman could be so treacherous and perfidious! Now he could see that all along I'd planned to bring him to the end he might have had if heaven hadn't taken pity on his plight.

"The moment don Gaspar said these words to Leonor, he left. Leonor was confused by it all but, even so, she followed him to find out the inn where he was moving. With this information she returned home. The happy thoughts I'd had of don Gaspar turned bitter; I was innocent of his charges. Now I was despised by the man I loved so much, the man for whom I'd risked my life and stared death in the face, holding a sword at my throat.

"These thoughts made me very melancholy. My husband was upset to see me sad and so far removed from any pleasure. Then don Luis began to pursue me. Learning of my weakness had given wings to his appetite, and he dared to express his desire to me nakedly. Without respect for God or his brother, he demanded that I reward his love. He threatened to expose everything he knew. He said that, since I'd opened the doors of my affection to one man, offending against my honor and my husband, I could do it for him. And, in fact, if I didn't, he'd tell his brother everything he knew about me.

"This situation was driving me crazy. It so depleted my strength that I ended up in bed with a serious illness. If only God had let my illness kill me, I would've been more fortunate!

"I spent a month in bed, forgetful of everything. I was so ill that the doctors held out little hope of saving my life. But heaven didn't permit me to die; it was saving me for further torment. During my illnes, my brother-in-law don Luis visited me frequently. He used threats, gifts, caresses, servility to try to bring me to his will. If I showed my aversion or lectured him in an effort to deviate him from his path, if I condemned his desire as wrong and sinful, then he would throw don Gaspar in my face. This was such torture for me that I felt like taking my own life to escape his persecution.

"One day I was with several of my friends who'd come to visit me, and don Luis entertained us with various games and distractions that, added to the mere sight of him, were like poison to me. He took up a guitar, which he played very well, and I recall that he sang this ballad that he'd composed on the subject of his desire and my ingratitude:

> Asking the sun for darkness
> when in the east he shows
> the beauty of his face
> across the flowery meadow;
> asking Flora herself
> while she combs her hair
> not to edge the green meadows
> with pearls instead of dew;
> asking all the elements
> to end their ancient war
> and turn their fierce conflict
> into total harmony;
> asking heaven for mercy
> and salvation for all the souls in hell
> is like asking your eyes
> to look on me more kindly.
>
> Asking the sea to contain
> its waves and to become
> gentle, calm, humble,
> when its way is cruel and proud;
> asking that its fishes walk
> freely over the sands
> and that all the shells
> pour forth pearls across the land;
> and that the sirens cease their song
> and their listeners not fall asleep,
> and for the Tritons and the sea nymphs
> to dwell in the meadows;
> asking heaven for mercy
> and salvation for all the souls in hell
> is like asking your eyes
> to look on me more kindly.

Asking the nightingales
not to sing their jealous plaints
and for the widowed turtledove
to seek a second husband;
asking the single phoenix
as it burns up in its flames
not to be reborn in its ashes,
not to remain its single self;
asking the royal eagle
whose glance pierces the sun
to cease looking into the light
and instead to look into darkness;
asking heaven for mercy
and salvation for all the souls in hell
is like asking your eyes
to look on me more kindly.

Asking the fierce fates,
haughty and proud,
not to cut with their scissors
the threads of life;
asking one who rages to taste
what can never reach his mouth
to eat the fruit
and sip the crystal waters;
asking the sad Ixion
for the wheel to cease its torture,
for Sisyphus to hold the rock
up on the peak he seeks;
asking heaven for mercy
and salvation for all the souls in hell
is like asking your eyes
to look on me more kindly.

"Imagine, don Garcia, my confusion to find myself in this bind that is the greatest torment a woman can suffer. On the one hand, I was now despised and abandoned by don Gaspar, which made me love him even more wildly than before. I knew that my love was absolutely hopeless for, even if he were to return my love, I no longer had the courage to take more risks. On the other hand, I was courted and pursued by my brother-in-law, and so threatened by him that, every time I opened my mouth to restrain or reprimand him, he reminded me that if I'd loved don Gaspar I could love him. Constantly intimidated and fearful, I contemplated giving in to him and closing my eyes to God. But when I thought about the offense against heaven and against my husband, I realized that there could be no remedy but death.

"The only way I could protect myself was to order my maids, and particularly Leonor, never to leave my side, never to leave me alone with don Luis for a moment, because he might resort to force. He saw his hopes frustrated and finally understood that I would never willingly accede to his pleasure. He decided upon the vilest, most treacherous plan you can imagine, which I shall describe to you.

"I've already told you that his house and mine were adjoining, divided only by a wall. Well, he decided to cut open a little door just big enough for one person to squeeze through up in an attic room so far removed that no one ever went up there. One night after we'd all gone to bed, don Luis came through the little door and entered my house. He knew the house well and, free of interference, he got the keys and, crafty as a burglar, he unlocked the main door to the street.

"After opening the door, he went to the stable and let all the horses loose; there were two riding horses and four coach horses. The frightened horses made such a racket that it woke up the stable boy. He yelled and called out for help. The horses had escaped and were running wildly down the street. My husband woke, got up, dressed, and called the other servants. Cursing the stable boy for his carelessness, don Pedro ran out after the horses.

"Don Luis, wearing only his nightshirt, watched him leave. He waited a little while and then came to my bed. Pretending to be my husband, he slipped between the sheets and began to caress me ever so tenderly and lovingly.

"Well, this happened night before last, and you know how cold it was. The traitor had come in his nightshirt and was so cold that I said to him:

" 'Heavens, my dear, how come you're so cold?'

" 'It's very cold out,' the crafty don Luis replied, disguising his voice as best he could.

" 'Did you catch the horses?' I asked.

" 'They're bringing them back now,' my treacherous brother-in-law replied, taking me in his arms. Then he proceeded to enjoy everything that he might ever have desired. He dishonored his brother, he injured me, he offended against heaven.

"When don Luis finished, knowing it was time for his brother to return, he led me to believe he was going to make sure the servants had gotten the horses in. He got up and went back to his own house the same way he'd come, without my ever suspecting a thing.

"Soon thereafter don Pedro came in, having seen that the horses were taken care of and the servants had retired. He crawled into bed and, as he was chilled to the bone, he snuggled up to me. I said reprovingly:

" 'Good heavens, my dear, how mischievous you are this evening! Why you just finished and here you are again!'

" 'You must have been dreaming, Hipolita,' don Pedro replied. 'I haven't been back here since I left to catch the horses.'

"This reply left me terribly confused, as I knew I hadn't been dreaming. The more I thought about it, the more I almost suspected the treachery. I couldn't go back to sleep for thinking about the mystery, but I didn't dare say a word to don Pedro.

"The next morning I slept much later than my worries usually let me sleep. I dressed and went to mass. This was yesterday morning, because my tragedy occurred night before last. I entered the church and saw don Luis standing by the holy water font. As I approached, arrogantly he offered me holy water. He appeared triumphant, he was all puffed up, and so, aptly, it was his own hubris that moved me to take vengeance. Primly and courteously, I accepted the water he offered from his hand. He pressed my hand in his. Laughingly he said in a low voice:

" 'Heavens, my dear, how come you're so cold?'

"The instant I heard those words, I understood everything. I heard mass and went back home more troubled than you can imagine. Don Pedro went out after dinner. I left no place in the whole house unexamined, no matter how hidden it seemed. I searched every window, tested every door, and found everything locked and unmarred. I began to suspect that don Luis had managed his daring feat with the help of one of my maids. I went up to the attic to finish my search, not expecting to find what I did find, which was the little door he hadn't bothered to close up, probably because he intended to use it again. Feeling satisfied with my discovery and without saying a word to anyone, I returned to my room and began to plan my vengeance. I stayed there till don Pedro came home for supper. After supper, he went to bed and I with him. I waited calmly for the household to become quiet.

"Once my husband was sound asleep, I got up and dressed. I took his dagger and a light, climbed up into the attic, passed through the little door, and went to don Luis's bedroom. He was fast asleep, feeling no guilt for his treachery and sleeping as soundly as my vengeance required. Having satisfied his desire, his sated lust let him sleep carefree. I aimed at his heart and, with my first thrust, he gave up the ghost, instantly, without time to ask God to have mercy on his soul. I stabbed him five or six more times with such rage and violence that I wished that each new blow would end his vile life all over again.

"I returned to my room and, without considering that it might cause harm to my innocent husband, I put the dagger back into its sheath without even cleaning off the blood or thinking about the consequences of what I was doing, so disturbed and enraged was I. If the law should catch me, truth was on my side and crime on don Luis's.

"I opened my desk and put all my jewels, worth more than two thousand ducats, into a scarf. Soundlessly, I opened the front door and, without anyone's being aware of my folly, I left the house and went to don Gaspar's inn. My maid had told me where it was. I knocked at the door, and a servant who knew about our disastrous affair opened it. When he set eyes upon me, he was terrified and told me his master hadn't yet returned from gaming.

" 'That doesn't matter,' I said. 'I'll wait for him.'

"And I did, with God knows how many fears, not because of what I'd done, for I couldn't even think about that, but because I was afraid don Gaspar no longer loved me. I hoped my visit would fix that and he'd return to his former love of me. I also feared what might happen to my husband and servants, not in regard to don Luis's death, but because I'd left the house and thus ruined our good name. I trusted that don Gaspar's love would save me. Despite the fact that he'd let it be known that he despised me, I couldn't really believe that, although it did give me cause to fear. Even if he didn't love me, being noble, he had to be courteous to me because, even where there's no love, one must always show courtesy to a lady.

"Don Gaspar finally came home. He entered, saw me, and crossed himself a thousand times. In a terrible rage, he said:

" 'What liberty is this, my lady Hipolita? What are you doing in my room? Aren't you satisfied with the trials you've put me through, the dangers you've placed me in? The cruelest and most vicious thing you did was your last trick when, with cruel and treacherous intent, you sent for me only to put me at the mercy of your brother-in-law and lover.'

"I had previously told the wretch how don Luis loved me, that's why he'd attributed these motives to me. To interrupt his fiendish attack against me, I said in a sea of tears:

" 'Alas! don Gaspar, my lord! How different things are from what you imagine! I realize now it was a mistake for me to ask my brother-in-law for help no matter how upset I was. But what else would you expect a poor weak woman to do with what she believed to be a corpse right when she expected her husband to come home? But you don't know what's happened in the meantime. I've just killed don Luis with my own hands. With his blood, I cleansed the offense against my honor which his desperate love attempted and finally accomplished. You'll find out tomorrow that my life is in peril and my house is threatened by what people will say. You must get me out of Valladolid immediately, you must take me to Lisbon! I'll sell these jewels and pay for everything.'

" 'Ah, you treacherous whore!' don Gaspar said. 'Now I know I was right! When you tired of my devoted love and became irritated by my courtship, you turned me over to your new lover for him to kill me. Now you tire of him, just like lascivious Lamia, adulterous Flora, and cruel, faithless Pandora, so you kill him and want to do me in too. Well, I'll show you! Where once I felt love, now I feel hatred, and I'll make you pay for your mistreatment of me.'

"With these words, he tore off my clothes down to my petticoat. Using his belt, he beat me as you can see." As modestly and chastely as she could, the beautiful lady showed don Garcia horrible bruises all over her body. They looked like they were ready to burst open and gush blood.

"Even don Gaspar's servant couldn't stop his cruel beating. I swallowed my cries to keep from being heard, and finally I fell to the floor, overcome by his violent punishment. When the traitor saw me collapse, he flung open the door and threw me into the street. He yelled after me that the only reason he didn't kill me was that he didn't want to dirty his sword with my vile, perfidious blood. If it hadn't been for your compassion, I might still be lying in the street, or maybe I'd be dead, or in the hands of the people who're looking for me.

"This, compassionate don Garcia, is my unhappy story. Now you must advise me. What can a woman who has caused such terrible harm do with herself?"

"Indeed, beautiful Hipolita," don Garcia said, enamored of her beauty and deeply troubled by her tears, "I'm terribly sorry about your misfortunes and furious with the ungrateful don Gaspar. Would to God it were in my hand to remedy both, even if it cost me my life! Given his vile abuse of you, I can't believe that don Gaspar has noble blood! Even if he didn't remember his former love for you, or take into account that you were at his mercy, he should've shown you consideration and courtesy simply because you're a woman. I promise you he'll not go unpunished; heaven will avenge you of don Gaspar as it did of don Luis. Now rest. If you'll tell me the address of your house and grant me permission, I'll go try to find out what's happened with regard to your absence and don Luis's death. Then we can decide what's the best thing to do."

The lady thanked him as warmly as she could. Don Garcia, feeling somewhat repaid for his love and obligated by her response, went to doña Hipolita's house to find out what was happening. Just as he arrived, he saw the police lead don Pedro out, under arrest for his brother's murder. His guilt had been proved by the little door in the attic and the bloody dagger in its sheath. Furthermore, the maids testified that don Luis had been courting their mistress. The police were very good at such investigations. They searched the house and took detailed statements from all the servants.

Not only was the poor gentleman innocent of the crime of killing his own brother, but he was confounded by his wife's absence. Her missing jewels and cloak and the unlocked door made him fear the worst. He was carried off to jail without making any statement. Both houses, the victim's and the prisoner's, were put under guard, and doña Hipolita's parents and all the servants were taken into custody.

Seeing that sight filled don Garcia with pity and with rage. He longed to punish don Gaspar's vile behavior. Impelled by the love he felt for doña Hipolita, don Garcia felt that don Gaspar should pay with his life for having beaten doña Hipolita and stolen her jewels. He went to don Gaspar's inn and inquired. The innkeeper told don Garcia that that very morning don Gaspar had left on the stage for Lisbon. He'd told his servant he had to leave because his father had fallen ill.

Don Garcia recognized the fruitlessness of pursuit and also that it was urgent to place doña Hipolita in safekeeping for her own protection and to avoid the danger to them both of her being found in his keeping. By this time, town criers were promising a hundred escudos to whoever might find her and threatening death to anyone

who harbored her. Besides, he needed to protect her from his own
love, for he loved her so madly he didn't trust himself; he almost
understood don Luis's criminal passion.

He went to a clothing store and bought a rich elegant dress and
all the other things doña Hipolita needed to be able to appear in
public. Not trusting the parcels to a messenger, he himself carried
them back to the inn. He told the beautiful Hipolita all the news,
including the fact that her husband was to be tortured until he confessed his crime. This news so distressed doña Hipolita that she wanted
to give herself up to the police to keep the innocent don Pedro and
her servants from suffering for her sake. Don Garcia reproved her for
this decision and tried to talk sense to her. He made her get dressed
and eat breakfast. Then he went out to get a litter to take her to a
convent. Liberally he paid all her expenses. Don Garcia advised doña
Hipolita that she should negotiate her husband's release, since he was
truly innocent, after she was safe in the convent.

That's what she did. She wrote a letter to the president of the city
council and told him that, if he wanted to know who don Luis's
murderer was, he should come see her and she would tell him.

The president was particularly anxious to learn the truth because
all the parties were prominent and also because doña Hipolita was a
relative of his. He came to the convent accompanied by other gentlemen of the council. Doña Hipolita told them everything we've said
here and confessed that she'd killed her treacherous brother-in-law.
She told them that her husband and all the servants, including don
Luis's, were innocent. They could understand what had happened because she was so beautiful.

The president told this story to the king. When the king saw how
rightly doña Hipolita had avenged herself, he pardoned her and set
her husband and all the other prisoners free. Within four days, they
were out of jail. Doña Hipolita, however, refused to go back to her
husband even though he begged and pleaded with her. She told don
Pedro that suspicious love couldn't lead to perfect love or to conjugal
harmony. He must suspect her not because of don Luis's treachery—
she'd avenged herself of that dishonor and was satisfied—but because
of her love for don Gaspar of whom her husband would always be
jealous. The only thing she asked of don Pedro was to provide for
her support in the convent, which he liberally granted.

This terrible tragedy caused the poor gentleman such sorrow that he fell gravely ill and died within the year. Since he never felt offended by his wife, he left her heir to his whole estate. Indeed, for all the time he lived, he visited her as often as he could.

Doña Hipolita was free, young, and wealthy. She felt obligated to don Garcia for having helped her so much. He'd visited her regularly and kept up her spirits all the time she was in the convent. Moved by the love she knew don Garcia felt for her, which he'd clearly shown while she was in the convent, pleased by his appearance, satisfied with his intelligence, certain of his nobility, and sure that he valued her person, she married him and made him master of her beauty and of her rich estate. The only thing he'd lacked to be a perfect match was wealth; of course, he had a modest income, but it wasn't really enough to meet all that his nobility required. He, always thankful to heaven for his good fortune, is still alive today and very much loved by his beautiful Hipolita. Their children, schooled in don Garcia's generous nobility, are proof of their love.

Some time later, a highwayman was brought to Valladolid. At the foot of the gallows, he confessed that he merited the death penalty, not for the crime he was accused of but for having killed his master, don Gaspar, and stolen from him a hoard of jewels that don Gaspar had taken from a lady who'd come to him for help. In a few sentences, he told doña Hipolita's story. That's how it came to be known that heaven had brought don Gaspar his well-deserved punishment at the hands of his own servant, the man about to be hanged.

These events happened in our own times and I heard about them from the very people to whom they happened. I decided to write the story down so that everyone can learn from their experience that, in the end, everyone gets his "just desserts."

The enchantment narrated by don Miguel gave such pleasure that his audience applauded loudly and thanked him heartily with a thousand words of praise. Don Lope, confident that his story would not give less pleasure than his companion's, began with these words:

"Noble audience, I don't want to praise the enchantment I'm about to tell you, not its plot, its poetry, or its moral, because all the stories told so far on these delightful evenings have been narrated in a plain style and everyday language, avoiding exaggeration, leaving such adornment to those who wish to be considered 'artistic.' In the tale I'm about to tell, what I hope you'll appreciate is that it's absolutely true. I don't include a single detail that didn't really happen. I assure you that today the son of our heroes lives in Salamanca, and close relatives of theirs sit on the Royal Council. Not to keep you in suspense, let me begin":

Triumph over the
Impossible

Salamanca is known as the noblest, most pleasant and beautiful city in Castile. Her nobility competes with her beauty, her letters with her arms, and she abounds in these attributes more than any other city of Spain. Salamanca was mother and progenitress to don Rodrigo and doña Leonor. Both were noble and wealthy; don Rodrigo was a prodigy of nature and doña Leonor was the epitome of beauty. These two became exemplars of love and of fortune, as this tale will tell. Don Rodrigo was the second son in his family, which was a great misfortune because, for this reason alone, the merit he deserved for his elegance and discretion was discredited. This defect could be overcome only by doing great deeds, not the least of which would be to win doña Leonor, her parents' only child and heiress to their vast estates.

The two families were neighbors and such close friends that the relationship between the two children was almost as close as if they belonged to the same family. The children loved each other from their tenderest years. When they reached the age of discretion, love, tired of make-believe, became real (it took full possession of them). The two lovers had been born under the sign of the tragic lovers Piramus and Thisbe. When doña Leonor's parents finally noticed what was developing, they began to fear not the end of this love, but its beginning. Her parents thought that, if they nipped it in the bud, it would go no further; so, as best they could, they tried to cut off all communication between doña Leonor and don Rodrigo. These restrictions did at least keep their relationship from being as free as it had been during their childhood.

Instead of quelling the fiery love that burned in them, however, the restraint fueled their passion so that its flame burned stronger in their hearts. When love turns serious, it becomes cautious and self-protective; consequently the two lovers began to fear even their own thoughts, and they sought out the most hidden places for their conversations. Youthful love took possession of their souls in the face of their parents' opposition and so inflamed their passions that soon the only thing they talked about was their love and the fulfillment of their desires. The two together and each alone were determined to die before giving up this love. Their gifts insured the loyalty of the servants, and love arranged frequent encounters. Their meetings were supplemented by amorous letters in which the young lovers expressed themselves freely, without any of the inhibition or sense of shame that sometimes lead lovers astray. They told each other their most secret thoughts.

Doña Leonor's beauty increased with each passing day, as did the number of don Rodrigo's competitors for her hand, young men who openly declared themselves her suitors. Don Rodrigo became haunted by the fear that one of them might win his beloved mistress. Trusting in his merits, which were many in spite of the fact that he was the younger son, don Rodrigo decided to ask his parents to request doña Leonor's hand in marriage. He urged them as his intermediaries to present a strong case, attesting to his nobility and his inheritance, for, discounting the entailment to his older brother, his parents had provided amply for his comfort. They felt optimistic about the outcome of their petition, but it turned out just the opposite of what they'd envisioned.

By the time the negotiations had concluded, don Rodrigo and doña Leonor were left totally without hope. Doña Leonor's parents had responded that their daughter was their only heir and that, although don Rodrigo was certainly worthy, he was not a suitable match because he was the younger son. They said that this alone had decided them against him; if the family could guarantee that his elder brother would never marry, they'd gladly accept don Rodrigo as their son-in-law. To complicate the matter, however, doña Leonor had already been betrothed to a gentleman from Valladolid named don Alonso. At that moment, don Alonso was at court seeking investiture in one of the noble orders, which was the only thing delaying doña Leonor's marriage to him.

Don Rodrigo's parents deeply regretted this turn of events and considered it an affront that their close friends preferred another man to their son. A terrible feud arose between the two families. No longer did they visit or talk to each other as they had in the past. The news devastated don Rodrigo; he almost went crazy and thought of doing wild things to win his beloved doña Leonor. Then he found out, to his despair, that his parents, in an effort to stifle his love through absence, had arranged for him to go to Flanders, exchanging his student robes for a soldier's uniform. Don Rodrigo looked so very handsome in his military regalia! If only he'd been as well endowed in his fortune, his love would never have been thwarted.

Doña Leonor remained unaware of these events. Don Rodrigo had feared that her father would answer just as he did because he cared more about earthly goods than his daughter's wishes, so don Rodrigo hadn't told her of his decision to ask for her hand. He hadn't wanted to upset her. The day don Rodrigo received her father's ill-fated reply to his unsuccessful petition and learned of his imminent departure, he wrote a letter to doña Leonor that was delivered to her by the hand of the slave who served as the messenger of their love. The letter read:

Beautiful mistress mine, your father has denied my father's request that you be mine, alleging that I am the second son in my family, a fault willed by heaven so that I should lose your beauty. Knowing that my love for you, kindled by your lovely presence, will never end, our parents have decided to prevent me from seeing you in order to thwart my hopes and put an end to my only desire. The hopelessness of our love is aggravated by the fact that they say you're already promised to a gentleman from Valladolid now at court seeking a title, and I've received orders to depart for Flanders within six days. Trying to express my sorrow is like trying to count the grains of sand or the stars in the sky; you know I love you more than life itself. You know my pain. The only possible remedy would be for you to say that you've already promised to be my wife and, if that's your pleasure, I pledge to you my word, not just once but a thousand times.

People who know the pain when two lovers separate will understand that this news brought doña Leonor terrible sorrow and grief. She took to her bed with a sudden dangerous illness that worried everyone. One morning (while her mother was out), doña Leonor made a great effort and answered her lover's letter as follows:

My illness proves to you the great sorrow your news has brought me. I can find no remedy, because the nearness of your departure allows no time to plan anything and I don't have the courage to cause my father such great displeasure. Don't lose heart, for I do not. Obey your parents and I promise you that I shall not marry for three years, even if it costs my life. This will give you time to achieve through brave deeds the merit—not to win me for I've already been won—and the necessary goods and money to satisfy my father's avarice. May heaven protect your life so I may see you again, as loyal and loving as always. I shall wait for you no matter how long you are gone.

When don Rodrigo read this letter, he sighed and wept as copiously as had doña Leonor when she composed it. It's not a sign of weakness but of strength for men to cry when their troubles have no remedy. Don Rodrigo wrote doña Leonor again, begging to see her one last time, even from a distance, to relieve his sorrow a little and help him bear his pain during his long exile.

Doña Leonor wanted to please her lover. Despite her illness and against the advice of her parents and the doctors (maybe love worked this miracle), doña Leonor got up the very day that don Rodrigo was to depart and begged her mother to take her to mass. She wanted to pray to a statue that was famous in Salamanca for its miracles. At times misfortune lets some things turn out well so that afterward the pain and grief that invariably follow happiness will penetrate more deeply.

Don Rodrigo was waiting by the church for the arrival of the coach carrying his mistress, her mother, and their maids. Handsomely dressed in black and gold to symbolize his uncertain fortune, he looked as elegant and attractive as he felt sad and unfortunate. Don Rodrigo was loved by the whole city because of his splendid appearance. The coach drew up to that place of death (as we must describe it), because it is death to separate the soul from the body. Their farewell consisted of one final glance. Doña Leonor, overwhelmed by love and emotion, directed her glance toward her lover, already wearing boots and spurs for his departure. The instant she looked at him, she realized she was losing him. This realization struck her so deeply that, in response to don Rodrigo's courtly and loving bow, her lover saw her collapse into her mother's arms in a swoon.

Her noble mother knew nothing of what had transpired because her husband had never mentioned don Rodrigo's proposal or his own refusal. She, therefore, attributed doña Leonor's collapse to her having gotten up from her sickbed too soon. Quickly they turned the coach homeward and, when doña Leonor recovered from her swoon, she found herself in her own bed surrounded by doctors and maids, all trying desperately to restore a life they thought was lost.

Although don Rodrigo was about to depart, his love wouldn't let him go while his mistress hovered between life and death. He waited for the slave, intermediary to their love, to inform him that doña Leonor, somewhat improved in health but not recovered from her grief, was resting, if one who suffers hopelessly can ever rest.

Don Rodrigo departed the moment he heard this news. He left his lady to combat her father's power alone. Being wise, her father was not unaware of the cause of his daughter's illness; he knew that don Rodrigo's departure had caused the great unhappiness he saw in her. This knowledge, however, didn't keep him from arranging everything so that, when don Alonso should arrive, he would find no impediment to the marriage. The lady kept giving excuses, repeating that she was too young to marry, that they should wait until she was in better health and older so she could enter into marriage with greater assurance. Her parents went along with these excuses; they had no other choice, seeing how long it was taking their proposed son-in-law to accomplish his mission at court.

When don Rodrigo arrived in Flanders, he was welcomed by the duke of Alba, governor of the Low Countries at this time. The duke was pleased to receive such a noble gentleman as don Rodrigo and immediately began to charge him with duties appropriate to his station and his many qualities. With each assignment, don Rodrigo demonstrated his valor and his capability and the duke, well pleased with don Rodrigo's accomplishments, rewarded him lavishly with favors and honors. Given don Rodrigo's good looks, elegance, discretion, and nobility, he became a favorite in the city, and there wasn't a lady who set her eyes upon him who didn't want him for her suitor or for her husband. Although don Rodrigo responded courteously to them all, deep down in his heart he prized, loved, and worshiped his absent doña Leonor. He adored her so truly, firmly, and tenderly that his love might have brought back the Golden Age.

It so happened that one day many important gentlemen and brave soldiers, including don Rodrigo, were with the duke of Alba. A very noble Flemish lady, named doña Blanca, appeared and knelt down at the duke's feet. She asked him to hear a most singular and amazing thing that she had come to tell him.

The duke knew doña Blanca, her quality and nobility, because she'd been married to a brave Spanish gentleman who'd served his majesty with great ability as Master of the Field. She also merited respect and esteem because of her incomparable beauty, adorned by impeccable purity. She arose from her curtsey and the duke welcomed her with his wonted courtesy. He offered her a seat and urged her to tell the story she'd mentioned.

In the presence of all the courtiers, doña Blanca described how, ever since the death of her husband the year before, she'd been hearing a dreadful noise. During the past four months, a huge and fearsome ghost had appeared in her house. Every night at eleven (that was the hour when it would appear), she and her maids locked themselves in a small dressing room and waited until it struck twelve, when the ghost would disappear. The ghost never entered the room where they were hiding. Doña Blanca ended this account and requested that the duke conduct an investigation into the matter to free her from that terrible fright.

The duke, being wise, knew that if it were really a ghost as doña Blanca said, there would be no place safe from it, no lock that could prevent it from entering into her hiding place. He thought about this for a moment and then ordered everyone present to keep the matter secret. Because the duke was impressed with don Rodrigo's prudence, courage, and spirit, he ordered him to attend to doña Blanca's problem and investigate the ghost that was harassing her, for there had to be an explanation.

Don Rodrigo kissed the duke's hand for the favor he showed him in selecting him for that assignment when there were worthier and braver people in the room. This humble response only made his noble spirit shine brighter. Doña Blanca returned home, instructed to tell no one that don Rodrigo would investigate the ghost that appeared every night, because the duke believed that through secrecy they could find out who the mysterious being was.

Night came, but more slowly than the valiant don Rodrigo wished, so anxious was he to solve this great mystery. He went to doña Blanca's house well armed and prepared for any eventuality. They chatted until ten without any reference to the matter at hand. When it came time to get ready, he spoke privately with her, asking how the ghost appeared. He asked her to call her steward to keep him company as he didn't find his own servants suitable, but don Rodrigo didn't want the steward to know why he was there.

Doña Blanca assented, feeling so attracted by don Rodrigo's elegance that she would willingly have made him master of her person and all her possessions. She spoke to him in such a way as to let him know her feelings. The servant, unaware of the plan, entered, and doña Blanca ordered him to prepare a torch, which he assumed was to light the gentleman home. He gave the lighted torch to don Rodrigo, the two went down and locked the front door, and don Rodrigo pocketed the keys. Back upstairs, don Rodrigo didn't leave the steward for an instant, nor did he permit the servant to leave the room. He commanded doña Blanca to retire with her maids and she obeyed, shutting herself in the same little dressing room as usual. It adjoined the room where don Rodrigo and his companion waited for the ghost. The lady, who was now in love, no longer felt the fear that had previously haunted her. She didn't even want to lock the dressing room because she wanted to watch don Rodrigo.

The steward couldn't figure out what was going on, and he was mystified when don Rodrigo concealed himself behind the door and ordered the servant to sit down and keep him company. The steward tried to get out of obeying but he couldn't, which only confirmed don Rodrigo's suspicions. The servant excused his agitation by explaining that he was afraid. Unable to escape, he settled back to await his fortune good or bad. He held the lighted torch in his hand as don Rodrigo had commanded. The clock struck eleven, and they heard a fearsome moaning and a loud knocking approaching them. The servant trembled from fear. Don Rodrigo was no fool and felt more suspicious than before. He held up his shield, drew his sword, and said:

"You, sir, take care that that light doesn't go out, for I must fight the ghost. Mind what you do, as I'm not a man for jokes."

That moment they saw the ghostly figure enter. The servant, pretending to faint, fell to the floor. As was later learned, he hoped in this way to extinguish the light, but his plan didn't work. The torch fell to the floor but didn't go out. Don Rodrigo quickly snatched it up with his shield hand and lunged at the ghost, which by then had reached the center of the room. This figure was so tall and deformed that it reached all the way to the ceiling. It carried a long cane from which dangled many chains that banged against the floor, making a dreadful noise intended to frighten the weak and credulous women.

Holding the torch in one hand and his sword in the other, don Rodrigo attacked, noticing that the ghost wore gloves. He slashed at its legs, instantly vanquishing it. It had walked on tall stilts like the ones used in some dances to elevate the dancers high above the ground. Because the foundation was false, the whole edifice came tumbling down with a terrible crash. This racket brought doña Blanca and her maids rushing into the room with a candle. The torch don Rodrigo was carrying had gone out with the force of his attack. Don Rodrigo stood over the fallen form, which was dazed and semiconscious. To identify the ghost, they removed the mask it was wearing over its face. It turned out to be a man both doña Blanca and don Rodrigo knew, a Flemish gentleman who was doña Blanca's neighbor. In love with her, he had courted and pursued her ever since her husband's death. The beautiful doña Blanca had harshly rejected him because he was married and her nobility and honor would never permit such an illicit relationship.

The maids brought water and put it on his face to bring him out of his faint. When he came to his senses, he was very embarrassed to see his trick discovered. Don Rodrigo said to him:

"Sir Arnesto, what kind of disguise is this, so unsuitable to your good name and your dignity?"

"Oh, don Rodrigo!" Arnesto replied, "if you know what love is you won't be surprised by what I do but rather by what I don't do. Since I must explain this disguise, as you call it, the deception was inspired by doña Blanca, whom my misfortune has made me love. Because she is who she is and I'm married, winning her was impossible. Tired of courting her and hearing harsh words from her lips, I consulted with this servant, collapsed here on the floor. Together we worked out this charade. The plan was for him to let me in through his room. With the fright caused by my moaning and the clanking of chains, the maids would run and hide, and I could have my way with the woman who's caused all my madness. Although I've been frightening them for a long time now, and fruitlessly, still I've persevered, hoping that just once fortune would favor me, so here I am.

"Tonight I came, as on every other night, not thinking that anyone might find me out. The servant always kept me informed of everything. Although he did tell me you were here this evening, I saw the torch wave, which was our signal, and everything seemed quiet, so I thought you'd gone and I could safely enter. Despite the fact that he didn't come back to his room, I thought he was doing his nightly duties as he'd done before, and I decided to run the risk. I entered, and now my trick has been discovered; things don't look good for me, being caught in a lady's house where I've never been invited. I'll surely be punished for this crime."

Don Rodrigo listened to the Flemish gentleman, feeling more pity than surprise and almost excusing his amorous error because of doña Blanca's great beauty. If the lover hadn't been married, don Rodrigo would've made a great effort to make her return the gentleman's love so he might win her. But the fact that he was married and the seriousness of his crime, especially for a noble, tempered don Rodrigo's feelings. Don Rodrigo told Arnesto that he was very sorry he suffered so hopelessly, but doña Blanca was a woman of high rank. This was not the time for discussion, as he had to take the Flemish gentleman to the duke to give account of the whole case, since the duke had commanded him to investigate.

Arnesto feared the duke more than death itself. He warned don Rodrigo of the danger to his life. Don Rodrigo replied that he had no choice but to take him before the duke. He gave Arnesto his word that he would help him in every way he could.

Don Rodrigo picked up a lighted torch, opened the window, and signaled to four brave and courageous friends waiting outside to assist him. When they saw the signal, they came to the door that don Rodrigo opened for them. They seized doña Blanca's servant and took Arnesto between them; then they all went to the duke's palace. He hadn't yet retired and, upon learning of don Rodrigo's arrival, he came out to receive him and all his company. The duke instantly recognized the Flemish noble, whom he knew to be doña Blanca's neighbor, and at once comprehended the situation. The duke heard the whole account from don Rodrigo's lips. He decided that the crime of a married man inventing such an elaborate deception in order to force the will of a woman as noble and important as doña Blanca didn't merit pardon. Paying no heed to don Rodrigo's plea for clemency, he ordered Arnesto placed in the tower and his companion sent to the public jail, where they were to remain until their trial brought a verdict. The crime was verified by statements from doña Blanca's servants and by Arnesto's own confession. Doña Blanca remained firm in her request for justice. Within a week, the two men were punished, one beheaded, the other hanged, a proper reward for those who dare to dishonor women of such worth and renown as the beautiful doña Blanca.

During this time, doña Blanca had fallen so in love with don Rodrigo that, although she did everything possible to get him out of her mind, she found herself head over heels in love. He was the only thing she could talk about, on every occasion, so all her friends became aware of her love. Her love was increased by the several calls our don Rodrigo paid her out of courtesy.

Doña Blanca, besides being surpassingly beautiful, was also young, wealthy, and of good family, qualities that might well have made don Rodrigo want to marry her had he not left his heart in Salamanca. His constant memories of doña Leonor kept him so heartsick that he didn't know how he could go on living without her. Indeed it was almost a miracle that he was still alive. When he became aware of doña Blanca's love for him, in order not to seem discourteous or so mean as to appear timid, cool, or distant, he acted appreciative but not loving. Sometimes the beautiful lady felt favored and happy, sometimes she felt put off and sad. The attentions of a man who is more courteous than loving are the torments of hell to the poor woman who has to suffer them without hope. They are felt deeply, and there is no end to them.

Don Rodrigo visited doña Blanca, obligated by her invitations and gifts. He complained about accepting so much but often he would give in so as not to seem ungrateful. He sent her gifts of greater value to keep from feeling in her debt. Sometimes he visited her simply to avoid her recriminations and desperate complaints, which, in a woman scorned, can be heartrending. Poor doña Blanca! What marble statue do you try to vanquish? With what invincible enemy do you struggle? You want a man who's in love with another woman!

One day when don Rodrigo went to repay her great kindness to him, he found her singing to the accompaniment of her harp. She sang this ballad, in which she expressed the circumstances of her love and her suspicion that don Rodrigo loved another woman:

> Listen, woods, to my misfortune
> if, perhaps, you know of love;
> hear about the madness
> of that tyrannical god.
> I adore a harsh master
> and, from fear and shame,
> I keep within my heart
> the secret of this flame.
> The man I love
> was so in love with another
> that I feared to put my love
> into such competition.
> Only in loving him could I repay

my heart for all it had lost:
its pleasure, repose, sleep,
loving without reward.
Would to heaven that my heart
had remained mute till now,
for experiencing his scorn
has caused me greater pain!
Woods of mine, I told him my love,
my passion was deceived
for all I've won is empty courtesy,
his disfavor clearly shown.
Graciously he responds
but, woe is me, he feigns,
for did he love me truly
I wouldn't feel as I do now.
In his appearance I see Adonis,
in his wit, Mercury,
in his greatness, Alexander,
in his valor, the brave Mars;
but, if he's surrendered all these charms
to another fair damsel,
it would have been a kindness of heaven
for me never to have seen them.
If, my tyrannical lord,
you adore the divine Leonor,
seeking your favor is like seeking
darkness from the sun itself.
Friendly woods, let us cry
for this impossible love
and this hopeless jealousy;
let us sing in sad tones
how unfortunate love is
when passion is born of jealousy.

The beautiful doña Blanca was the daughter of a Spanish father and a Flemish mother. She inherited her mother's beauty and her father's wit and elegance. She spoke the Spanish tongue as if she'd been born in Castile. Doña Blanca sang this ballad with such grace and charm that her beautifully stated and well-sung plaints almost won don Rodrigo's heart as he listened to such a beautiful woman sing his praises. Such flattery never sounds bad to men, especially when the flattery comes from a great beauty. I think, if doña Blanca had been alone instead of accompanied by all her maids, don Rodrigo might not have kept such faith with his absent mistress. Indeed, he gave her to understand that this was so and, when he left, he seemed so affectionate that she almost went crazy from joy.

But love was on the beautiful doña Leonor's side more than on doña Blanca's, perhaps influenced by the great sacrifices the distant lady was making for the sake of her love. The love between doña Blanca and don Rodrigo was snuffed out in the following way.

In the same city there lived a Spanish gentleman named don Beltran. He equaled the lovely doña Blanca in his good looks and in his nobility; although he couldn't match her in wealth, he'd been well brought up and left a small estate by his parents, both of whom had died in this land. Don Beltran was well respected and highly regarded and, when idle souls set out to marry off the ladies of the city, they all agreed that the beautiful doña Blanca and the gallant don Beltran belonged together. He loved her madly.

Doña Blanca had not looked upon don Beltran with disfavor until she met don Rodrigo. The moment love captured her will, she forgot all about don Beltran, and the mere mention of his name filled her with scorn. Her disdain almost killed the poor gentleman. He sought to discover the cause of doña Blanca's change of heart. Gifts to servants often buy their loyalty, since they're not very good at keeping secrets. Don Beltran learned from one of doña Blanca's maids that his lady had fallen in love with don Rodrigo. He also found out that don Rodrigo responded to her love more from courtesy than genuine desire. Believing this report, don Beltran decided to try to win doña Blanca by using reason instead of bravado and daring.

That same night as don Rodrigo left doña Blanca's house feeling more moved by her love than ever before, don Beltran approached him and asked to have a few words with him. Don Rodrigo recognized don Beltran because soldiers, although they may not all be friends, all know one another, so he politely replied that his inn was nearby if don Beltran would like to go there, or was it a matter that required a different place more suitable for a duel?

"Your inn will serve very well, don Rodrigo," don Beltran responded. "Among friends, it's not necessary to go to the kind of place you suggest."

Together they went to don Rodrigo's lodging, entered, and sat down. Don Beltran began with these words, or others almost like them:

"I'm sure, don Rodrigo, that you know about love and aren't unaware of the pain suffered by a heart that cannot attain what it desires even though it loves well. A heart that serves faithfully and remains silent achieves sufficient merit to deserve some reward. If you will listen to me sympathetically, my misfortune will touch you tenderly, for you are the cause of my suffering.

"I'm hoping, if not for a remedy, at least for your help. I shall not bore you, don Rodrigo, with proofs of my nobility. Simply by telling you that I'm the son of one of the worthiest gentlemen from the city of Guadalajara, I need say no more. I will tell you that, from my tenderest years, I have loved the beautiful doña Blanca; even before she married I adored her. She responded to my love in every way that such a noble woman could show favor without compromising her good name. Her love, however, must not have been as strong as I thought it was for, when I went to Spain on business, doña Blanca gave her hand in marriage to her late husband, with whom she lived for scarcely a year. He died, but my love did not; it survived its disillusionment.

"When I saw my mistress widowed, my hopes renewed their flame and again I was favored by the lady as before. Just when I thought I'd find myself bound to her in the yoke of matrimony, her affections changed suddenly. Dramatically, as you know, for she's loved only you since the night you conquered that ghost, fabricated for my misfortune. I'd have conquered him myself, relieving you and the duke of Alba of any concern, if only doña Blanca had told me of that nefarious trick. But fortune decides one's luck, and one person's misfortune may bring good fortune to another. Your victory has placed me in a more miserable position than anything I could imagine. My anger has advised me to kill you, but I resisted the temptation. Not because I think I'm braver or in any way superior to you, but because I had the advantage in that I controlled a situation of which you knew nothing. I've met your mistress doña Leonor, and I know that she is and will always be your true love. So I decided to beg you, for her sake and because you prize her highly, to please take pity on my woes. If doña Blanca is not to be yours, let her be mine. In giving up her beauty, you'll acquire a devoted slave, which I shall be so long as I live."

With these words, don Beltran ended his speech, shedding a few tender tears. Deeply moved, don Rodrigo felt great compassion and obligation. Given his own experience with love, he needed to hear no more to understand how don Beltran felt and to sympathize. Don Rodrigo said he wished he loved doña Blanca more so he had more to give up in ceding his place to don Beltran. To tell the truth, don

Rodrigo had never returned her love, he'd simply shown her a restrained affection and a prudent courtesy. Don Rodrigo offered to do everything in his power on don Beltran's behalf. He did think, however, that doña Blanca was so in love, so impassioned, that the only way for don Beltran to win her would have to be through some deception. They decided that don Rodrigo, always gracious, should continue the affair until don Beltran could gain possession of the heartless lady. This don Rodrigo did. He visited her the very next day. Doña Blanca was thrilled with the favors she'd received the evening before and with the thought that now she had him within reach.

Don Rodrigo, if ever he had felt any desire for doña Blanca, was now obligated to don Beltran because the latter had asked him for his help, so he forgot any feelings he may have had. She was so intent upon favoring him that he begged her to grant him an audience that night without witnesses, for love needs no witnesses. Don Rodrigo dared to ask her this favor before they married because it would displease the duke if they married while the war lasted. But, of course, when it was over, the reward he'd ask for his services would be to marry her.

In order not to lose her chance, doña Blanca accepted the proposition. She told him to come at eleven, the hour when all her maids retired. To signal her, since he was musical, he should sing her a song so she could enjoy all his charms. She herself would open the door for him and he, having promised to marry her, would know how much she loved him in possessing her.

Don Rodrigo kissed her hands numerous times (a favor she greatly esteemed and a daring liberty on his part, as he later told don Beltran). He asked her permission to let a friend whom he trusted absolutely accompany him to be witness to their good fortune. Doña Blanca acceded because she believed that she was winning a treasure and could be profligate with her favors.

Don Rodrigo took leave of his deceived lady and went to look for don Beltran to tell him about the arrangements. Don Beltran acted as pleased as he could with such good news. At the appointed hour, the two gallants went together to the lady's house. Her household had already retired. She was waiting for them on her balcony, beautifully dressed, for she had set aside her widow's weeds for the raiment of a bride. I suspect, if don Rodrigo could have seen her, he might have regretted giving her up. Furthermore, I think love was kind to doña Leonor, for the dark night suited don Beltran's purposes. Love seemed to want to make him happy and thus ensure the good fortune of the poor woman in Salamanca who imagined and feared just such situations.

In the street in front of doña Blanca's house, don Beltran, who boasted of a magnificent voice, signaled with his lute and then sang this ballad:

> Woods who, once upon a time, were
> witness to my good fortune
> when I was happier
> and my mistress more constant,
> if ever, perchance,
> my desires obliged you,
> my praises flattered you,
> my verses sang your glory,
> turn your leaves into eyes
> to see how I come back
> to bring you with my tears
> new and greater suffering.
> Woods of mine, a second time
> I offer you my tears
> for you to use
> to swell your gentle streams.
> I loved Laura; fear not
> that I don't say I love her still
> because I want to trick her
> by saying that I scorn her.
> I learned how to love
> by loving her, for
> all my gallantries were true
> and great was my passion.
> You know how she treated me,
> I cannot repeat it;
> my unlucky star was to blame
> or my gallantry insufficient.
> Sorrow pursues true love
> and jealousy kills it.

Doña Blanca had completely forgotten about don Beltran so, although she knew his voice, she didn't recognize it and, believing him to be don Rodrigo, she whispered to him:

"This fortress doesn't surrender so easily. You can only win what you desire by singing another song."

Don Beltran was quick to respond and sang this sonnet:

I love and I fear; if I fear it's because I love,
for it wouldn't truly be love if there were no fear;
I'd like to feel brave, if I could,
but if I do, then I heed not my true love.

If I call upon Love himself to succor me,
he haunts me with great fears.
I want to love, I don't want to be afraid,
because my love is demeaned by my fear.

My fear has been fear of losing you
because love has always been unfortunate,
but never doubt that I fear because I love.

Well I know that love is won by daring,
it's also true that one who's loved forgets;
one who fears, loves, and loves truly.

Thus, I love and I don't love;
I fear and I don't fear;
the more I burn, the greater my chill,
for if the one I love
I win being cowardly and I lose by bravery,
do not refuse me because my love is clever.
Truly I adore you
and would be very happy
if I knew how to conquer as I know how to love.

Doña Blanca saw that it was time to reward her lover by letting him in, so she came down and opened the door for don Beltran to enter. The lady asked him if he came intending to be her husband. The loving gallant, desiring nothing more, said yes and embraced her. He called out to his friend who was waiting further down the street. Don Beltran promised to be her husband in his friend's presence, which, according to Flemish custom, constituted as proper a marriage as if they'd been wed formally. With this assurance and believing that her new husband was don Rodrigo, doña Blanca surrendered herself to don Beltran, letting him enjoy all he'd desired and won through his persistence, which took most of the night. For honor's sake, there was no light in the room, making it easy for doña Blanca to be deceived and believe that she was with don Rodrigo and not don Beltran.

At last don Beltran noticed that it was almost dawn. Alleging the discourtesy of leaving his friend so long in the street, he took leave of his new wife. The two went downstairs, and the noise of the key in the door roused don Rodrigo, who saw it was time to reveal his deception. He identified himself to the lady and presented the man she had taken for him. Ardently, he begged her to forgive his deception, but don Beltran's great love for her and her harsh treatment of him had forced them to use such means. Furthermore, he could never marry anyone except the beautiful doña Leonor, to whom he'd given his promise of marriage.

The beautiful doña Blanca wept sorrowfully as she listened to don Rodrigo's statement. Finally, realizing that she couldn't do anything about it, she asked don Rodrigo, the matchmaker to her deception, to make arrangements with her family and the duke so that everyone could celebrate her marriage to don Beltran. She bade the two men good-night. Don Rodrigo negotiated his new friend don Beltran's good fortune with such dispatch that within three days doña Blanca and don Beltran were wed to everyone's great delight.

Meanwhile, in Salamanca, doña Leonor was leading a sad, almost inconsolable life. The three years she'd agreed to wait for don Rodrigo had passed; now almost four had gone by and all she'd had to entertain her love was an occasional letter. (Don Rodrigo was aware of the danger she was in, but he didn't dare ask the duke for leave as the war wasn't yet over and no leaves were granted during wartime.) Doña Leonor had been putting her parents off with the excuse of her tender age and her poor health (which had deteriorated because of her constant unhappiness). Her parents, not wanting to upset their daughter, used the same excuses with her fiance, who had now been in Salamanca for over a month. She was their only child and they loved her dearly. They were concerned about her health, but they still suspected that don Rodrigo's absence was the real cause of her melancholy.

One day the beautiful lady, feeling embattled by her parents, torn by her love, and desperate because of his prolonged absence, went into her dressing room where, she thought, no one could hear her, and she uttered these laments:

"Oh, Love, what cruel punishments you use to consume me and wear down my patience! Why do you mistreat those who serve you and torment those who obey you? Does my constancy offend you? Does my loyalty displease you so much that you must unseat me from the happy state I enjoyed in my childhood, destroying my happiness in my age of discretion? Why did you take from me the joy that I now recognize and appreciate? Hope, what gives you encouragement?

Desire, what feeds your growth? Loving passion, how can you persist when your absent master not only doesn't keep the promise he made to come back but even denies you the few letters he used to send to encourage your weakness? Alas! Don Rodrigo, how different your actions from your words! You, the true lover? You, constant? Faithful? You, who said that the memory of our love would live on even after death? You've had three years to confirm your words by your deeds. Believing in your words, I've endured a flood of pressures, a century of unhappiness, and more threats and sorrows than the sands of the seas and the stars in the skies. I've endured, not just the three years we agreed upon, but even a fourth year now drawing to its end and my own. I can't put off my parents any longer nor can I forget you. What other excuses can I give? What other means can I use? If I obey them, I lose you. Even if I displease them, I do not gain you; you remain absent and forgetful of me while I live in this chaos and confusion where love struggles with obedience, constancy with absence, and this conflict threatens and consumes my life.

"Oh, deceitful men! How wretched are the women who believe in you! If we discourage you, you call our modesty cruelty, our discretion disdain, our purity ingratitude, and our chaste thoughts perverse. If we accept you, your attentions are deceitful, you hide behind pretense, you conquer us with lies. When, at our own expense, we surrender and grant you possession, then your pleasure diminishes and you no longer prize us, you get bored and treat us coldly. When you're jealous, you insult us; when you're weary, you offend us; when you scorn, you cause grief. In sum, when you see yourselves loved, you remain disaffected. When you wish to shake off the yoke, closing your eyes to all obligation, you find rationalizations to repay us for all we've done for you. And we're so foolish that we don't learn from each other. We repeat the very same mistakes we've seen a friend or a relative make. To cover up your own faults, you complain of our inconstancy, you offend against our loyalty and call our love persecution, our regard nagging, our scruples offenses.

"Who would ever have thought, ungrateful don Rodrigo, given my youth, nobility, and modesty, that you'd be the one to cause my torment and teach me how false men are! Loving, you forget; pledged, you scorn; loved, you offend. In the end, you wound the tenderest woman in her honor, in her very life. How did Daphne offend Apollo that he should call her ungrateful and ignoble instead of chaste and modest? How did Dido offend Aeneas that he should charge her with being dull and irritating and so excuse his abandoning her and causing her suicide when she loved him truly? How did Olympa, who gave up her family, country, and honor to love Virenus, offend him? And look how he repaid her in the end!

"How have my nobility, my constancy, my loyalty, and my firmness displeased you that you treat my love with such ingratitude? What can I tell my parents that they'll believe? What excuse can I give that they'll accept? Shall I allow their pleading to overcome my will? Yes. They are my parents and they desire nothing but my welfare; even if their wishes were harmful, I owe them my very being and more love than I can imagine. How else can I repay them, except by obeying them and giving them pleasure? But if I obey them, how can I be true to my love and keep my promise to don Rodrigo? It is possible that some terrible exigency has kept him from coming at the appointed time. Can I live without him? No. Well, if I must die without don Rodrigo, I prefer to die having had no other master to take his place in my heart or in the life that, in my mind, I've promised to him. I must refuse my parents; I'll suffer their harshness and not evade their punishment. When I die, I shall die constant. It's impossible that my beloved, although he may forget me now, will not be moved by my constant love when I die for him. What are four years or four thousand? Am I to be less brave than Penelope, failing to withstand those who try to marry me off against my will, who won't let me wait for my beloved to return? Certainly not. If there's no other remedy, death will be my final solution."

In saying these words to herself, the beautiful Leonor gathered such strength that all the power in the world seemed small to her. She felt sure that she could turn things to her will. She dried her tears and, feeling much better for having vented her passion, went to join her maids. Everything seemed better since she'd withdrawn to her dressing room and expressed her complaints. But, as we mentioned, her mother, anxious to find out the cause of doña Leonor's melancholy, had listened to the whole lament and heard all the reasons why she refused to marry. To make sure, that same night after her daughter was fast asleep, doña Leonor's mother took the keys to her daughter's desk and inside she found more than enough proof in don Rodrigo's letters. When she'd read them all, she put them back as she'd found them, locked the desk, and replaced the key.

She recounted what she'd learned to doña Leonor's father. The two of them realized they could never talk her out of her love, so they decided to have a letter written in the name of don Rodrigo's servant, whom they all knew, which reported that his master had married a very beautiful, very rich Flemish woman whose dowry had suited his needs. This letter was delivered to don Rodrigo's parents. They didn't really believe the news, as their son hadn't written himself; even so, they told their friends, and the word spread throughout the city. Bad news travels fast, so it soon came to doña Leonor's ears. She measured the inconstancy of men with her own unhappiness. She calculated that the time that had passed since she received his last letter was more or less the same as the time she'd agreed to wait for him to return. She believed the news of his marriage. Desperately seeking some remedy for her unhappiness and desiring vengeance, it seemed to her that her only option was to surrender to her tyrannical fiance, as she considered the husband her parents had chosen for her. Sad and tearful, tasting her misfortune, at last she gave her hand to don Alonso. They were wed in Salamanca with the most splendid feasts and parties the city had ever seen.

Whoever looks at doña Leonor, now married to a different master than the one her love had promised, may want to blame women's fickleness. Others will say you shouldn't be so easily fooled by unsubstantiated news. Doña Leonor is innocent of the charge of inconstancy; she had even waited an extra year beyond the time the lovers had agreed upon. Furthermore, don Rodrigo was certainly lax in not writing to her. Her parents' insistence was powerful, and their deception was convincing. What really exonerates doña Leonor and proves her love is what happened after her marriage. To her displeasure, she had to put up with her husband's maddening attentions. She'd hated him before her marriage, and no sooner had she given him her hand than she was sorry, and afterward even sorrier. From this unhappiness she fell prey to a profound melancholy that infuriated not only her husband but also her parents.

We'll leave doña Leonor, victim of a terrible deception, and go to Flanders where don Rodrigo, fearing just such an eventuality, saw don Beltran in possession of his beloved doña Blanca. Don Beltran was more in love than ever, and doña Blanca quite content with her new husband. Don Rodrigo valiantly performed his military duties. The duke had excellent troops under his command, and he observed that don Rodrigo consistently distinguished himself in the execution of his duties. The duke honored don Rodrigo by giving him command of a cavalry troop; in the field, don Rodrigo performed even greater deeds and earned eternal fame and praise from everyone.

At this time, the well-known sack of Antwerp took place, which was famous and celebrated everywhere. Don Rodrigo realized that some Spaniard would be appointed to return to Spain carrying the news to the wise and Catholic King Philip II. He thought this was the perfect opportunity for him. Trusting in his outstanding record, he requested the duke to grant him the favor of performing this mission. Don Rodrigo also told the duke of his personal reasons for leaving his service prematurely.

The duke granted don Rodrigo's request and granted him other favors to acknowledge his merit. Don Rodrigo, happier than he'd felt in his whole life, set out immediately for Spain. He made the journey faster than anyone else could have, as he was carried on the wings of his love.

Don Rodrigo arrived at court and submitted his report. To reward him for the good news, his majesty honored him in many ways and awarded him the habit of the Order of Santiago with its four thousand ducats of annual income. The moment don Rodrigo completed his mission at court, with all these rewards, he returned on leave to his native city, intending to ask for the hand of his beloved mistress Leonor in marriage. Should her parents refuse, he planned to reveal her written vow to the vicar.

Don Rodrigo reached Salamanca and enlightened his parents as to the false news they'd received of his marriage. Immediately he asked them to try to arrange his marriage to the beautiful doña Leonor. The answer he received was cruel: namely, that she was already married. Don Rodrigo felt sad, desperate, and terribly confused. Finally, tired of feeling sorry for himself and lamenting his misfortune and tormenting himself with all kinds of imaginings, he left his house intending to speak to doña Leonor. He wanted to tell her of his sorrow and blame her inconstancy. Then he planned to return to Flanders to die in the service of his king, where he'd enjoyed better fortune than with his faithless lady.

When don Rodrigo got to doña Leonor's house, the sad lady was on her balcony. She was feeling unusually dominated by melancholy thoughts about the unhappy marriage she'd entered to vent her anger against her faithless lover. Marriages made under such circumstances always end up bitter.

Her husband don Alonso was a jealous man and also, not being any better than most of his kind, he enjoyed satisfying his appetites and other vices by womanizing and gambling, which made doña Leonor despise him even more. Because of her coldness and overt scorn, he didn't treat her very lovingly; this made her life so unpleasant that not a soul in the house had seen her laugh since the day she married.

When don Rodrigo saw her looking so melancholy, he stopped, feeling very distressed. The lady came out of her abstraction and noticed the attentive, gallant soldier who was gazing up at her. The instant she recognized don Rodrigo, she uttered a loud, sharp, scream and fell in a paroxysm to the floor. Doña Leonor's reaction so upset don Rodrigo that he regretted his decision to gaze upon her, which had caused her such a shock.

The noise of her fall brought her mother and the maids rushing to the balcony. Because she was unconscious, they thought she'd fainted. They carried her to her bed, undressed her, and placed her under the covers. Quickly servants were sent to fetch her husband and a doctor. Several doctors came and examined her carefully. They tried a thousand remedies, with no result. They massaged her and slapped her; and finally, having exhausted all remedies, they declared doña Leonor dead. This news shocked her family and the whole city. As soon as the news of her sudden death became public, people wept over the loss of such a beautiful lady, almost as if she'd belonged to them. When strangers felt her death so deeply, you can imagine how it affected the man who held her in his heart, don Rodrigo. After she'd swooned, he couldn't tear himself away from her street, waiting for some news about her condition. The sudden crying and wailing from within his mistress's house communicated the dreadful news to him. In an effort to find out more certain information, he questioned one of the servants leaving the house. When don Rodrigo heard that doña Leonor had dropped dead, he almost did likewise. Don Rodrigo took refuge in his house and said such pitiful things as you can imagine.

The doctors, to make no mistake, ordered her family to wait thirty-six hours before burying her.

The appointed time passed, and her family saw it was useless to delay longer. Doña Leonor's body was taken to the church, the funeral mass was said, and she was buried. Her lovely body lay in a coffin lined with black velvet. As with all her family, her coffin was placed in a vault in a beautiful underground chapel lined with niches to contain the coffins. At the front of the chapel there was a richly adorned altar with a life-size crucifix and many lamps that the sacristan lighted each evening. Many masses were said in that place where they left doña Leonor forever.

Don Rodrigo learned that his beloved doña Leonor had been placed in the vault and, driven by the sorrowing love that weighed heavy on his heart, he went to the church the moment night fell. He encountered the sacristan just locking the doors to the vault, having lighted the lamps on the altar. Don Rodrigo begged the sacristan to let him have one last look at the beautiful doña Leonor. He gave the sacristan a chain worth a hundred escudos. Because of the reward, which makes the difficult easy, the sacristan willingly agreed. He closed the church, and the two went down together to the funeral chapel. They opened doña Leonor's coffin, and the loving gentleman embraced her lifeless body tenderly, as if it were alive. Bathing it with his tears, he said:

"My dearest Leonor, who ever would have thought that when at last I held you in my arms, you would be dead and have no ears to hear me? Woe is me! How cruelly you've had to pay for your error in marrying while I was still alive! It was cruel for you to have taken such enormous vengeance! Beautiful mistress mine, you should've stayed alive, even if you belonged to another master, for all I needed to live happy was just the sight of you. I didn't want you gone! I don't take my own life only because I'm Christian, but I shall go where the enemy can kill me on the battlefield. You'll soon be accompanied in death by the man who adored you in life."

Don Rodrigo said these and many other heartfelt words so sad that the sacristan began to weep. Don Rodrigo looked up at the crucifix on the altar. He had never faltered in his devotion whether he was in love or despondent. Don Rodrigo knelt down before the crucifix and prayed for pardon for having spoken like that to the lovely doña Leonor in His divine presence. With a fervent prayer, don Rodrigo prayed for her to come back to life, just as Christ had sacrificed His life on the Cross in order to grant everlasting life. He made a solemn promise. Oh, the power of prayer! It can do so much! Oh, merciful God, who heeds the prayers of those who call out to Him!

The very instant don Rodrigo ended his devout and fervent prayer, it was mercifully heeded. He heard a sound from the coffin where doña Leonor was lying. He turned his head and saw that the lady was moving her hands to her face. She uttered a faint sigh. Don Rodrigo and the sacristan hovered over the coffin and observed that she hadn't opened her eyes, but she was beginning to breathe. They agreed that they should remove her from the funeral vault so that, if she did recover her senses, she wouldn't find herself in such a frightening place. Don Rodrigo gave heartfelt thanks to God and promised the Holy Christ silver lamps and rich raiment. Gently he picked up the beloved form. He ordered the sacristan to close the coffin and put it back as it had been before. He carried doña Leonor up into the church and laid her on a soft carpet. He handed a doubloon to the sacristan and sent him to get some wine and biscuits to nourish her when she recovered. The moment the sacristan left the church, don Rodrigo took his lady in his arms and carried her to his house. He carried her to his room without anyone knowing, took off the habit she was wearing, and put her in his bed.

The sacristan came back and didn't find the gentleman or the lady. He had no idea who the loving thief was. He locked the church, went back to his room, where he packed some shirts and clothes, the chain, and the change from the doubloon and, leaving the keys hanging on a nail, he went to a friend's house where he could stay in hiding until he saw where that would end.

Don Rodrigo, thrilled that doña Leonor was gradually recovering the warmth of life, began to call out her name and sprinkle wine over her face. He applied compresses to her nose, and she came to her senses. She opened her eyes and saw don Rodrigo alone, with no other people around. She was overwhelmed to find herself with don Rodrigo, knowing where she'd been, as you'll find out. Amazed, she asked where she was, she didn't remember exactly what had happened. Don Rodrigo responded telling her everything he knew. Doña Leonor confirmed the miracle that she had come back to life, and other things that you'll soon find out.

The lovers decided to go the next day to Ciudad Rodrigo where don Rodrigo had relatives. From there, they would publish their wedding banns and marry after the proper time. To make sure that everything was properly done, don Rodrigo consulted with a theologian who advised him to go ahead with his plans and have the banns read in Salamanca as well. He believed that God had returned doña Leonor to life so that the lovers could keep their first vows. What an example for those people who never keep any vows!

Don Rodrigo informed his parents that he was going to Ciudad Rodrigo to visit relatives and, with their permission, he departed with his lady that very night, which was the second one after she'd come back to life. Doña Leonor regained strength but not her color; that never came back to her face.

As soon as our gentleman and his lady arrived in Ciudad Rodrigo, he sent a messenger to his parents asking them to come to Ciudad Rodrigo for a week to treat matters of great importance. When they arrived, they'd learn the details justifying such an odd request. His parents had often journeyed to visit those relatives and relax with them, so they took a coach and went to see their son. They entered the house where he was staying, which belonged to his mother's sister, a rich widow, and they beheld doña Leonor. They couldn't believe their eyes and asked who she was. Don Rodrigo answered. He told them the whole story. Happy, they all gave thanks to God who had blessed them in so many ways.

His parents drew up the banns and sent them to Salamanca to the priest of their church, which was the parish of all the parties concerned. The priest had, of course, missed the sacristan but, finding the silver and all the church ornaments in their proper place, he decided that something urgent had come up that required the sacristan's sudden absence. No one missed the lady.

It so happened that the three times the banns were read doña Leonor's parents and her husband were in church. They heard their daughter's name and their own names but, believing her dead and buried, they didn't react. They probably thought that in a city as big as Salamanca there must be others with the same names.

The banns were read publicly, the term expired, and there was no objection to the marriage. The lovers did in fact marry, and don Rodrigo at last enjoyed his beloved. They decided that they'd celebrate the nuptial mass in Salamanca a month later. That was the time for the city's big festival with bullfights and jousting. Don Rodrigo's parents returned home to prepare everything for the celebration; they also invited all the nobles and beauties from Ciudad Rodrigo.

Don Rodrigo and his bride, accompanied by many other ladies and gentlemen, arrived secretly in Salamanca and stayed at his parents' house. Four days later was the appointed day. Dressed in their richest and most elegant best, don Rodrigo and doña Leonor and their party entered the church for the nuptial mass at the very moment when the bride's parents and husband arrived to hear mass. Don Alonso had taken a fancy to a lady who attended that church and he was punctilious in serving her.

When doña Leonor's family saw such an elaborate and grand wedding, they looked at the lovely, splendidly attired bride and naturally they recognized her, being her very own parents and husband. But they couldn't believe their eyes! They asked everyone who the bride was because they recognized the groom. When they were told doña Leonor's name they were astounded, incredulous, they couldn't believe it was doña Leonor herself, whom they'd seen dead and buried. During this time, the two were wed.

Don Alonso left the church and asked some friends to call the police. He realized that he'd just witnessed his wife being married to another man. He called the police not because of any love for doña Leonor, but because of his desire to retain the vast dowry she brought.

As the newlyweds and their party were leaving the church, doña Leonor's mother, not as unhappy as the rest of the family, stood up and, staring at her daughter, approached. The mother recognized her daughter full well. She embraced her saying:

"Dear Leonor, daughter mine, how can your heart not let you speak to me?"

When doña Leonor saw her mother so close, she hugged her and burst into tears.

Then doña Leonor's father and don Rodrigo's father came over and, seeing the tumult, they tried to straighten out the matter. They led the two women outside and put everyone into the waiting carriages. In the time it took to get to the house where the celebration and banquet were to be held, doña Leonor's family learned the whole story just as I've told it here. Her parents were prudent and realized that don Rodrigo and his parents wouldn't do such an unheard of thing without good advice and opinions from theologians and jurists. They also commented on the many ways God has to achieve His will. Her parents thanked don Rodrigo's parents for all they'd done and agreed to defend their cause if don Alonso, as they thought he would, should try to sue them.

Together they arrived at the party. The tables were waiting, and everyone ate with much pleasure. Afterward they went out on the balconies to watch the festivities. The lavishly dressed and festive bride and groom sat together on the lowest balcony.

Don Alonso had hoped that would be the situation. Accompanied by his friends on horseback, he rode around the square, staring straight at the bride and groom. They ended their promenade at the foot of the balcony where the newlyweds were sitting, feeling apprehensive about don Alonso's intentions.

After a long pause, don Alonso, surrounded by the group that included the mayor and other ministers of justice, decided that that woman was indeed his wife, the woman they'd all seen dead and buried two months before. Don Alonso made a formal complaint against doña Leonor and don Rodrigo and asked the mayor to judge the case. Some people began to get stirred up and cause trouble. The mayor moved forward to arrest don Rodrigo. Don Rodrigo had been expecting just that, and he leaned over the balcony and said:

"My lords, I do not deny that this lady is my wife doña Leonor, daughter of don Francisco and doña Maria who are here present, and the previous wife of don Alonso. I hereby state that I am legitimately married to her by order of the ecclesiastical vicar. How I came to marry her I shall tell you another time. May your graces accept my word and allow the festivities to continue. This case must be proved by documents that are so much in my favor that I have no fear of an adverse decision."

Don Alonso kept shouting for the police to take doña Leonor into custody. The mayor did just that, commanding his wife who was present in the plaza to take doña Leonor home with her. He removed don Alonso's and don Rodrigo's swords and ordered them, on their oath, to stay within their houses, which would be under guard until the festivities were over. Then the jousting and the bullfights continued. The next day, don Rodrigo's parents, considering this matter more appropriate to ecclesiastical authority than to civil courts, sent a petition to the bishop asking him to take jurisdiction over the prisoners, which he did. Don Alonso made his case to the bishop. He stated that doña Leonor, the same woman whom don Rodrigo now called his wife, was really don Alonso's wife who had swooned. Because of the doctors' error, she had in fact been buried. But obviously she was no longer in the tomb where she'd been placed and was, in fact, alive, so he demanded that she and her dowry be returned to him. He'd been dispossessed of the dowry because of the false news of her death. He presented proof.

Don Rodrigo responded that doña Leonor was his legal wife. The two had loved each other from their earliest childhood and had pledged their troth to each other in writing. Doña Leonor had been unable to keep her vow because her parents had forced her into marriage. They had deceived her by telling her falsely that he'd gotten married in Flanders. Doña Leonor had had to obey them. Furthermore, even if there had been no deception, her first husband had no rights, as death dissolves the bonds of matrimony. Therefore, doña Leonor was properly his and not don Alonso's. She had in fact been dead and not simply in a swoon, as the testimony of the three doctors proved. Her family had waited thirty-six hours after her death to bury her, twelve more than required by law.

When don Rodrigo saw that doña Leonor had been buried, he'd bribed the sacristan to let him hold in his arms the dead body he had never held while alive. Having exhausted his tears, he'd turned to the statue of Christ there in the chapel and had prayed fervently and devoutly, asking Him to return her to life. And His Divine Majesty, the most Just of Judges, had answered his prayer, as they could see, granting doña Leonor a new life to enjoy with her true husband. Don Rodrigo had gone to great lengths to establish his proper title and prove that he was her true husband; he'd consulted with theologians and jurists, he'd followed all the proper procedures as ordered by the Council of Trent, as her parents and her first husband could attest. The banns had been read in their presence, and they'd made no objection and had even attended the nuptial mass, so they couldn't plead ignorance or make reclamations. God in His great wisdom had taken from don Alonso the wife who wasn't properly his and had restored her to her true and legitimate husband so that doña Leonor and don Rodrigo could enjoy life together.

After taking statements from the two men, the bishop had doña Leonor appear and asked for her statement. She declared that she was don Rodrigo's true wife for many reasons. First, she'd given him her promise, which she'd been unable to keep because her parents forced her into marrying don Alonso by means of threats and the false information that don Rodrigo had married. Under these circumstances, she had perforce given her consent. Don Alonso himself could support this as he'd never succeeded in getting her to consummate the marriage. This had caused much anger and argument, which his greed for her dowry had obliged him to dissimulate. She had indeed died a real death, as she proved by telling things that aren't important here and so aren't described. Lastly, she was now in don Rodrigo's possession, and she recognized him and no other as her true husband.

The bishop heard their case and then consulted with a famous law professor from Salamanca's great university. The case had serious implications, so the professor didn't wish to be alone in rendering a

270 TRIUMPH OVER THE IMPOSSIBLE

decision. He laid it before his students and asked each of them what was just. Loudly and unanimously, the students acclaimed: "Rule in favor of don Rodrigo! Grant her to don Rodrigo, for she's truly his!"

The bishop ordered doña Leonor to be delivered to don Rodrigo, and so it was done. Don Alonso was dispossessed of his wife and her dowry. Don Rodrigo enjoyed the beautiful doña Leonor for many years although they seemed few in light of their great love. The lovely lady never recovered her color in reminder of her death.

Doña Leonor died shortly before don Rodrigo, who followed her within a few months. They left one son who lives today, married and much loved in Salamanca.

I heard this story from one of the judges of the case who were, as I said, the students in the university of the renowned city of Salamanca. He's still alive and he calls the people by their own names. I don't use their real names because they have relatives who sit on His Majesty's Royal Council. Through don Rodrigo's intercession, the sacristan returned to his church.

In this eighth and absolutely true enchantment, you have seen a "triumph over the impossible."

Fifth Night

To set off the fifth and final night of the savory entertainment Lysis's friends had arranged for their beautiful friend, day dawned happier and more splendid than the human mind can imagine. It seemed like spring instead of winter, May and not December. To celebrate the lovely day, the pleased and happy ladies dressed in their most elegant finery, and, seeing such art combined with such beauty, it would be no exaggeration to say that they shone like stars. Or perhaps we should say that each lovely lady looked like heaven, for her eyes, like the sun, gave life to all who beheld her. The ladies went to Lysis's house. She was feeling thankful to be at last rid of her irksome quartan fever, thanks to vows she'd made to the Virgin of Carmen, and had donned a lavish new dress. The bodice, mantle, and pettiskirt were of fine, soft, golden wool; across the fabric silver embroidery in figures and loops made a lovely pattern on the rich tawny color. The overskirt was of white wool embroidered with the same figures but in thread of gold, as was the trim. She wore a diamond belt and around her neck a large cameo encircled with diamonds set off the tawny dress. Lysis was so stunningly beautiful that the sun, king of the earth, would have wanted her for his queen, a desire reflected in don Diego's happiness and don Juan's despondence.

After the ladies heard mass they greeted the other guests who were arriving, and soon it was time to dine. Seated at the tables, the many guests were served savory appetizers followed by abundant delicious concoctions, and the meal ended with a variety of artfully prepared fruits. It turned out to be one of the most splendid and sumptuous banquets that could be imagined by taste or by the mind's eye.

After the tables were cleared, the guests spent the afternoon playing parlor games and dancing until night fell. When it came time to begin the enchantments, Lysis took up her instrument. The musicians did likewise, as they prepared to sing. Much to don Diego's relief, it was made clear that these were occasional verses intended to erase the memory of the ill-intentioned verses that had been sung before. Everyone fell silent as they sang this ballad:

> Now across the eastern balcony
> appear the golden tresses
> of dawn, lifting the curtain
> of night from the sun's face.
> Here comes the beautiful reflection
> rich with perfumed flowers
> adorning the fields
> with pearls and dewdrops.
> Now the sun spreads his rays
> and gilds the haughty peaks,
> embroiders the proud mountains,
> and glances at the bordering beaches.
> Now the earth blooms with carnations,
> acanthus, and calendulas,
> honeysuckle, wallflowers,
> pinks, lilies.
> The birds are cheerful
> singing their loving songs,
> the gentle brooks leap in joy,
> the bubbling springs whisper.
> While nature overflows with gladness,
> only Marfisa weeps.
>
> She worships a thankless master
> whose fickle nature
> captures the most carefree heart,
> vanquishes the freest life.
> What is this, beautiful nature,
> she asked tearfully;
> it seems as if your glory
> is born from my sorrow.
> If you laugh because I weep,
> cease, nature, your laughter,
> for you should pity
> and lament my sad love.
> Woods who listen

to the grief that dwells in me
and cover with cold ash
all my dead hopes,
if these tears you see
do not fill you with pity,
when I call you thankless
the fault is yours, not mine.
While nature overflows with gladness,
only Marfisa weeps.

The music ended, but the song did not because Lysis and the musicians saved the second half of the ballad for the last enchantment.
Don Juan took his place and all eyes were upon him, especially Lisarda's, because she was his mistress and responded to his charm. When
don Juan saw that everyone was hushed and waiting, he began like
this:

"I considered it a joke, discreet listeners, to have to tell a story, so
I didn't have one prepared. But last night the beautiful president of
this assemblage commanded that I obey, so I took pen in hand and
wrote out several drafts, products of my feeble wit. Letting your wit
fill in for my faults, I shall begin like this":

Judge Thyself

The noble city of Valencia counted among her many wonders and marvelous splendors the incomparable beauty of Estela, an illustrious lady rich in grace, virtue, and every good quality. Indeed, even if the city could boast of nothing but having Estela as a daughter she would still be praised among all the cities of the world for this great boon. Estela was her parents' only child and heiress to the great wealth that heaven had bestowed upon them, and they were thankful and praised heaven for these blessings.

Among the many gentlemen who sought to honor the beautiful Estela with their noble attentions was don Carlos, young, noble, wealthy, and entirely suitable for Estela to choose as her husband. Of course Estela cared only to please her parents because she knew that what they wanted was best for her. Of all her suitors, don Carlos's gentility and courtesies attracted her most, but she showed such discretion and modesty that neither her parents nor don Carlos were aware of her inclination. She didn't scorn his attentions nor did she lightly accept his courtesies; she received them with an open gaze and reserved goodwill. This satisfied the gallant who happily continued his courtship, adored his beloved, and praised her beauty. Don Carlos tried through his appearance, his presence, and his continual promenades to let the lady know how much he esteemed her. He believed that once he was assured of her acceptance, which he considered an important part of such negotiations, Estela's parents would give her to him in matrimony.

There also lived in Valencia a woman of freer customs than appropriate for such a noble and well-to-do lady. She watched don Carlos pass by her house with regularity, as it was on his way to Estela's. She felt so attracted to him that, without heeding anything but her own desires, she decided to let him know of her love in any way she could, indirectly with her eyes, the soul's tongue, or directly with words. She decided to put all her money, effort, and time into this endeavor. She would appear in his presence as often as she could, trying always to arouse his passion with her beauty. But, since don Carlos's passion was directed elsewhere and held captive by Estela's beauty, he never noticed the solicitude with which Claudia (this was the lady's name) pursued him. She took note of his lack of interest in her and, given her knowledge of love, she realized that don Carlos must be in love with another woman.

Claudia began to make inquiries and soon discovered exactly what she'd been trying to hide from her heart, to avoid tormenting it with the raging illness of jealousy. Don Carlos was so devoted in his attentions to Estela that Claudia had to acknowledge the hopelessness of her love, but still she hoped to break up his affair any way she could. She could no longer live without the man she adored. The constant sight of him inflamed her love, and his unresponsiveness to her was bringing her close to death. So Claudia made up her mind to win his love or die in the attempt, a notion not uncommon among lovers. It's madness to despise life for the sake of a fantasy and to desire death because of lascivious desires.

Claudia found out that don Carlos's page had recently died. He was the servant who accompanied don Carlos everywhere and served as his loyal advisor in matters of the heart. To accomplish her own ends, Claudia consulted a servant previously in don Carlos's employ who was more interested in her money than her welfare or her beauty. Claudia asked him to help her obtain the dead page's position, explaining to him that she wanted it so she could try to win don Carlos's love away from Estela. If he could get her this position, she promised him a large reward, and she began by giving him a handsome gift.

The greedy old man saw that this was an easy way to get Claudia's wealth for himself. In less time than it would have taken him to advise her against such a course of action, he negotiated everything: he obtained the position in don Carlos's household with all its rights and obligations, and he acquired appropriate male attire for her. The old servant's resourcefulness overcame all obstacles, and within a few days

Claudia found herself serving as page to her lover. By being pleasant and performing many services, she soon won his confidence and became the repository of don Carlos's most secret thoughts. Don Carlos so favored his new page that "he" became the one charged with satisfying don Carlos's every wish.

By this time, Estela was beginning to accept don Carlos, and his love was winning out over the lady's extreme modesty. Claudia would weep when she saw how happy the two lovers were. Some nights don Carlos managed to speak to Estela when she was out on her balcony. Estela accepted his letters with delight, and she would listen to the songs with which he occasionally serenaded her. Their courtship unfolded at the expense of Claudio (this was the name the page had chosen), given that "he" was the messenger and intermediary to these encounters as well as witness to them all.

One night when don Carlos wanted to serenade his beloved Estela, he asked his page Claudio to play and sing. Instead of singing of her master's love, however, she decided, by means of this sonnet, to express her own love, because she was to the point of bringing things to a head:

> Let the one who's had his love
> and his senses enchained enjoy liberty,
> and let the one condemned to loving sorrow
> enjoy all the favors he's desired.
>
> In sweet embraces, because he is true,
> with his heart full of love's pleasures,
> let him who beheld his love from afar
> triumph over distance without fear of rejection.
>
> Let the jealous one, unfavored, live in love,
> let the scorned one conquer scorn,
> let the one who hopes fulfill his hopes.
>
> Let the fortunate one be glad with his joy,
> and let the victorious lover delight in his prize,
> and the one who loves the impossible, like me, let him die.

The gallant don Carlos of course noticed how inappropriate the sonnet was to his purpose; he'd been accepted by his lady and it was unsuitable for him to complain about impossible love. But he thought that Claudio, being a man, was in love, or maybe "he" had sung those verses because "he" couldn't think of any others, so don Carlos let it pass without comment.

Their courtship progressed for a while in this fashion, and don Carlos waited for Estela's permission to ask her parents for her hand in marriage. Then a young, elegant Italian count arrived in Valencia and took lodging at an inn near Estela's house. Since her beauty affected everyone who set eyes on her, she captured the count's affections. Confident in his many fine qualities, his gentility, because he was who he was, the count decided to ask Estela's parents for her hand in matrimony. Don Carlos submitted his petition on the very same day as the count. Don Carlos was motivated by the lady's loving encouragement and also by his jealousy of the count, whom he saw often in her street; he hoped to put a happy end to his jealousy.

Estela's parents listened to both sets of intermediaries. They realized that don Carlos was worthy of becoming Estela's husband but, preferring to see their daughter become a countess, they rejected don Carlos's petition and betrothed her to the count. It was arranged that the wedding should take place in a month; the papers and agreements were signed without informing Estela until after everything was finalized. Her parents were sure she'd go along with their decision as she'd always been accommodating and obedient. When Estela learned of her marriage, it had all been settled.

The lady naturally regretted this misfortune. She tried to get out of the marriage, but her efforts were in vain. When don Carlos told her his petition had been turned down, their love seemed hopeless. It appears that Love isn't doing his duty if he doesn't create impossible situations. When the two lovers saw each other as usual that night, Love disposed their hearts to agree that a week later, after don Carlos made preparations, he would take her from her house and together they'd elope to Barcelona and get married. By the time her parents found out what had happened, Estela would already have a husband every bit as noble and rich as they could have desired, if only such a strong competitor as the count and their own ambition had not gotten in the way.

Claudia heard this conversation and their plans touched the depths of her heart. She took refuge in her room and, thinking she was alone, she began to weep and uttered the following lament:

"Now, unhappy Claudia, how can you have any hope? Carlos and Estela will marry. Love is on their side and has cruelly decreed that I must lose him. Can my eyes bear to see my ungrateful lover in the arms of his beloved, she so happy and I so sad? To see her favored, and myself scorned? To see her fortunate, and myself unfortunate? To see her in possession and me dispossessed? No, certainly not. I'll tell him who I am and then take my own life. That's the only solution. That's what I'll do. Tomorrow I'll tell don Carlos who I am and then I'll kill myself. It's better to die once and for all than to suffer these little deaths."

Claudia said these words and others in the same vein, lamenting her misfortune. Suddenly she heard a knock at her door. She went to see who it was and found that the person knocking was a handsome, attractive Moor who had belonged to don Carlos's father. He'd just been ransomed and was waiting for a boat to take him to Fez, which was his home. When Claudia saw him, she asked:

"Amete, why have you come to intrude and interrupt my complaints, which you must have heard. Knowing my affliction and my misfortune, leave me to suffer; you can do nothing to console me. There can be no consolation for my deep sorrow."

The clever Moor, a nobleman in his own country where his father was a wealthy pasha, had, in fact, heard Claudia's lament. He also knew who she really was. He replied:

"Claudia, I did hear what you said. I know a lot, although you may not think so because I'm a Moor. Perhaps I can suggest a better solution than the one you've decided upon. If you kill yourself, what injury do you do your enemies? What you're really doing is removing one obstacle to their happiness. What you should do is take Carlos away from Estela. If that's what you'd like to do, it's easy. Just listen to my plan and, if you don't think it'll work, don't do it.

"You're a woman determined to go to any extreme, as I can tell from the fact that you've given up your feminine dress and your good name in order to achieve your desire. To encourage you, let me tell you a secret that I've never before put into words. Several times I've seen Estela, and her beauty has captured my heart. Look at what I've said in those few words! You complain that you've lost your repose because of Carlos, you accuse him of being ungrateful, but you're making a mistake. If you'd told him of your love, then maybe Estela would never have won him, and I wouldn't be dying of unrequited love. You think there's no solution now that they've decided to elope to Barcelona, but you're wrong, for in this very fact, if you will it, is your salvation and mine.

"My ransom has been paid and tomorrow I'm to depart from Val-

encia. I have a ship ready to take me home; it dropped anchor last
night in the shallows near Grao, and I'm the only person who knows
about it. If you want to take don Carlos away from his lady and
thereby make us both happy, you must do this: Estela believes everything you say because you're her lover's messenger, so you will go tell
her that your master has arranged passage to Barcelona as agreed but,
to ensure the success of the venture, he doesn't want to wait the whole
week as they'd planned and she should prepare to leave tomorrow
night. You set the time and tell her don Carlos will be waiting for
her at the dock. Then you'll bring her to the place I'll indicate and
I'll carry her off to Fez, and you'll stay here without any obstacle to
your love. You can cajole don Carlos and bring him around to loving
you, and I'll be rich with my great beauty."

The Moor's plan astonished Claudia but, because she cared about
nothing but getting rid of Estela and getting her hands on don Carlos,
she agreed to it and hugged and thanked the Moor all at the same
time. She promised to put this treachery into effect the next day. It
wasn't hard because Estela believed she was giving herself into the
hands of the man who was to become her husband. By midnight,
carrying all her jewels and money, Estela was on board the ship and
with her was Claudia, for Amete repaid her for her betrayal by taking
her captive as well.

At first Estela was unaware of her misfortune, although she noticed
that she was surrounded by Moors, including don Carlos's slave. When
they began hurriedly raising the sails, and don Carlos did not appear,
she wasn't sure what was happening but she began to suspect her
misfortune. Her terror at finding herself in such danger caused her to
fall into a deep swoon that lasted until the next day. Her terror increased when she regained consciousness and overheard a conversation
between Claudia and Amete. The Moor was afraid Estela had died.
Claudia, holding her in her arms, was saying to the perfidious Moor:

"Amete, why did you make me expose this poor woman to such
danger if you never intended to leave me in the desirable company of
don Carlos? I betrayed Estela by placing her in your hands only so I
could enjoy don Carlos. How can you call yourself noble when you've
been so cruel with me?"

"Claudia," Amete replied, "the traitor always gets what he gives.
That's the wisest advice in the world. Furthermore, one should never
trust a person who's not loyal and true to his own land and nation.
You love don Carlos and he loves Estela. To gain your love, you have

deprived your beloved of his very life by removing her from his presence. Well, what does the kind of person who'll do such a dreadful deed as to betray her beloved for a whim deserve? How can you expect me to be sure you wouldn't turn around and tell the whole city what happened to Estela; then they'd be after me and sentence me to death? To avoid that probability, I've brought you with me. This way I protect my own life and Estela's, the woman I adore. She'll survive, especially when she realizes that you can't enjoy what she's lost."

As Estela came to her senses, the two traitors were saying these and other such things and she heard most of what they were saying. She asked Claudia to explain the mystery of her abduction, which she couldn't understand. Claudia gave her a lengthy account of who she was and how they came to be captives and told Estela everything that had taken place.

Estela heard her misfortune confirmed and shed oceans of lovely tears. Amete reveled in his good fortune. He tried to console the lady as best he could. He promised that she'd be mistress of everything he possessed and even more, if she'd give up her religion. This comfort the lady considered torture rather than solace, and she cried even harder.

Amete ordered Claudia to change into women's dress and serve and coddle Estela while they sailed across the high seas to Fez.

Let's leave them for a while and return to Valencia and the moment when Estela's parents discovered she was missing. Crazy with fear, they couldn't imagine what had happened to her. With mournful faces and tears streaming from their eyes, they searched even the most hidden corners of the house. They all acted as if there'd been a funeral. On her dresser, they found the key to her desk. They opened it, and inside they found a letter that read:

My dear parents, love and ambition do not go well together, being contrary to one another. For that reason, I've chosen to reject one and surrender myself to the other. My lack of interest in the count's wealth leads me to place myself in the hands of don Carlos, whom I recognize as my legitimate husband. His nobility is so renowned that, if such a powerful competitor as the count hadn't intervened, you couldn't have wanted or asked for a better person to marry me than don Carlos. If my error in doing this, and in doing it this way, deserves any forgiveness, we shall come back to you together to ask for it. In the meantime, I shall pray to heaven to protect our lives.

Estela

You can imagine the fright and sorrow this letter caused, considering how much Estela's parents loved her and how precious she was to them. They ordered the household to remain silent, for they hoped she hadn't yet left Valencia and they required secrecy to make cautious investigations into the lovers' whereabouts. They reported the case to the viceroy. The first thing he did was go to don Carlos's house. Don Carlos, totally unaware of all that had transpired, was sound asleep in his bed, to his misfortune. Because all the parties concerned were wealthy and prominent, the viceroy himself, accompanied by the officers of the law, woke don Carlos from his sleep. He was taken to a castle and charged with abducting the beautiful Estela and offending against the honor and nobility of her parents. The charge was signed by her parents and her husband, for thus the count considered himself. The evidence used was Estela's letter and others found in the desks of the two lovers, as well as the testimony of neighbors and servants, who are like knives to one's honor and amplifiers of each liberty love takes.

Don Carlos was truly innocent of the charges that placed him in prison, and he made great efforts to prove his innocence. He was told that Estela had disappeared and that her parents had found a letter written by their daughter explaining that he, as Jupiter to this beautiful Europa, was the author of her abduction. Because of this, don Carlos would be held accountable for her whether she was dead or alive. Don Carlos was so grief-stricken that he almost took his own life. The punishment for his crime was so serious that already the knife was at his throat. Don Carlos's father, being noble and rich, defended his son with all the power he could command.

Let us leave don Carlos at this point and return to Estela and Claudia who, in the company of the cruel Amete, were sailing with favorable winds toward Fez. When they arrived, the ladies were taken to the house of Amete's father, where the beautiful Estela continued to grieve over her captivity and separation from don Carlos. When Amete realized that his kindness and cajoling wouldn't win Estela, he began to use force. He thought to obtain her favors by punishing her, so she could put a stop to her suffering only by being nice to him. He treated her like a wretched slave; he dressed her in rags; he gave her leftovers to eat and made her serve the entire household, which consisted of Amete's father, his four wives, and two other younger sons.

The elder of Amete's brothers felt very attracted to Claudia. When she assessed her situation and realized she had no freedom, no way to get herself back home to Carlos, she felt sure they'd treat her as cruelly as they treated Estela if she didn't accept Zayde, as Amete's brother was named. So she closed her eyes to God and, abjuring her holy faith, married Zayde. Because of this, Estela gained another cruel tormentor. The poor woman lived this sad and desperate life for over a year, all the while suffering a thousand griefs. What was most difficult for her to bear was Amete's persecution. He never missed a chance to pursue and chase her. Finally, desperate for some remedy, Amete pleaded with Claudia to arrange things so that at least he could have her by force.

Claudia promised to do this for him. To set her plan in motion, she feigned melancholy and unhappiness and began to pamper Estela and treat her lovingly. One day, when all the other women had gone to the baths and the two were left alone, the perfidious Claudia spoke these words, false as she was herself:

"Beautiful Estela, I don't know how to tell you the sadness and sorrow I feel in my heart, finding myself in this strange land leading a sinful life with my soul in terrible jeopardy. If death should catch me by surprise in my present state, my soul would be damned to hell. It's really depressing me to be so far from home, dependent on these infidel dogs who live contrary to God's laws and who make me live godless like them. So I, my friend Estela, have decided to run away. I haven't become such a Moor that my Christian faith doesn't still draw me; the only reason I did what I did was from fear, and not free will.

"Fifty Christians have a boat ready in which we can leave for Valencia tonight. Since we came together, we can return together if you like. All you have to do is say yes and we can go with God, for I have hope in Him that He will save us. If you prefer not to go, you can give me a message for Carlos, whom I expect to see a month from today. But I should warn you, so you can see how fond of you I am, that if you don't come with me, it may so happen that Carlos will come to love me. If you do come, you will complicate things for me. I tell you this so you'll know that I'm moved more by pity for your misery than by my own desires."

Estela threw herself at Claudia's feet and kissed them over and over. She had already made up her mind, and she begged Claudia not to leave her behind. Claudia would see how loyally Estela served her.

The two women decided they'd leave together that night after everyone had gone to bed, and they went to pack their few possessions in order not to go unprepared.

If only someone had said to Estela: "Innocent lady, what are you doing? Look at the person in whom you've placed your trust! If Claudia betrayed you when she was a Christian, what can you expect of Claudia the renegade? If she arranged for you to be abducted from Valencia and placed you in Amete's hands once, why can't you see that she's taking you out into the country to place you in his hands again?" But what innocent heart isn't fooled by crocodile tears and a few treacherous words spoken with kindness and affection? Claudia's ploy did deceive Estela's noble heart because she could think only of her desire for freedom.

Claudia informed Amete of the arrangements and the place she intended to take Estela. The time passed, but it seemed to all three to go by more slowly than they would've liked. At midnight, with a full moon brighter than the moon in May, Estela and Claudia, carrying their little bundles with their dresses, clothing, and other necessities for the journey, left the house and headed toward the harbor where Claudia said the boat, or ship, in which they were to escape, was lying at anchor. Amete followed behind them from the moment they left the house. They stopped at some large boulders, where Claudia said they were to wait for the rest of the group. The two women settled down in the most comfortable place the crafty Claudia could find suitable to her designs. While they waited, Claudia encouraged the terrified lady, who feared that every little sound was Amete or someone else from the household who'd discovered their absence and had come out searching for them. They spent over an hour talking and waiting. Although Amete was close by, he stayed in hiding so Estela would gain more confidence. At last Amete approached, a cruel and hateful sight to the beautiful Estela. When he saw the two women, he feigned an infernal wrath and shouted:

"Oh you disloyal dogs! What kind of escape are you attempting? Now you won't get away with the treacherous escape you'd planned."

"It's not treachery, Amete," Estela replied, "for a person to seek freedom, just as you'd do if you found yourself in my position, mistreated and beaten by you and everyone in your house. Besides, if Claudia hadn't encouraged me, I'd never have had the courage to attempt such a thing. But my bad luck seems to want to place me in your hands; I fear this will happen every time I trust in it."

"That's certainly true, you little bitch!" the renegade Claudia interrupted. "And I want you to know that my real purpose in bringing you here tonight was not to help you escape but to deliver you into the hands of the gallant Amete so he can enjoy you willingly or by force. You will satisfy his desire; tonight he will possess your body or leave you here torn to shreds. There's no boat to freedom except Amete's arms. Your only road to liberty is in surrendering to him. If you do, you'll go from slave to mistress, from being a mistreated servant to being served. Just think about it and it will happen."

After Claudia said these words, she moved away, ceding her place to the Moor. He took up where she left off and continued in the same tone, trying to persuade Estela first with kind words and then threats, caresses and then blows. Estela, bathed in tears, made no response whatsoever, and all Amete's efforts were in vain, for she was determined to lose her life before she lost her honor.

Amete became furious, his tenderness turned into rage, and he began to beat her, striking her beautiful face and threatening her with every kind of death imaginable if she refused to give in to his will. When this failed, he decided to overpower her with force and exhaust her so he could rape her. Estela's courage at this point was greater than you might have expected in such a frail maiden but, as Amete was using his full strength to subdue her, her own strength finally gave way and she fell to the ground, unable to defend herself any longer. Then she took recourse to the only real defense women have: she began to scream.

Her screams were heard by Xacimin, son of the king of Fez, who was returning home from the hunt. Deeply affected by the screaming, he ran to the place where he thought it was coming from, leaving behind the many servants who accompanied him. He arrived and saw instantly how the fierce Moor was brutalizing a beautiful woman. The prince was twenty, a very gallant, noble, and soft-spoken man. He was well loved by all his subjects because of these fine qualities and because of his courage and generosity. Xacimin also tended to favor Christians and, when he found out that they were being mistreated, he would punish this crime severely.

Dawn was by now beginning to break, so he could see quite clearly what was taking place between the Moor and the beautiful slave. He saw her stretched out on the ground with her hands tied while the cruel Amete tried to gag her mouth. By the light of the new day, the

prince saw every detail of that vile and dishonorable act. His voice
filled with anger, he shouted:

"You cur, what are you doing? In the court of the king of Fez you
dare to rape a woman? Leave her this instant or, by the king's own
life, I'll kill you."

As he said this, he drew his sword.

When Amete heard these words, he leapt to his feet and of course
recognized the prince, but he acted as if he didn't. With the prince's
sword at his throat, he swiftly drew his own and attacked. He would
have killed Xacimin if the prince hadn't leapt back, dodging his blow.
In a fury, the prince turned and said:

"You traitorous cur! You dare attack your prince!"

Amete was now blind with rage and cared about nothing. He attacked the prince a second time, and again he would have killed him
if the prince hadn't turned the blow aside, but not quickly enough to
prevent a slight wound to his head. The valiant Xacimin, realizing that
the Moor was not going to accord him the respect he owed his prince,
retreated and blew the hunting horn he wore around his neck. His
gentlemen and huntsmen, who had thought him lost and were looking
for him, quickly rushed to his side just as Amete tried to put an end
to his life with a third attack. Xacimin was rescued by his men, and
they took the traitor Amete prisoner. Estela threw herself at the feet
of prince Xacimin, as did the false turncoat Claudia. The gallant Moor
saw Estela's beauty more clearly but, instead of feeling attracted by it,
it made him feel sorry for her suffering. He asked her who she was
and how she came to be in such a place.

Estela told him she was a Christian and went on to recount as
briefly as possible her story and how she'd gotten into that situation.
The compassionate Xacimin angrily ordered that all three be taken to
his palace immediately. Even before he had his wound bandaged, he
told the story to his father, the king, and asked him to punish Amete's
crime.

The prince had his wound dressed and, even though it wasn't a
serious injury, Amete and Claudia were sentenced to death for their
disrespect to the prince and their treason. Both were impaled that very
same day. All the money and bribes Amete's father offered couldn't
save him, and Claudia died just as wickedly as she had lived.

After justice had been done, the prince had Estela brought into his
presence. He was kind and consoled her, and asked her what he should

do with her. The lady knelt down beside his bed and requested that he send her where there were Christians so that from there she could return to her own land.

The prince granted this petition; he gave her money, jewels, and a Christian slave to accompany her. Then he ordered two of his servants to take her wherever she directed.

This incident occurred when Charles V, king of Spain and Holy Roman Emperor, was fighting Barbarossa in Tunis. Estela knew about the presence of Spanish troops in north Africa. She cut her hair and, abandoning feminine garments, she donned masculine attire. Accompanied only by the Spanish captive the prince had given her, who was sworn not to reveal her identity, the two Christians took their leave of the Moorish gentlemen who had guided them out of the city. Estela and her servant went to Tunis to find employment in the service of the emperor. Estela earned a reputation for being a valiant and courageous soldier and came to serve always at the emperor's side. She won such high regard from the emperor that he rewarded her by giving her command of a cavalry troop; that's how greatly she was favored!

Estela served the emperor not just on this campaign when he restored the kingdom of Tunis to its prince Roselo, whom Barbarossa had driven to the sea, but on many other campaigns as well. She took part in all the emperor's military operations in France and Italy. Once, when Charles had to fight on foot because his horse had been killed, our valiant hero (she used the name don Fernando and was considered a hero and not a heroine) gave him her horse and fought at his side, defending him until he was safe. The emperor was so grateful for this service that he honored don Fernando with lavish favors and rewards, among which was investiture in the prestigious Order of Santiago and also the title of duke with its income. Even then the emperor didn't feel that he'd repaid her sufficiently and, if she'd asked for half his realms, he would've given them to her.

During all this time, Estela had had no news from her parents or from home. One day she recognized her beloved don Carlos among the soldiers in the army. The moment she set eyes upon him, the wound of her former love, if it had ever really healed over, burst open and began to bleed. She sent for him and, containing the great emotion the sight of him caused in her, she asked him what his name was and where he was from. Don Carlos willingly responded to Estela's questions, feeling flattered by her attention and struck by her re-

markable resemblance to Estela. He presented his letters of introduction and told her all about himself and how he came to be in the
army.

Don Carlos didn't exclude the account of his tragic love affair and
his term in prison. He told her that, although he'd intended to abduct
his beloved from her house so they could elope, she'd vanished from
sight as had his page, in whom he confided his every secret, and this
had made him suspicious. He wondered if she'd loved his page more
than him and so had run off with the servant. He questioned her
behavior, which caused his love for her to diminish. It was true that
in the letter written by the lady to her father, she said she was eloping
with don Carlos, that he was her true husband. Don Carlos couldn't
really believe that she would, in fact, run away with Claudio and say
it was don Carlos. That did make him wonder, and the only logical
explanation he could find was to think that she didn't really love him
because she'd put him in a situation for which he was almost hanged.
He'd spent two years in prison, charged with assaulting the honor of
a noble house, abducting Estela, raping her, and killing her.

During those two years she never appeared, dead or alive, and it
became impossible for him to avoid the death penalty any longer. Don
Carlos had to depend on his wits, which told him that the only way
to save his life was to break out of jail, trusting more in escape than
in any merit his case might've had. He spent the next year searching
everywhere for Estela, but all in vain. It seemed as if the earth had
swallowed her.

Estela listened to don Carlos with great astonishment, as she knew
what had happened to her. She hastened to reply to the suspicions
he'd voiced regarding her and the page, saying:

"Carlos, you shouldn't think that Estela would be fickle, that she'd
deceive you and run away with Claudio because she loved him. Women
as noble as she is don't behave that way. What's most probable is that
she was deceived herself. Maybe things happened in such a way that
she couldn't defend herself. Perhaps some day God will let her prove
her innocence and then you'll learn the truth. Now I'd like to ask you
to work for me as long as you remain a soldier. I want you to serve
as my secretary. As such you'll be treated like a friend, which is what
I'll consider you from this day on. I know that with my help—and
everyone knows the many ways the Emperor Charles has honored
me—your enemies will cease pursuing you and, when this campaign
is over, we'll obtain a court order exonerating you of all charges. The

only thanks I ask in return is that you hold Estela in higher esteem than you have, particularly considering the fact that you were the cause of her perdition. What moves me to say this is my conviction that gentlemen should think highly of women and always speak well of them."

Carlos listened attentively to don Fernando, thinking all the while that he'd never in his life seen a greater likeness to his Estela. But it didn't occur to him to think that don Fernando might be Estela herself. When don Fernando finished "his" speech, Carlos expressed his appreciation for such a great favor and asked for "his" hand to kiss. He said he would forever be don Fernando's servant. Estela raised him up from his knees, and from this day on Carlos remained in her service and was so favored that the other servants were envious.

Several months passed like this: don Carlos served his lady not only as secretary but also at the table and in the bedchamber. Always don Carlos was specially favored, and always the two would talk about Estela. They talked about her so much that don Carlos began to think that the duke was in love with her "himself." "He" kept asking don Carlos if he loved Estela as much as before, if he'd be glad to see her again, and other such things that certainly made him wonder. Sometimes don Carlos's answers satisfied Estela, sometimes they made her unhappy.

One day the emperor received the news that the viceroy of Valencia had died very suddenly, and he needed to appoint a successor to serve in that position, for he couldn't let that kingdom remain long without a governor. Immediately he thought of don Fernando, who had served him so well.

Estela had also heard about the death of the viceroy, and she didn't want to let this opportunity slip through her fingers. She went to the emperor and, kneeling down, requested that she be honored with this appointment.

The emperor felt it proper that don Fernando had made this request, but he hadn't yet made up his mind because it saddened him to lose "his" company. The emperor realized, however, that this was a well-earned and proper reward for don Fernando's services, so he granted "his" request and ordered "him" to depart immediately, bearing the new title and other necessary papers.

So now our Estela is viceroy of Valencia. Don Carlos is still her secretary and the happiest man in the world because he believes he no longer has to fear his enemies, especially now that his father is

mayor of the city. All this he confided to his benefactor. He felt satisfied that the viceroy believed in his innocence in the matter of Estela,
and he was feeling as good as free, trusting in don Fernando's promises.

They set out filled with anticipation, and their pleasure increased
when they arrived in Valencia, where the new viceroy was received
with rejoicing.

She assumed her position, and the first matter placed before her to
judge was her own case. Once again the same charges were brought
against her secretary, don Carlos. The viceroy promised to hear the
case. She ordered an investigation, and all the witnesses were examined
again. The complainants wanted don Carlos imprisoned to hold him
secure, but the viceroy satisfied them by saying that "he" trusted don
Carlos and his only prison was doing the viceroy's will. She took the
case so much to heart, as I've mentioned, that in less than six days
everything was ready for the hearing and sentencing, which was to
take place the next day.

That night don Carlos came into the room where the viceroy was
in bed and, kneeling down, he said:

"Tomorrow your Excellency is to hear my case, reach a verdict, and
declare my innocence. Besides all the witnesses who have testified on
my behalf and all who have sworn in my favor, the best, surest, and
truest evidence is the oath I've given into your hands, under pain of
perjury, that I not only didn't abduct Estela, I hadn't even seen her
since the day before her disappearance. I don't know what became of
her or where she is. Even though I did intend to elope with her, I
never had a chance to do so, as my misfortune took her from me first,
to my own ruination, and maybe also to hers."

"Enough, Carlos," Estela said. "Go home and sleep secure. I am
your master and your friend, which should relieve all your fears. I
have more confidence in you than you know. Even if I didn't, my
bringing you here with me where your life is in danger and keeping
you in my employ should be reason for you not to despair. Your case
is in my hands and well I know your innocence. You are my friend,
that's all you need think of; I'll take care of the rest."

Don Carlos kissed "his" hands and left; the viceroy kept thinking
of what she had to do.

Who can doubt that don Carlos looked forward to the day that
would bring him his freedom? Scarcely had the universal father of all
that lives loosed his rays across the balconies of the dawn, when don

Carlos arose and dressed in his finest clothes, as if to prove that this was his day of glory, as if to demonstrate his elegance and nobility more splendidly on this day than ever before. After he dressed, he went to help the viceroy dress so that "he" could reassure him of his innocence.

The viceroy emerged from "his" bedroom half-dressed with an amused scowl on "his" face. With a hollow laugh, "he" looked at "his" secretary and said:

"You've gotten up early, friend Carlos. Your anxiety makes your innocence look a little suspicious; the free man sleeps with a clear conscience while guilt is a harsh accusor."

This statement upset don Carlos but, calming himself as best he could, he replied:

"Oh, your Excellency, liberty is so dear that even if I didn't have enemies as powerful as I do, the joy of seeing myself free at last because of your kindness was enough to keep me from sleeping. Just as great sorrow prevents sleep so too does great joy. Fear of evil and hope of good have the same effect."

"You look very elegant," the viceroy responded. "On the very day you are to see your tragedy played in court in the mouths of all the witnesses against you, you dress in your finest clothes? Indeed, it seems that Estela's parents and her husband may not be far from right when they say that you must have raped her and killed her afterward, trusting that no one saw you do it. Even if Claudio, that vile intermediary to your affair, should appear, I'm not sure you can prove your innocence and, to tell you the truth, every time we speak of Estela, you reveal such little feeling, such coldness, that I think your lady owes more to me than to you. I care deeply about her loss, and you seem not to care."

What a terrible blow this was to don Carlos's heart! It sank! Suddenly despairing of any good outcome, he was about to plead time as an excuse since time brings forgetfulness to amorous passion when, with severe mien and angry expression, the viceroy said to him:

"Silence, Carlos, don't say a word. I've considered this matter thoroughly, and I find that you aren't entirely open about it, as evidenced in your great desire for freedom. Estela is gone, lost, and you're alive. Estela may be dead, and you're still sane; yet you say that when she vanished you loved her passionately. You must have a new lover now; it seems obvious that you want to be free in order to enjoy your new love more freely. Well, I shall see that justice is done, unmoved by either affection or personal interest. I wouldn't want anyone to complain to the emperor about my judgment. Judges know the importance of impartiality better than anyone, so be careful not to try to influence my judgment. I can't make promises, I can only hold you secure, which is important, for one who broke out of prison might easily break his word to me."

As Estela said these words, she signaled to a page, who left the room and returned with a squad of soldiers. They took don Carlos's weapons from him and placed him in custody. If you had seen don Carlos at this moment you couldn't have helped feeling sorry for him. His eyes downcast, his color gone, his face dejected, he could only blame himself and regret having trusted the unpredictability of the powerful.

The viceroy finished dressing. Knowing that all the parties to the trial and the other judges were waiting, "he" entered the hall where the case was to be heard. Surrounded by soldiers, Carlos entered behind the viceroy.

The viceroy took "his" seat and the other judges sat down alongside. Then the court reporter began to read the suit, stating the charges and describing the evidence to the effect that don Carlos had abducted Estela. This was corroborated by the letters found in their desks, by the servants who knew about their affair, by the neighbors who'd seen them converse through the grating. What was most damaging was Estela's letter in which she clearly stated that she was eloping with don Carlos in order not to marry the count.

To all this, the best witnesses on don Carlos's behalf were the servants of his household who declared that, the night when Estela disappeared, they'd seen him go to bed even earlier than on other nights, and don Carlos's own statement under oath that he had not seen Estela that day. But none of this contradicted the allegation that he could have gone to bed in the presence of his servants, dressed again, and gone out to abduct her. It seemed clear that don Carlos had killed both Estela and Claudio, as neither of them had ever turned up again. So don Carlos must have killed his intermediary, the page, as well. As far as the validity of his own oath was concerned, naturally he wouldn't give testimony against himself.

The viceroy saw that up to this point, it appeared well established that Carlos was guilty of assaulting the honor of Estela's parents, abducting Estela, and killing both her and Claudio. Only the viceroy could get Carlos out of this bind. Although Estela was determined to do just that, first she wanted to back him into a corner so that his passion would lead him to confess his love publicly and make him hold her in higher esteem. Estela called Carlos forward. As he stood before all the people assembled in the hall, she said to him:

"Friend Carlos, if I had known how little justice you had on your side, I give you my word and I swear by the life of the emperor, I would never have brought you back here to Valencia with me. I can't deny that my mistake grieves me, as you can tell from my tears. Please believe that I deeply regret seeing your life in such danger. If I'm to judge this case on the basis of the present evidence, then I'd have to find you guilty, seeing no other alternative. The complainants are noble, their charges serious, and their case so strong with regard to the loss of Estela that it would be a miscarriage of justice for them to accept a lesser verdict. The only solution would be for Estela herself to appear; then they would be satisfied and I could help you. But unless she does, I can do nothing but condemn you to death."

The heartbroken don Carlos was terrified to hear this sentence and, despairing, he knelt down and said:

"Your Excellency well knows, ever since we met in Italy, that every time we've discussed this case I've told it in the same words and in the same way. I wouldn't deny the truth to you as judge, even as I repeatedly told the truth to you as my master and friend. And I'll say the same thing again: I confess that I adored Estela."

"Say that you adore her," the viceroy whispered. "It looks suspicious for you to speak in the past and not feel in the present."

"I mean, I adore her," don Carlos repeated, surprised at the viceroy's insight. "I used to write her and talk with her. I promised to be her husband and agreed to take her from her house and this city to go to Barcelona. But I didn't take her away. I didn't even see her that day, may lightning strike me dead where I stand! I may die, but if I die, I die innocent! My only error may have been for me to love a fickle, false, inconstant, woman, a deceitful siren who, in the middle of her sweet song, has brought me to this shameful, bitter death. I die because I love her, not because I know anything about her whereabouts."

"Well, what could have happened to this woman and your page?" the viceroy asked. "Did they fly up to heaven? Did the earth simply swallow them?"

"How am I to know," the distressed don Carlos replied. "The page was handsome and Estela beautiful. She a woman, and he a man. Perhaps . . ."

"Traitor!" the viceroy cried out. "In this 'perhaps' you reveal your false and devious thoughts. How quickly you let yourself be carried away by your evil imagination! God help the woman who gives you the slightest pretext for denigrating her! You leap quickly to conclusions because you think that what a woman does for you, obliged by your courtship and your attention, she'd do with just any man who happens down the street. Estela wasn't a woman and Claudio wasn't a man. Estela was noble and virtuous, and Claudio a villain who, as your servant, was heir to all your falsity. Estela loved you and regarded you as her husband. Claudio hated Estela because she loved you. And, I repeat, Estela was not a woman, because the woman who's modest, discreet, and virtuous, isn't a woman but an angel. Claudio was not a man, but rather a woman who, madly in love with you, sought to break up your relationship with Estela by removing her from your sight. I am Estela. I've endured a thousand trials for your sake, and you reward me by harboring false suspicions about me!"

Estela went on to relate everything that had happened to her since the day of her disappearance from home. Everyone was astounded, and above all don Carlos. He felt most ashamed that he hadn't recognized her and that he'd impugned her honor. Still kneeling, he grasped her beautiful hands and kissed them over and over, bathing them with his tears and begging her to forgive his error. Estela's father and Carlos's begged her to forgive them, and everybody crowded around to embrace her and greet her lovingly.

The count came up to congratulate her and asked her please to keep the word her father had given him that she would become his wife. Don Carlos awaited her answer with his heart in his hand, and his hand was placed on the hilt of the dagger at his waist so that, if Estela failed to answer in his favor, he could kill the count and anyone who came to his defense. Or he'd kill himself rather than see her in another man's possession.

But the lady loved and cherished don Carlos more than her own life. Very courteously, she begged the count to excuse her from this agreement because she'd always considered herself Carlos's true wife. She wanted to give to him everything she possessed. It only grieved her that she wasn't master of the whole wide world to give it all to him. Indeed, all her brave deeds had been born from the courage that being his had given her. She asked her father for his approval.

Stepping down from the judge's bench, Estela embraced everyone. She went over to Carlos and placed her brave and beautiful arms around his neck and gave herself into his possession. The two lovers got into a carriage together and went to her mother's house. She'd already heard the incredible news and contributed to the celebration with tears of thanksgiving.

The marvelous news spread quickly throughout the city. Everybody was amazed that the viceroy was a woman and, most of all, that the woman was their Estela. People rushed to the palace or to her house to congratulate her.

A letter was immediately sent to the emperor, who was in Valladolid at the time, communicating this great news to him. Charles was more astonished than anyone, as he'd witnessed Estela's many valiant deeds on the field of battle. He could scarcely believe it was true. He answered the letter sending his congratulations and many jewels. The emperor confirmed on Estela the estates he'd previously granted her and added a new title: princess of Buñol. He transferred to don Carlos Estela's habit of the Order of Santiago with its income and the appointment as viceroy of Valencia.

The new lovers, rich and honored, performed all the ceremonies and other rites of the church. The celebration of their wedding gave much pleasure to the city; it also gave beautiful heirs to their marriage, and to storytellers it gave good material for writing an enchantment, with special praise for the beautiful Estela's valor. Her wisdom and prudence made her a severe judge, especially considering that she had to judge her own case. That's no less marvelous than anything that happened. Long live the person who can judge himself, for better or for worse; usually we judge the faults of others without seeing our own.

As don Juan ended his clever enchantment, which everyone praised lavishly, the exquisite Lysis's discreet mother occupied the special seat. She deferred to her heavenly daughter to finish the ballad she'd begun earlier, accompanied by the musicians:

> Jealous I am and, since jealousy
> is the very seed of hell,
> it's no great wonder
> that it sows sorrow in the soul.
> Alas for the heart burned
> and bedeviled by such a flame!
> And alas for the poor soul
> whose only relief lies in death!
> For the unfortunate lover to die

is not really death but mercy;
but cruel death flees
from those who are unfortunate.
The misfortunes I suffer are so great
that I am misfortune personified;
life for me is living death.
But if Fabio is both life and heaven,
why do you, Marfisa, fear
that heaven will hear your sorrows,
that life will grant you death?
While nature overflows with gladness,
only Marfisa weeps.

When the discreet Laura saw that her lovely daughter and the musicians had ended the ballad, she began her enchantment charmingly:

"Discreet listeners, I do not wish to present to you as proven facts the events of this story, although well they might be, because it's nothing new for a brother to kill a brother or for a sister to betray a sister if they're driven by jealousy, love, and envy. From the very beginning of the world there've been invidious and treacherous brothers and sisters, as we see in a thousand stories that have been written down. Neither is it new for poverty to produce ingenious trickery, particularly when inspired by blind passion. Nor is it novel for a lover to risk his soul to get what he wants, or for a woman trying to protect her honor to ask a lover to do the impossible. I don't even find it startling for the devil, always trying to win captives for his horrible and fearsome prison, to arrange extravagant displays, pretending to satisfy men's desires. What is most amazing is that the devil should ever be capable of a good deed, as you will see in my enchantment. To explain this there must have been other, secret causes we can't understand. At any rate, I'll not ask you to believe any more than you wish to. I'm telling it only to make a point and to warn people to be careful. So with your permission, here's how it goes":

The Magic Garden

Not many years ago in the beautiful, noble city of Zaragoza, a miracle of nature and the glorious crown of the kingdom
of Aragon, there lived a rich and noble gentleman who, because of
his outstanding qualities had won in marriage an equally fine woman
to be his wife. Her nobility and virtue matched his in every way, and
this is the greatest reward any man can have. Heaven gave them as
the fruit of their marriage two celestial suns, which is how they considered their two daughters. The older was named Constanza, the
younger Theodosia, and both were remarkable in their beauty, discretion, and grace, and both were so outstanding that neither sister
excelled the other. These two beautiful young ladies, renowned for
their wealth, their beauty, and because they were so accomplished and
perfect, were considered the pride and joy of the city.

The girls reached the age of discretion when a maiden's beauty and
grace begin to blossom. Don Jorge, a young, wealthy nobleman, also
a native of the city of Zaragoza, fell in love with Constanza. He was
the only heir to his parents' estate for, although he had a younger
brother named Federico, he was the elder son.

Federico loved Theodosia, although he hid it so carefully from his
brother that the latter never knew about his love. The two brothers
didn't get along, and Federico feared his older brother might ruin his
courtship of Theodosia.

Constanza did not look on don Jorge with disfavor; indeed, she
felt grateful for his affection and accepted it with modesty. She realized

that soon her parents would arrange her marriage, and she didn't think there was anyone in the world as deserving as don Jorge. Trusting in this belief, she appreciated and even favored his courtship. She felt sure that the moment he asked her father for her hand, their love would reach its happy culmination. Of course, she comported herself with such dignity and modesty that, if her father didn't accede to her desire to have don Jorge as her husband, she could, without any offense against her honor, give up this pretension.

Things didn't go so well between Federico and Theodosia; he could never obtain even the slightest favor from her; rather, she showed great scorn for him. The reason for this was that Theodosia was suffering from her impossible love for don Jorge. Jealous of seeing her sister so happily loved, Theodosia began to ponder and plan ways to separate the two lovers. She was so astute and clever that neither don Jorge nor Constanza ever suspected that she was in love with don Jorge, let alone suspected her of plotting against them.

Her rejection of him made Federico so sad and unhappy that everyone knew he was miserable, even though they didn't know the reason. Constanza noticed Federico's melancholy for, although she loved don Jorge with all her heart, she was also fond of his brother. Constanza came close to suspecting that Theodosia was the cause of his great sorrow because she'd noted telltale signs in the way he glanced at her sister. Constanza wanted to find out for sure. This was easy because both gentlemen and their parents were good friends of the house, and the close friendship between their families made it difficult to keep anything hidden.

One day Constanza took Federico aside to talk with him and learned from him how much he loved her sister and how coldly Theodosia treated him. But Federico warned her that don Jorge shouldn't know of his love because, as we've already said, the brothers didn't get along.

Constanza was amazed that Theodosia should scorn Federico because he was in every way worthy of love. But, since Theodosia kept her own love for don Jorge so well hidden, it never occurred to Constanza that don Jorge might be the cause. Rather she blamed it on Theodosia's unloving nature, which she told Federico every time the two talked, and they talked together frequently. Ultimately don Jorge became somewhat annoyed and began to feel jealous of his brother. Constanza's reserve made him more jealous because, even when there was an opportunity, she would never let him take her hand.

Don Jorge's jealousy inspired Theodosia with a plan to make him reject her sister. She thought don Jorge would merely come to despise Constanza. It never occurred to her that he might take revenge. If don Jorge came to hate Constanza, then she could fill the place her sister had formerly occupied. This kind of wrong-headed thinking is typical of people who do evil: they see only the harm they do to their enemy and cannot imagine the harm that might be done to the one they love.

With this plan in mind and not imagining the bloody conclusion it might lead to, Theodosia decided to tell don Jorge that Federico and Constanza were in love with each other. No sooner said than done, for blind Love rules blindly and is likewise served by the blind. One who isn't blind can't rightly consider himself Love's captive.

Fortune soon gave Theodosia her chance. One day, Constanza and don Jorge were alone; he was angry with her and, you might say, jealous, because he'd found her in conversation with his detested brother. So don Jorge told her all his worries and accused her of a waning affection for him. He refused to believe that her reluctance to let him hold hands was simply discreet modesty on the part of the lady. She replied as follows:

"Don Jorge, I'm sorry you don't appreciate my affection and the great favor I grant you in allowing you to love me. But you stoop to such a low opinion of me that you suspect me falsely and entertain unfounded jealousies that you've just mentioned. Furthermore, you dare to ask more favors from me than the ones I already permit, knowing full well that I won't grant them. I can't reply to such unfounded suspicions as yours for, if I'm not more giving to you than I am, how could you think I'd be giving with your brother? As for your complaints about my reserve, I'll tell you once and for all, to keep you from pestering me, that so long as you aren't my husband, you can expect no more from me. I have parents and I shall do their will. Given your many fine qualities, my parents' wishes should not differ from your own wishes. In saying this, I'm telling you what you should do if you want to please me and, if you don't, then things will turn out otherwise."

After Constanza said these words, she left him and went into the next room where there were people and servants present. She didn't want to encourage him to take any amorous liberties.

Theodosia couldn't have wished for a better occasion to work her deception. She'd been watching and listening to every word they said, and she saw don Jorge so downcast and despondent at Constanza's firmness that she went up to him and said:

"Don Jorge, I can no longer hide my sorrow at seeing you so madly in love with my sister. I can't bear knowing how she deceives your love. If you'll give me your word never to repeat what I tell you, if you'll never tell a soul that I've told you what I know and what you also should know for the sake of your honor, then I'll explain why Constanza's affection for you seems so reluctant."

Suspecting exactly what the treacherous Theodosia was intimating, don Jorge reacted eagerly, anxious to find out what would only cause him grief to learn, which is typical of lovers. Swearing many oaths, don Jorge vowed to her that he would keep her secret.

"Well," Theodosia said, "your brother Federico and Constanza love each other so deeply and so firmly that, to prove it, I need say only that they've agreed to marry. They've promised each other, and I think they've even exchanged other favors. I witnessed this without their knowing. I saw and heard everything that I'm describing to you because I was afraid that might happen. Now that you know the truth and there's nothing you can do about it, I urge you to bear this setback and accept the fact that Constanza wasn't born to be yours. Heaven is saving you for someone who really deserves you, and love made in heaven, human beings cannot set asunder. You'll find the woman you deserve, and your brother will find himself punished for having dared to take away your lady."

Theodosia ended her betrayal at this point, not wanting to tell don Jorge about her love for him at the moment so he wouldn't suspect her treachery. Don Jorge went into a desperate, jealous rage, thinking about his brother's offense against him and Constanza's disloyalty to him. Don Jorge allowed his jealousy to act as judge: his outraged love joined forces with his hatred of Federico to act as prosecutor and, without asking any more questions about the offense, he came to a harsh, cruel sentence. Dissembling, so as not to upset Theodosia, he thanked her courteously for the kindness she'd done him. He promised to repay her by taking her advice and abandoning his courtship of Constanza, now that he knew her affections were directed toward his brother and not himself.

Don Jorge took leave of Theodosia, and she felt extremely pleased with herself. She thought, with don Jorge disillusioned in his hope of winning her sister, it would now be easy for her to get him for her husband. But that's not what happened, for the greater the offense against a jealous man, the more strongly he loves.

The moment don Jorge left Theodosia's presence, he set out to find his detested brother. First he spoke with the page in whom he confided his closest secrets. He gave him jewels and a large sum of money and told him to prepare a horse and wait for him at a certain place in the outskirts of the city. Then he approached Federico and told him he had certain matters to take up with him that necessitated their meeting outside of town.

Federico agreed to meet his brother, although he wasn't so incautious that he didn't fear his brother, considering the bad blood between them. Fortune, who arranges things as she pleases, without regard for innocence or merit, had already cast her luck in favor of don Jorge and against poor Federico. When Federico came to the designated place, which was very isolated, don Jorge drew his sword and, without giving Federico time to draw his, he called him the robber of all he held dear and ran his brother through the heart with such force that the sword pierced his body and came out his back. The unfortunate Federico instantly surrendered his soul to God and dropped to the ground stone dead.

After the unfortunate youth had died at the hand of his cruel brother, don Jorge went to where his servant was waiting with the horse. He mounted, took the page up behind him, and set out for Barcelona. From there, he embarked on the galleys for Naples, saying farewell forever to his native Spain.

That same night, the ill-starred Federico's body was discovered and brought home to his parents. They and the whole city lamented the dreadful murder whose author remained unknown. It was true that his brother was missing, but it never occurred to anyone that don Jorge might be responsible for such an awful deed. His absence did, however, make people think that he might have had some connection with the misfortune. Only Theodosia, the real cause of the tragedy, could have told the truth about what had happened, but she remained silent because it was important to her honor and her plans.

Constanza deeply lamented don Jorge's absence, but even she never suspected anything unfavorable to his honor and so, waiting to have news of him, she put off all thought of marriage.

Then her father died. He left great wealth to the two girls and their mother to take care of them. For over two years their mother kept busy managing their affairs and never thought to arrange her daughters' marriages. They didn't initiate anything because they were waiting for the return of their beloved don Jorge, despite the fact that they never heard a word from him during all that time. Neither did the girls want to lose the loving care their mother provided. Time gradually worked its natural effect of forgetfulness on Constanza's love. Not so with Theodosia, who remained steadfastly in love with don Jorge and wanted her sister to marry so she'd feel more secure when don Jorge returned.

Then it happened that a gentleman from Santander, named Carlos, came to Zaragoza on business. He was between thirty and thirty-six years old, better endowed by nature than by wealth, elegant, discreet, and in every way worthy of love. He took lodging right across the street from Constanza's house. The first time he set eyes on the lady's great beauty, he surrendered his freedom to her. His heart was so stricken by love that death alone could have shaken it. His love was only increased by her noble birth, her wealth, her modesty, and her attractive reserve.

Our Carlos was a stranger in this land, and he was poor. Although he had noble ancestors, what he lacked was money, so there was no way he could ask for Constanza's hand in marriage; he knew that her family wouldn't give her to him. But, since there doesn't exist a love without its art, a smart man knows how to use it to his advantage. So Carlos thought up a stratagem that he hoped would get him what he wanted. To put it into effect, he began by making friends with Fabia, which was Constanza's mother's name. He regaled her with gifts that he bought just for that purpose, and the noble lady returned his kindness. He visited the three women from time to time, earning the goodwill of all three with his pleasant company and gracious conversation. Finally, they could scarcely get along without him.

Now that all this had worked out according to Carlos's design, he revealed his plan to an old servant who waited on him, promising to pay her handsomely for her help in this matter. He pretended to be ill, not just a minor temporary affliction but one so serious that he took to his bed.

The old woman, his maid, had already made arrangements with a doctor to whom they'd given a nice present, and he came to attend Carlos. He diagnosed the illness as a dreadful fever. When the noble Fabia learned of her neighbor's illness, feeling very sorry for him, she immediately went to visit. She took care of him as if he were her own son, attending to all his needs. The feigned illness got worse, according to the complaints of the patient and the doctor's reports, until finally he was urged to make his will and take the last sacraments. This scene took place in Fabia's presence. The seriousness of his illness upset her terribly. The clever Carlos took her hand and, preparing to make his will, he said to Fabia:

"My lady, you can see that I'm closer to death than to life. I don't regret it so much for my sake, even though it arrives at the midpoint in my life, as much as I regret that it will prevent me from serving you, which has been my greatest pleasure since meeting you. For my soul to depart this life with some comfort, please let me reveal a secret to you."

The good lady told him to tell her anything he wanted and to remember that she loved him as if he were her own son and would listen carefully to what he had to say.

"My lady Fabia," Carlos continued, "for six months I have lived across the street from your house, and all this time I have adored your daughter Constanza because of her great beauty and virtue, and I've wanted her for my wife. I haven't mentioned this before because I was waiting for the arrival of a relative of mine who I hoped would serve as intermediary and make all the arrangements. But God, who knows what's best, has, as you can see, seen fit to put an end to my desires without permitting me to enjoy my heartfelt wish. The permission that I'm requesting of you is that you allow me to leave my entire estate to Constanza, that she be allowed to accept it, and that you, my lady, serve as executrix. After my will has been executed, what remains shall be her dowry."

With loving words Fabia thanked him for the great favor he did her. She wept and lamented losing him.

Carlos made his will and mentioned more than a hundred thousand ducats and named fine estates in various parts of Santander. He left everything to his only heir Constanza. Her mother was so grieved that she prayed to heaven to save his life. Fabia went to tell her daughter the news and, throwing her arms around Constanza's neck, she said:

"My darling daughter, how much you owe Carlos! You should consider yourself terribly unfortunate from this day on because you're losing such a fine husband."

The beautiful lady, impressed with Carlos's many fine qualities and also feeling obligated by the wealth he'd left to her, responded:

"Heaven forbid, mother, that Carlos should die, or that my happiness should be so short-lived as to witness his death. I pray that God will grant him life so that we can repay the great kindness he has shown us."

With these fervent wishes, mother and daughters prayed to God to save his life. Within a few days, Carlos, who had his health under control, began to get better and, by the end of the month, he was completely well. Not only was he healthy but also married to the beautiful Constanza because, when he recovered fully, Fabia had taken him into her house and married him to her daughter.

Constanza was very happy because her husband knew how to win her love with gifts and loving caresses. But he'd earned all this through his deception. When Carlos felt fully assured of Constanza's love, he dared to reveal his trick to her, offering as excuse her great beauty and the true love he felt from the moment he first saw her.

Constanza was discreet so, instead of resenting his deception, she considered herself fortunate to have such a husband and felt thankful for his trick. She believed it had been heaven's will, which cannot be thwarted no matter how one tries. Furthermore, the splendid estates she possessed more than made up for what he didn't possess. The only thing that had been lacking to complement her beauty, discretion, and wealth had been a good husband like the one she now had, equally discreet, genteel, of noble blood and fine character. Her mother and sister, seeing Constanza so happy that she truly considered herself blessed, also loved him dearly and, instead of ruing the deception, they considered it a stroke of fortune.

Four years must have passed after Federico's death and still don Jorge remained absent. During this time Constanza had married, and the exquisite lady received as gifts from her husband two lovely children. She was even happier than at the beginning of her marriage, which made her consider as wasted all the time before she'd belonged to Carlos.

Then don Jorge, who'd wandered all over Italy, Piedmont, and Flanders, could no longer bear his absence from his beloved mistress. The people he'd met in those parts assured him that his name hadn't been connected with the death of the unfortunate Federico, so he returned home and presented himself to his parents. Although his absence had made them wonder, don Jorge managed to explain his disappearance and, pretending it was all news to him, he lamented the death of his brother with feigned tears and dissimulated sorrow and put to rest any suspicion they might have felt about his disappearance.

Don Jorge's loving parents received him with all the joy one feels upon finding a prized possession long after having lost it with no hope of its recovery. The beautiful Theodosia shared in that joy because of her passionate love for don Jorge, but she kept her deception secret, particularly from her beloved, so he would never suspect her.

The person who was least happy about his return was Constanza, almost as if she divined what was to happen. She truly loved her husband, so what made everyone else happy made her unhappy, for don Jorge, terribly distressed to find her married, gathered up his nerve and began to serve and court her despite the fact that she couldn't become his wife. Although marriage was impossible, at least he could enjoy her beauty and not belie the many years he had loved her. He haunted her street, sent her gifts, serenaded her, and courted her so attentively that people in the city began to gossip. The lady was deaf to all don Jorge's advances. She wouldn't accept a single gift or letter, nor did she acknowledge his attentions. When she ran into him in church or at a party, she wouldn't respond to his many complaints about the fact that she'd married another man, or to any of the other tender, heartfelt words he'd utter every time he found himself in her presence. On occasion, she tired of hearing his endless complaints and spoke to him so harshly and with such displeasure that her response only served to increase his unhappiness.

The sorrow that Theodosia felt when she saw these amorous extremes in her beloved don Jorge was so great that, if she hadn't been encouraged by her sister's disdain for him, she would have died a thousand deaths. She had good cause for, although she frequently intimated her love to don Jorge, all she received from him in return was rude harshness, which saddened her and brought her to despair.

Constanza was not unaware of what was causing her sister's unhappiness, and she wished don Jorge were inclined to remedy it, because she hated to see Theodosia suffer and she wanted to be free of his importunate courtship. Such a solution seemed more and more impossible, however, as don Jorge became so extreme and crazy in pursuing his desire that he no longer cared if his love for Constanza became common gossip in Zaragoza or if Constanza's husband learned of it.

For over a year, don Jorge behaved in this mad fashion, ignoring the fact that Constanza fled from the sight of him. She never left her house except to go to mass and then only in the company of her husband so don Jorge wouldn't dare address her. She did everything to discourage the precipitous gallant and get him to desist from obsessively pursuing her. At last Theodosia's melancholy reached its limit, and she took to her bed with a dangerous illness so serious that her family began to lose hope that she would survive. Constanza, who loved her sister dearly, knew that the only remedy for her illness lay in don Jorge's hands. She decided to speak with him and, for the sake of her sister's life, to try to change his cold, cruel attitude. One day, when Carlos had gone hunting, she sent for don Jorge. Don Jorge received the happy message from his beloved lady and was wild with joy. Not wanting to miss his chance, he went immediately to see what the mistress of his heart wanted of him.

Constanza greeted don Jorge with a smile on her face and sat down with him in her parlor. Trying to oblige him and bring him to her will, she said as modestly and amiably as she could:

"Don Jorge, when I look dispassionately at your merits and the affection I owe you, I cannot deny that I was unfortunate the day you left this city, for then I lost hope of having you for my husband. Given the honest affection with which I accepted your courtship, favors, and attentions, I had never expected you to disappear. Of course I am well contented with my husband and thank heaven that I came to merit him, as you can tell from the coldness with which I've treated your attentions since your return. It wouldn't be right for me to deny the obligation in which you place me, but the obligations of my honor are such that I cannot risk exposing myself to your pretension. I can't deny that my first love was powerful and, if there were any way I could correspond and retain my honor and my husband's, be assured that I would have rewarded your perseverance as it deserves.

"But that's impossible, and you exert yourself in vain, even if you devoted a whole century to loving me and trying to obligate me. Because this is the case, I've decided to repay you by giving you in my place another me, since I cannot give you my person. If you grant me this request, you will gain not only my true friendship but also my perpetual debt. Not to keep you in suspense, the beauty I want to give you in exchange for my beauty, which belongs to Carlos, is my sister Theodosia. Despairing because of your scorn, she has come to the end of her days; the only remedy that will bring her back to life is you. Now is the time for you to show me how much I really mean to you, if you will only honor us all by giving your hand in marriage to Theodosia. By doing this you'll put an end to the gossip, my husband's suspicions, your own sorrows, and you'll bring my sister back from the brink of death. Without your acquiescence, there's no doubt that death will triumph over her youth and beauty. If you were my brother-in-law, I could gratefully repay you as now I cannot out of modesty."

Troubled and despondent, don Jorge listened to Constanza. Then, carried away by his amorous passion, he exclaimed:

"Beautiful Constanza, is this the reward you have in store for all the torment I've suffered for your sake, for the enduring love I have for you? I thought you'd sent for me because you felt obligated by my attentions, and it was only because you wanted to make my love totally impossible! I assure you that I refuse your request. No woman who is not Constanza will ever possess me. I shall die loving you, and I shall live loving you until death overtakes me. When you know how much I desire death for myself, how can you ask me to try to prevent your sister's death? My dear lady, if you don't want me to kill myself right here before your eyes now that I have the opportunity, you'd better take pity on me and deliver me from all the sorrows I suffer for your sake."

Constanza listened. Then she stood up and said jokingly:

"Don Jorge, let's make an agreement: if, between now and to-morrow morning, you will make for me in the square in front of my house a garden with flowerbeds full of perfumed flowers, trees, and fountains that, in all its beauty, freshness, and diversity of birds, sur-passes the famous gardens that Semiramis had built on the walls of Babylon, then I shall place myself in your hands for you to do with as you please. If you don't, then you must cease your mad courtship of me and in repayment you will give your hand in marriage to my sister. Unless the black arts assist you, Carlos and Constanza will not lose the honor they've worked so hard to earn and keep. This is the price of my honor; get to work; for a lover as devoted as you, nothing should be impossible."

When she finished, she went into her sister's room, feeling very unhappy about the way things had gone. She left don Jorge in such despair that it was a miracle he didn't kill himself.

He fled from Constanza's house like a man demented. Without seeing where he was going, with faltering step, he went out into the country and threw himself down at the foot of a tree. He cursed his bad luck and the day he'd first seen and loved Constanza. He remained in that state until night began to fall, uttering sad and painful sighs, calling her a cruel, harsh woman, weeping, thinking of suicide. Some-times he would cry out like a madman, sometimes he would fall silent.

Suddenly a man appeared out of nowhere and stood before him. He said:

"What's the matter, don Jorge? Why do you cry out and sigh in the wind when there's another way for you to solve your problem? What womanish tears are those? Doesn't a man of your courage have more spirit than you're showing? Can't you see, now that your lady has put a price on her love, the solution isn't as difficult as you thought?"

Don Jorge stared at the stranger as he said this, amazed to hear him speak of things he knew no one else could know. Don Jorge replied:

"Who are you who know things even I don't know? You, who promise me a remedy that's impossible? What can you do when my plight is impossible even for the devil?"

"And what would you say if I were the very one you've just named?" the devil himself asked. "Have courage! Take heart! Tell me, what would you give me if I make the wonderful garden your lady has asked for?"

You listeners, just imagine what a desperate man would promise to get what he wanted most, a man who cared little for his life or for his soul! Don Jorge replied:

"You set the price for your service and I'll pay."

"Promise me your soul," the devil said, "and write me an agreement signed by your hand that it will be mine the moment it leaves your body. Then you can go home knowing that before the sun rises you will have answered your lady's impossible wish."

Noble, discreet listeners, the ill-advised young man was in love, so it wasn't hard for him to do exactly what the evil enemy of our repose asked. The devil had brought the necessary implements, and he placed paper and pen in don Jorge's hand. Don Jorge wrote out the agreement as the devil had commanded. He signed it without thinking about what he was doing: to satisfy his monstrous appetite he was giving away his most priceless possession, which had cost its Creator such a dear price. Oh crazy youth! Oh ill-advised gentleman! What are you doing? Look at how much you lose and how little you gain; the pleasure you buy will end in an instant, and the pain you'll suffer will last for eternity. Your desire to possess Constanza lets you heed none of this, but you'll be sorry when it's too late.

After don Jorge signed the pact, he returned to his lodging, and the devil set out to build the fabulous artifact.

When morning came, don Jorge felt sure it would be the day of his glory. He got up at dawn and dressed as richly and as elegantly as he could. Then he went to the square where the garden was supposed to be. When he reached the beautiful Constanza's house, he felt happier than he'd ever felt in his life as he beheld the most magnificent garden he'd ever seen. Had it not been false like its maker, it might have been built by a great monarch. Don Jorge entered the garden and walked along the beautiful flowerbeds and down the splendid paths and waited for his lady to come out to see how he had satisfied her wish.

The day Constanza had spoken with don Jorge, Carlos had returned tired from the hunt. The next morning, in order to take care of some business that had come up, he awoke at dawn. Since it was scarcely daylight, he opened the window that gave onto the square to dress by its light. The instant he opened the window, he beheld the garden built by the devil to vanquish the fortress of his wife's honor. Carlos stood there astounded, thinking he was dreaming. But even though his eyes might have been deceived by the lavish flowerbeds, the beautiful trees, the intricate labyrinths, his ears couldn't have been, and they were delighted by the sweet song of the many different kinds of birds that, noticing the garden's magnificence in their morning flight, had flocked there to enjoy its splendid beauty. As if awaking from a dream, Carlos called out to his wife and everyone else in the house, telling them to get up and come look at the most marvelous wonder that had ever been seen.

At his astonished cries, Constanza, her mother, and everyone in the household got up, sure that Carlos was making things up. The lady didn't remember her offer to don Jorge, since it was impossible and so, without thinking, she went to see what her husband wanted. When she looked out and saw the garden filled with flowers and trees, the price of her honor, she realized that the garden she'd been given, filled with lovely fountains and bowers, was much more than she'd asked for. Everyone who looked at the garden was filled with wonder. Strolling about in it was don Jorge, very elegant in all his finery. Suddenly Constanza realized what she'd promised. She fell to the floor in a mortal swoon. The sound of her fall brought her husband and the rest of her family to her side. They all thought it was a bewitchment, given the prodigies they were witnessing.

Tenderly Carlos took his wife in his arms and ordered that the doctor be called immediately. He feared she might be dead, and he loved her dearly. Carlos and Theodosia began to weep and lament

Constanza's death. Their weeping attracted the people who'd gathered in the square to look at the garden. Don Jorge, who already imagined what must have happened, came in with them, and they all joined in the lament.

The beautiful lady's swoon lasted for over a half an hour, during which time the doctors attempted every remedy. Then, with shudder, she came to her senses and found herself in her loving husband's arms and surrounded by a crowd of people, including don Jorge. Constanza, pouring forth bitter tears from her beautiful eyes, looked at Carlos and then spoke:

"My lord, if you want to keep your honor, your children's, and the honor of all my noble relatives, then you must put an end to my life this instant. Not because I have, in any way, offended against you or them, but because, without thinking that honor is priceless, I set a price on my honor. I beg you to end my life in imitation of Lucrecia and even to surpass her, for she killed herself after she'd been dishonored, and I would die without losing my honor, but for having thought to put a price upon it. Since I must lose my life and you, who are my life, even though I'm innocent, I am Christian, and it would be wrong for me to lose my soul, which cost its Creator so dearly."

These words shocked Carlos more than anything else that had taken place. He asked Constanza to explain the meaning of what she'd said and to tell him why she was crying so uncontrollably.

Constanza calmed herself somewhat and told everyone assembled around her bed what had transpired between her and don Jorge from the time he'd begun to love her up to the present. In ending, she added that since she'd asked don Jorge for an impossibility, and he'd complied, although she didn't know how, there was no alternative but for her to die. If her husband killed her because his honor had been offended, the whole problem would be solved, and don Jorge could have no complaint. When Carlos understood the implications of this strange situation, he recalled that he enjoyed great wealth through his wife. Inequality can often serve as a restraint to a man's passion, for a man who marries a woman richer than himself doesn't buy a wife but agrees to serve a mistress. As Aristotle says, if the wife brings no other wealth than her virtue, then she must strive through her virtue and humility to earn her lord's esteem. So Carlos, more in love with his beautiful Constanza than ever, said:

"My lady, I cannot deny that you did wrong to put a price on that which can have no price, for there's no way in the world to pay for a woman's chastity and her virtue. Although you trusted in an impossibility, you should have realized that nothing is impossible for a real lover, who'll do the impossible to obtain the reward for his love. But you've paid for this fault with great suffering; furthermore, I can't put an end to your life, nor can I cause you more grief than you now feel. I'm the one who must die. Fortune, tired of favoring me, now seeks my downfall. You promised to give don Jorge the reward for his love if he made the garden. He has found a way to keep his word to you. The only solution is for you to keep your word to him and I, by doing what you're about to witness, shall not stand in your way. You can fulfill your obligations, and he can enjoy the reward for his great love."

As Carlos said these words, he drew his sword. He was about to plunge it through his heart without even thinking that, in doing such a desperate deed, he too would lose his soul. Don Jorge, anticipating his intent, quickly leapt to his side, grabbed the hilt of the violent sword, and said:

"Stop, Carlos, stop!"

Don Jorge held it firmly and, standing just as he was, he described what had happened between him and the devil. Then he said:

"It isn't right for me to offend against such a noble person as you. When I see that you will take your own life to keep me from dying, I feel such obligation to you that not one life but a thousand would I give to keep from offending against you. (There can be no crueller death for me than to deprive me of the woman I love so passionately, the woman who's cost me so dearly, for I've paid for my love with my soul.) Your wife is hereby free of her obligation to me: I release her from her promise. May Constanza enjoy Carlos, and Carlos Constanza, for heaven has made them equal in virtue and Carlos alone deserves her, just as she's worthy of being his. Let don Jorge die. He was born so unfortunate that not only has he lost his desire to love, he has also lost his priceless soul, which cost God His sacrifice on the Cross."

The instant don Jorge uttered these words, the devil appeared to them all, holding the pact in his hand. He shouted loudly:

"No matter how you try, you won't get the best of me! Where a husband tramples his own desire and, by conquering himself, seeks to put an end to his own life, giving his wife permission to keep her promise; where a crazy lover feels obligated by the husband's act and so releases his beloved from her promise, which has cost him no less than his soul, as you can see here in this pact in which don Jorge promises his soul to me; I can do no less than they. So that the whole world will be amazed that the devil can be virtuous, here, don Jorge, take this, take back your pact! I don't want the soul of a man who's learned to conquer himself. I release you from your obligation."

With these words, the devil threw down the pact. There was an enormous explosion, and the devil vanished, as did the garden. All that was left in its place was a thick, stinking, smoke that lasted a long time.

At the great noise of the explosion, so loud it sounded as if the whole city had blown up, Constanza, Theodosia, their mother, and all the servants, who'd been entranced at the sight of the devil, came to their senses. They saw don Jorge kneel down and, weeping copiously, he thanked God for the mercy He'd shown in freeing him from such peril. Everyone present likewise knelt down and gave thanks to God, believing that everything had happened for mysterious reasons known only to Him.

After don Jorge finished his devout prayer, he turned to Constanza and said:

"Now, beautiful lady, I recognize how right you've been to maintain your decorum, so well deserved by the husband you have. Obviously Carlos can entertain no doubts about the virtue with which you honor him. So that he can live with confidence in me, I want to ask your forgiveness for the trouble I've caused you and for threatening your good name with my importunate courtship. Now let me request what you offered me yesterday out of concern for my welfare, which I, like a madman, rejected. I'm asking for the beautiful Theodosia's hand in marriage. In doing this, the noble Carlos can live secure, and the whole city will know of your valor and your virtue."

When Constanza heard this, she went up to don Jorge with open arms and placed them around his neck. Her beautiful lips grazed the forehead of the well-intentioned young man who, through his virtue, had finally earned the reward he'd never been able to win through his impassioned desire. Constanza said:

"This favor I grant to you as my brother. It's the first favor you've enjoyed from me in all the time you've loved me."

Everybody joined in the rejoicing, some with exclamations of amazement, others with hearty congratulations. To the delight of everyone who heard their story, that same day don Jorge and the beautiful Theodosia were betrothed. Because they didn't want to wait, the next day the solemn wedding was held with Carlos and Constanza serving as sponsors. There were many parties throughout the city to celebrate the happy end of such a complicated story. At every gathering, Carlos and don Jorge were hailed as exemplars of elegance, nobility, and gentility, and everyone considered the ladies who had merited them to be very fortunate.

They all lived for many years and had lovely children. No one ever found out that don Jorge had murdered his brother Federico until after his death, when Theodosia told the story she alone knew. When she died, this enchantment was found written in her own hand. At the end she promised a laurel wreath as a reward to the one who could prove which of the three had been the noblest: Carlos, don Jorge, or the devil. If anyone wishes to win the laurel, let each person judge. Here I shall end the "Magic Garden," a title given to the enchantment because of that wondrous artifact.

As the noble and discreet Laura ended the last enchantment, all the ladies and gentlemen began to dispute who'd been the noblest, hoping to win the promised laurel for their cleverness as well as a jewel the lovely Lysis had contributed as a prize. Each person defended an opinion: some favored the husband, others the lover, and everyone agreed that the devil had outdone himself, because it's unheard of for the devil to do a good deed.

Don Juan played the devil's advocate divinely and won the proffered jewel, much to don Diego's discomfiture. Don Juan immediately presented the jewel to a triumphant Lisarda, which naturally aggravated Lysis.

Their discussion lasted until so late that there wasn't time to put on the play, so the guests all voted to postpone the play until New Year's Day, the Feast of the Circumcision, when don Diego and the lovely Lysis were to be formally betrothed. Then everyone flocked to the tables and dined with great pleasure. This ended the fifth and final night, and I end my well-intentioned and entertaining soiree, promising a second part if this one is received with the pleasure I hope. In the second part we shall see don Juan's ingratitude punished, Lisarda's change of heart, and Lysis's wedding. I hope my work is appreciated, valued, and praised, not my rough style but the will with which it has been written.

Designer:	U.C. Press Staff
Compositor:	Auto-Graphics, Inc.
Text:	10/13 Galliard
Display:	Galliard
Printer:	Edwards Bros., Inc.
Binder:	Edwards Bros., Inc.